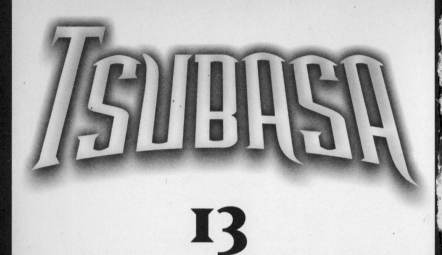

13

CLAMP

TRANSLATED AND ADAPTED BY
William Flanagan

LETTERED BY
Dana Hayward

BALLANTINE BOOKS · NEW YORK

Tsubasa, vol. 13 is a work of fiction. Names, characters, places, and incidents are the products of the author's imagination or are used fictitiously. Any resemblance to actual events, locales, or persons, living or dead, is entirely coincidental.

A Del Rey Trade Paperback Original

Published in the United States by Del Rey Books, an imprint of The Random House Publishing Group, a division of Random House, Inc., New York.

DEL REY is a registered trademark and the Del Rey colophon is a trademark of Random House, Inc.

Publication rights arranged through Kodansha, Ltd.

First published in Japan in 2006 by Kodansha, Ltd., Tokyo.

ISBN 978-0-345-48533-5

Printed in the United States of America

www.delreymanga.com

9 8 7 6 5 4 3 2 1

Translation and adaptation—William Flanagan

Lettering—Dana Hayward

Contents

Tsubasa crosses over with *xxxHOLiC*. Although it isn't necessary to read *xxxHOLiC* to understand the events in *Tsubasa*, you'll get to see the same events from different perspectives if you read both series!

Honorifics Explained

Throughout the Del Rey Manga books, you will find Japanese honorifics left intact in the translations. For those not familiar with how the Japanese use honorifics and, more important, how they differ from American honorifics, we present this brief overview.

Politeness has always been a critical facet of Japanese culture. Ever since the feudal era, when Japan was a highly stratified society, use of honorifics—which can be defined as polite speech that indicates relationship or status—has played an essential role in the Japanese language. When addressing someone in Japanese, an honorific usually takes the form of a suffix attached to one's name (example: "Asuna-san"), or as a title at the end of one's name or in place of the name itself (example: "Negi-sensei," or simply "Sensei!").

Honorifics can be expressions of respect or endearment. In the context of manga and anime, honorifics give insight into the nature of the relationship between characters. Many English translations leave out these important honorifics, and therefore distort the feel of the original Japanese. Because Japanese honorifics contain nuances that English honorifics lack, it is our policy at Del Rey not to translate them. Here, instead, is a guide to some of the honorifics you may encounter in Del Rey Manga.

-san: This is the most common honorific, and is equivalent to Mr., Miss, Ms., Mrs. It is the all-purpose honorific and can be used in any situation where politeness is required.

-sama: This is one level higher than "-san." It is used to confer great respect.

-dono: This comes from the word "tono," which means "lord." It is an even higher level than "-sama" and confers utmost respect.

-kun: This suffix is used at the end of boys' names to express familiarity or endearment. It is also sometimes used by men amongst friends, or when addressing someone younger or of a lower station.

-chan: This is used to express endearment, mostly toward girls. It is also used for little boys, pets, and even among lovers. It gives a sense of childish cuteness.

Bozu: This is an informal way to refer to a boy, similar to the English term "kid" or "squirt."

Sempai/Senpai: This title suggests that the addressee is one's senior in a group or organization. It is most often used in a school setting, where underclassmen refer to their upperclassmen as "sempai." It can also be used in the workplace, such as when a newer employee addresses an employee who has seniority in the company.

Kohai: This is the opposite of "sempai," and is used toward underclassmen in school or newcomers in the workplace. It connotes that the addressee is of a lower station.

Sensei: Literally meaning "one who has come before," this title is used for teachers, doctors, or masters of any profession or art.

-[blank]: This is usually forgotten in these lists, but it is perhaps the most significant difference between Japanese and English. The lack of honorific means that the speaker has permission to address the person in a very intimate way. Usually, only family, spouses, or very close friends have this kind of permission. Known as *yobisute*, it can be gratifying when someone who has earned the intimacy starts to call one by one's name without an honorific. But when that intimacy hasn't been earned, it can be very insulting

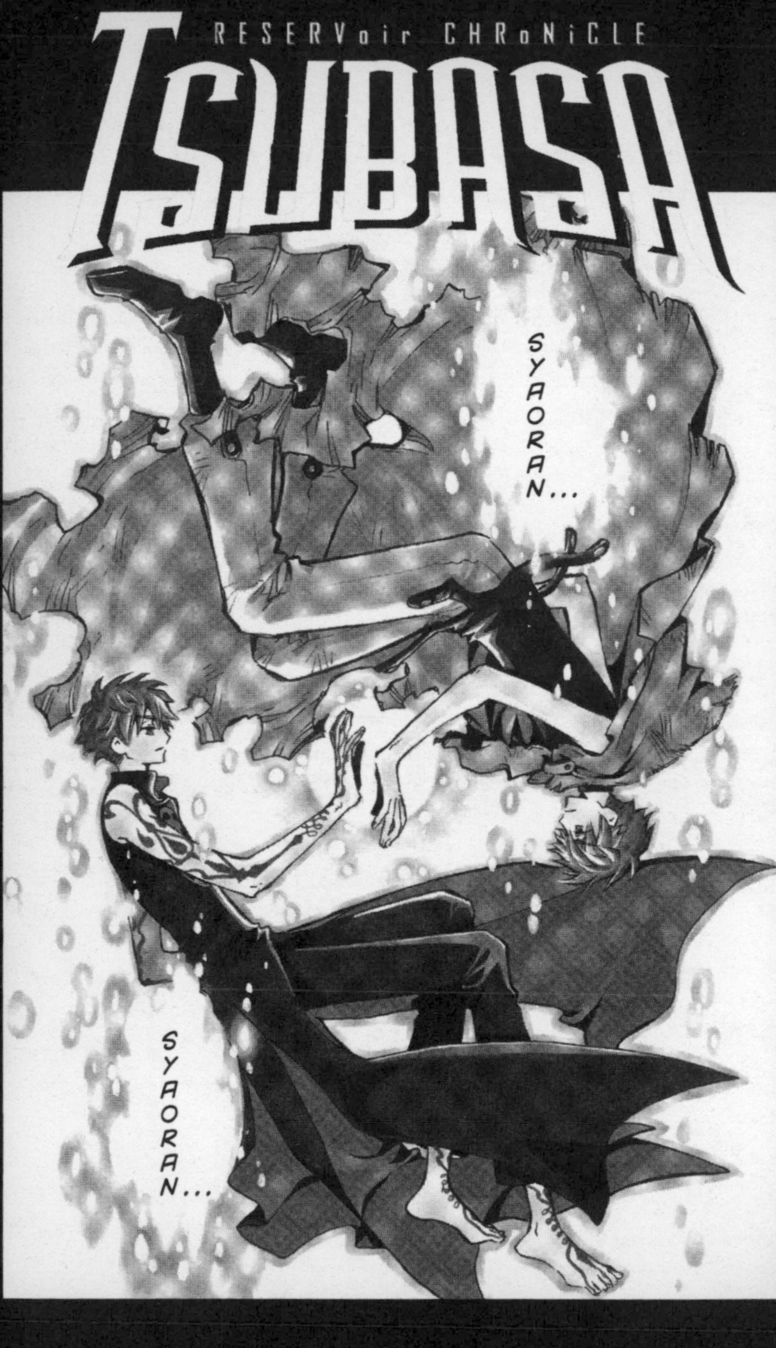
RESERVoir CHRoNiCLE
TSUBASA
SYAORAN...
SYAORAN...

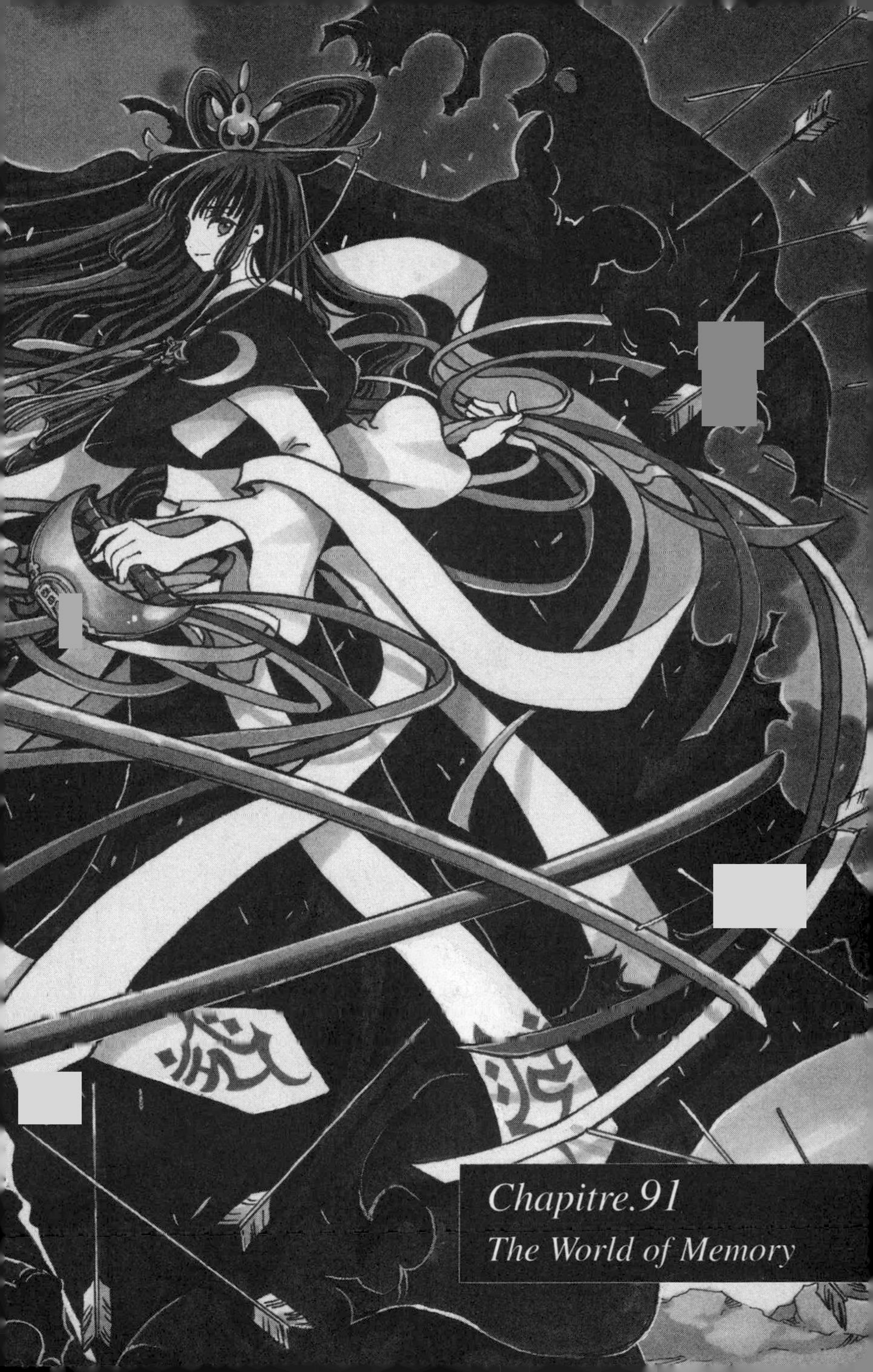
Chapitre.91
The World of Memory

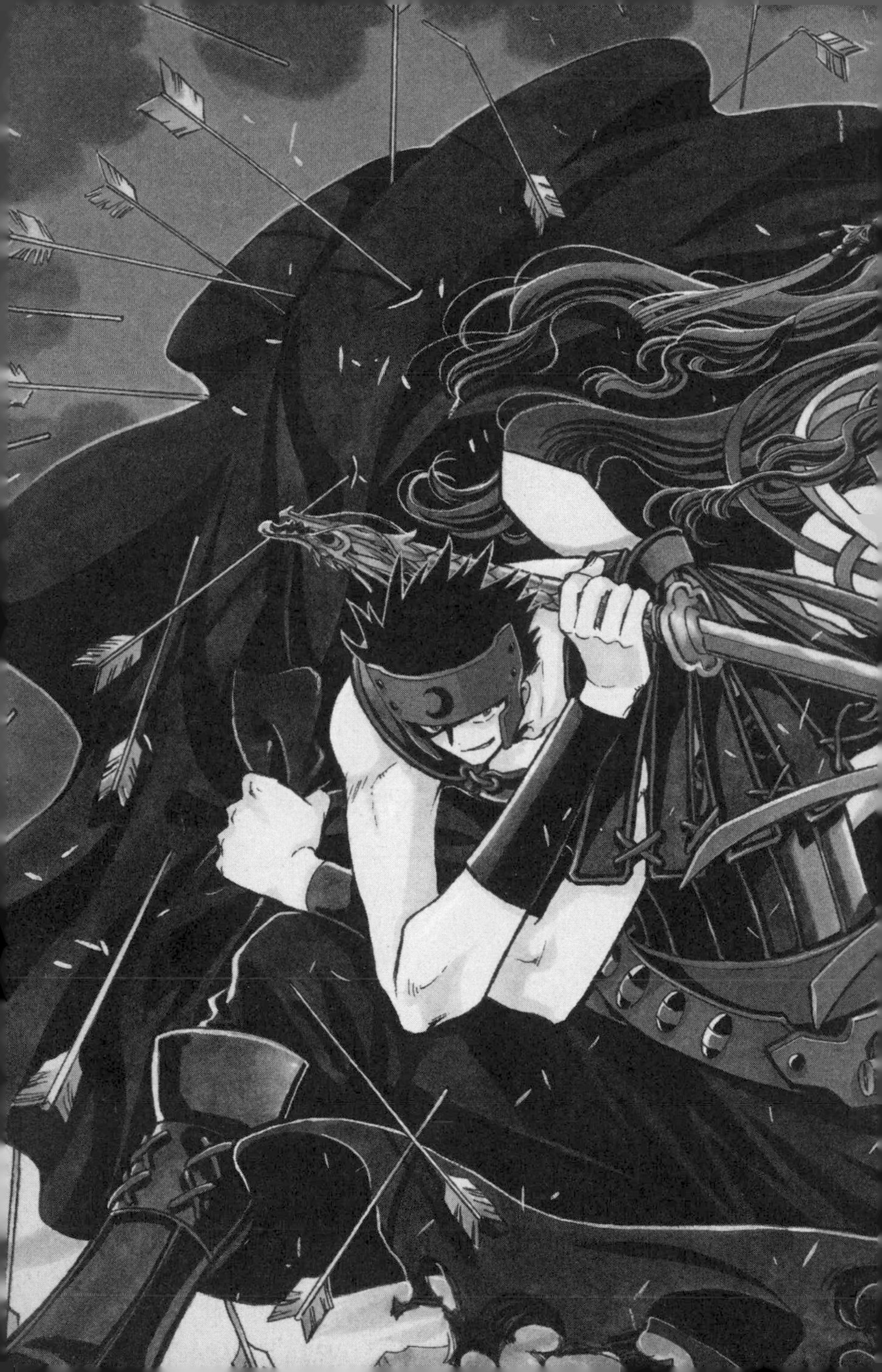

ツバサ

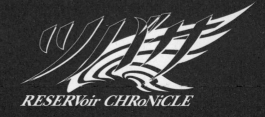

RESERVoir CHRoNiCLE

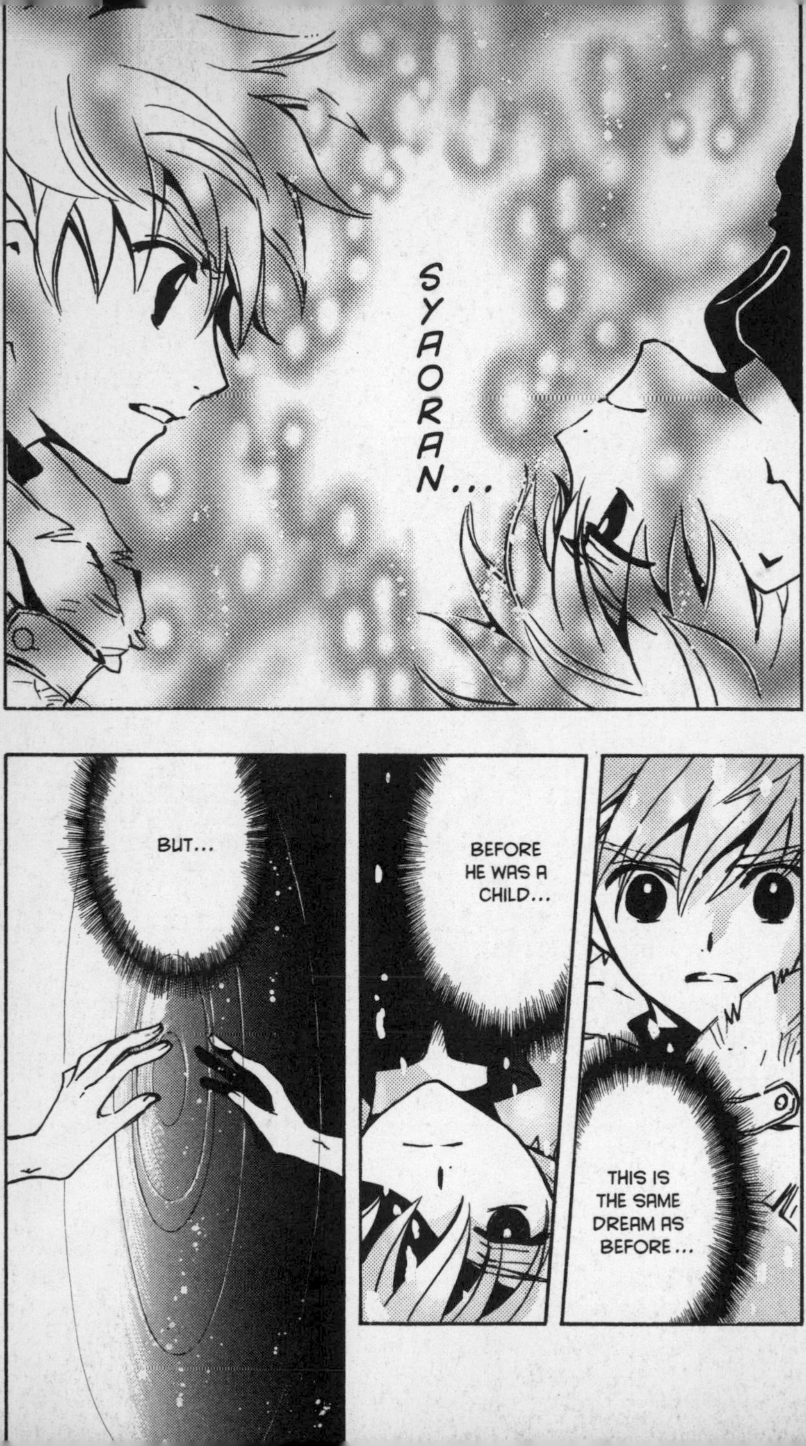
SYAORAN...
THIS IS THE SAME DREAM AS BEFORE...
BEFORE HE WAS A CHILD...
BUT...

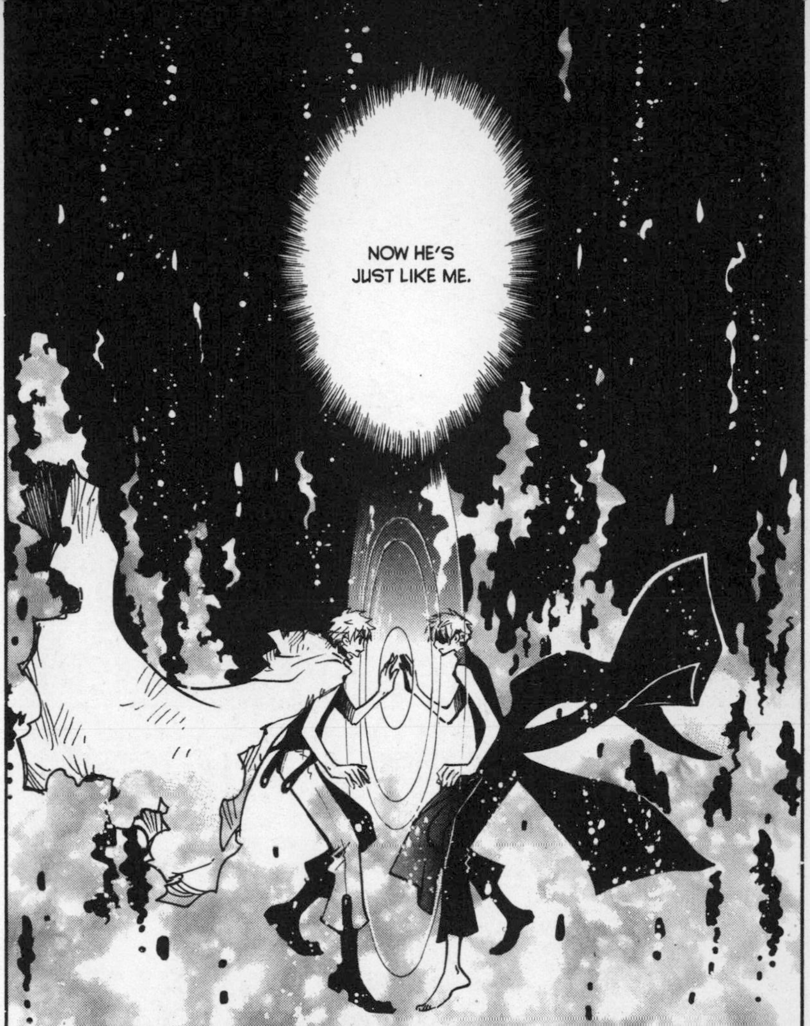
NOW HE'S
JUST LIKE ME.

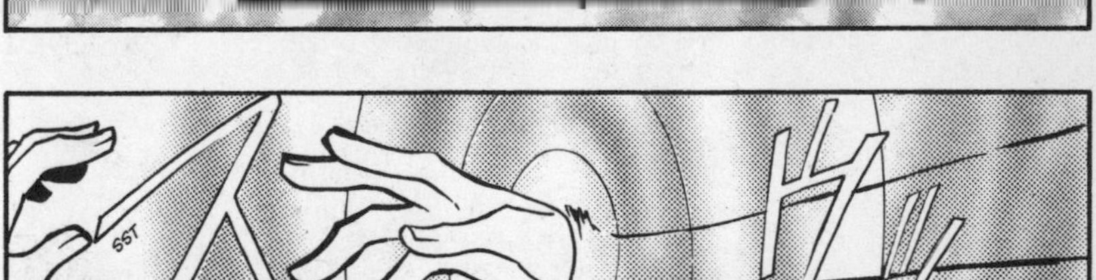
SST

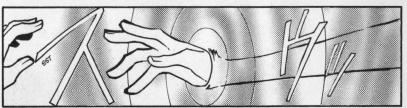

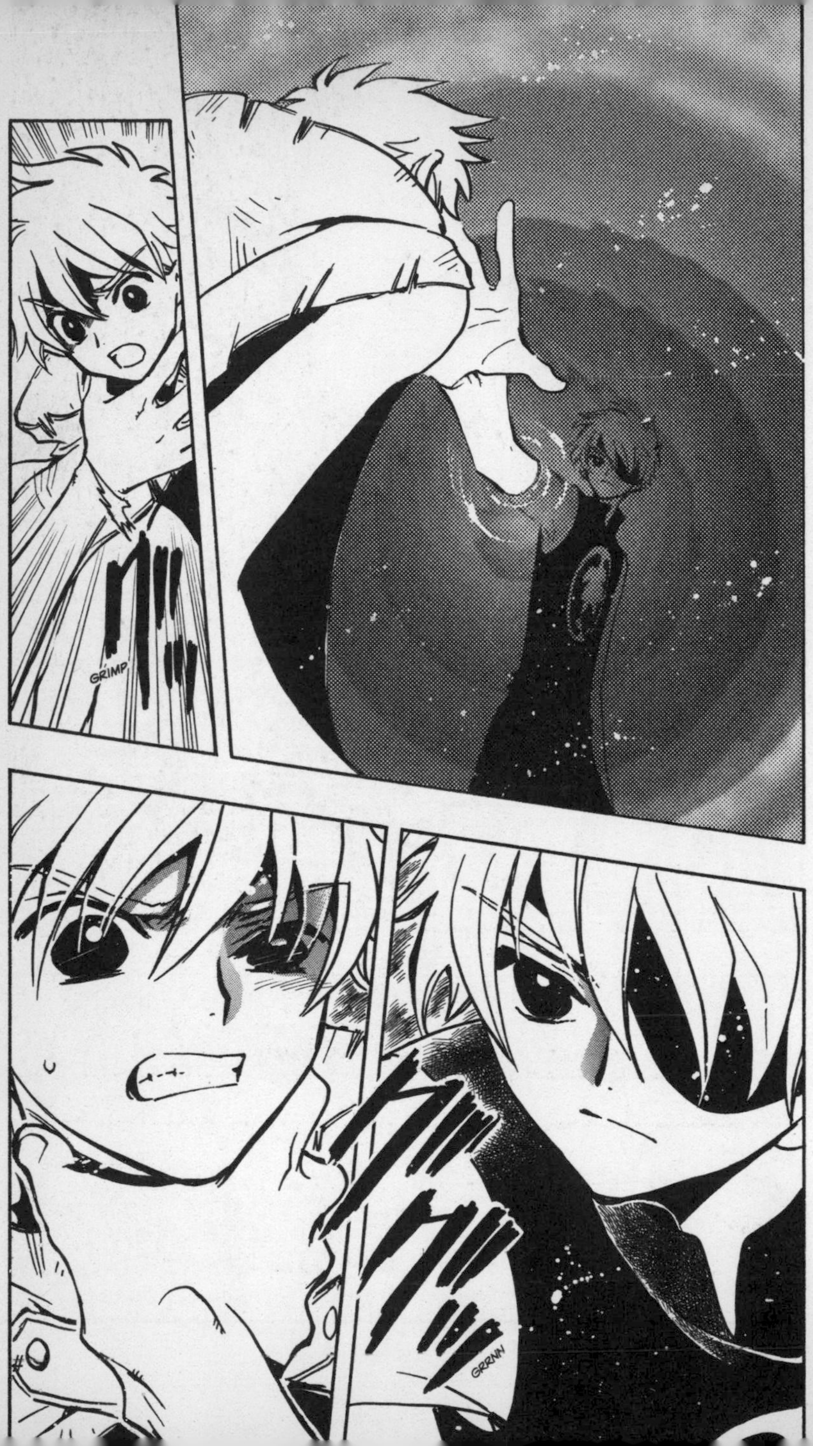
GRIMP
GRRNN

SYAORAN-KUN!!
VAMM

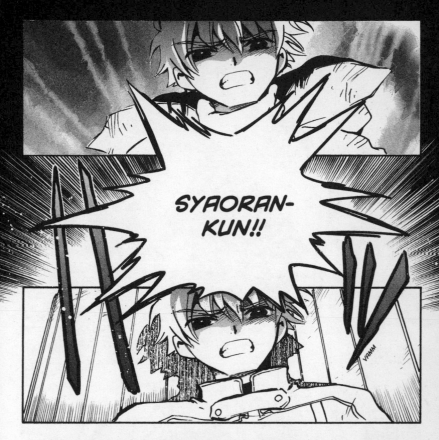

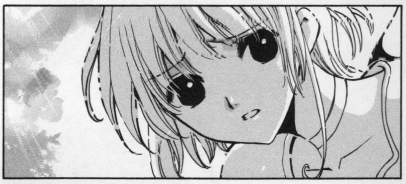

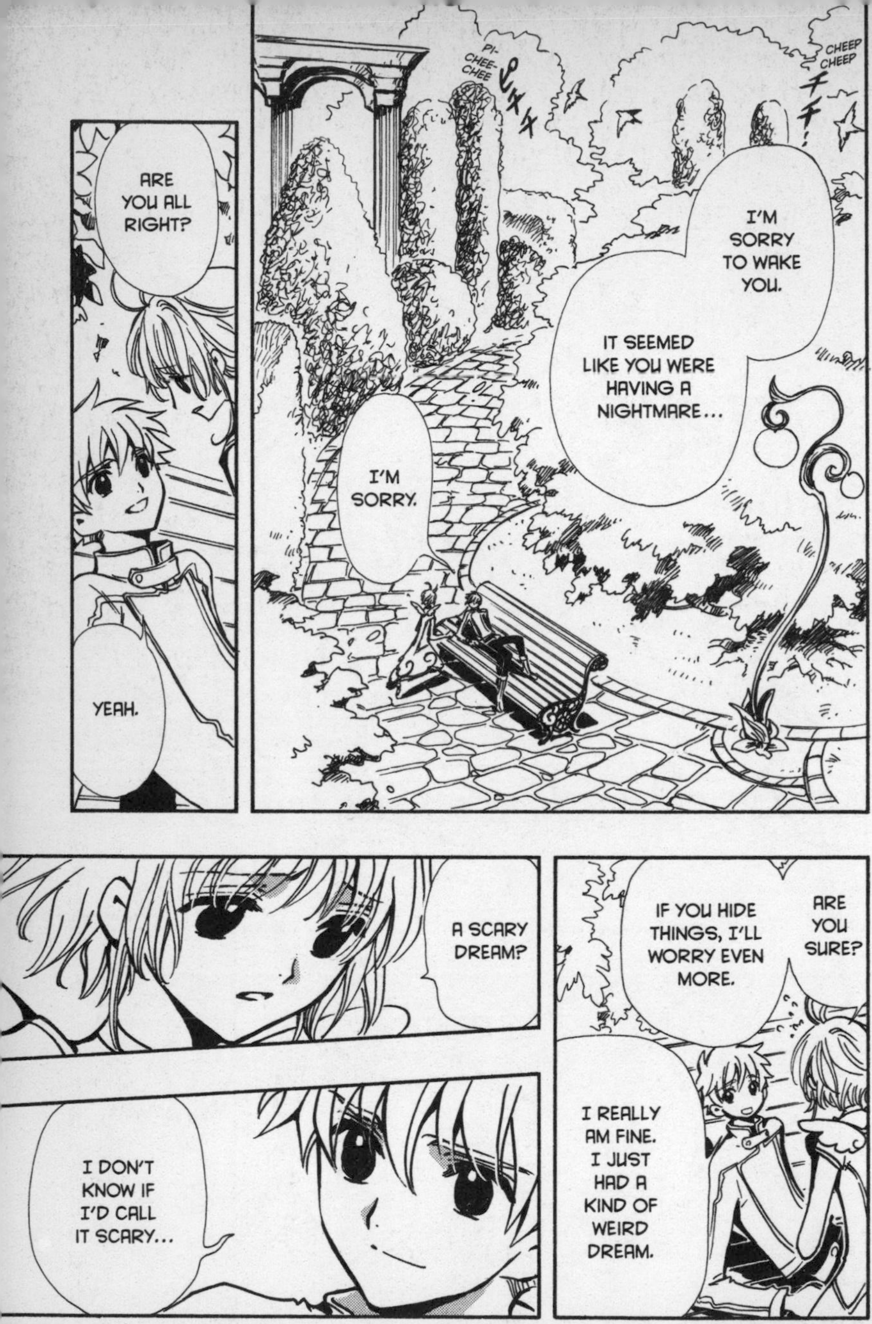
CHEEP CHEEP
チチ!
PI-CHEE-CHEE
I'M SORRY TO WAKE YOU.
IT SEEMED LIKE YOU WERE HAVING A NIGHTMARE...
I'M SORRY.
ARE YOU ALL RIGHT?
YEAH.
ARE YOU SURE?
IF YOU HIDE THINGS, I'LL WORRY EVEN MORE.
I REALLY AM FINE. I JUST HAD A KIND OF WEIRD DREAM.
A SCARY DREAM?
I DON'T KNOW IF I'D CALL IT SCARY...

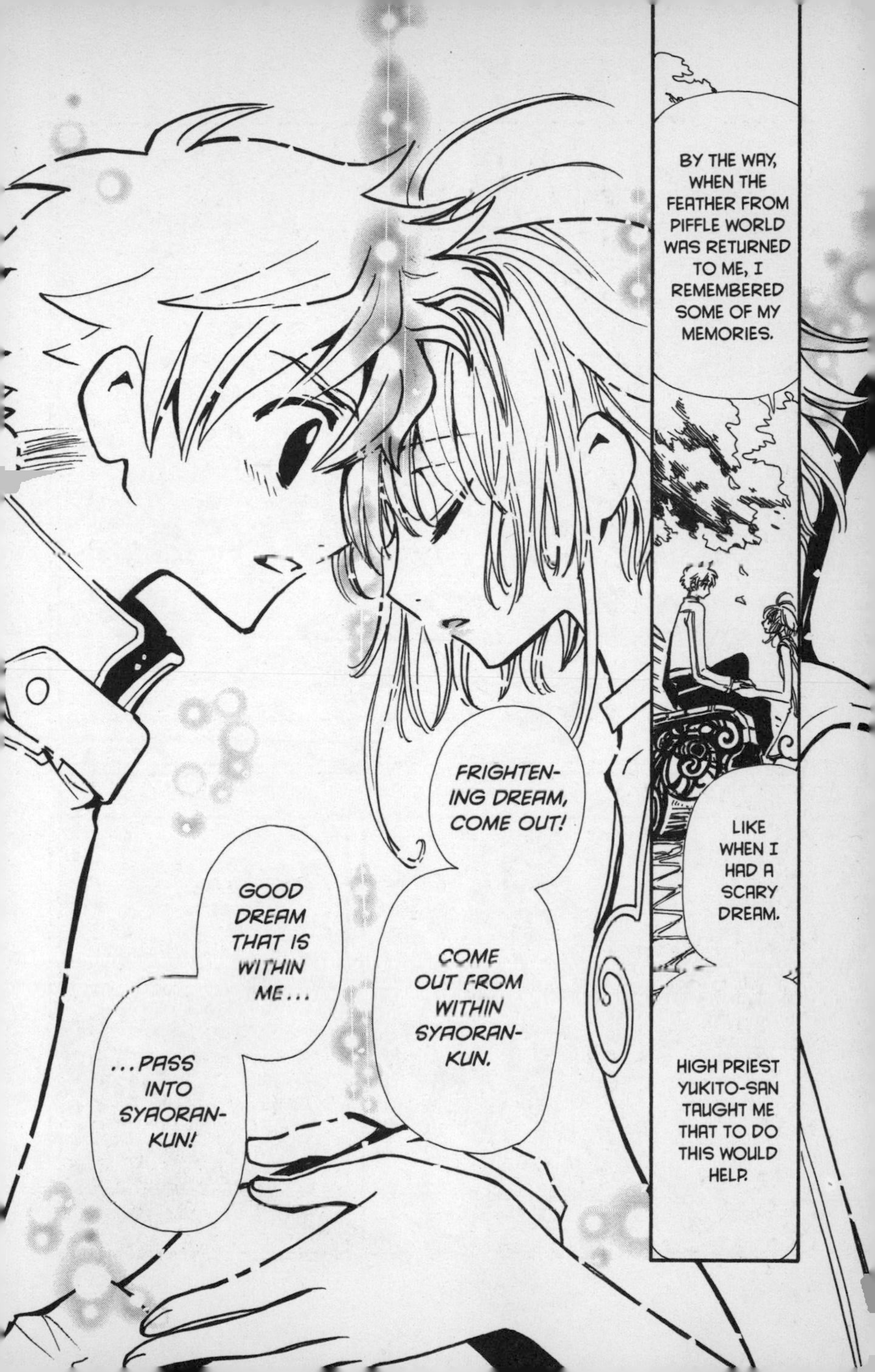
BY THE WAY, WHEN THE FEATHER FROM PIFFLE WORLD WAS RETURNED TO ME, I REMEMBERED SOME OF MY MEMORIES.
LIKE WHEN I HAD A SCARY DREAM.
HIGH PRIEST YUKITO-SAN TAUGHT ME THAT TO DO THIS WOULD HELP.
FRIGHTEN-ING DREAM, COME OUT!
COME OUT FROM WITHIN SYAORAN-KUN.
GOOD DREAM THAT IS WITHIN ME...
...PASS INTO SYAORAN-KUN!

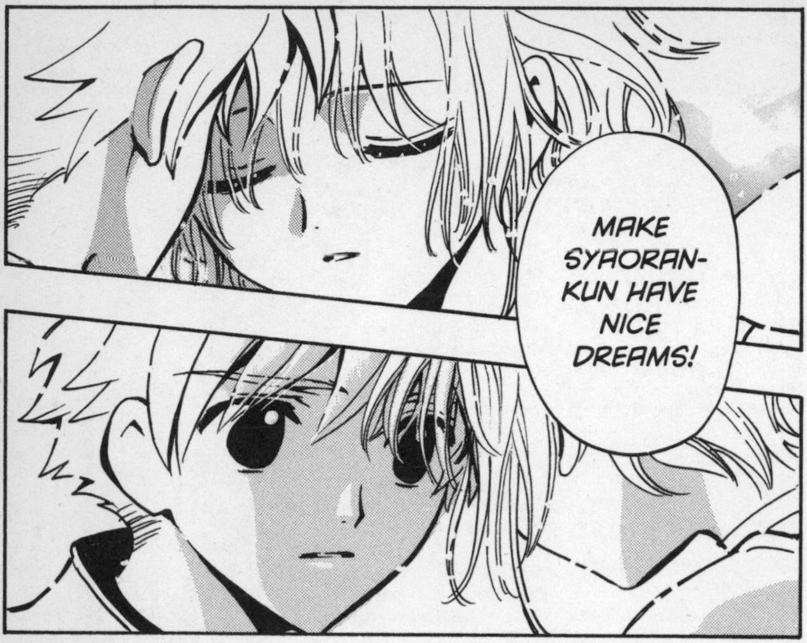
MAKE SYAORAN-KUN HAVE NICE DREAMS!

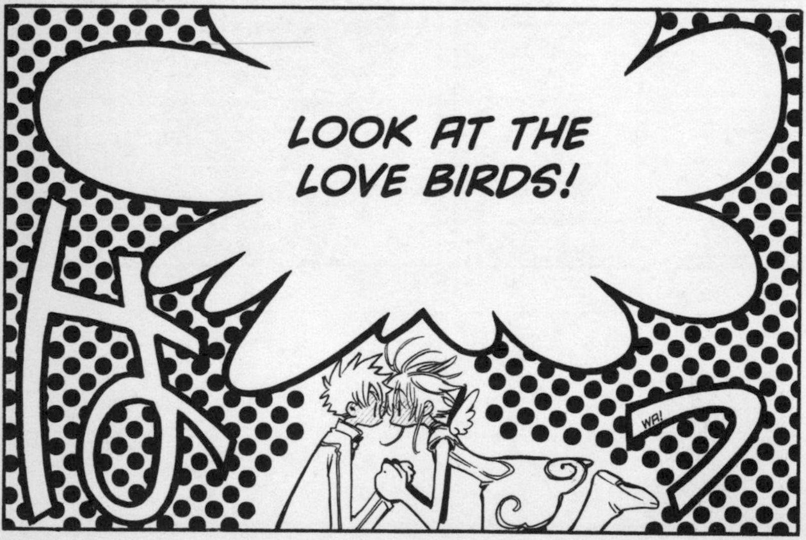
LOOK AT THE LOVE BIRDS!
WA!

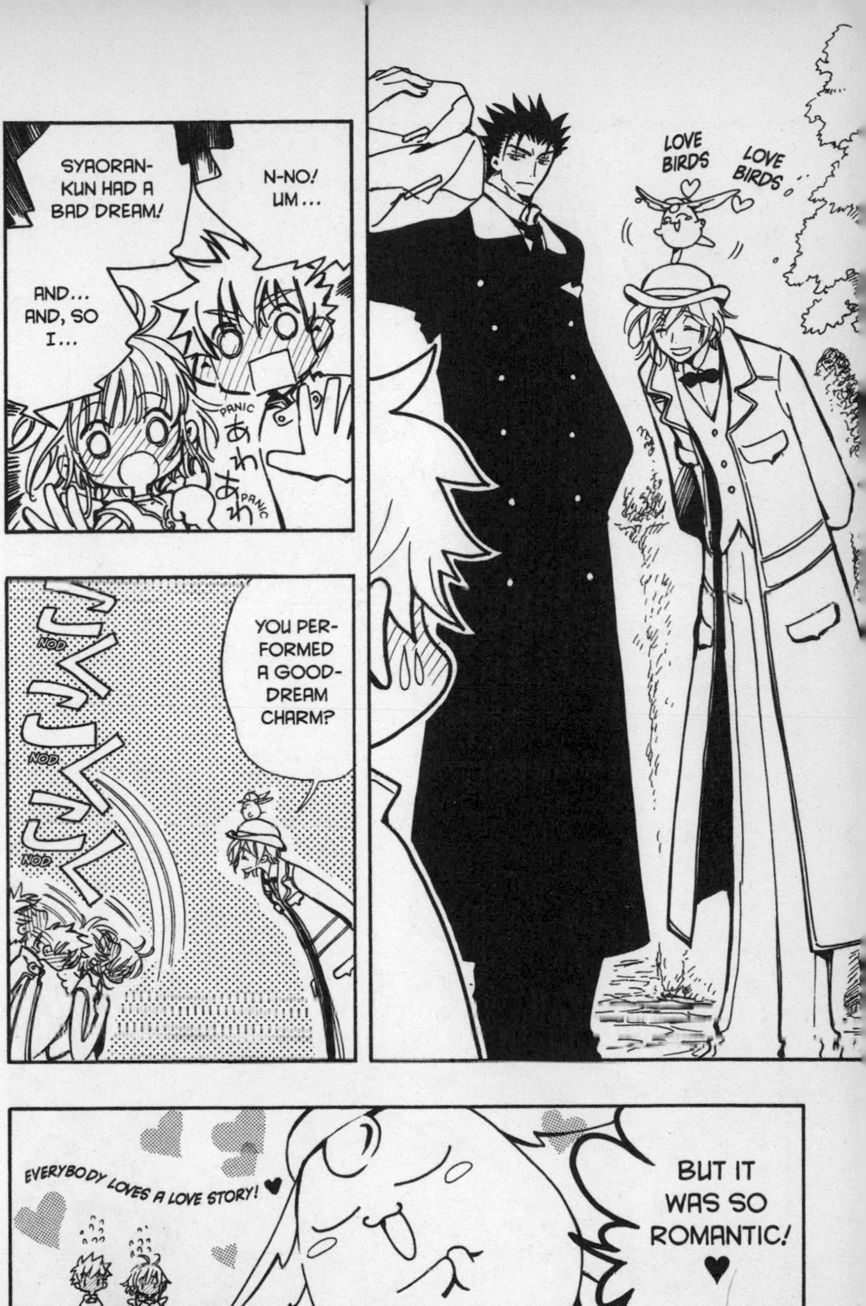
LOVE BIRDS
LOVE BIRDS
N-NO! UM...
SYAORAN-KUN HAD A BAD DREAM!
AND... AND, SO I...
PANIC
あわあわ
PANIC
YOU PER-FORMED A GOOD-DREAM CHARM?
NOD
NOD
NOD
BUT IT WAS SO ROMANTIC! ♥
EVERYBODY LOVES A LOVE STORY! ♥

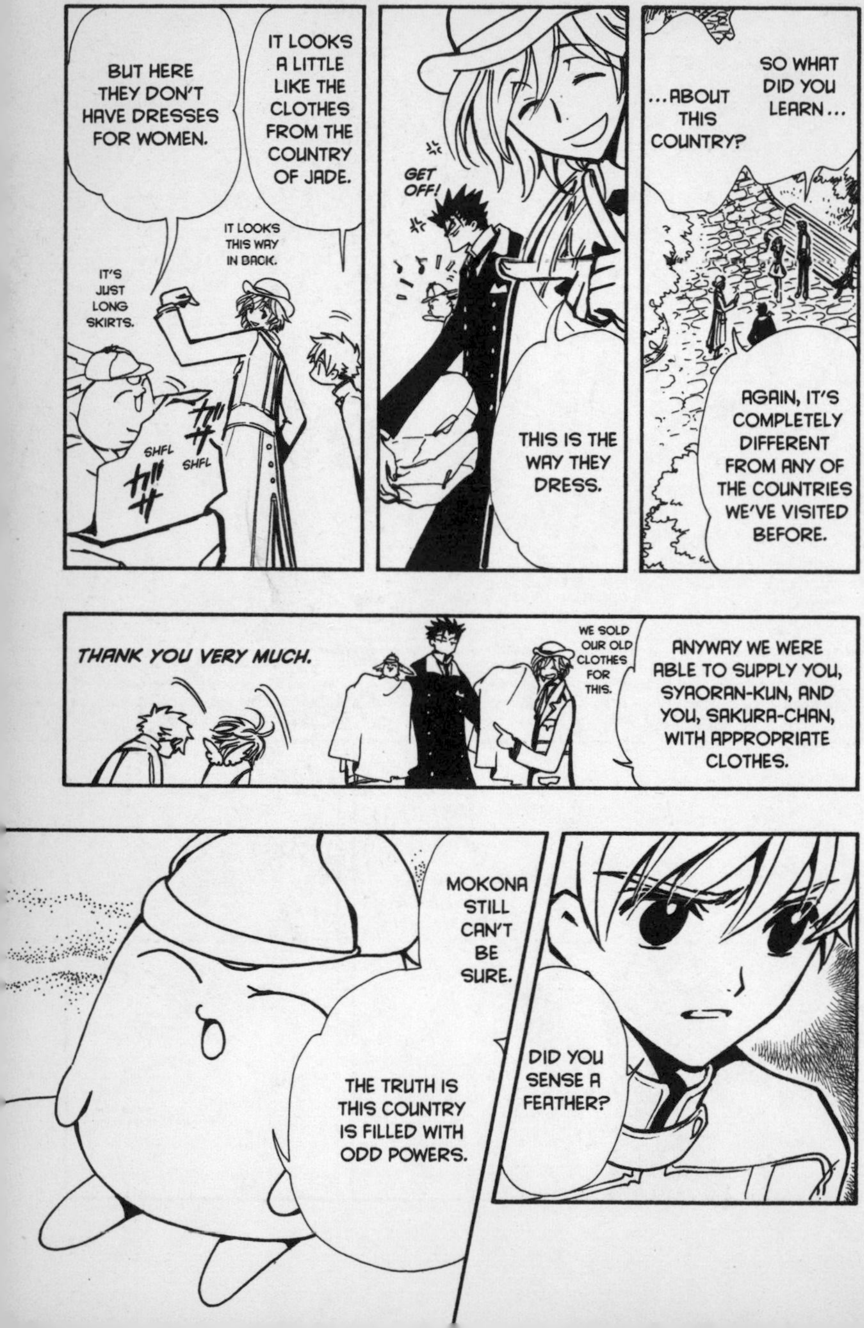
SO WHAT DID YOU LEARN...
...ABOUT THIS COUNTRY?
AGAIN, IT'S COMPLETELY DIFFERENT FROM ANY OF THE COUNTRIES WE'VE VISITED BEFORE.
THIS IS THE WAY THEY DRESS.
GET OFF!
IT LOOKS A LITTLE LIKE THE CLOTHES FROM THE COUNTRY OF JADE.
BUT HERE THEY DON'T HAVE DRESSES FOR WOMEN.
IT LOOKS THIS WAY IN BACK.
IT'S JUST LONG SKIRTS.
SHFL
SHFL
ANYWAY WE WERE ABLE TO SUPPLY YOU, SYAORAN-KUN, AND YOU, SAKURA-CHAN, WITH APPROPRIATE CLOTHES.
WE SOLD OUR OLD CLOTHES FOR THIS.
THANK YOU VERY MUCH.
DID YOU SENSE A FEATHER?
MOKONA STILL CAN'T BE SURE.
THE TRUTH IS THIS COUNTRY IS FILLED WITH ODD POWERS.

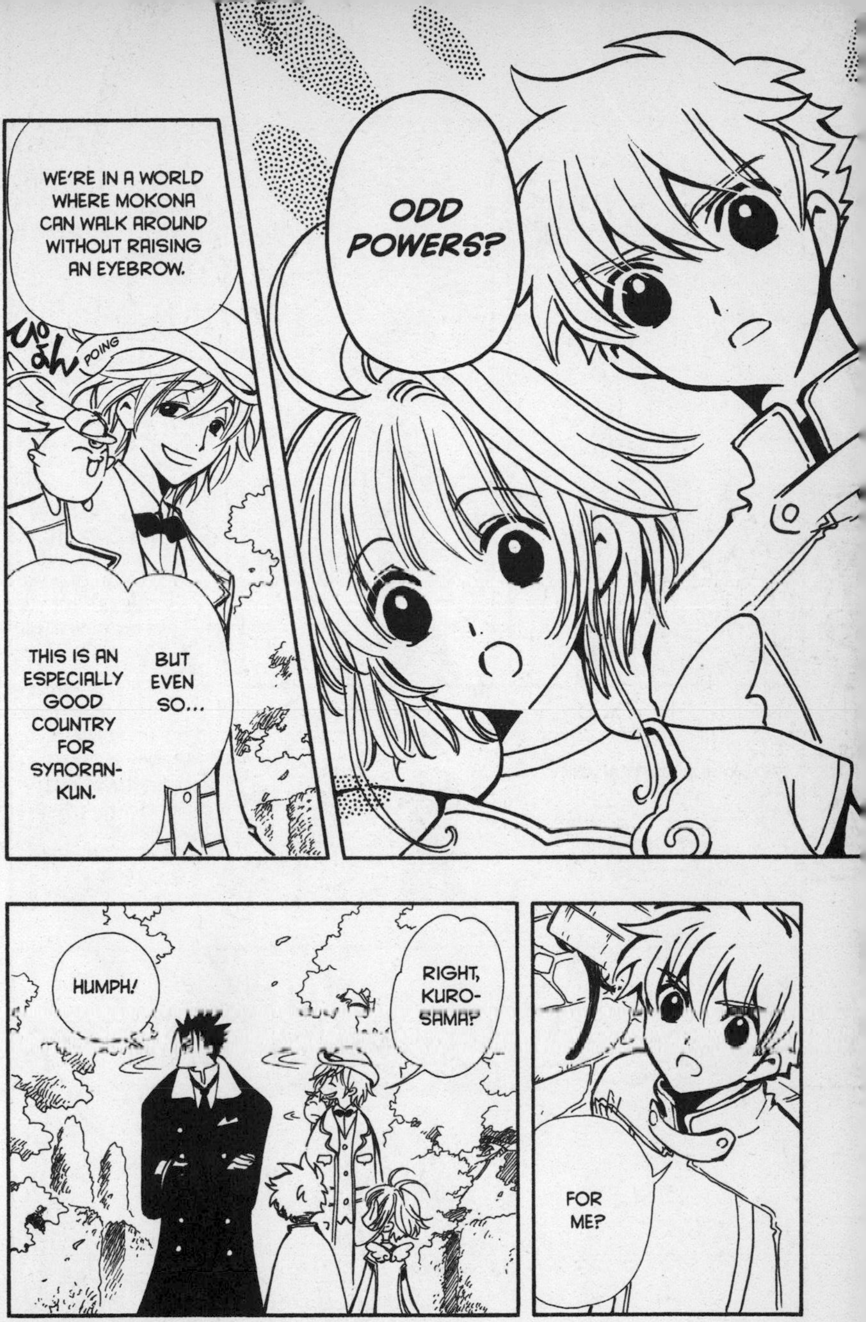
ODD POWERS?
WE'RE IN A WORLD WHERE MOKONA CAN WALK AROUND WITHOUT RAISING AN EYEBROW.
POING
BUT EVEN SO...
THIS IS AN ESPECIALLY GOOD COUNTRY FOR SYAORAN-KUN.
FOR ME?
RIGHT, KURO-SAMA?
HUMPH!

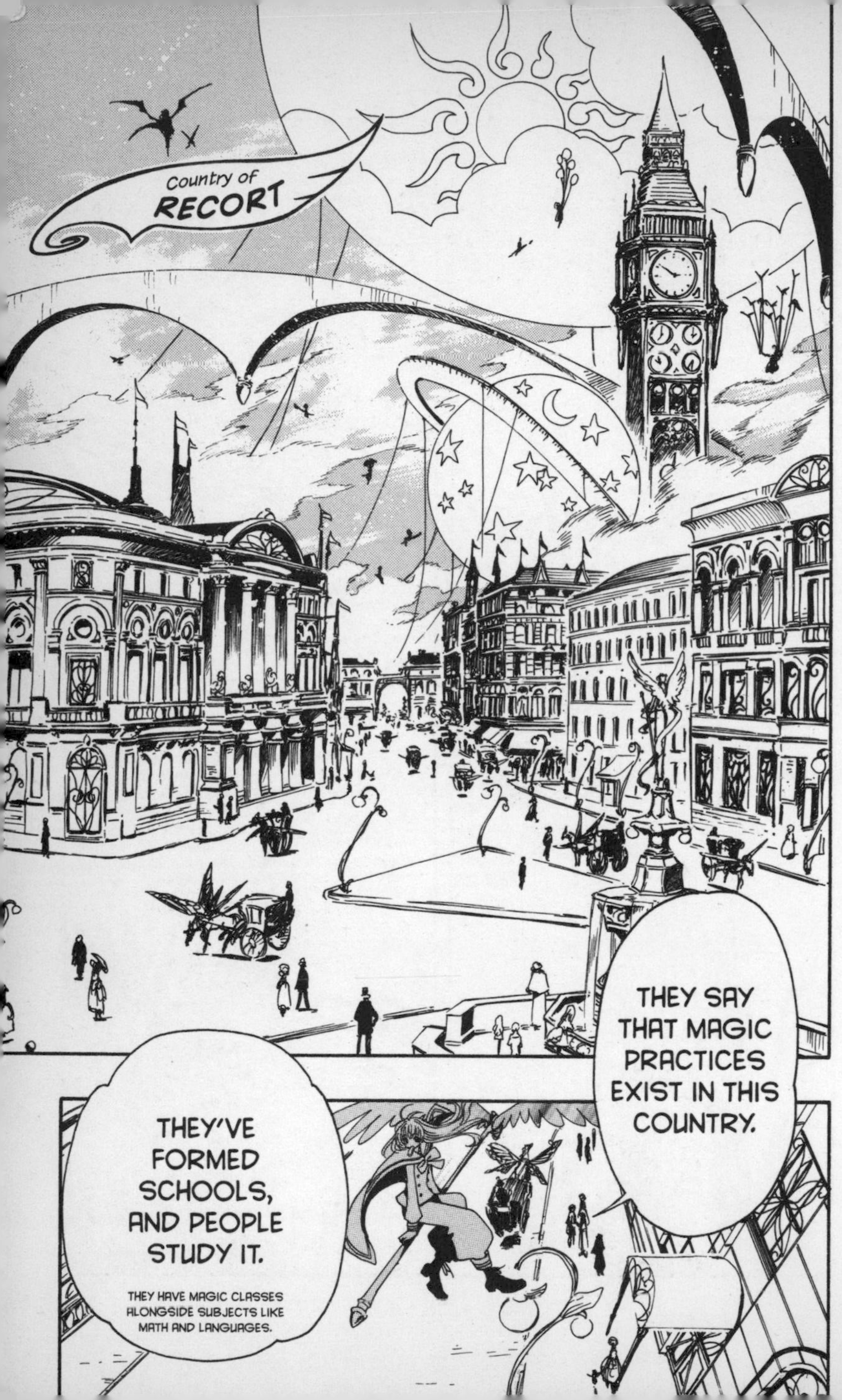
Country of RECORT
THEY SAY THAT MAGIC PRACTICES EXIST IN THIS COUNTRY.
THEY'VE FORMED SCHOOLS, AND PEOPLE STUDY IT.
THEY HAVE MAGIC CLASSES ALONGSIDE SUBJECTS LIKE MATH AND LANGUAGES.

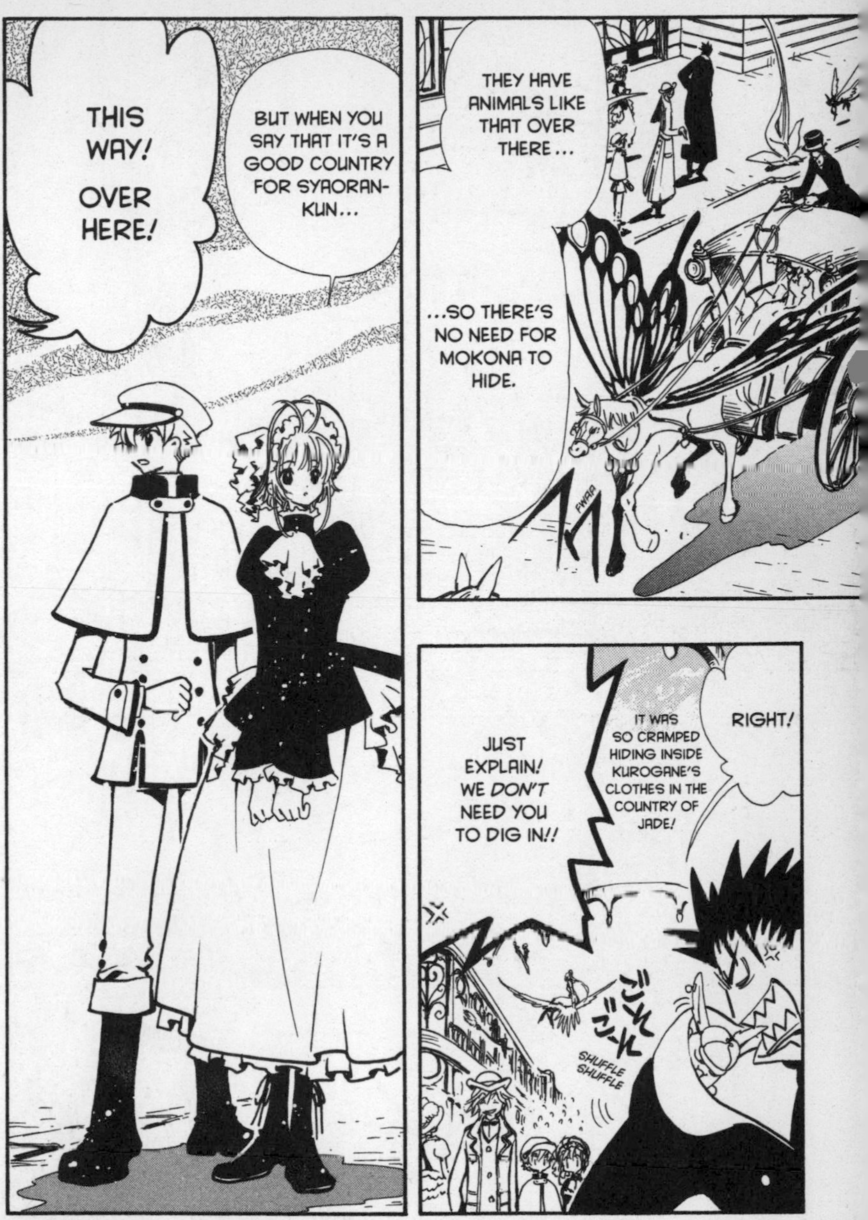
THEY HAVE ANIMALS LIKE THAT OVER THERE...
...SO THERE'S NO NEED FOR MOKONA TO HIDE.
FWAA
RIGHT!
IT WAS SO CRAMPED HIDING INSIDE KUROGANE'S CLOTHES IN THE COUNTRY OF JADE!
JUST EXPLAIN! WE *DON'T* NEED YOU TO DIG IN!!
SHUFFLE SHUFFLE
BUT WHEN YOU SAY THAT IT'S A GOOD COUNTRY FOR SYAORAN-KUN...
THIS WAY! OVER HERE!

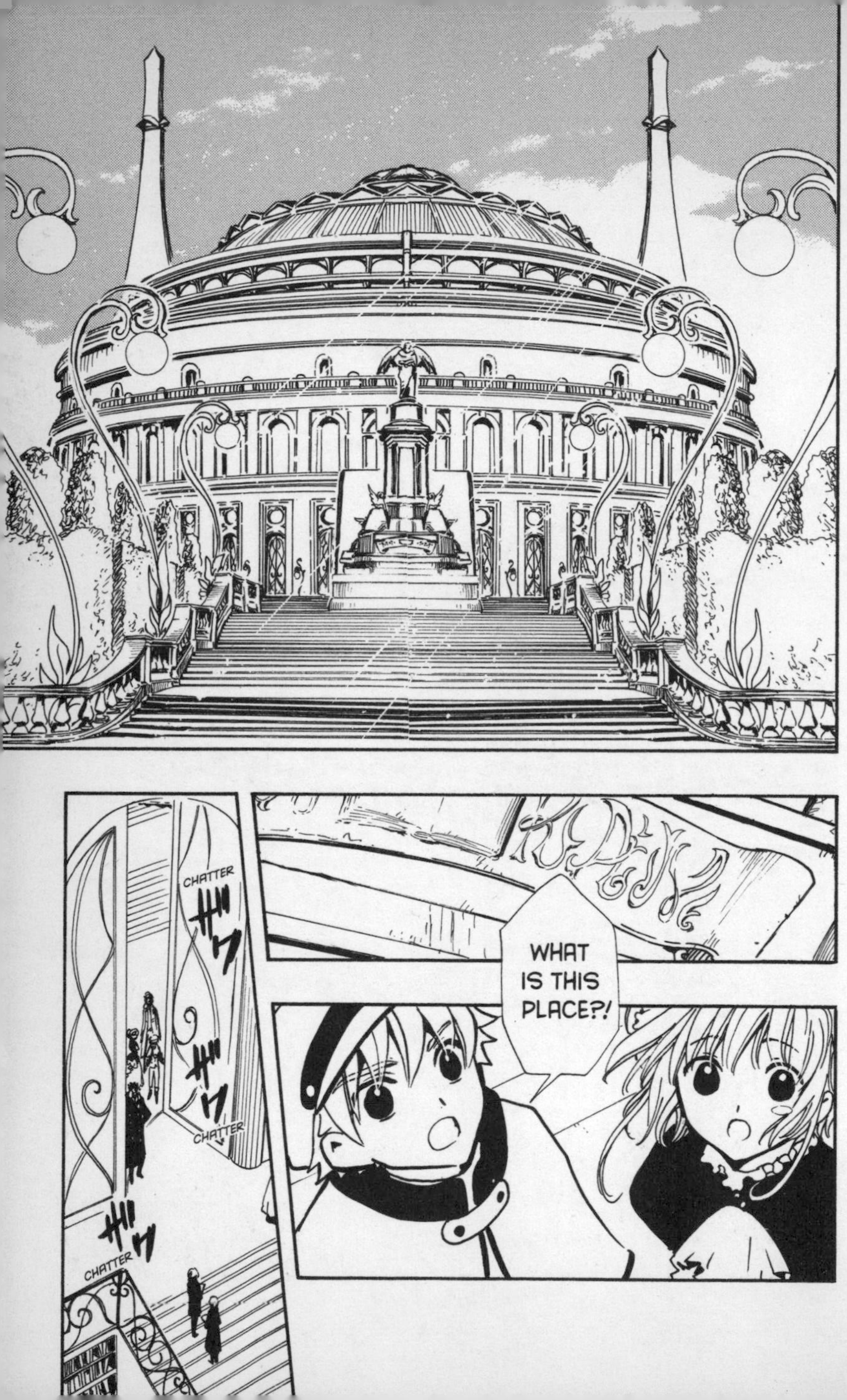
WHAT IS THIS PLACE?!
CHATTER
CHATTER
CHATTER

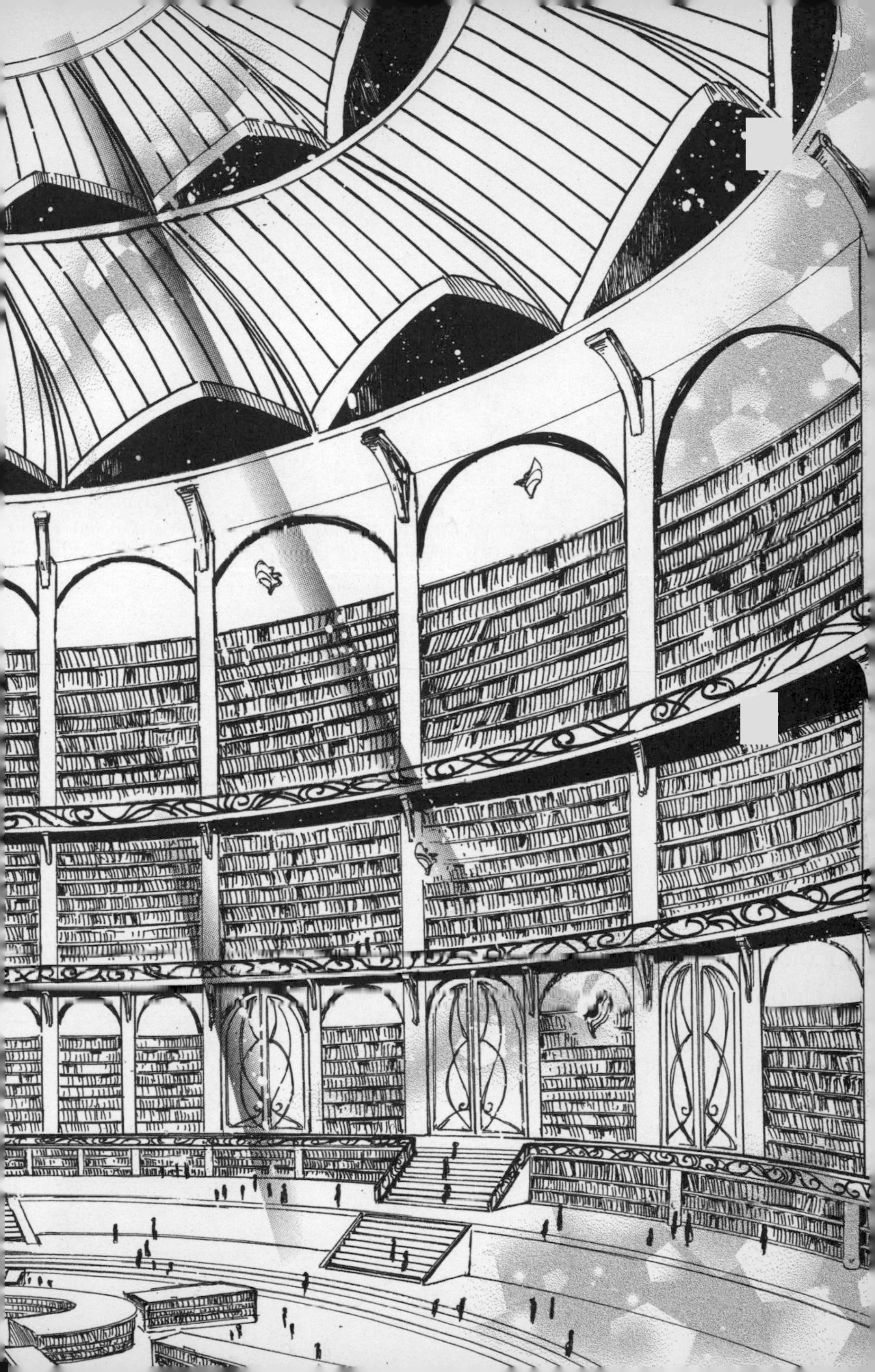

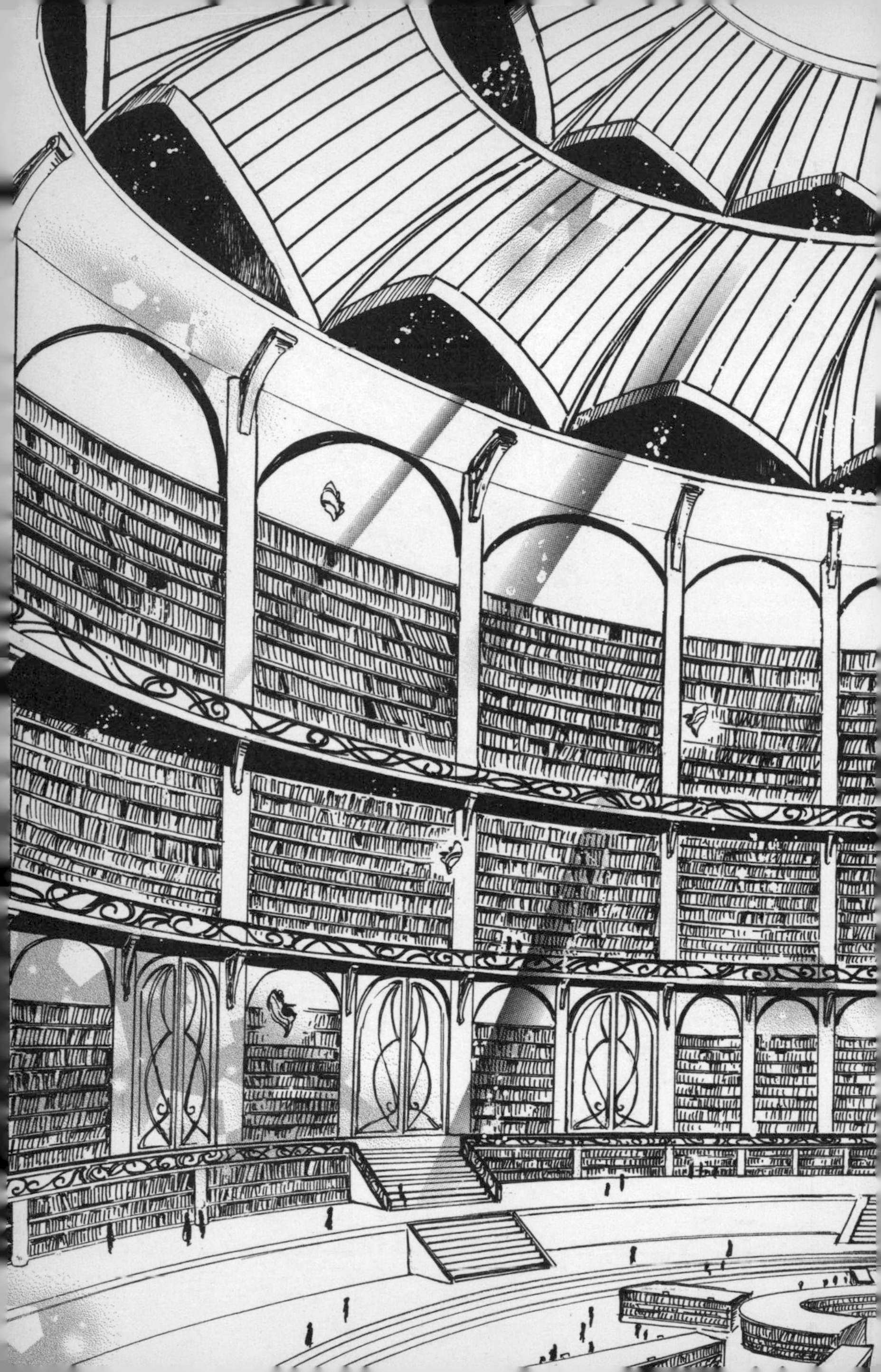

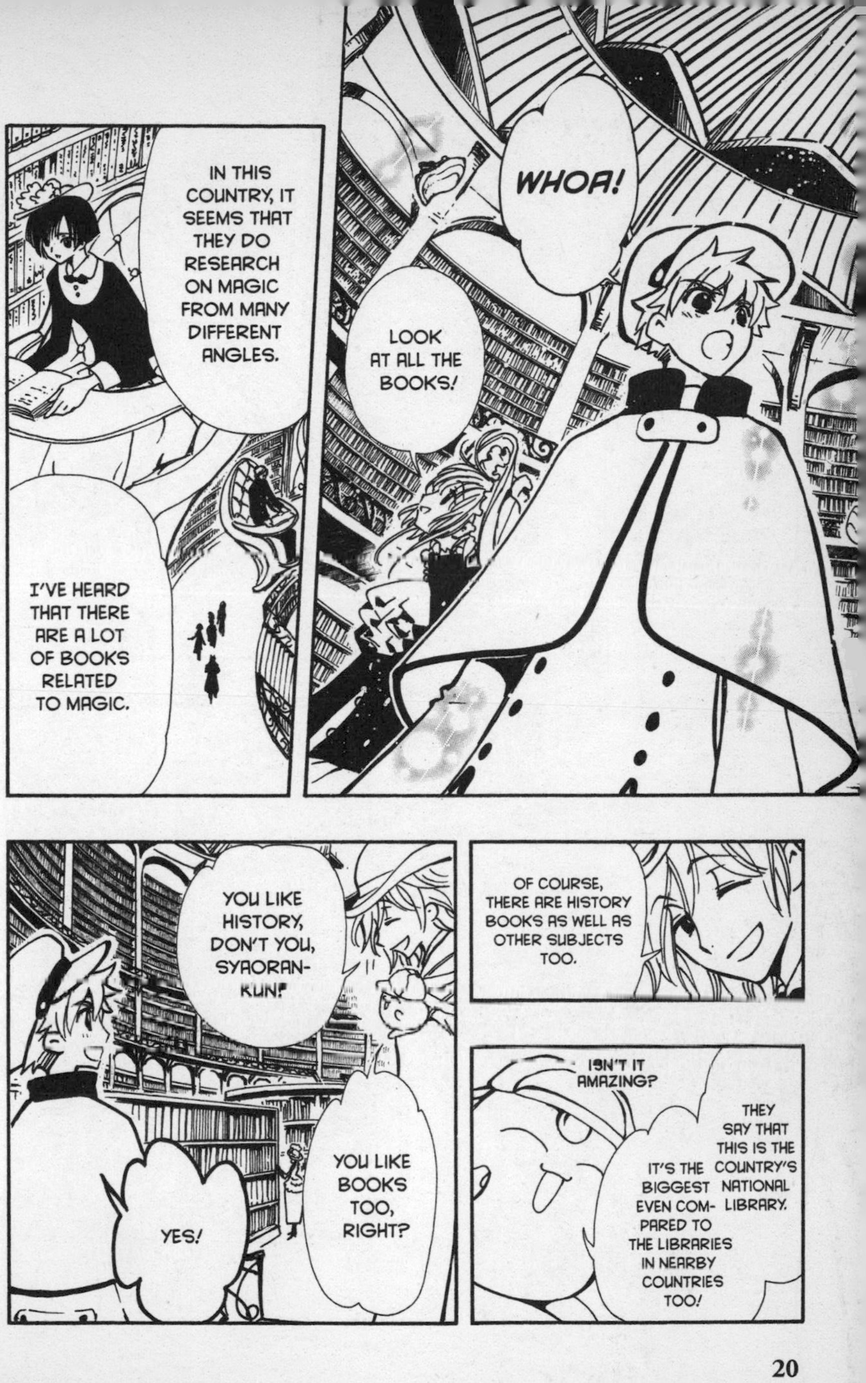
WHOA!
LOOK AT ALL THE BOOKS!
IN THIS COUNTRY, IT SEEMS THAT THEY DO RESEARCH ON MAGIC FROM MANY DIFFERENT ANGLES.
I'VE HEARD THAT THERE ARE A LOT OF BOOKS RELATED TO MAGIC.
OF COURSE, THERE ARE HISTORY BOOKS AS WELL AS OTHER SUBJECTS TOO.
ISN'T IT AMAZING?
THEY SAY THAT THIS IS THE COUNTRY'S NATIONAL LIBRARY.
IT'S THE BIGGEST EVEN COM-PARED TO THE LIBRARIES IN NEARBY COUNTRIES TOO!
YOU LIKE HISTORY, DON'T YOU, SYAORAN-KUN?
YOU LIKE BOOKS TOO, RIGHT?
YES!

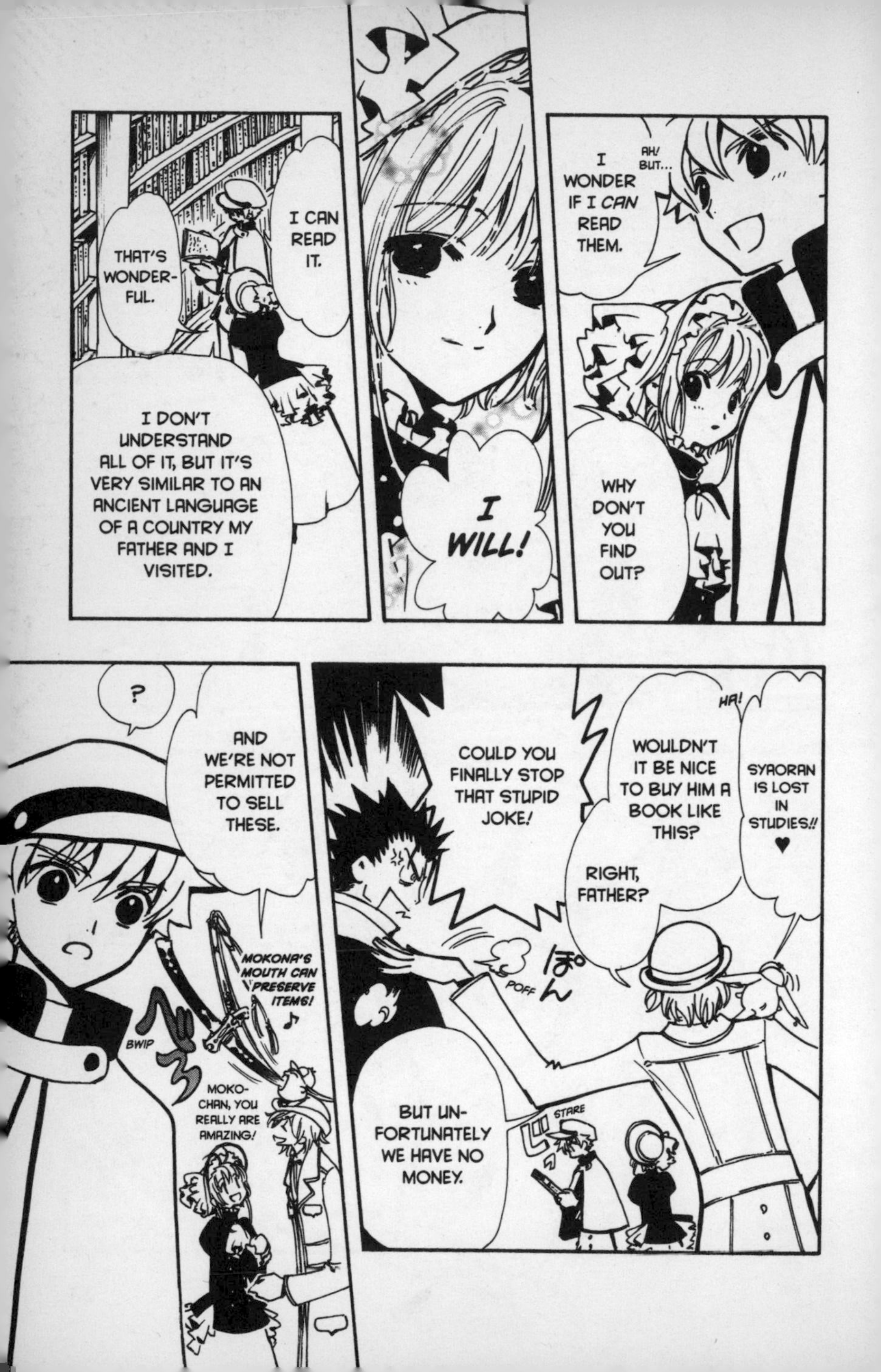
AH! BUT...
I WONDER IF I *CAN* READ THEM.
WHY DON'T YOU FIND OUT?
I WILL!
I CAN READ IT.
THAT'S WONDERFUL.
I DON'T UNDERSTAND ALL OF IT, BUT IT'S VERY SIMILAR TO AN ANCIENT LANGUAGE OF A COUNTRY MY FATHER AND I VISITED.
HA!
SYAORAN IS LOST IN STUDIES!! ♥
WOULDN'T IT BE NICE TO BUY HIM A BOOK LIKE THIS?
RIGHT, FATHER?
COULD YOU FINALLY STOP THAT STUPID JOKE!
ぽん
POFF
STARE
BUT UNFORTUNATELY WE HAVE NO MONEY.
?
AND WE'RE NOT PERMITTED TO SELL THESE.
MOKONA'S MOUTH CAN PRESERVE ITEMS! ♪
BWIP
MOKO-CHAN, YOU REALLY ARE AMAZING!

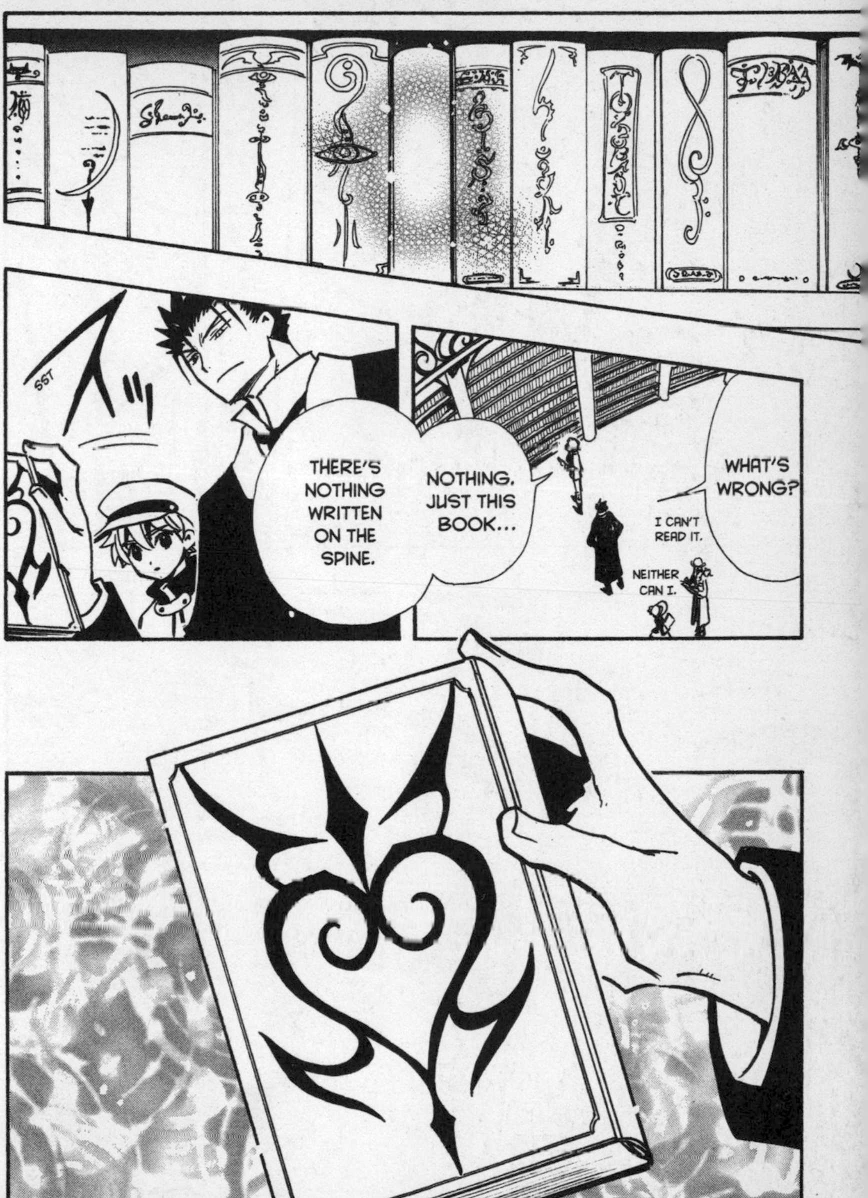
WHAT'S WRONG?
I CAN'T READ IT.
NEITHER CAN I.
NOTHING. JUST THIS BOOK...
SST
THERE'S NOTHING WRITTEN ON THE SPINE.

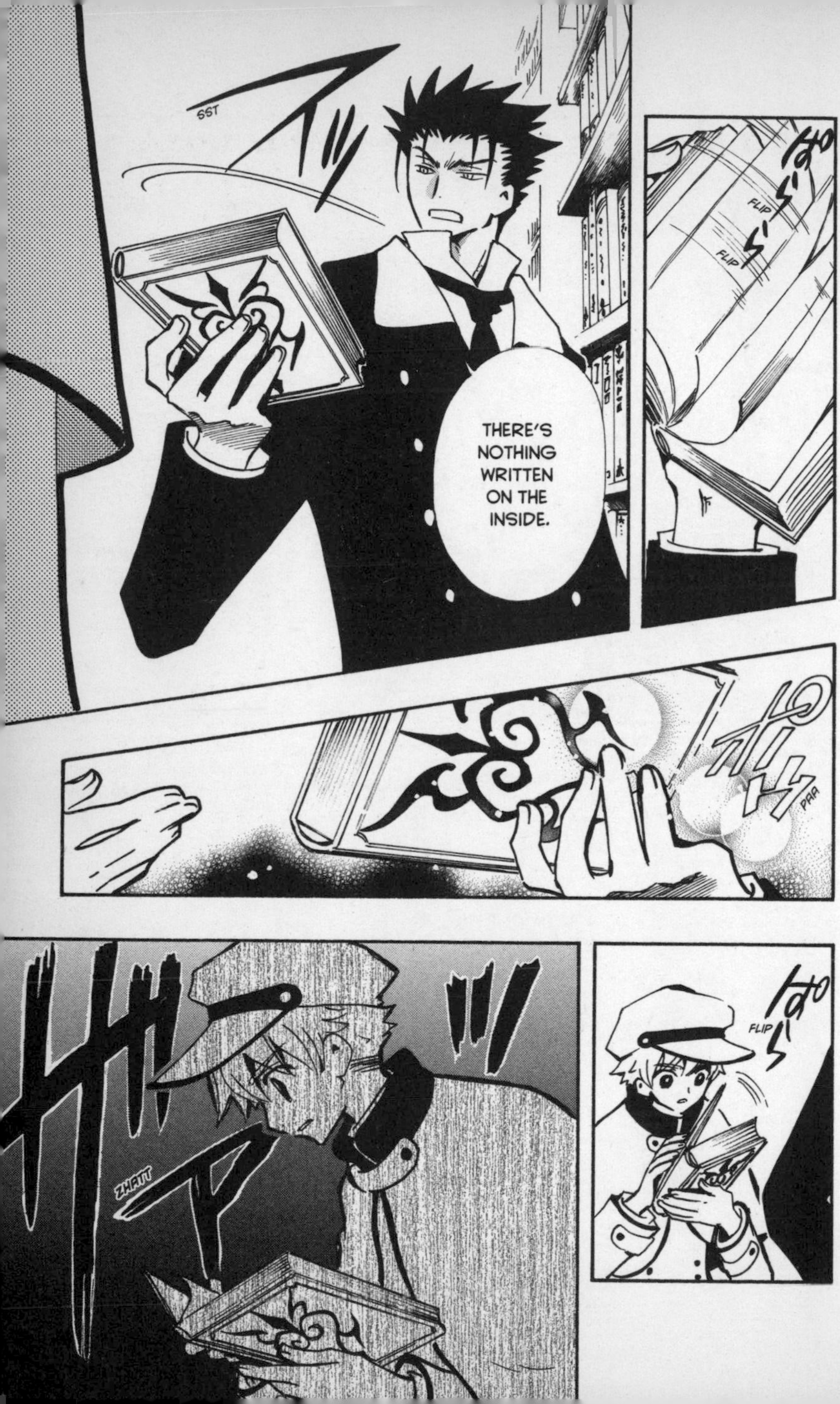
FLIP
FLIP
SST
THERE'S NOTHING WRITTEN ON THE INSIDE.
PAA
FLIP
ZHATT

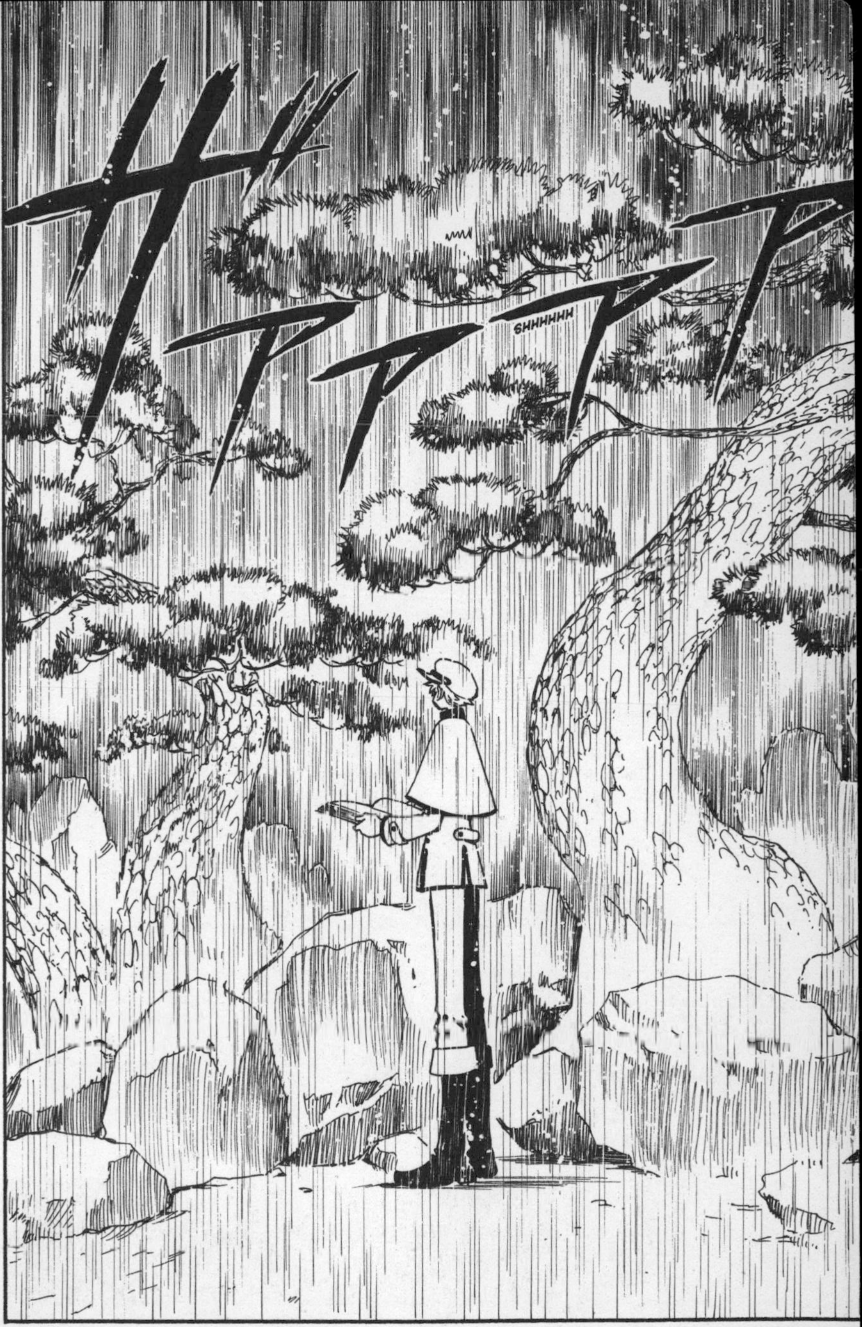
ザァァァァ
SHHHHHH

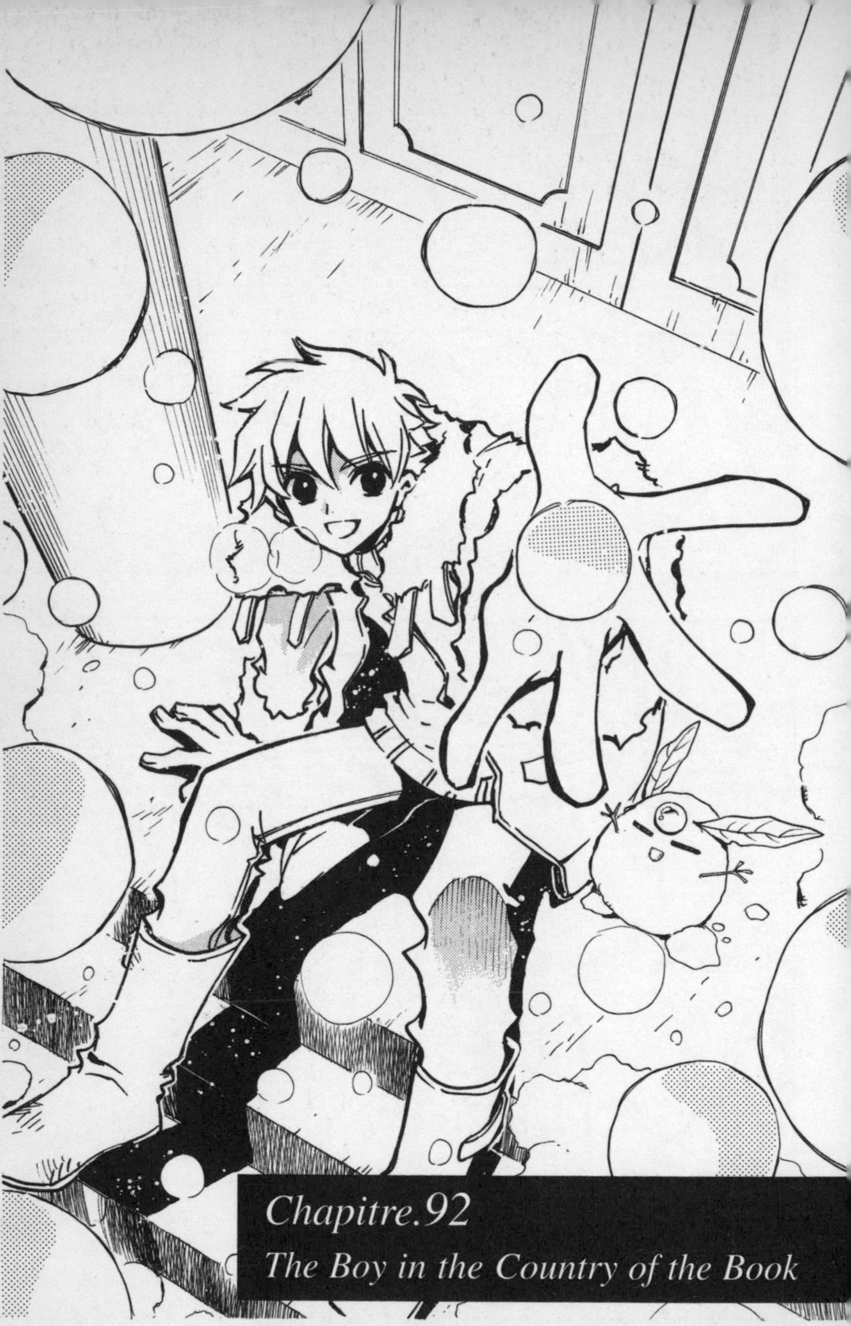

Chapitre.92
The Boy in the Country of the Book

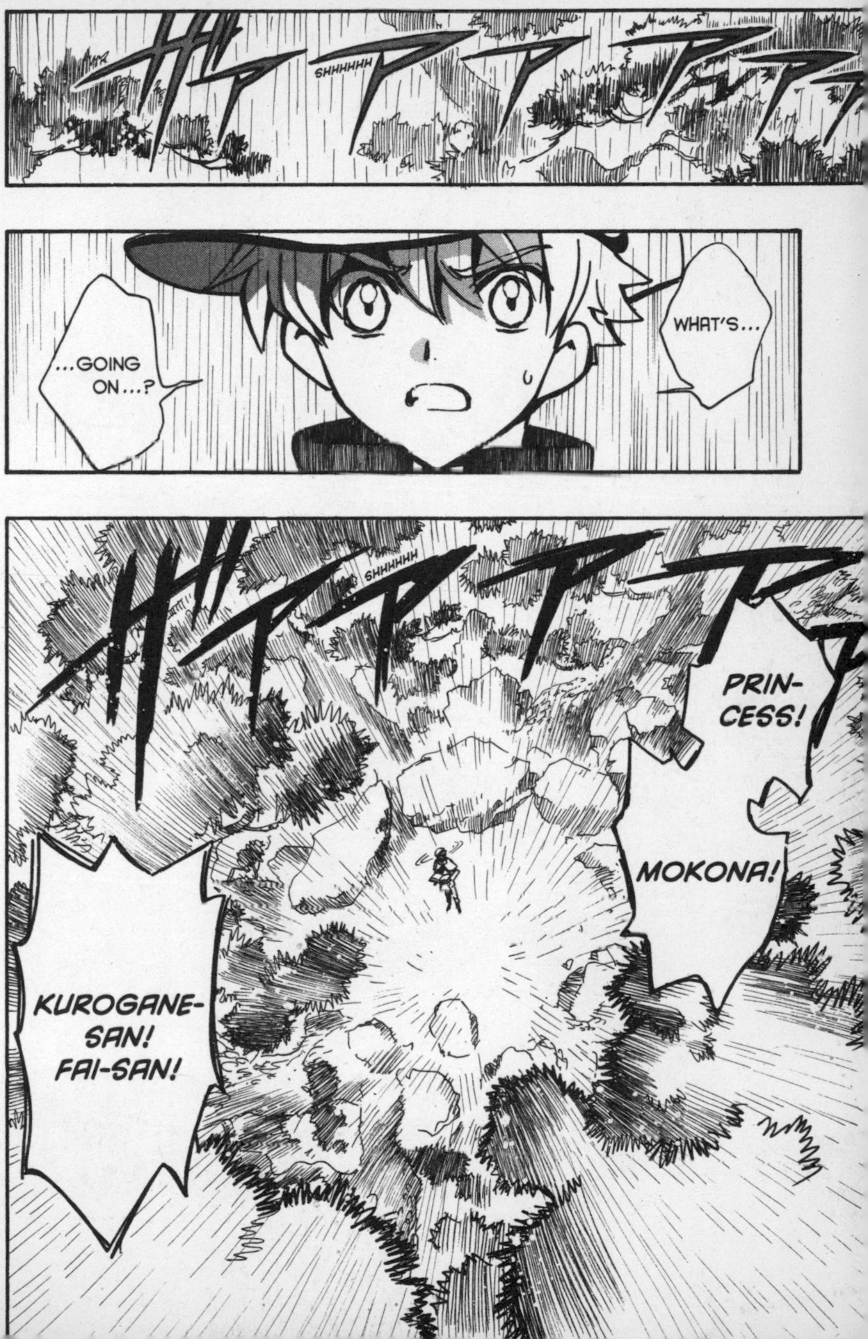
SHHHHHH
WHAT'S...
...GOING ON...?
SHHHHHH
PRIN-CESS!
MOKONA!
KUROGANE-SAN! FAI-SAN!

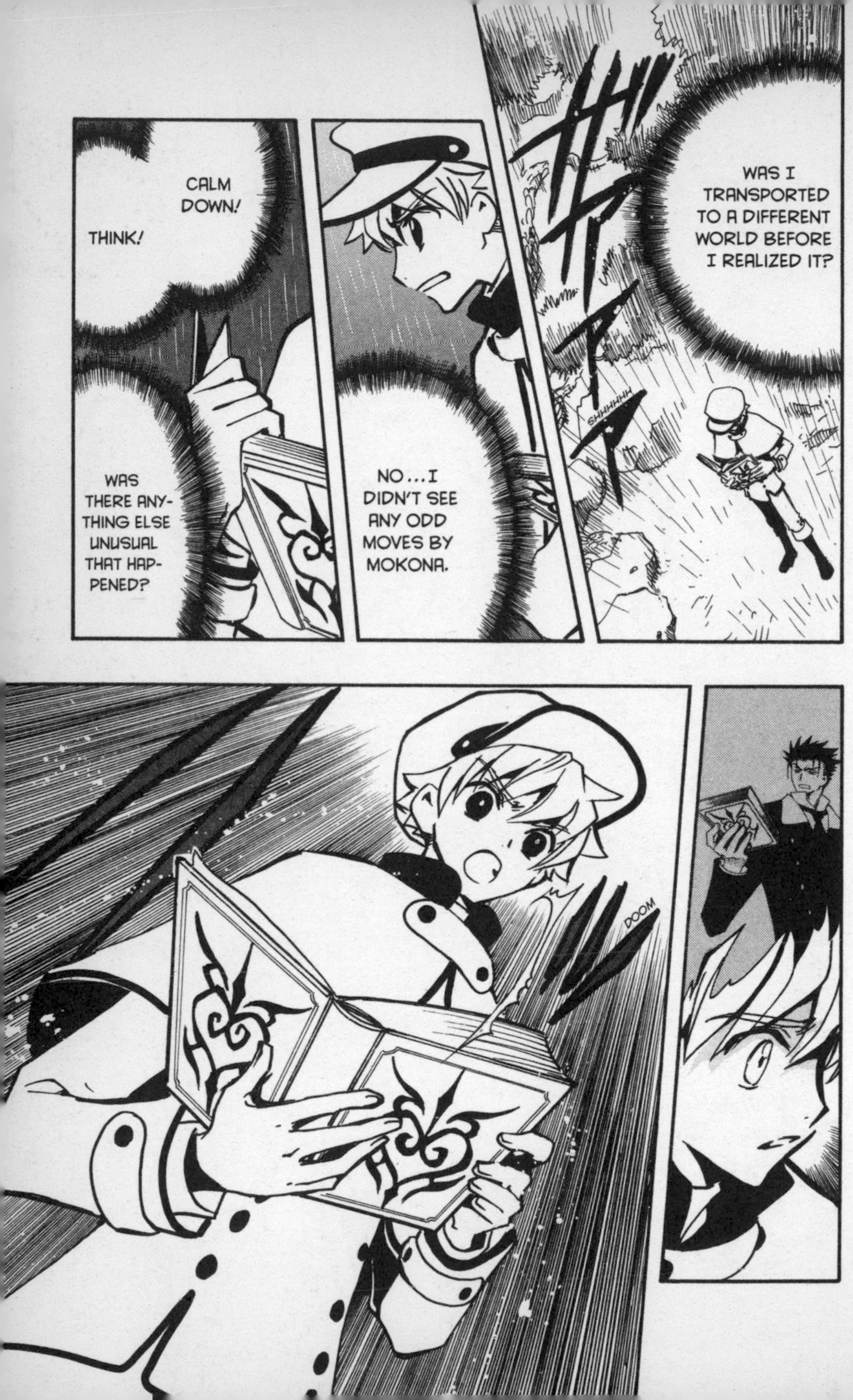
WAS I TRANSPORTED TO A DIFFERENT WORLD BEFORE I REALIZED IT?
SHHHHHH
NO...I DIDN'T SEE ANY ODD MOVES BY MOKONA.
CALM DOWN!
THINK!
WAS THERE ANY-THING ELSE UNUSUAL THAT HAP-PENED?
DOOM

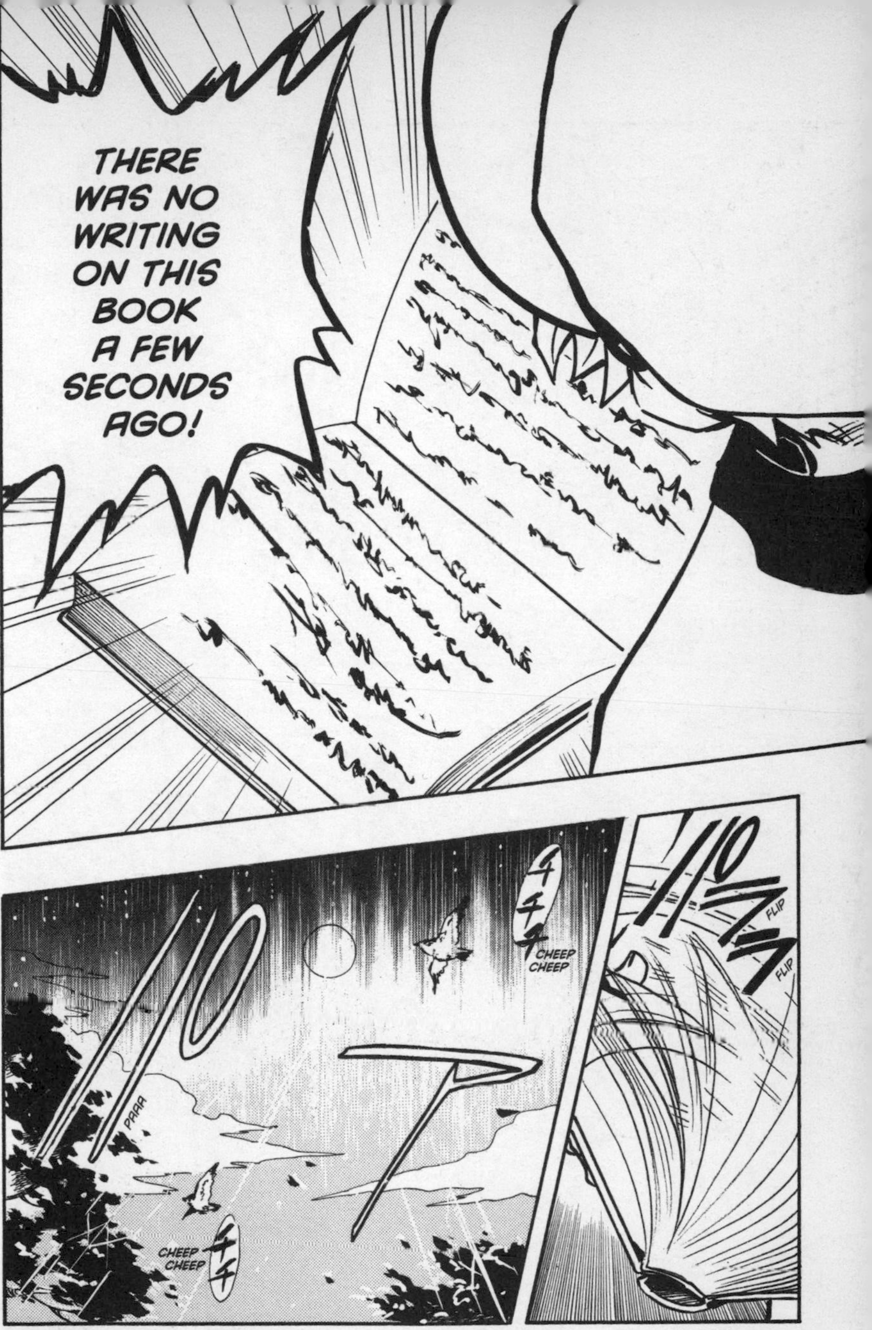
THERE WAS NO WRITING ON THIS BOOK A FEW SECONDS AGO!
FLIP
FLIP
CHEEP CHEEP
PAAA
CHEEP CHEEP

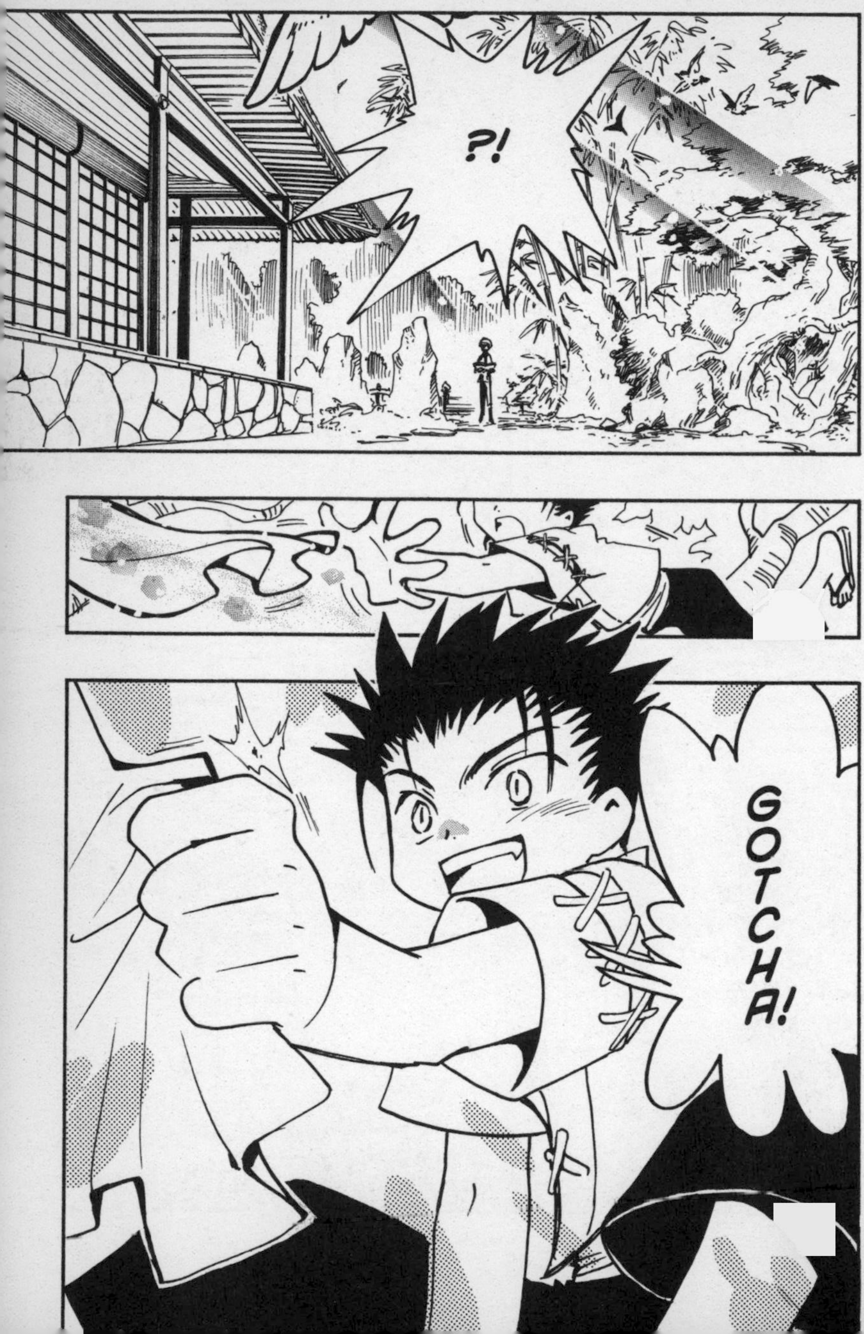
?!
GOTCHA!

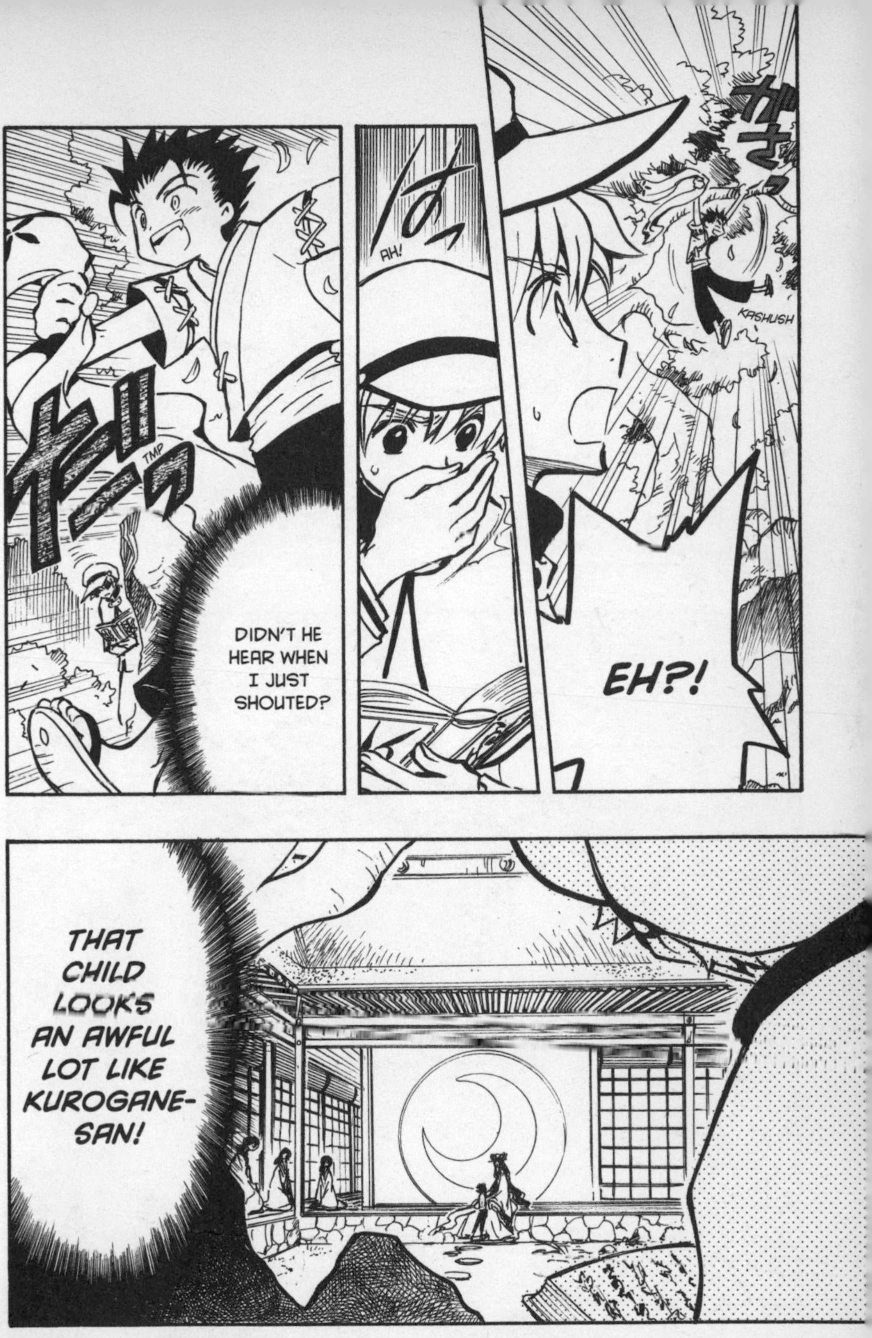
KASHUSH
EH?!
AH!
TMP
DIDN'T HE HEAR WHEN I JUST SHOUTED?
THAT CHILD LOOKS AN AWFUL LOT LIKE KUROGANE-SAN!

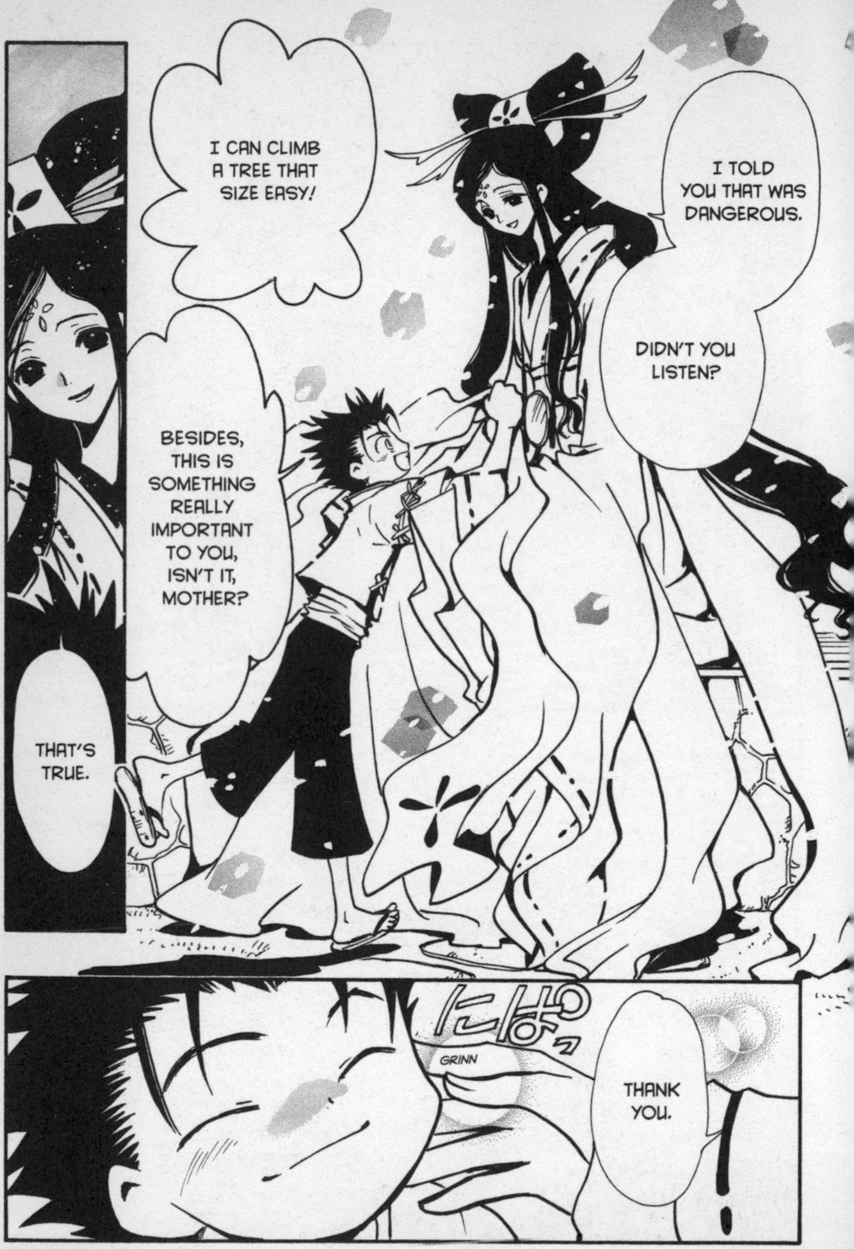
I TOLD YOU THAT WAS DANGEROUS.
DIDN'T YOU LISTEN?
I CAN CLIMB A TREE THAT SIZE EASY!
BESIDES, THIS IS SOMETHING REALLY IMPORTANT TO YOU, ISN'T IT, MOTHER?
THAT'S TRUE.
にぱっ
GRINN
THANK YOU.

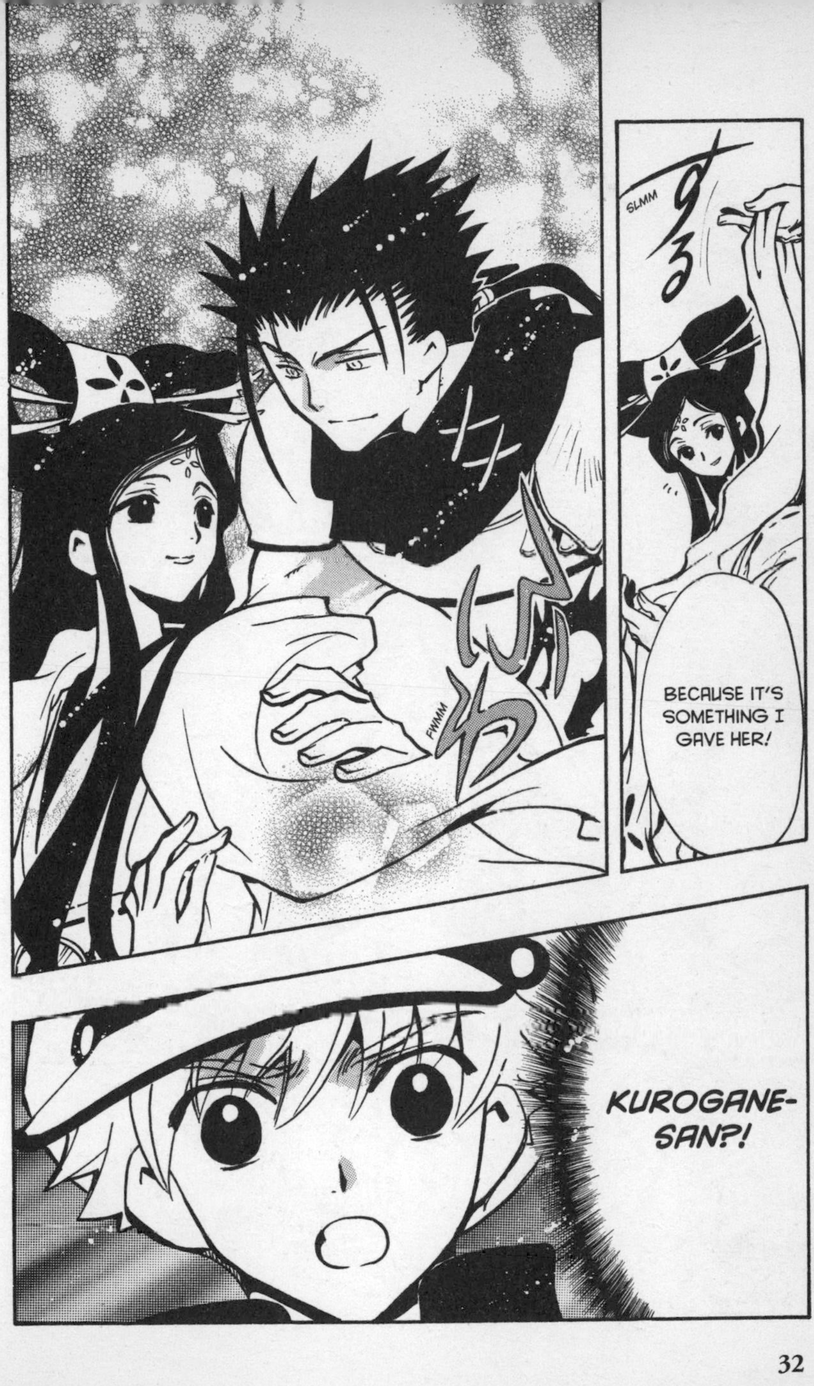

する
SLMM
BECAUSE IT'S SOMETHING I GAVE HER!
ふわ
FWMM
KUROGANE-SAN?!

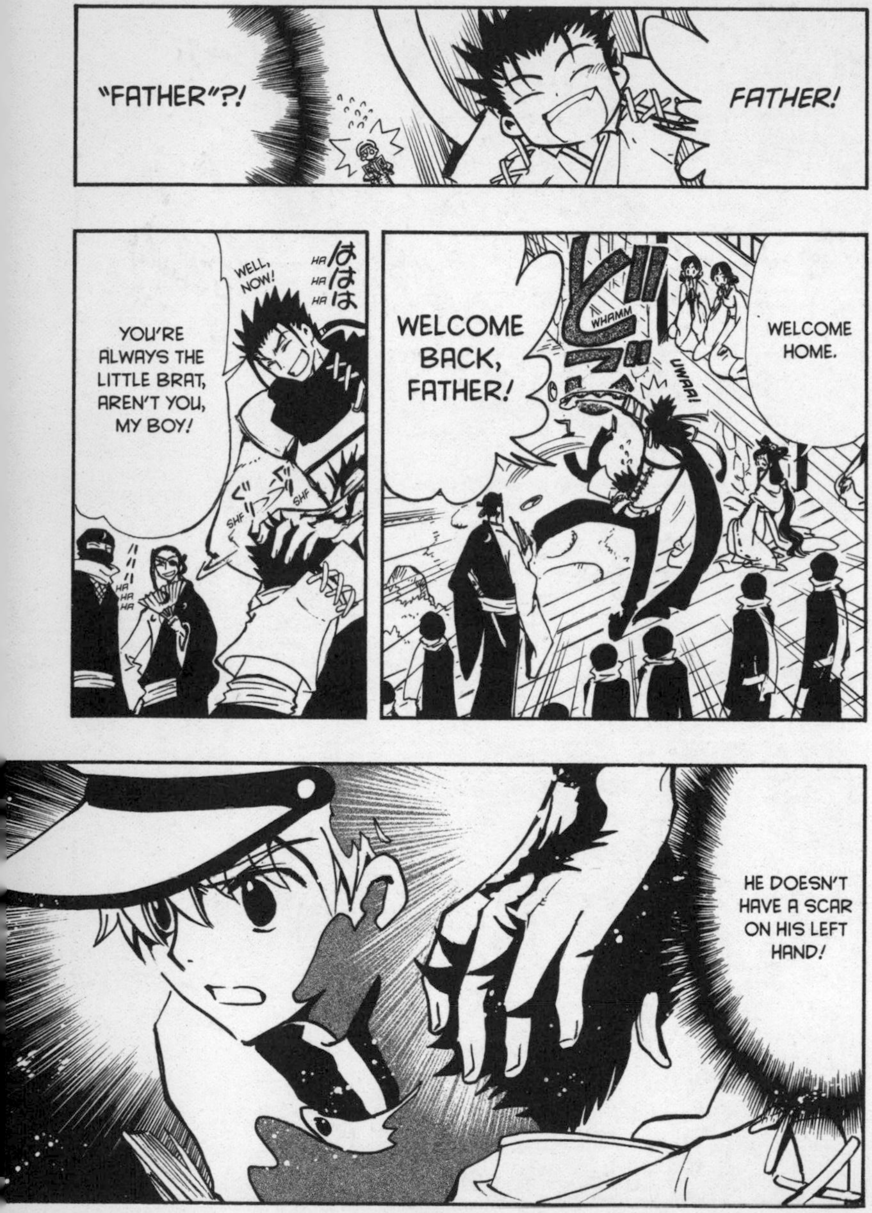
FATHER!
"FATHER"?!
WELCOME HOME.
WHAMM
UWAA!
WELCOME BACK, FATHER!
HA HA HA
WELL, NOW!
YOU'RE ALWAYS THE LITTLE BRAT, AREN'T YOU, MY BOY!
SHF
SHF
HA HA HA
HE DOESN'T HAVE A SCAR ON HIS LEFT HAND!

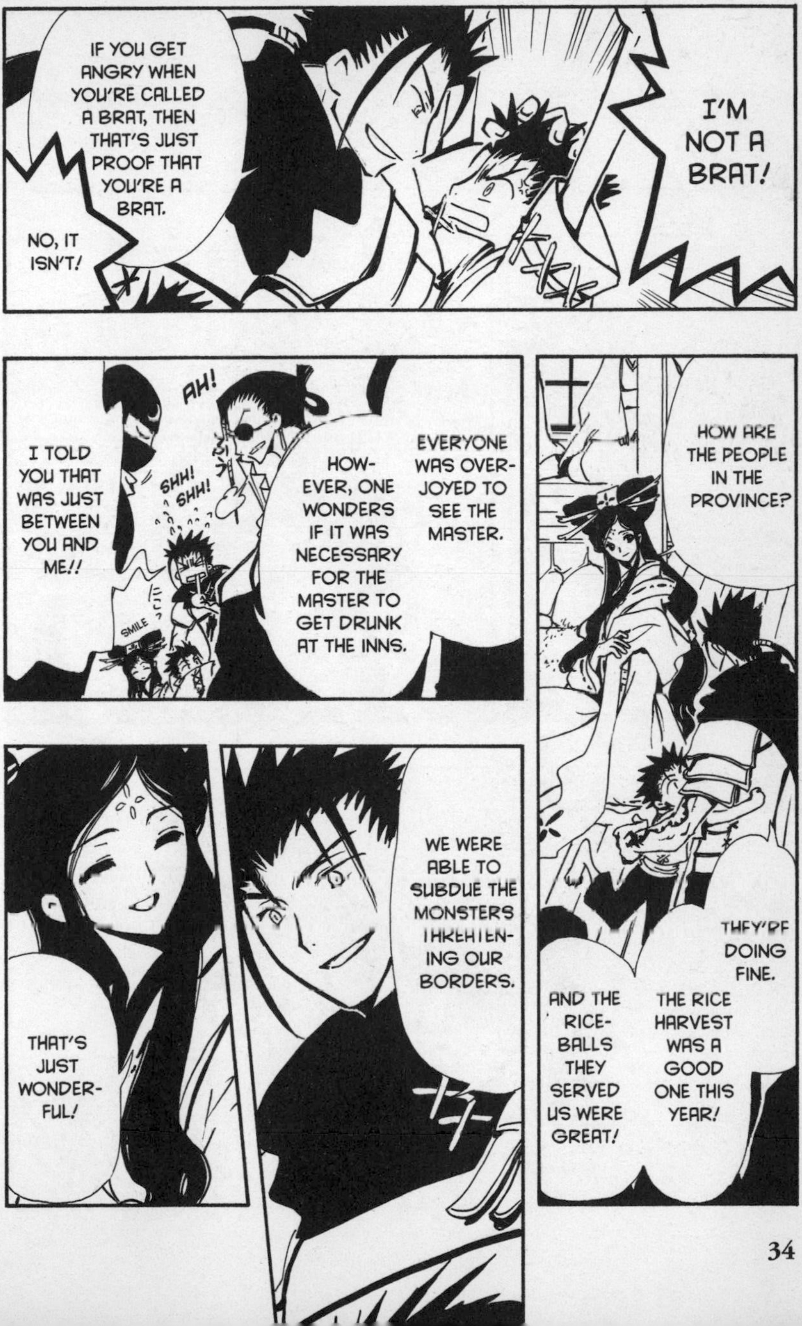
I'M NOT A BRAT!
IF YOU GET ANGRY WHEN YOU'RE CALLED A BRAT, THEN THAT'S JUST PROOF THAT YOU'RE A BRAT.
NO, IT ISN'T!
HOW ARE THE PEOPLE IN THE PROVINCE?
THEY'RE DOING FINE.
THE RICE HARVEST WAS A GOOD ONE THIS YEAR!
AND THE RICE-BALLS THEY SERVED US WERE GREAT!
EVERYONE WAS OVER-JOYED TO SEE THE MASTER.
HOW-EVER, ONE WONDERS IF IT WAS NECESSARY FOR THE MASTER TO GET DRUNK AT THE INNS.
AH!
SHH! SHH!
I TOLD YOU THAT WAS JUST BETWEEN YOU AND ME!!
SMILE
WE WERE ABLE TO SUBDUE THE MONSTERS THREATEN-ING OUR BORDERS.
THAT'S JUST WONDER-FUL!

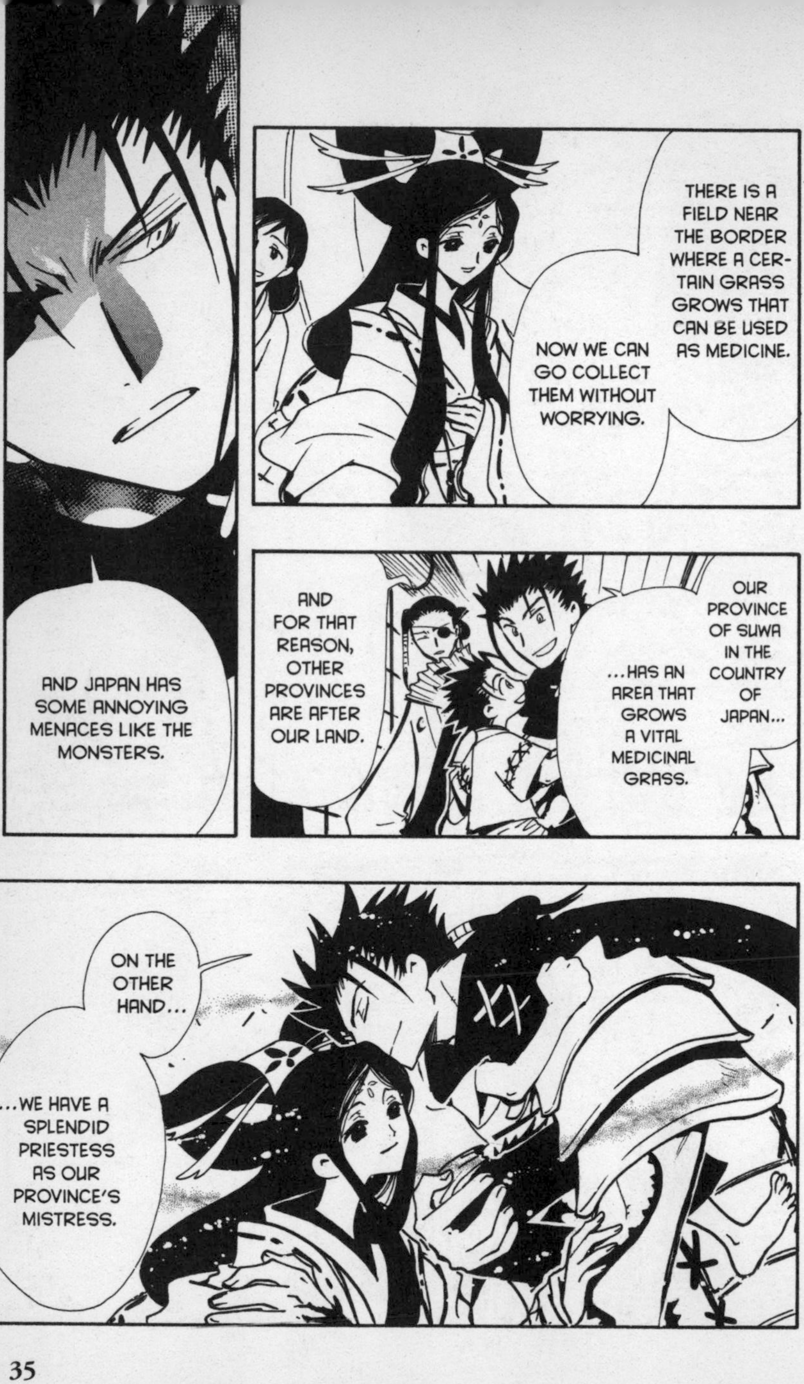
THERE IS A FIELD NEAR THE BORDER WHERE A CER-TAIN GRASS GROWS THAT CAN BE USED AS MEDICINE.
NOW WE CAN GO COLLECT THEM WITHOUT WORRYING.
OUR PROVINCE OF SUWA IN THE COUNTRY OF JAPAN...
...HAS AN AREA THAT GROWS A VITAL MEDICINAL GRASS.
AND FOR THAT REASON, OTHER PROVINCES ARE AFTER OUR LAND.
AND JAPAN HAS SOME ANNOYING MENACES LIKE THE MONSTERS.
ON THE OTHER HAND...
...WE HAVE A SPLENDID PRIESTESS AS OUR PROVINCE'S MISTRESS.

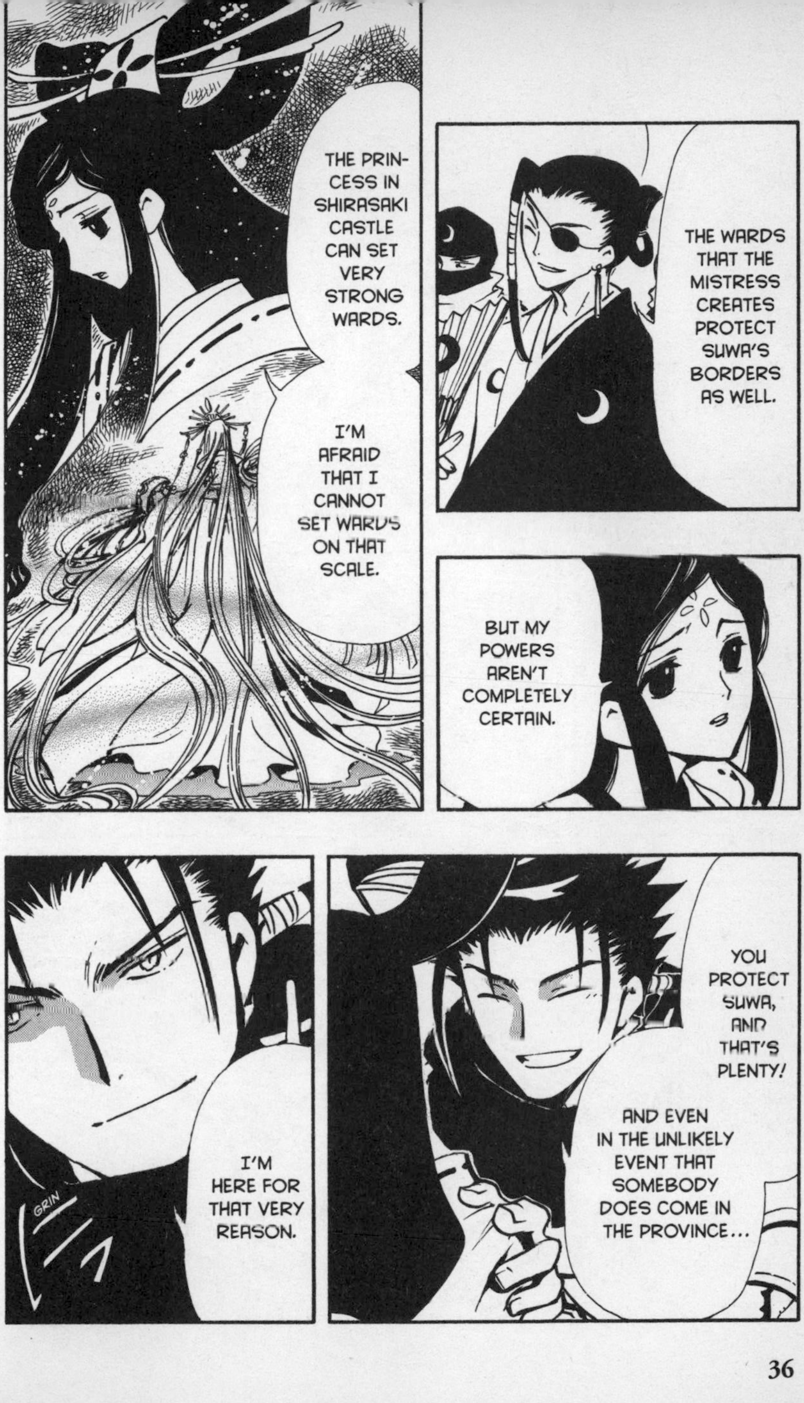
THE WARDS THAT THE MISTRESS CREATES PROTECT SUWA'S BORDERS AS WELL.
BUT MY POWERS AREN'T COMPLETELY CERTAIN.
THE PRIN-CESS IN SHIRASAKI CASTLE CAN SET VERY STRONG WARDS.
I'M AFRAID THAT I CANNOT SET WARDS ON THAT SCALE.
YOU PROTECT SUWA, AND THAT'S PLENTY!
AND EVEN IN THE UNLIKELY EVENT THAT SOMEBODY DOES COME IN THE PROVINCE...
I'M HERE FOR THAT VERY REASON.
GRIN

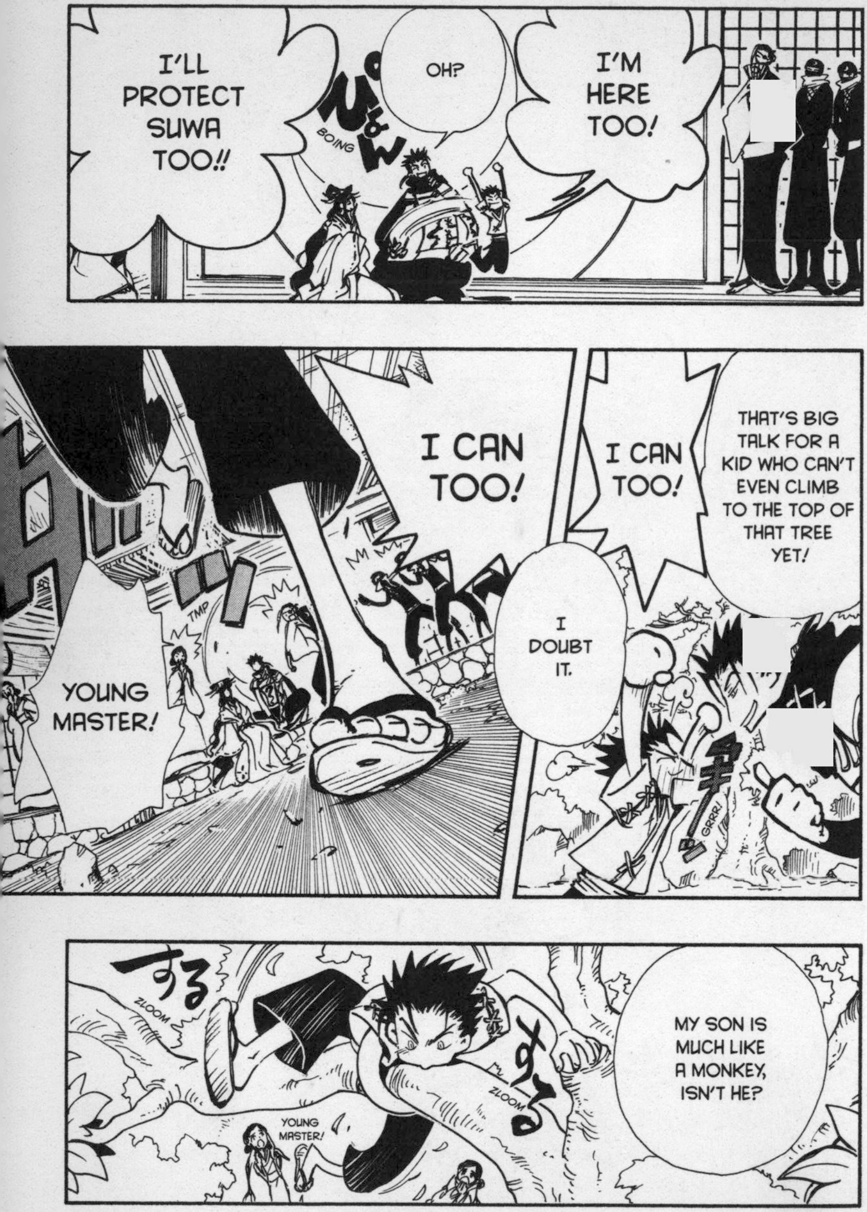
I'M HERE TOO!
OH?
BOING
I'LL PROTECT SUWA TOO!!
THAT'S BIG TALK FOR A KID WHO CAN'T EVEN CLIMB TO THE TOP OF THAT TREE YET!
I CAN TOO!
I DOUBT IT.
GRRR!
I CAN TOO!
TMP
YOUNG MASTER!
MY SON IS MUCH LIKE A MONKEY, ISN'T HE?
する
ZLOOM
する
ZLOOM
YOUNG MASTER!

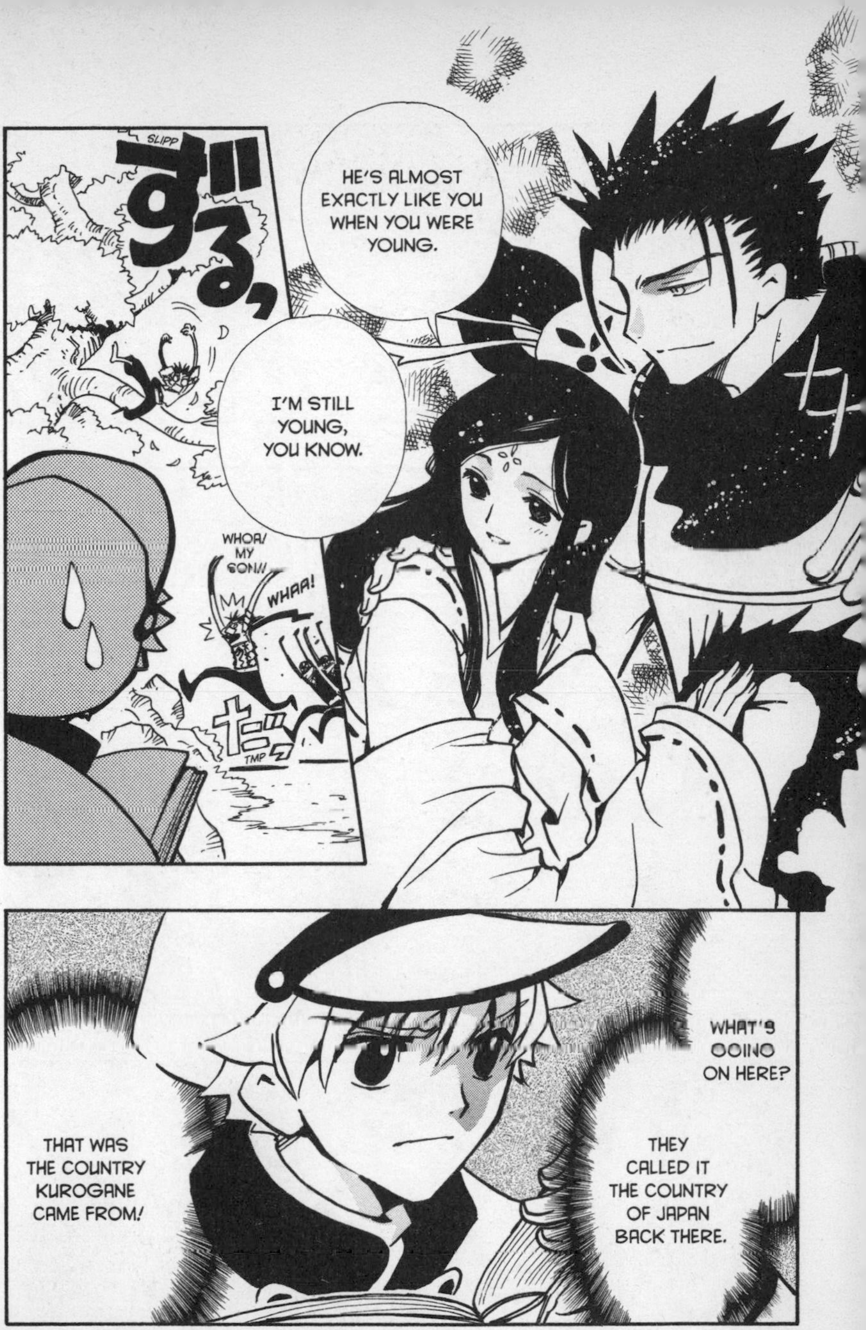
HE'S ALMOST EXACTLY LIKE YOU WHEN YOU WERE YOUNG.
I'M STILL YOUNG, YOU KNOW.
ずる
SLIPP
WHOA! MY SON!!
WHAA!
たっ
TMP
WHAT'S GOING ON HERE?
THEY CALLED IT THE COUNTRY OF JAPAN BACK THERE.
THAT WAS THE COUNTRY KUROGANE CAME FROM!

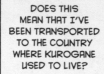

DOES THIS MEAN THAT I'VE BEEN TRANSPORTED TO THE COUNTRY WHERE KUROGANE USED TO LIVE?

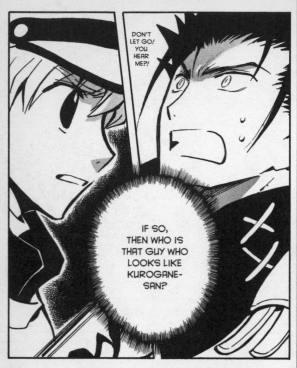

DON'T LET GO! YOU HEAR ME?!

IF SO, THEN WHO IS THAT GUY WHO LOOKS LIKE KUROGANE-SAN?

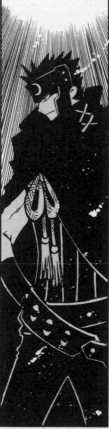

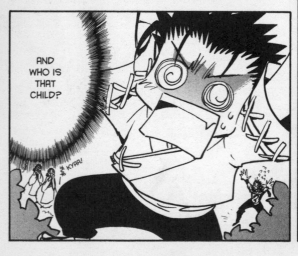

AND WHO IS THAT CHILD?

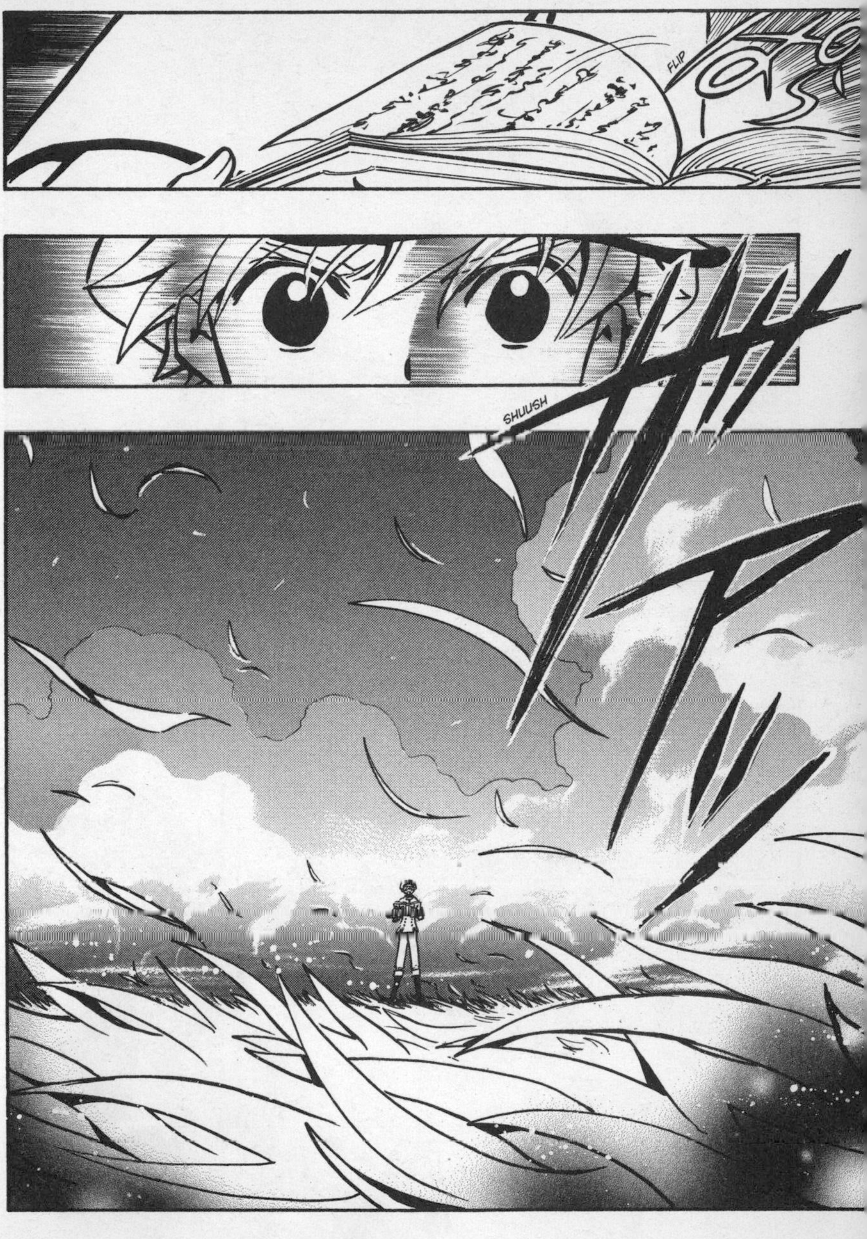
FLIP
SHUUSH

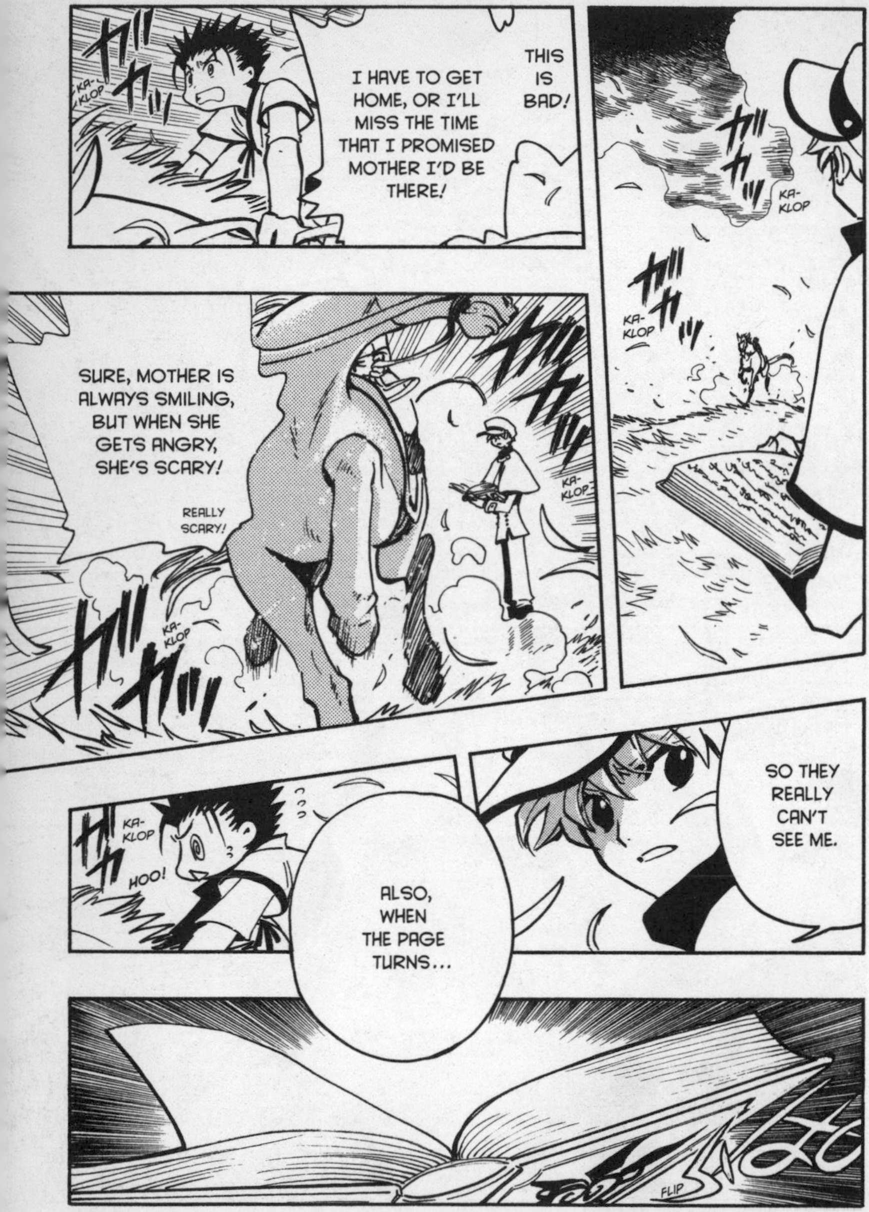
KA-KLOP
KA-KLOP
THIS IS BAD!
I HAVE TO GET HOME, OR I'LL MISS THE TIME THAT I PROMISED MOTHER I'D BE THERE!
KA-KLOP
KA-KLOP
SURE, MOTHER IS ALWAYS SMILING, BUT WHEN SHE GETS ANGRY, SHE'S SCARY!
REALLY SCARY!
KA-KLOP
SO THEY REALLY CAN'T SEE ME.
KA-KLOP
HOO!
ALSO, WHEN THE PAGE TURNS...
FLIP

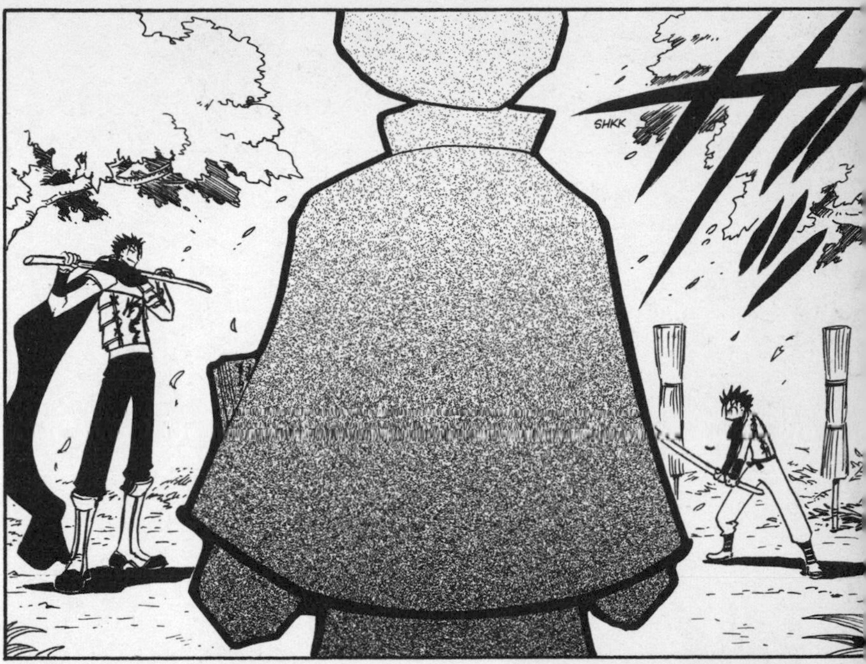
SHKK

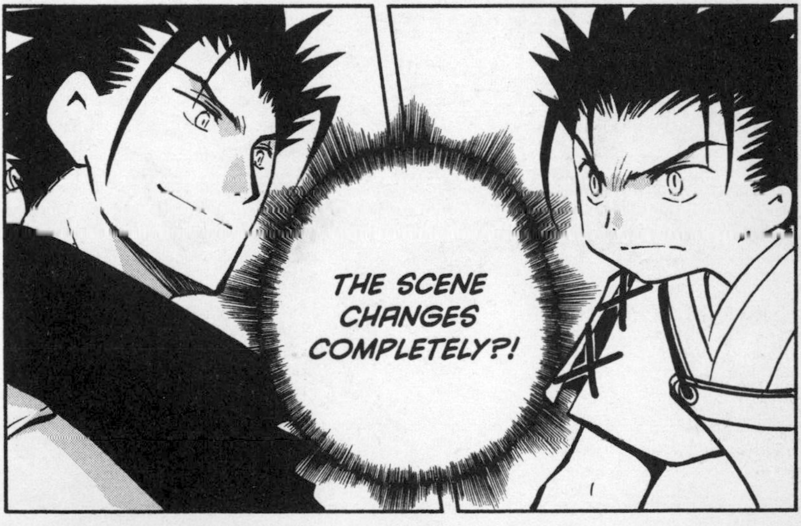
THE SCENE CHANGES COMPLETELY?!

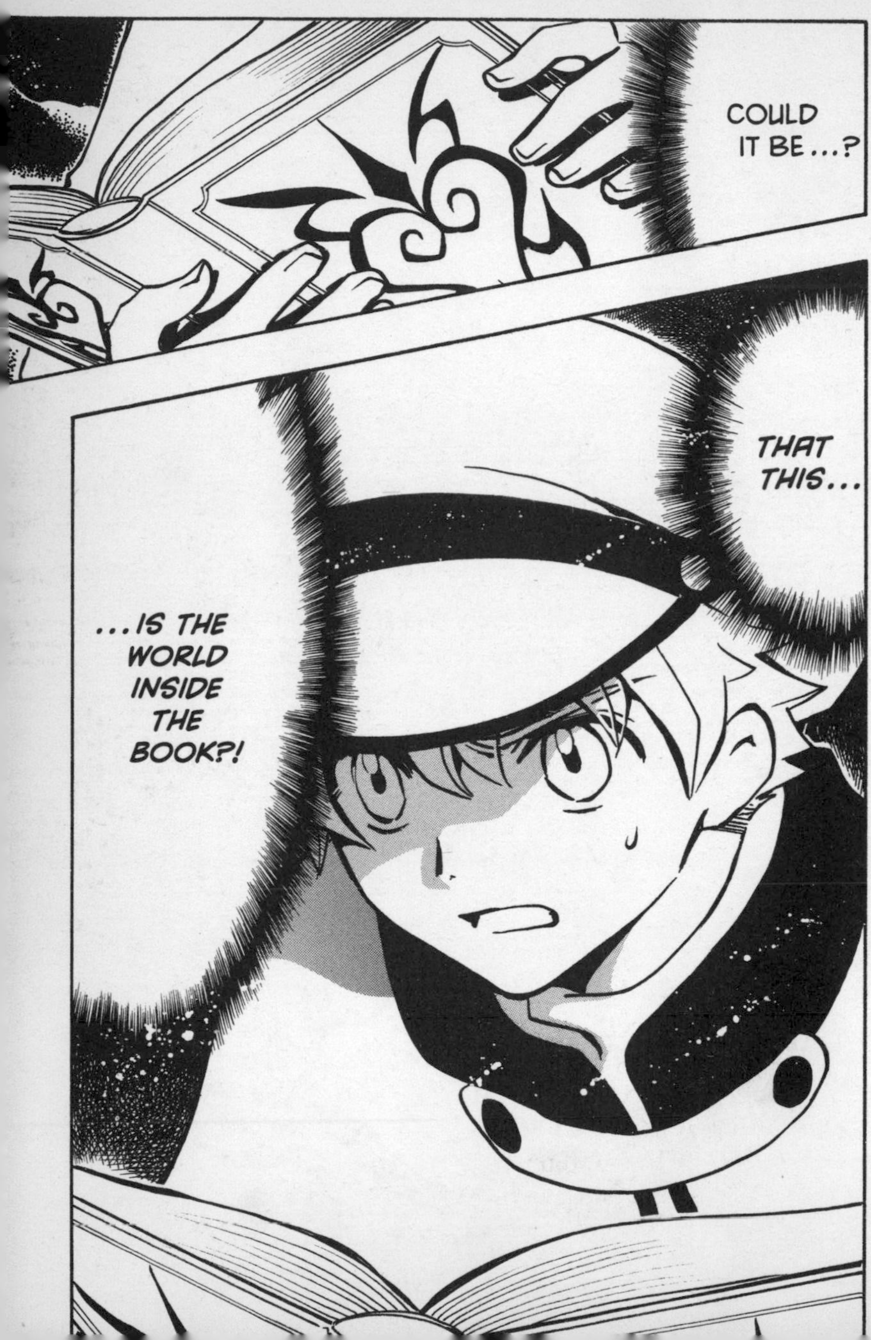
COULD IT BE...?
THAT THIS...
...IS THE WORLD INSIDE THE BOOK?!

ツバサ
RESERVoir CHRoNiCLE

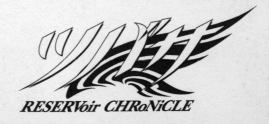

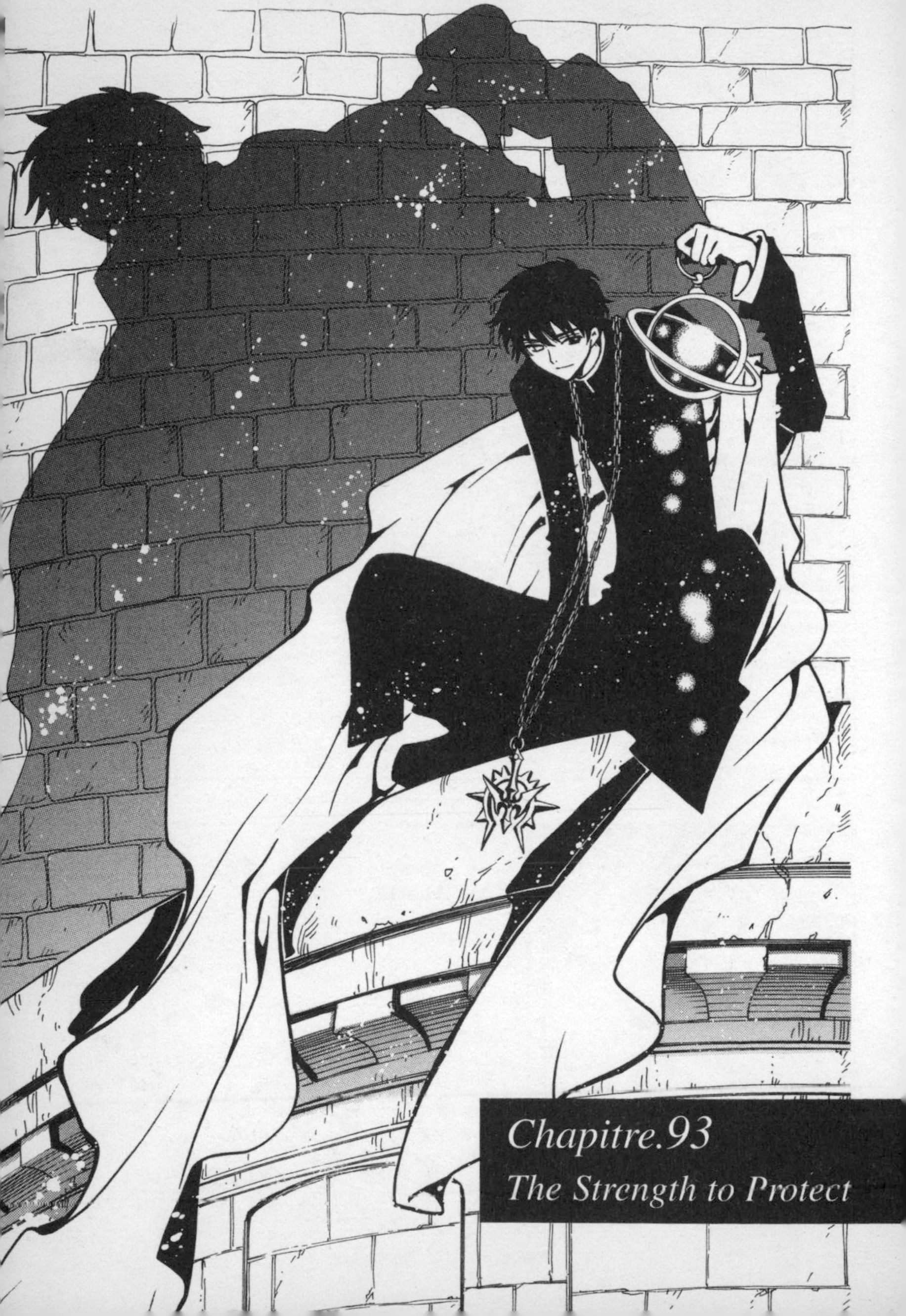
Chapitre.93
The Strength to Protect

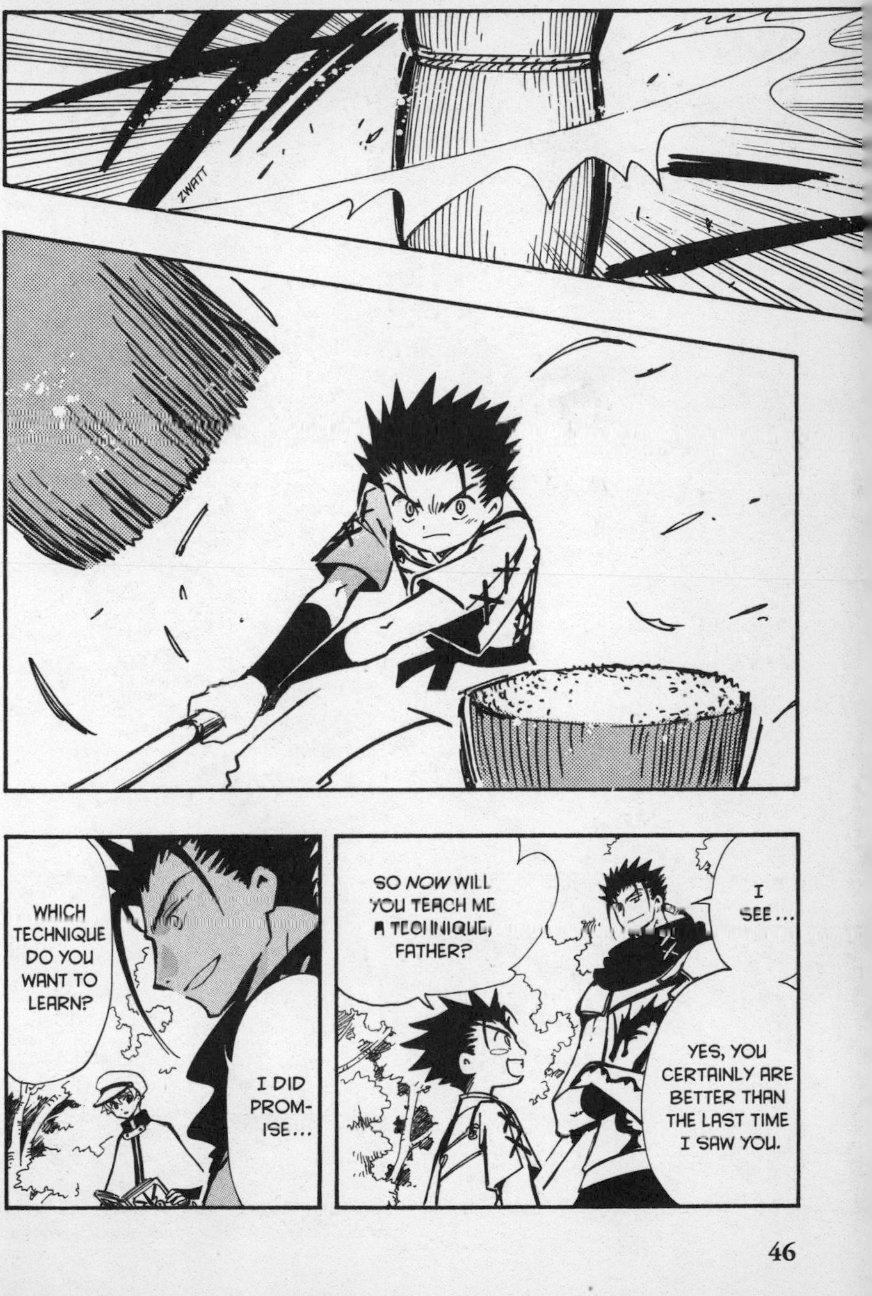
ZWATT
I SEE...
YES, YOU CERTAINLY ARE BETTER THAN THE LAST TIME I SAW YOU.
SO *NOW* WILL YOU TEACH ME A TECHNIQUE, FATHER?
I DID PROMISE...
WHICH TECHNIQUE DO YOU WANT TO LEARN?

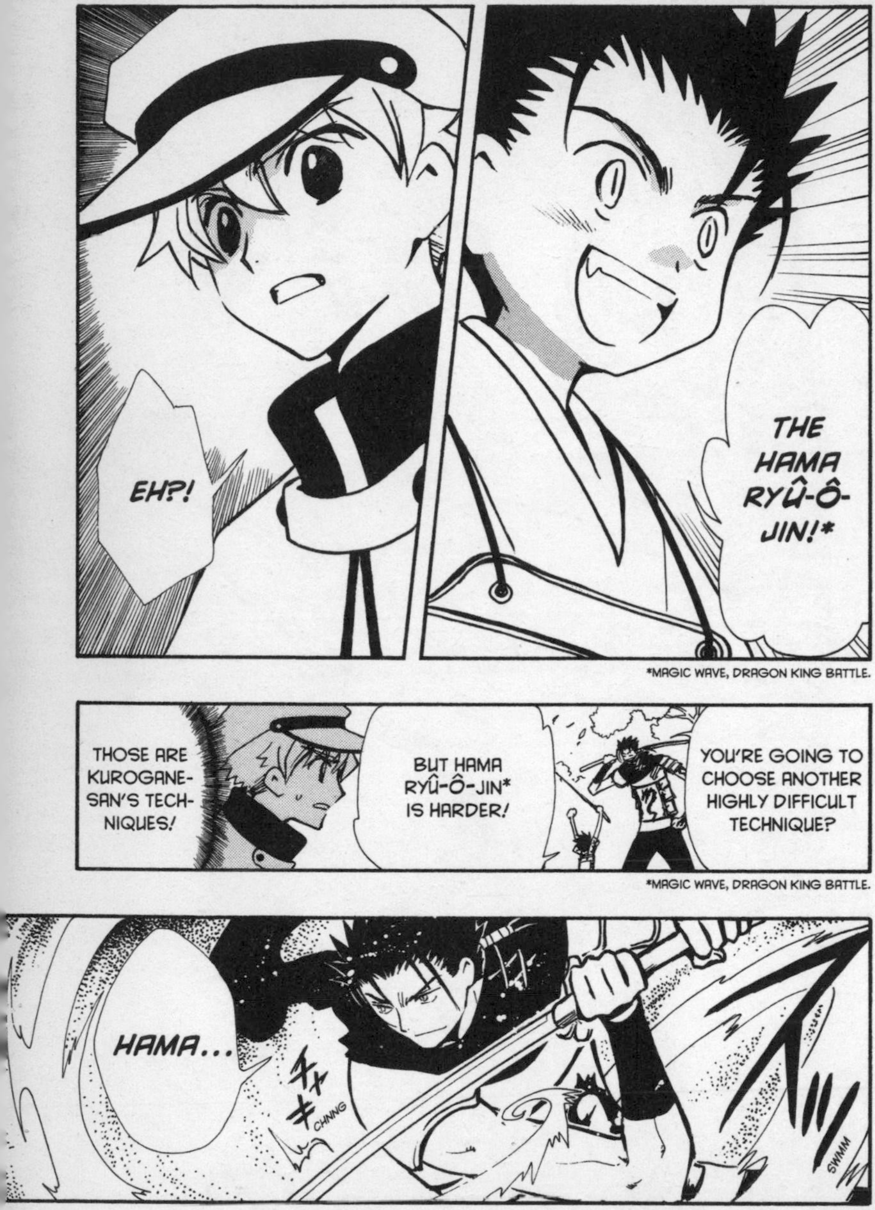
THE HAMA RYÛ-Ô-JIN!*
EH?!
*MAGIC WAVE, DRAGON KING BATTLE.
YOU'RE GOING TO CHOOSE ANOTHER HIGHLY DIFFICULT TECHNIQUE?
BUT HAMA RYÛ-Ô-JIN* IS HARDER!
THOSE ARE KUROGANE-SAN'S TECHNIQUES!
*MAGIC WAVE, DRAGON KING BATTLE.
SWMM
HAMA...
チャキ
CHNNG

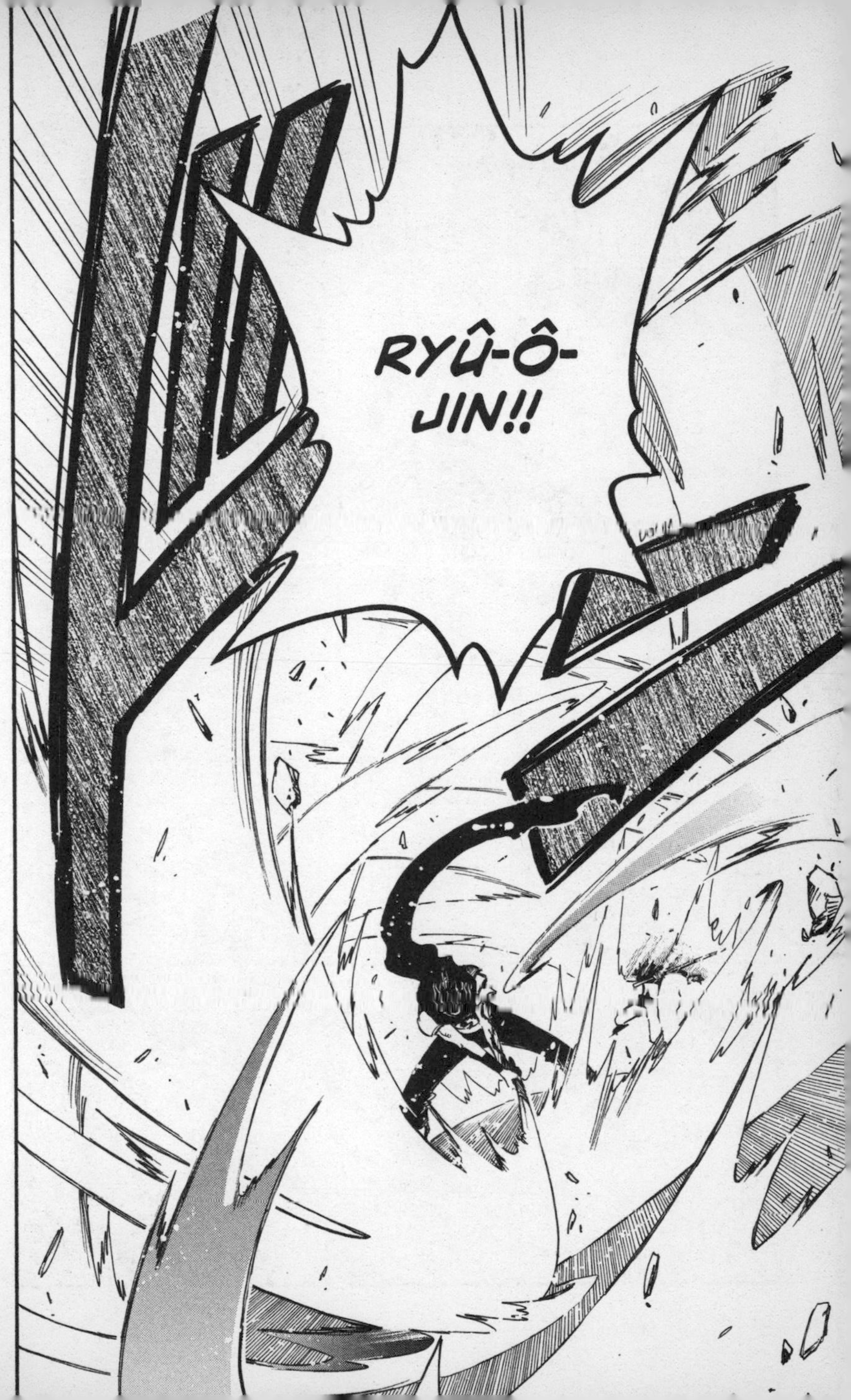
RYÛ-Ô-JIN!!

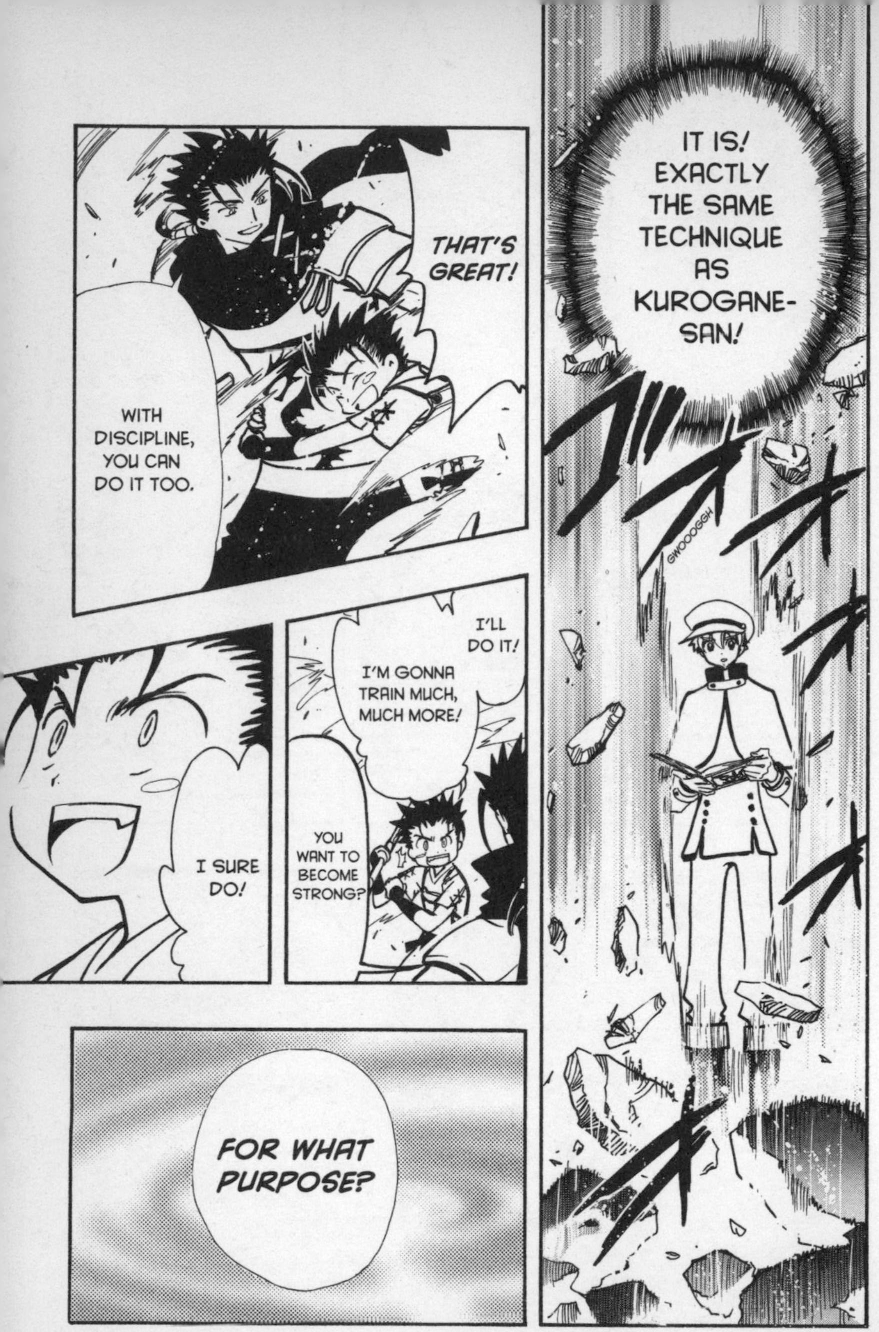
IT IS! EXACTLY THE SAME TECHNIQUE AS KUROGANE-SAN!
GWOOOGGH
THAT'S GREAT!
WITH DISCIPLINE, YOU CAN DO IT TOO.
I'LL DO IT!
I'M GONNA TRAIN MUCH, MUCH MORE!
YOU WANT TO BECOME STRONG?
I SURE DO!
FOR WHAT PURPOSE?

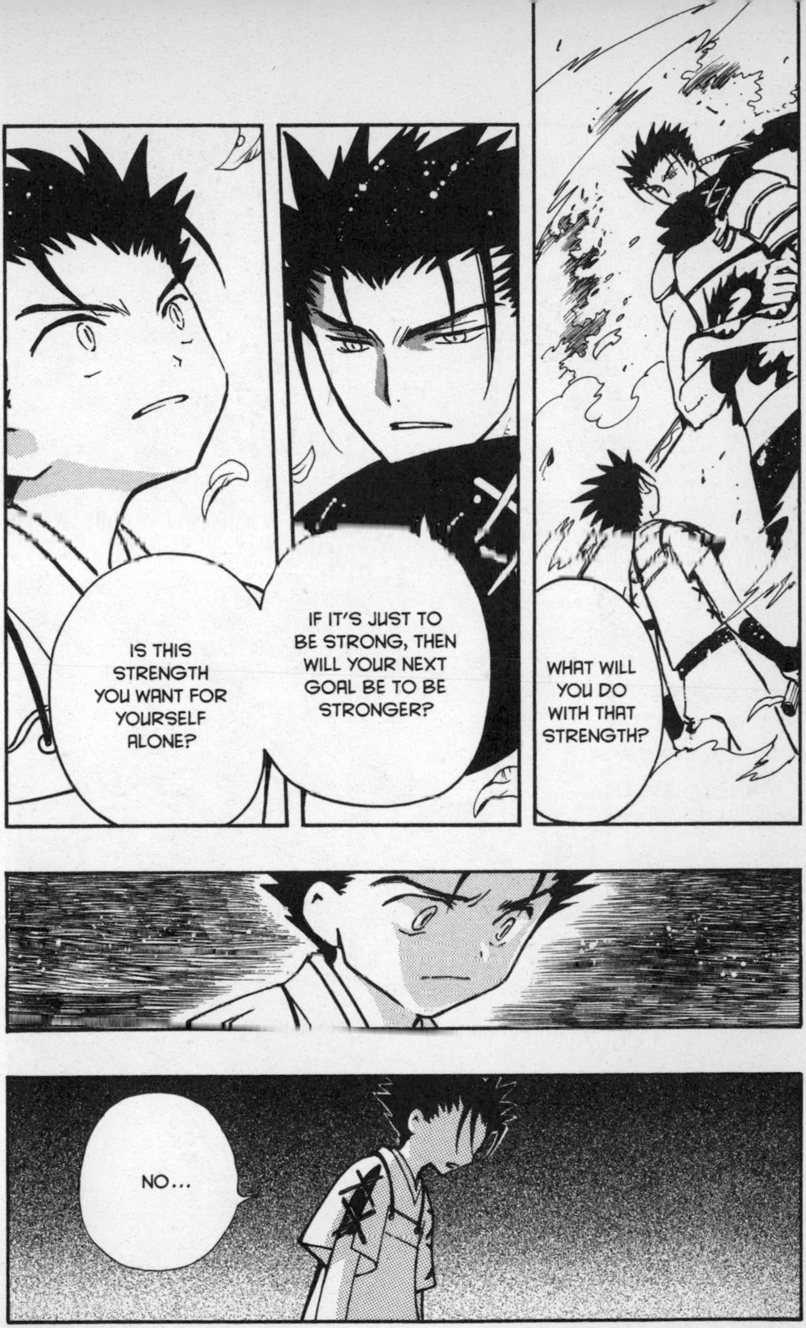
WHAT WILL YOU DO WITH THAT STRENGTH?
IF IT'S JUST TO BE STRONG, THEN WILL YOUR NEXT GOAL BE TO BE STRONGER?
IS THIS STRENGTH YOU WANT FOR YOURSELF ALONE?
NO...

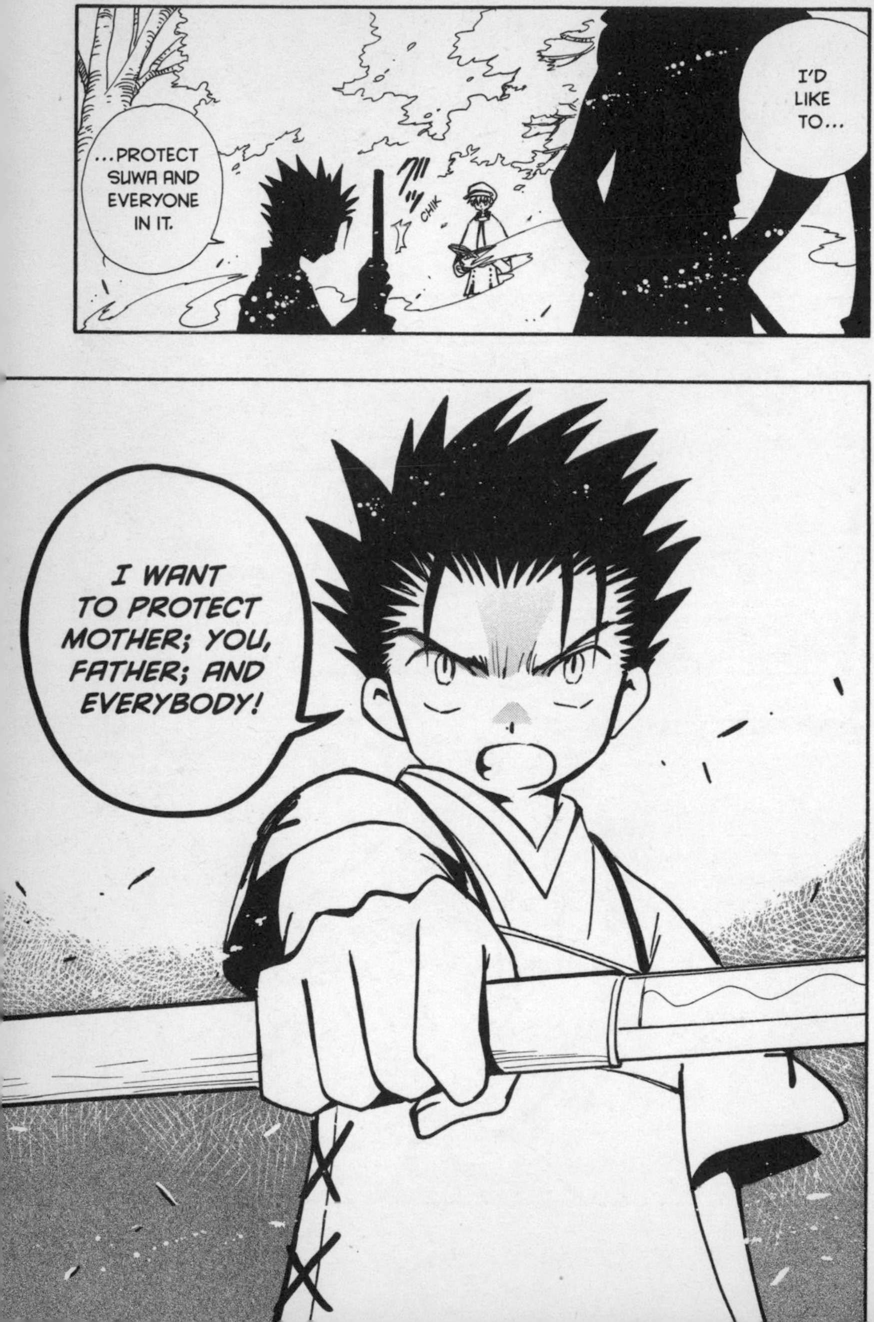
I'D LIKE TO...
CHIK
...PROTECT SUWA AND EVERYONE IN IT.
I WANT TO PROTECT MOTHER; YOU, FATHER; AND EVERYBODY!

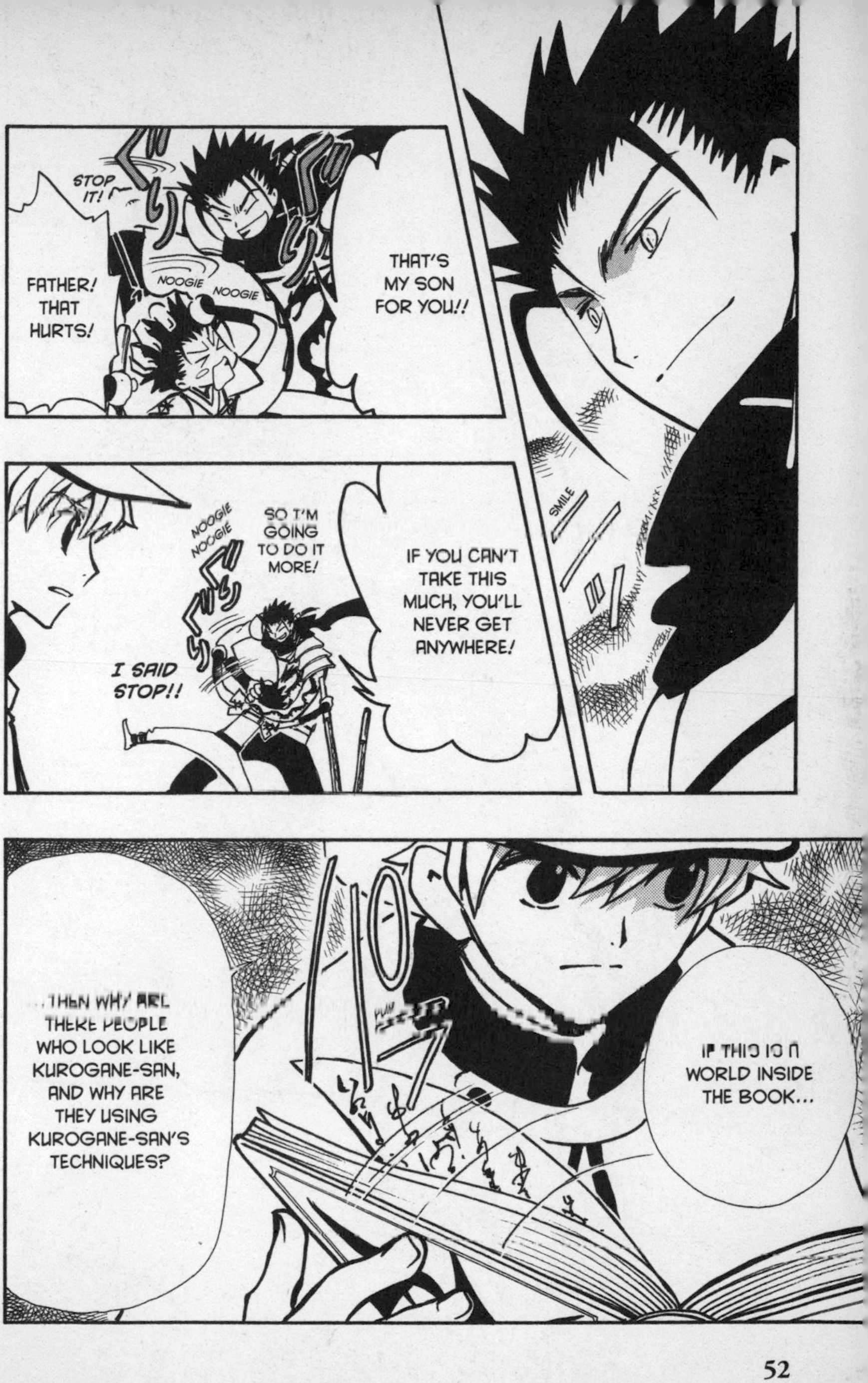
SMILE
THAT'S MY SON FOR YOU!!
NOOGIE NOOGIE
STOP IT!
FATHER! THAT HURTS!
IF YOU CAN'T TAKE THIS MUCH, YOU'LL NEVER GET ANYWHERE!
SO I'M GOING TO DO IT MORE!
NOOGIE NOOGIE
I SAID STOP!!
IF THIS IS A WORLD INSIDE THE BOOK...
...THEN WHY ARE THERE PEOPLE WHO LOOK LIKE KUROGANE-SAN, AND WHY ARE THEY USING KUROGANE-SAN'S TECHNIQUES?

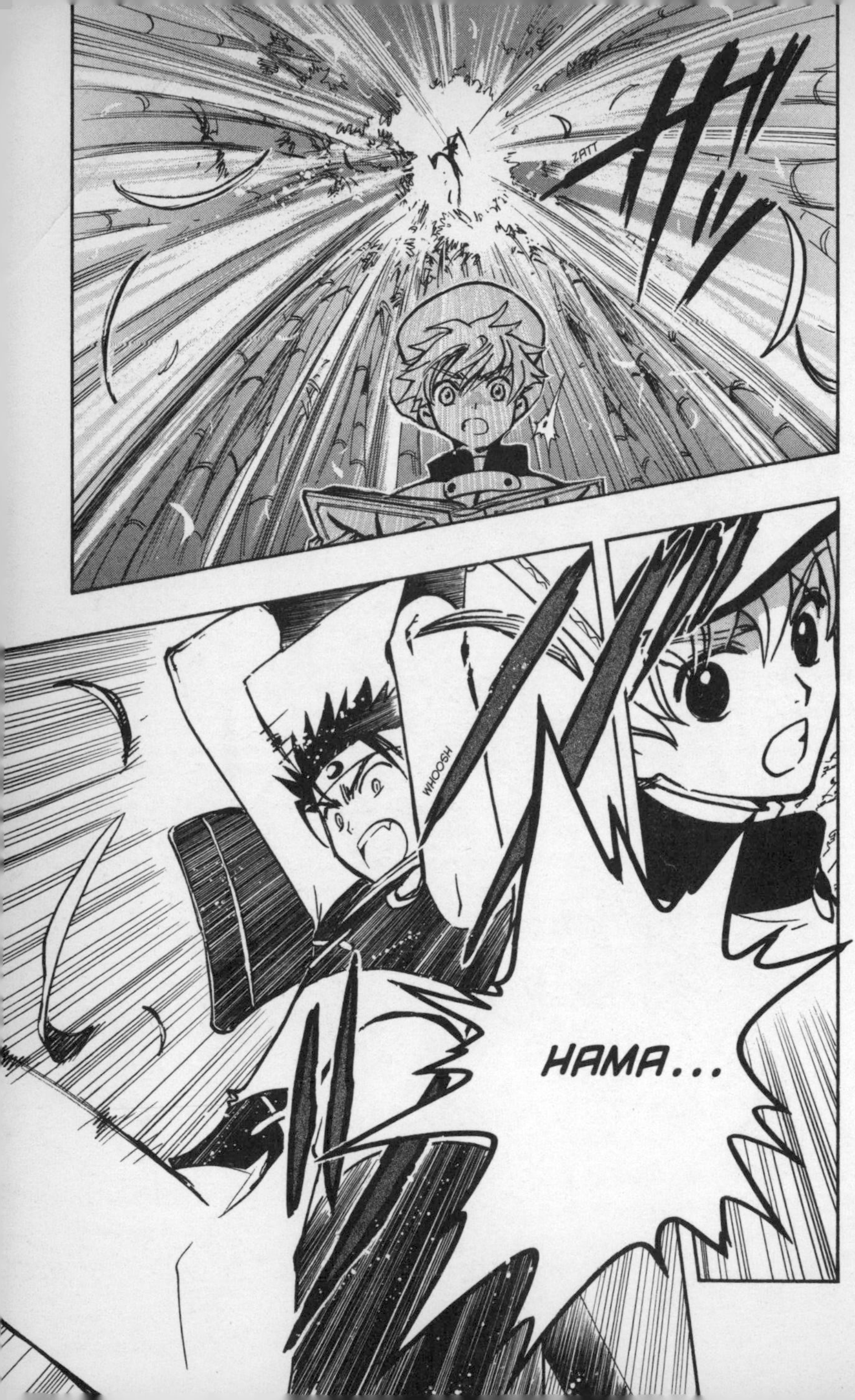
ZATT
WHOOSH
HAMA...

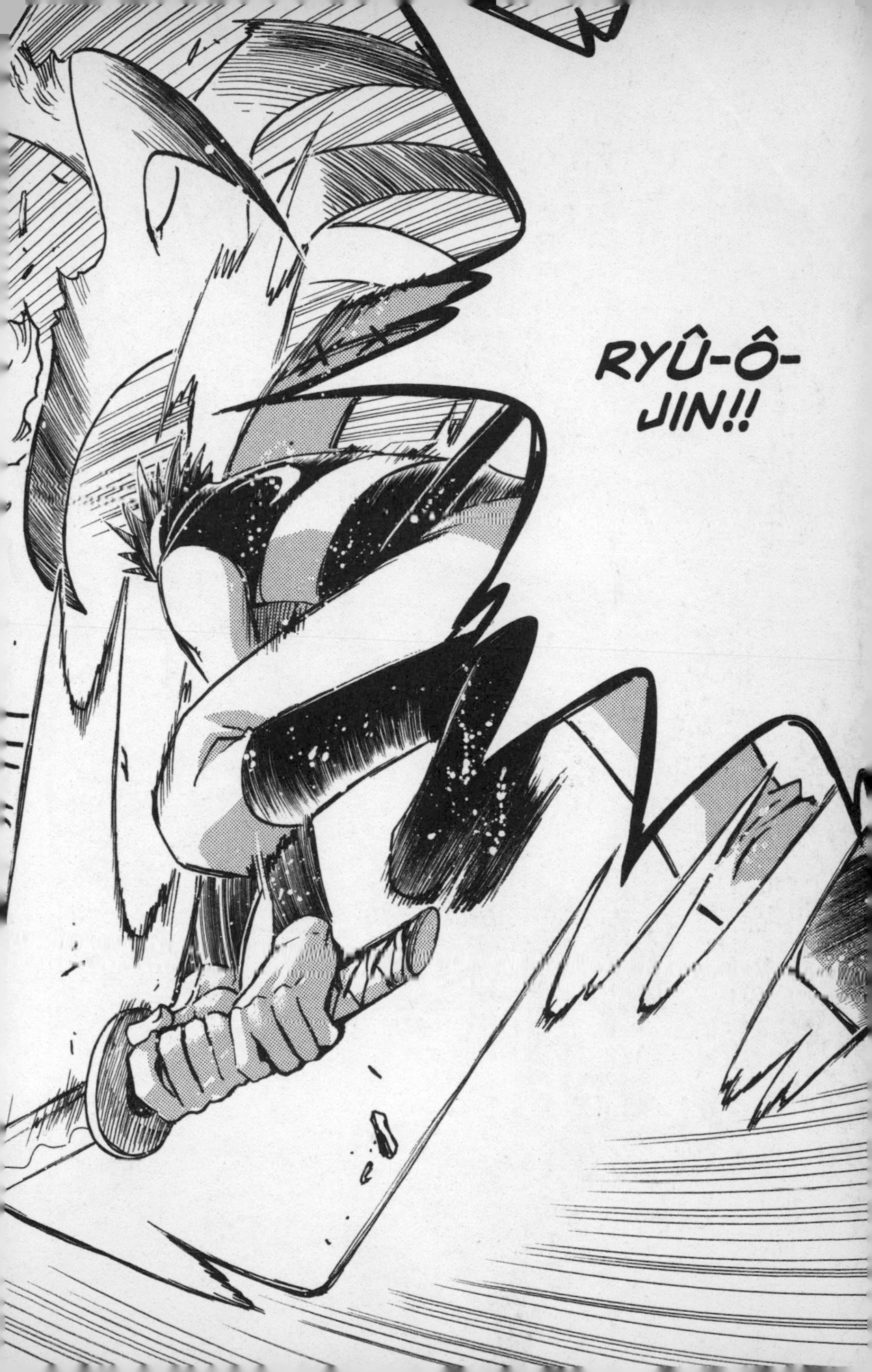
RYÛ-Ô-
JIN!!

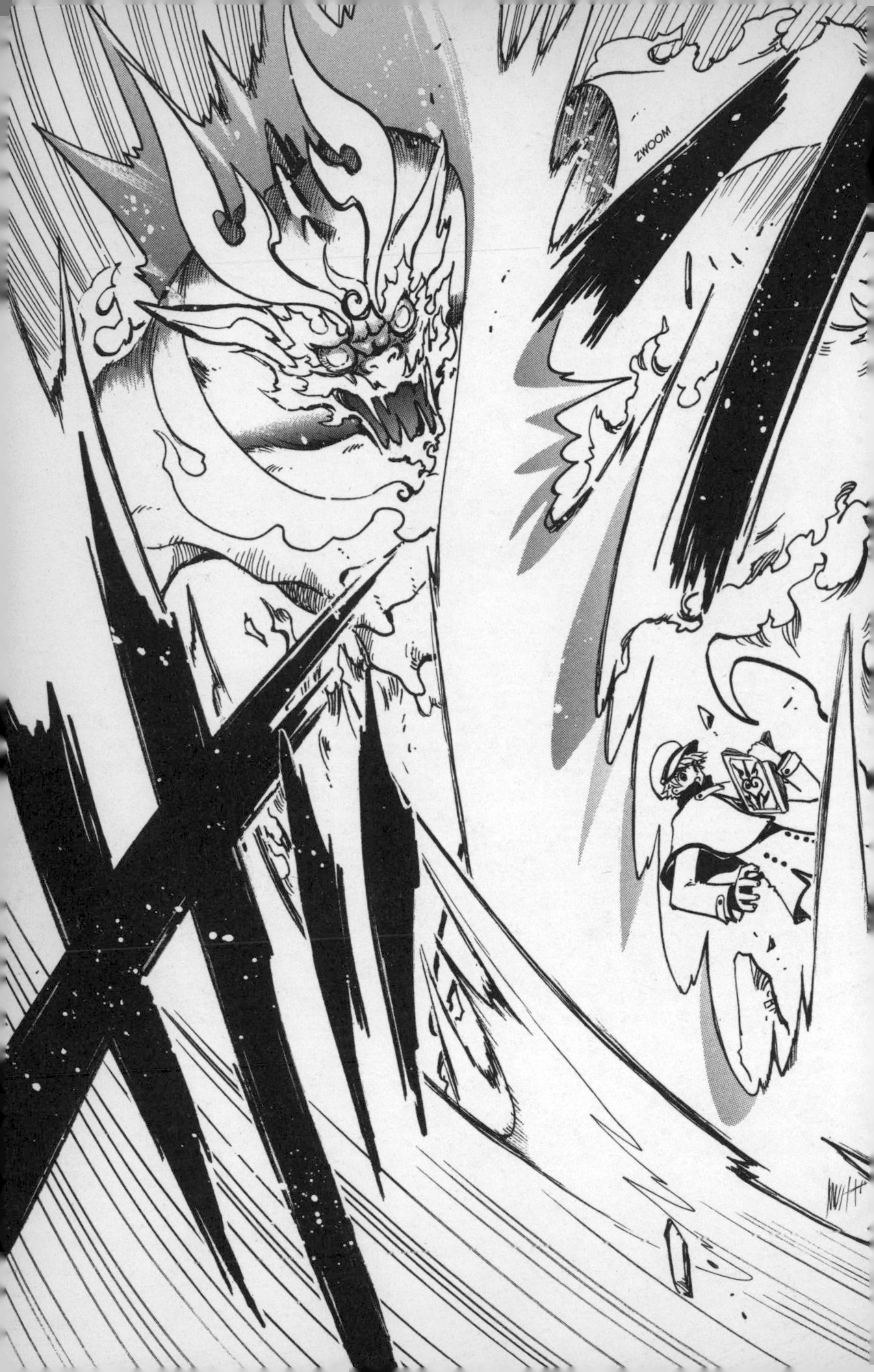
ZWOOM

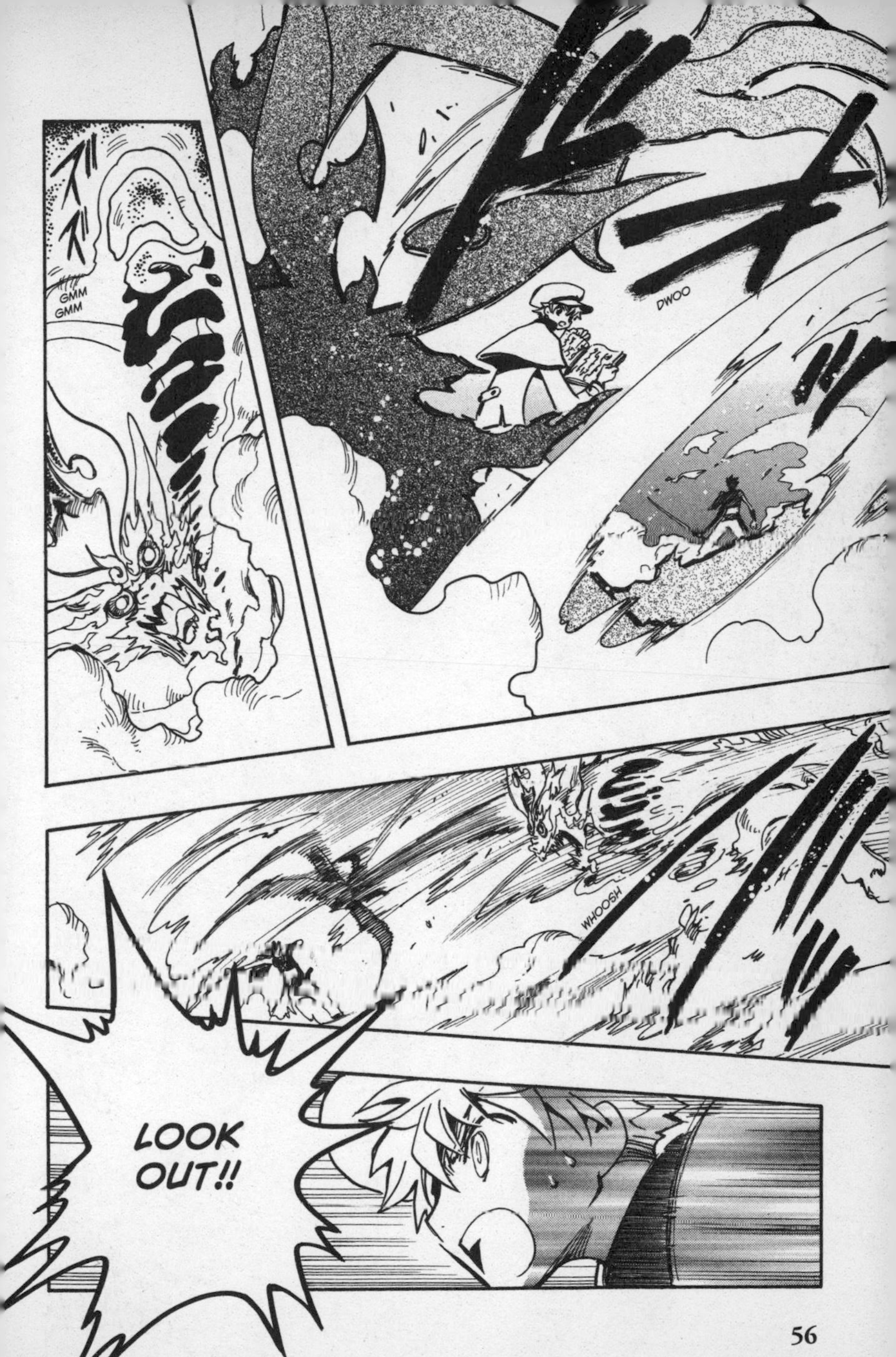
DWOO
GMM GMM
WHOOSH
LOOK OUT!!

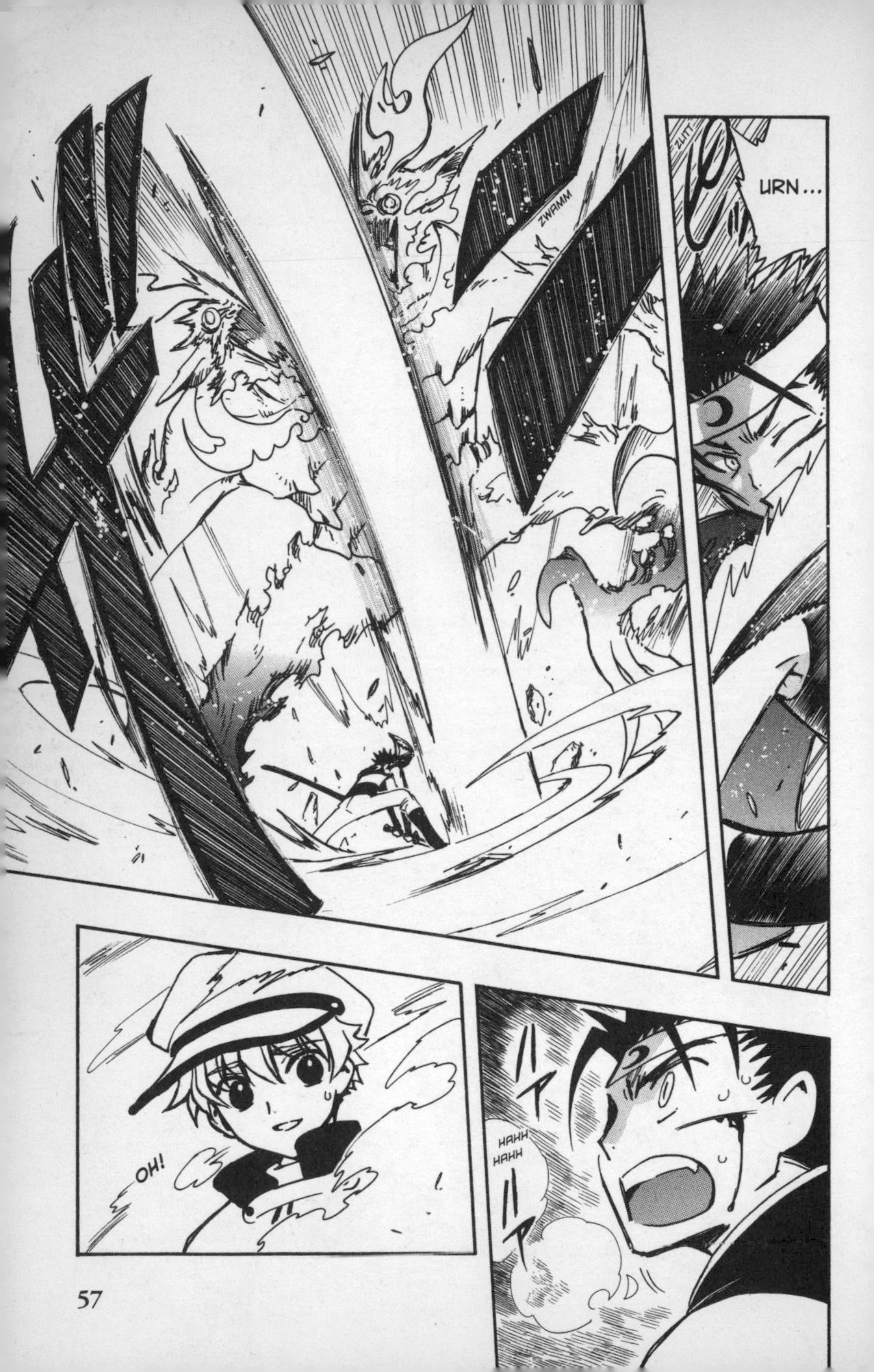
ZUTT
URN...
ZWAMM
HAHH HAHH
OH!

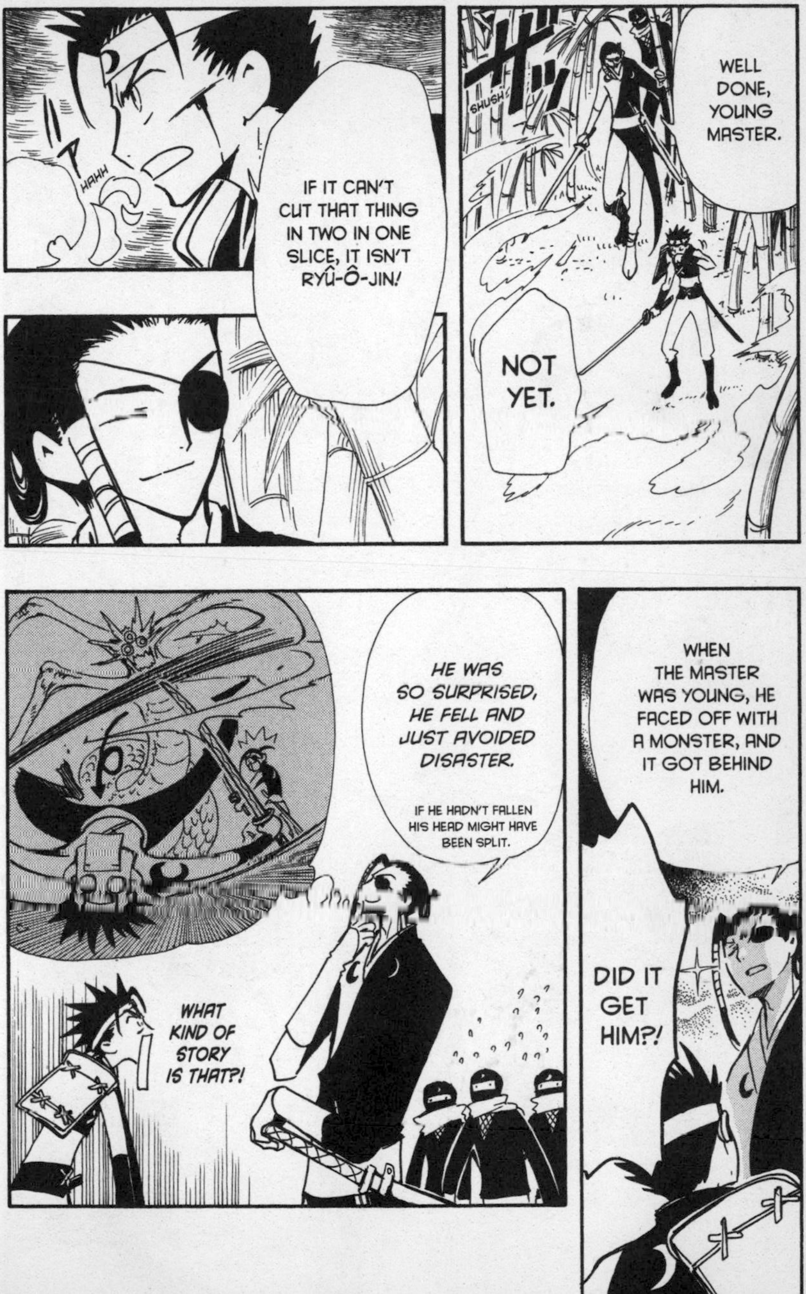
SHUSH
WELL DONE, YOUNG MASTER.
NOT YET.
HAHH
IF IT CAN'T CUT THAT THING IN TWO IN ONE SLICE, IT ISN'T RYÛ-Ô-JIN!
WHEN THE MASTER WAS YOUNG, HE FACED OFF WITH A MONSTER, AND IT GOT BEHIND HIM.
DID IT GET HIM?!
HE WAS SO SURPRISED, HE FELL AND JUST AVOIDED DISASTER.
IF HE HADN'T FALLEN HIS HEAD MIGHT HAVE BEEN SPLIT.
WHAT KIND OF STORY IS THAT?!

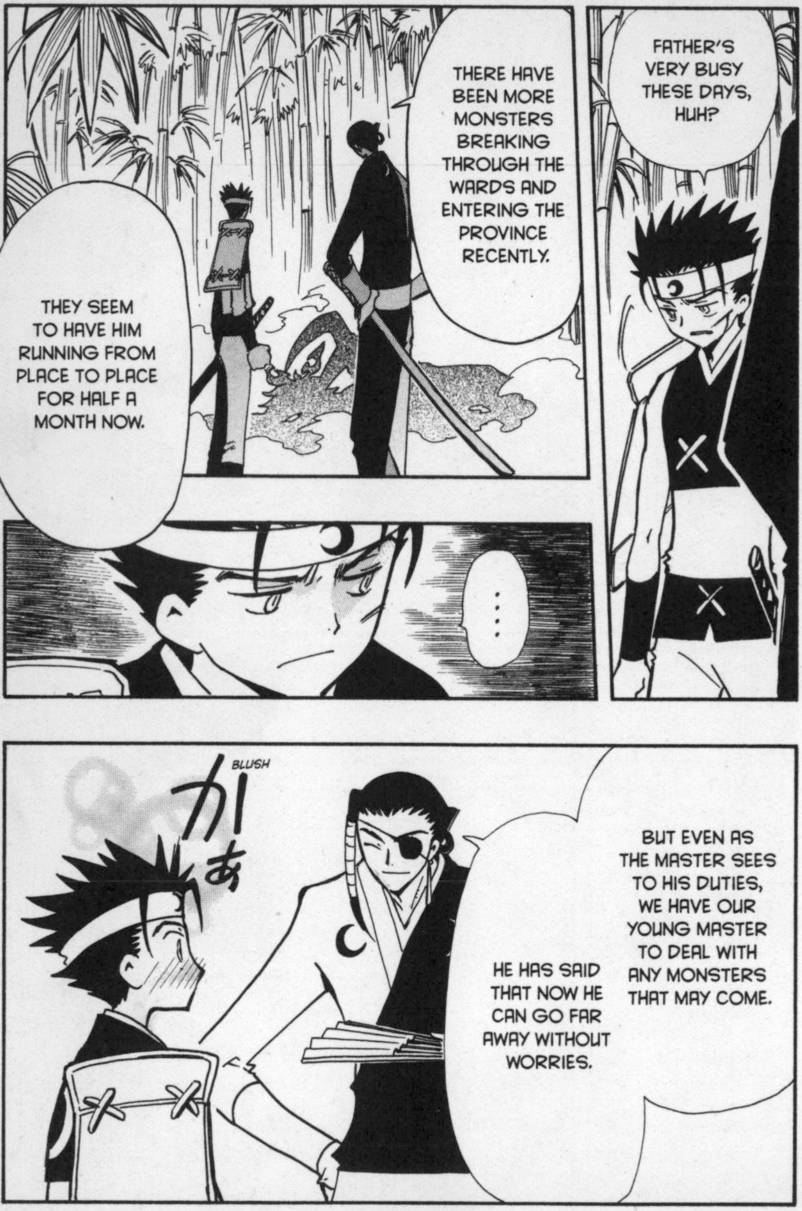
FATHER'S VERY BUSY THESE DAYS, HUH?
THERE HAVE BEEN MORE MONSTERS BREAKING THROUGH THE WARDS AND ENTERING THE PROVINCE RECENTLY.
THEY SEEM TO HAVE HIM RUNNING FROM PLACE TO PLACE FOR HALF A MONTH NOW.
....
BUT EVEN AS THE MASTER SEES TO HIS DUTIES, WE HAVE OUR YOUNG MASTER TO DEAL WITH ANY MONSTERS THAT MAY COME.
HE HAS SAID THAT NOW HE CAN GO FAR AWAY WITHOUT WORRIES.
BLUSH
かあ

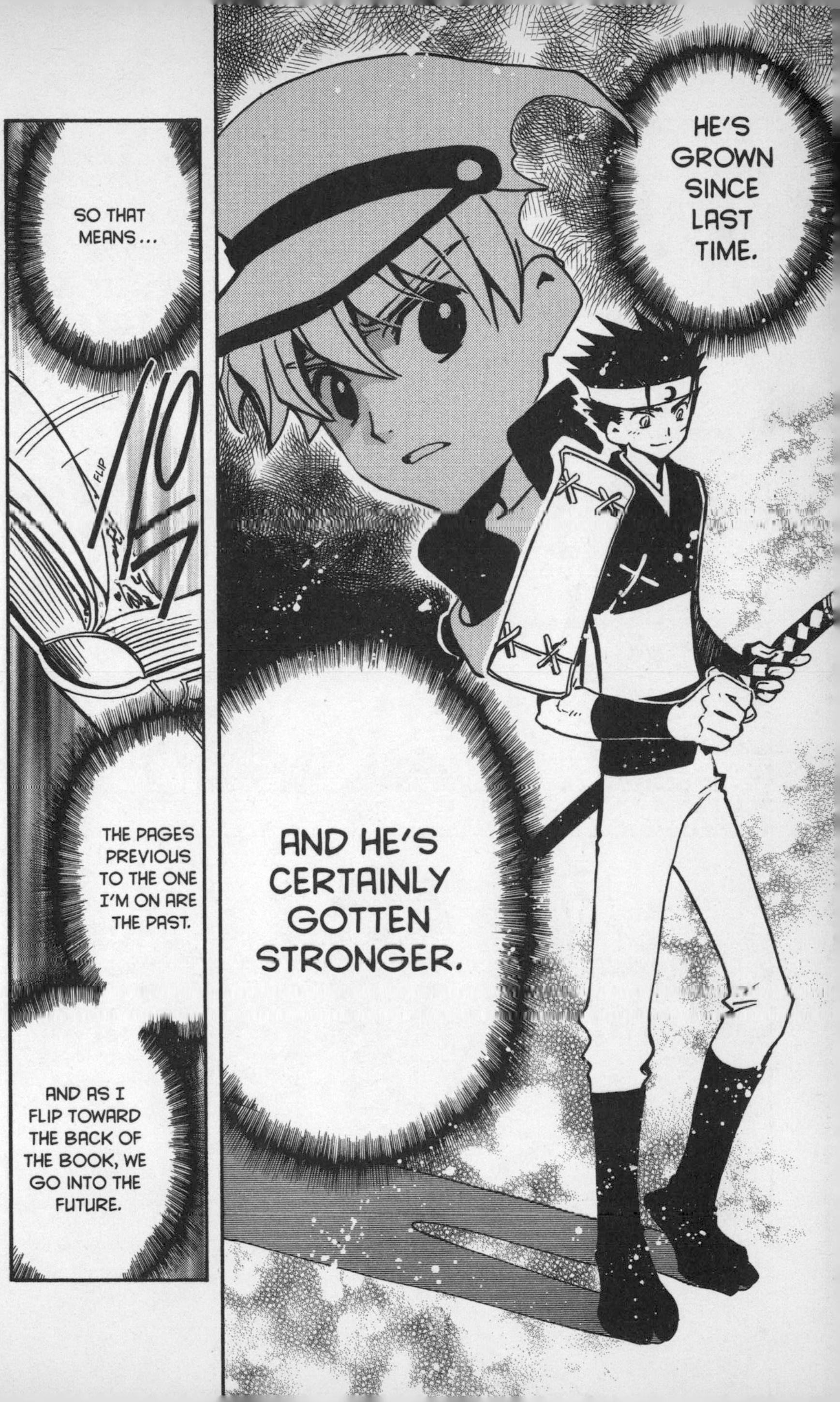
HE'S GROWN SINCE LAST TIME.
AND HE'S CERTAINLY GOTTEN STRONGER.
SO THAT MEANS...
FLIP
THE PAGES PREVIOUS TO THE ONE I'M ON ARE THE PAST.
AND AS I FLIP TOWARD THE BACK OF THE BOOK, WE GO INTO THE FUTURE.

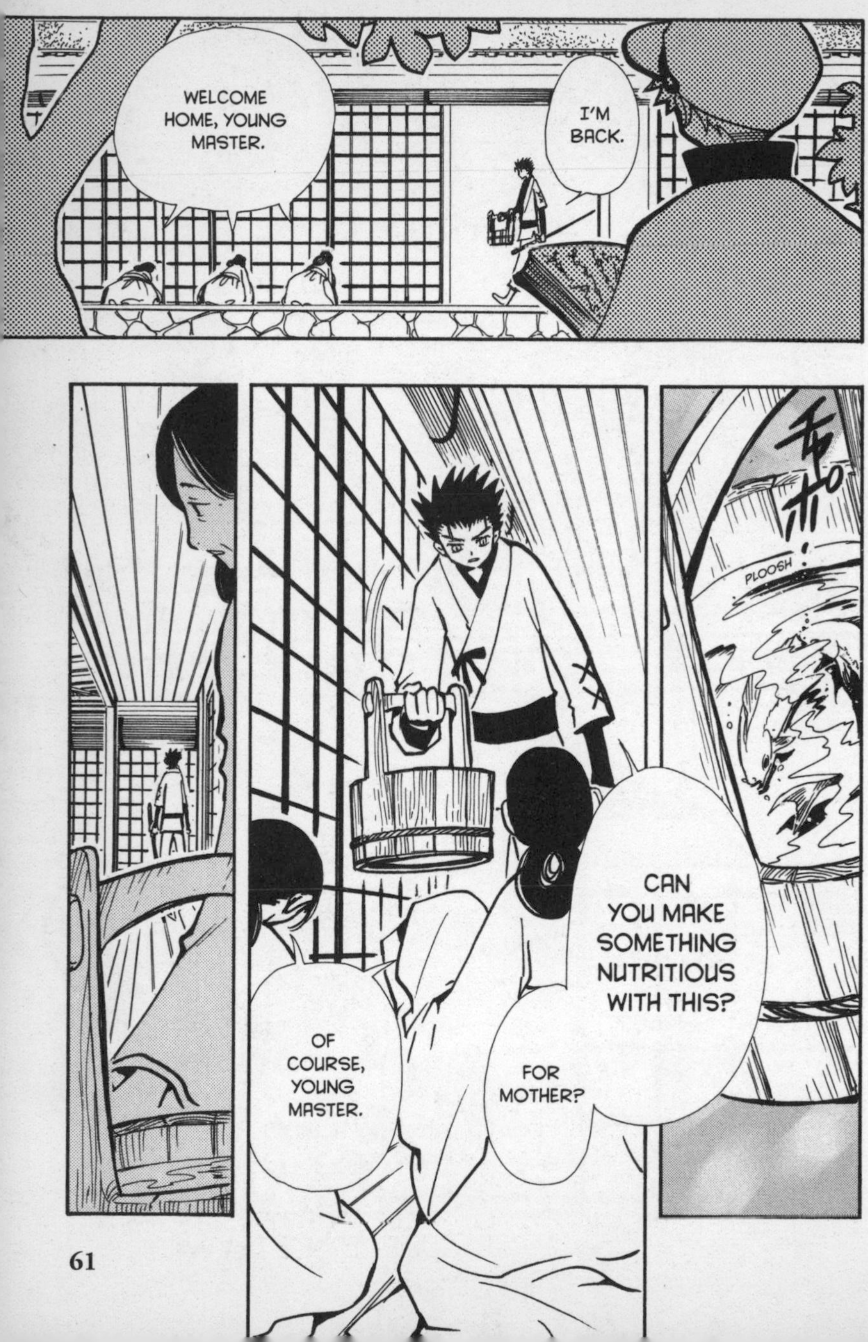
I'M BACK.
WELCOME HOME, YOUNG MASTER.
PLOOSH
CAN YOU MAKE SOMETHING NUTRITIOUS WITH THIS?
FOR MOTHER?
OF COURSE, YOUNG MASTER.

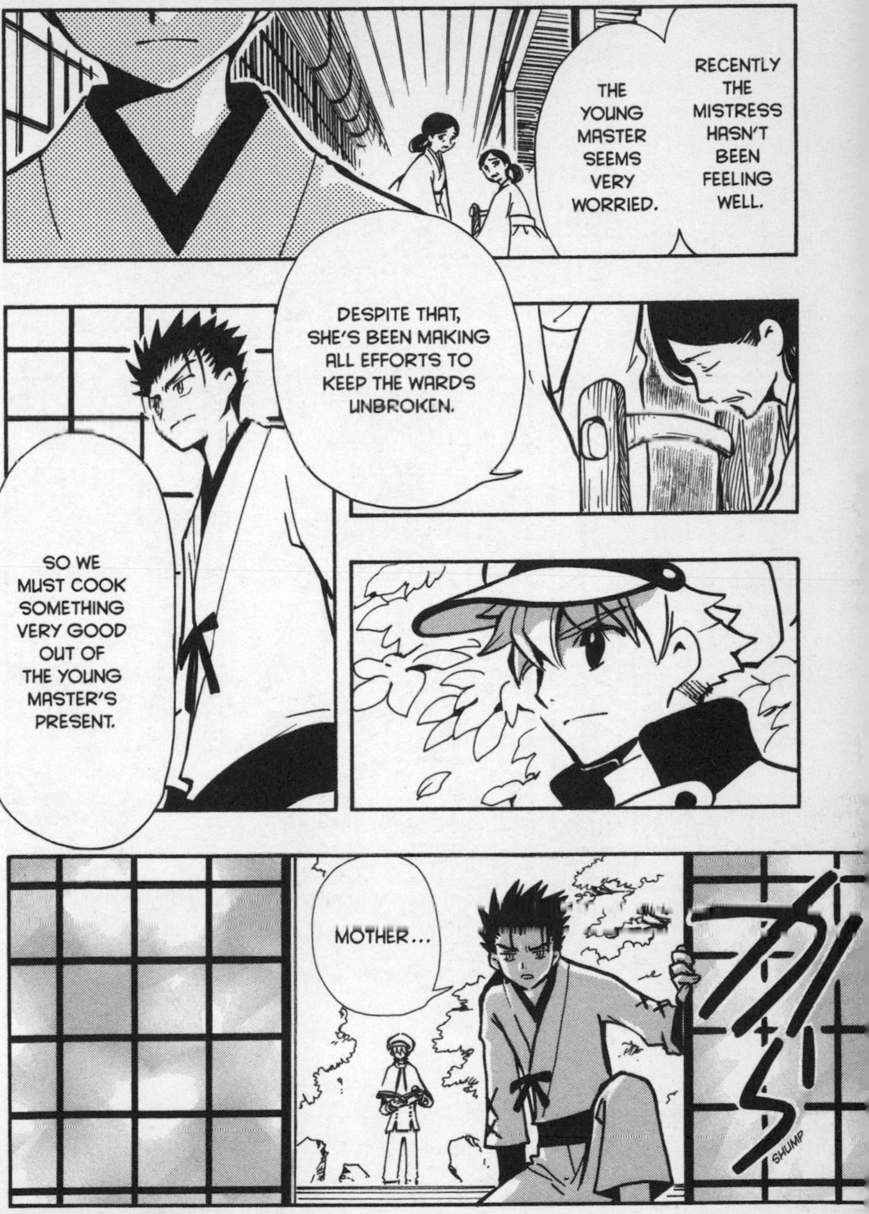
RECENTLY THE MISTRESS HASN'T BEEN FEELING WELL.
THE YOUNG MASTER SEEMS VERY WORRIED.
DESPITE THAT, SHE'S BEEN MAKING ALL EFFORTS TO KEEP THE WARDS UNBROKEN.
SO WE MUST COOK SOMETHING VERY GOOD OUT OF THE YOUNG MASTER'S PRESENT.
MOTHER...
SHUMP

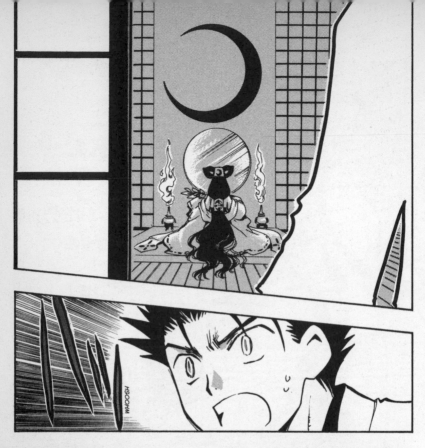

WHOOSH

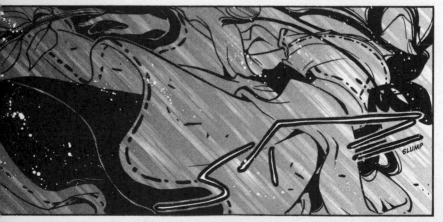

SLUMP

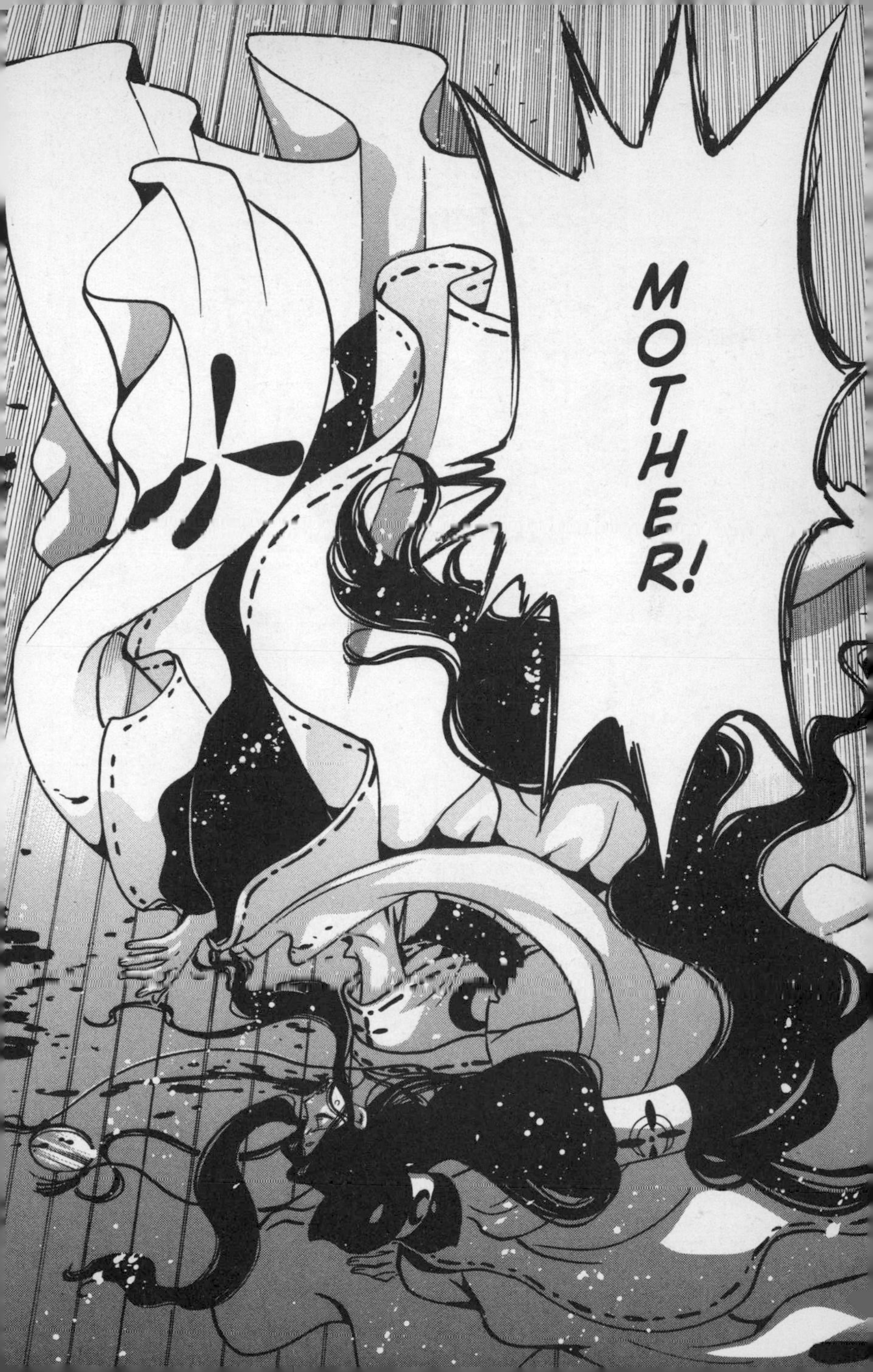
MOTHER!

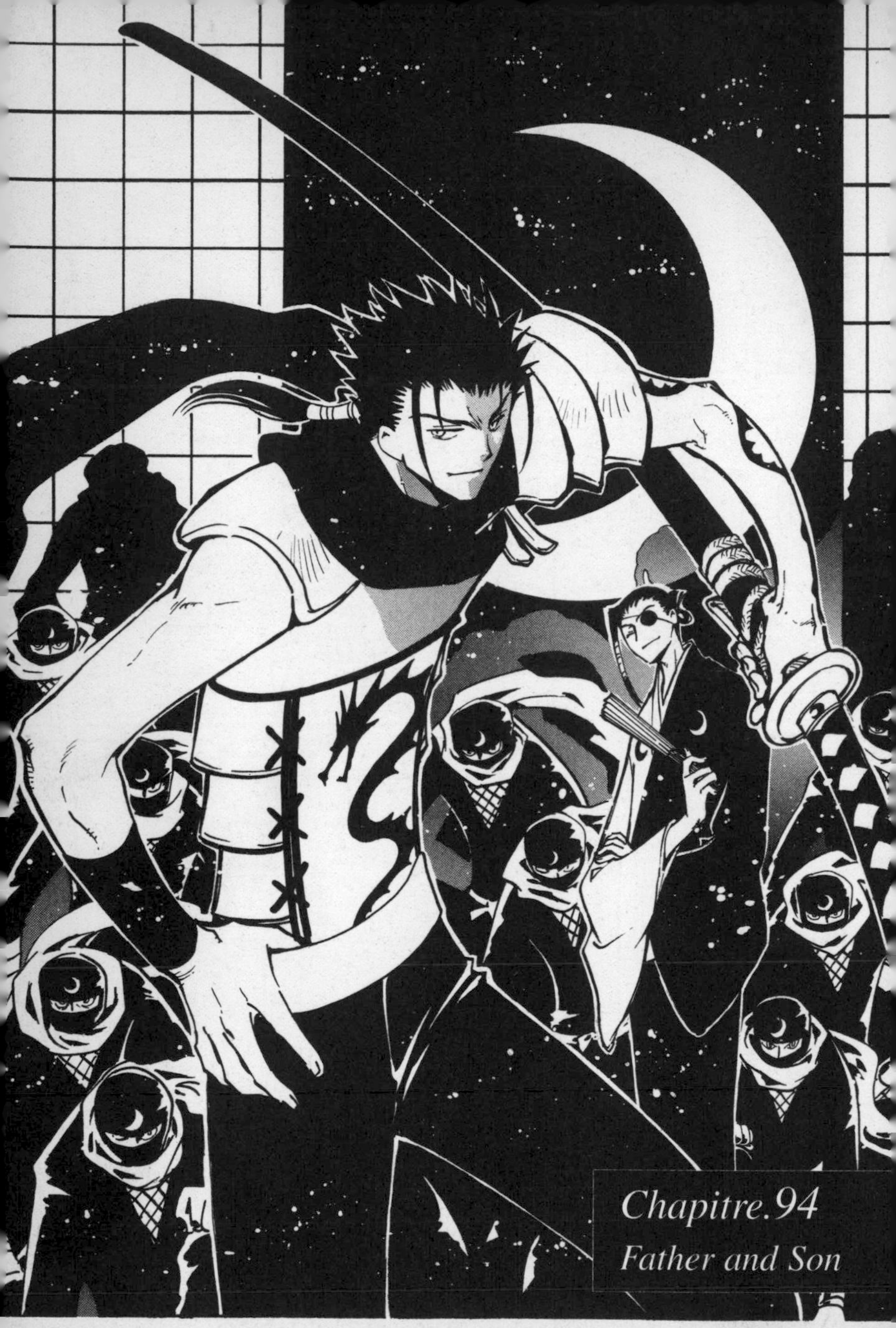
Chapitre.94
Father and Son

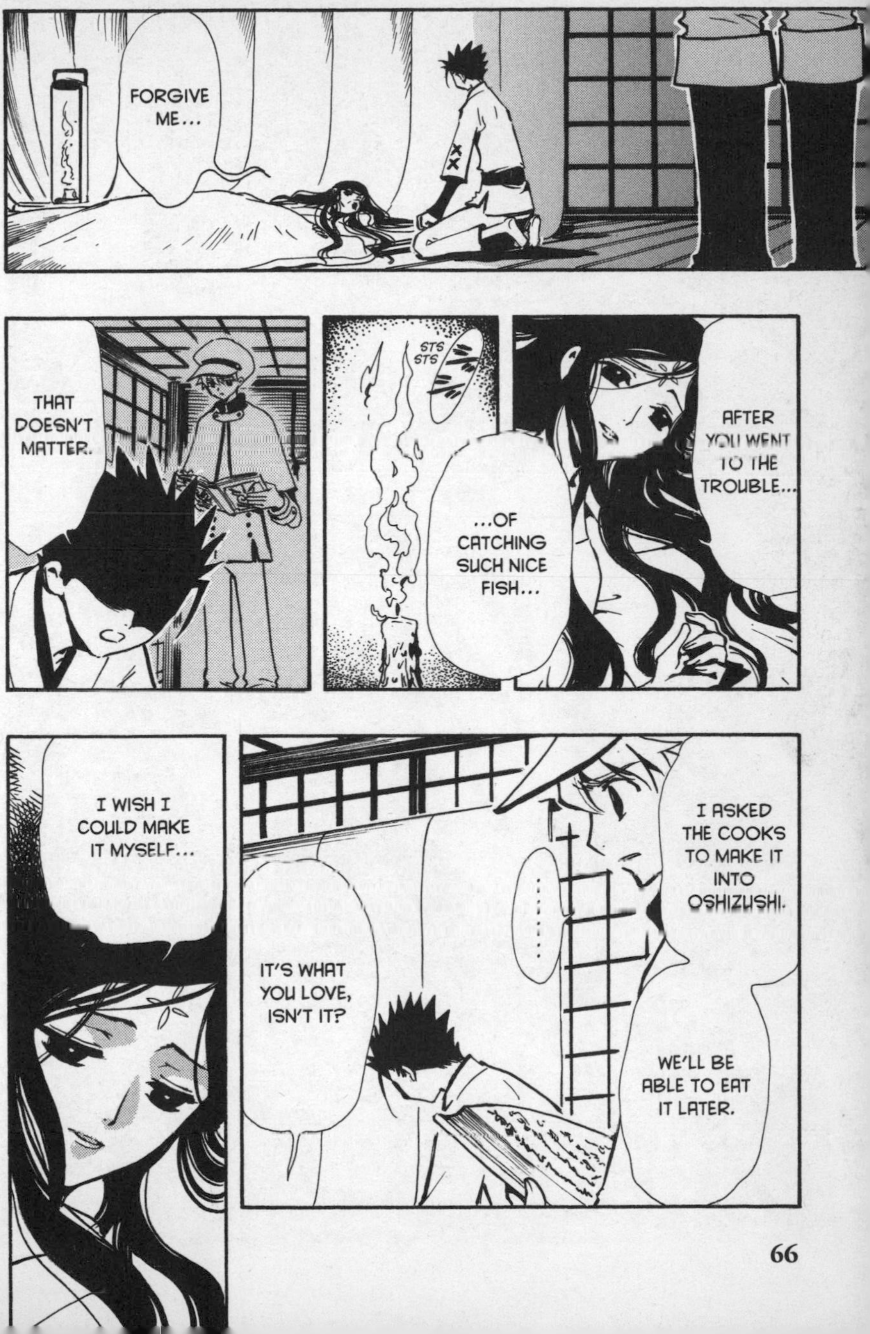
FORGIVE ME...
AFTER YOU WENT TO THE TROUBLE...
...OF CATCHING SUCH NICE FISH...
STS STS
THAT DOESN'T MATTER.
I ASKED THE COOKS TO MAKE IT INTO OSHIZUSHI.
WE'LL BE ABLE TO EAT IT LATER.
......
IT'S WHAT YOU LOVE, ISN'T IT?
I WISH I COULD MAKE IT MYSELF...

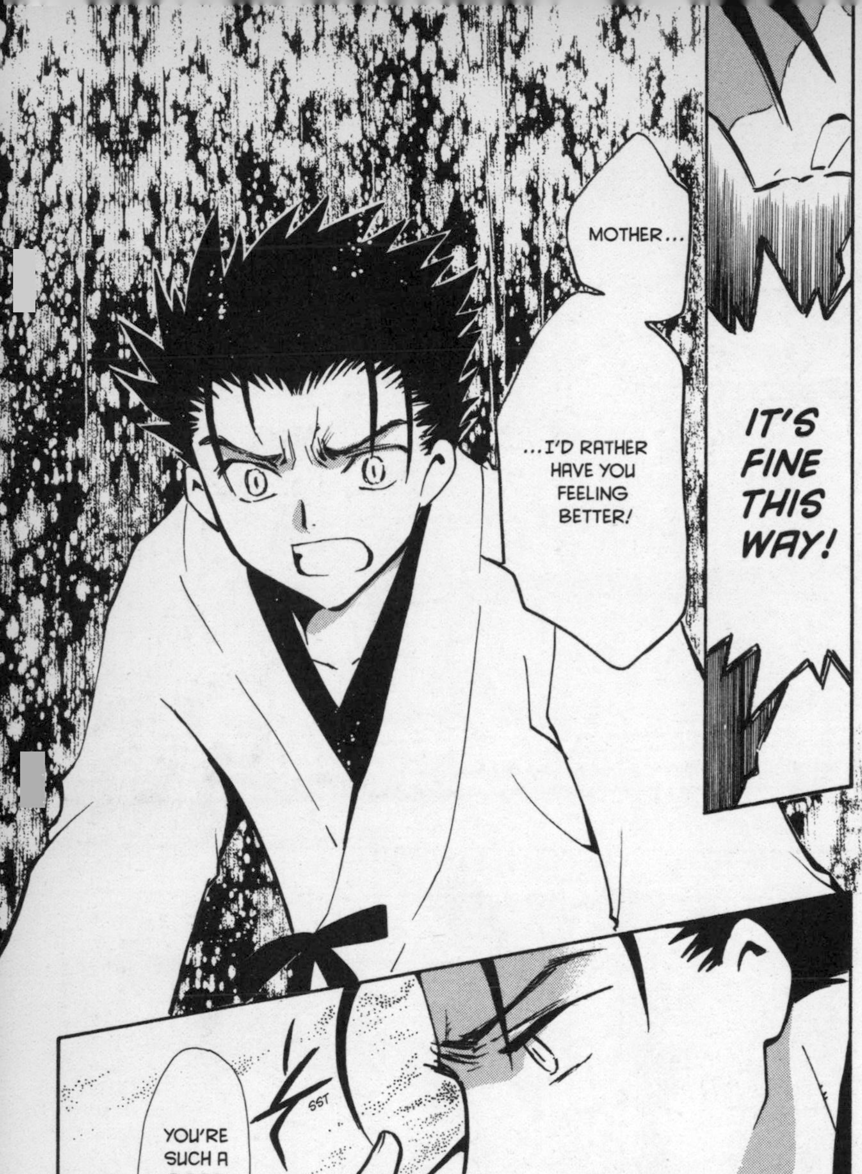
IT'S FINE THIS WAY!
MOTHER...
...I'D RATHER HAVE YOU FEELING BETTER!
SST
YOU'RE SUCH A GOOD CHILD.

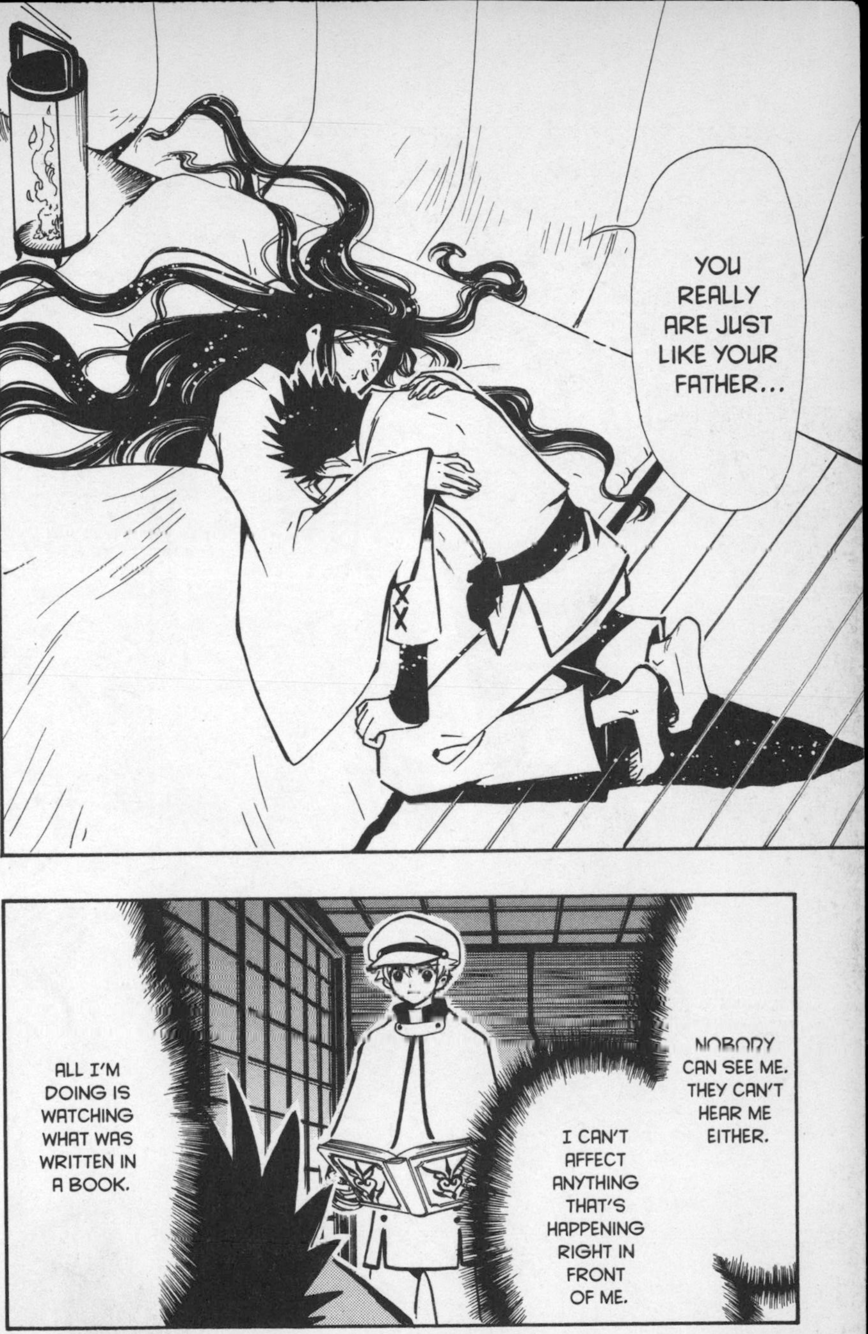
YOU REALLY ARE JUST LIKE YOUR FATHER...
NOBODY CAN SEE ME. THEY CAN'T HEAR ME EITHER.
I CAN'T AFFECT ANYTHING THAT'S HAPPENING RIGHT IN FRONT OF ME.
ALL I'M DOING IS WATCHING WHAT WAS WRITTEN IN A BOOK.

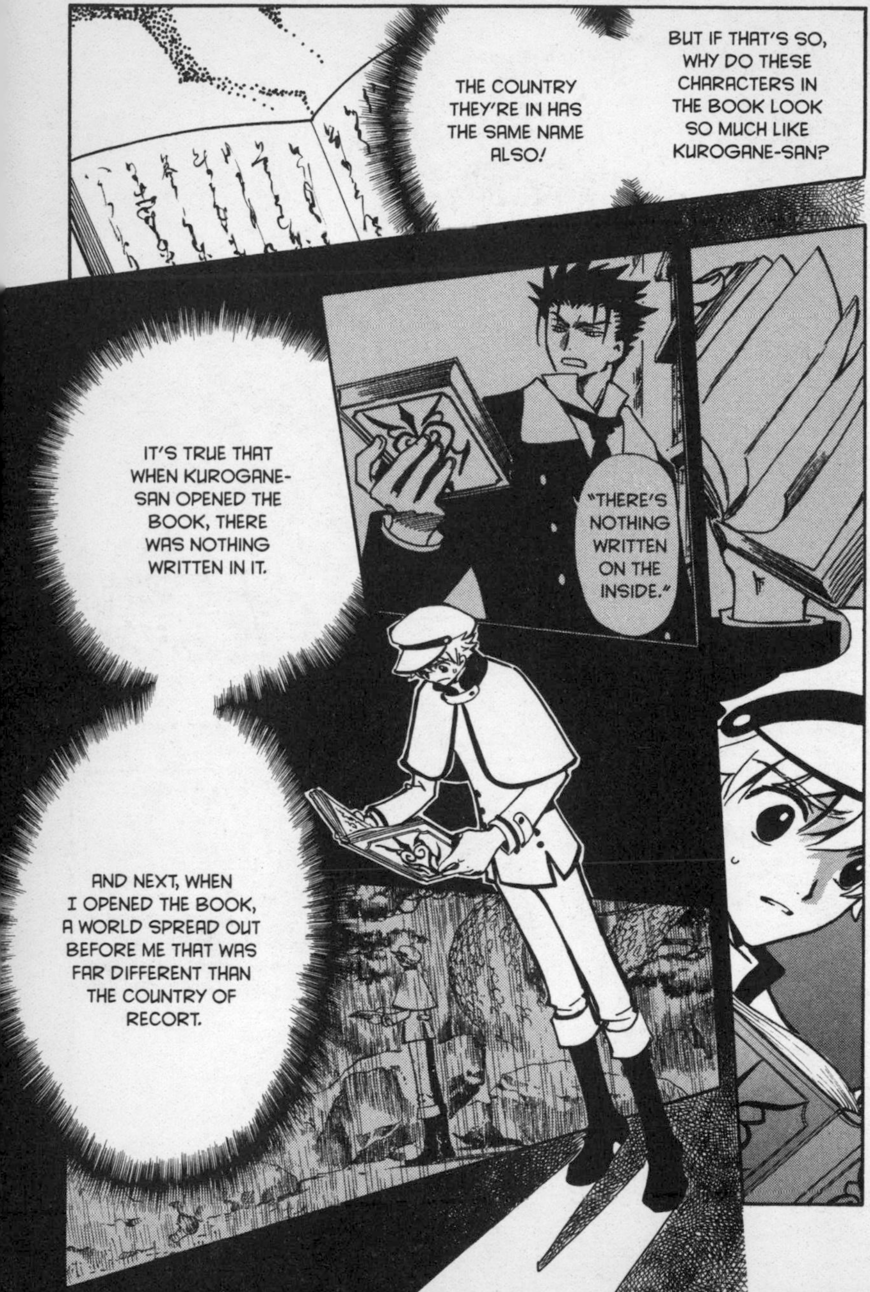
BUT IF THAT'S SO, WHY DO THESE CHARACTERS IN THE BOOK LOOK SO MUCH LIKE KUROGANE-SAN?
THE COUNTRY THEY'RE IN HAS THE SAME NAME ALSO!
"THERE'S NOTHING WRITTEN ON THE INSIDE."
IT'S TRUE THAT WHEN KUROGANE-SAN OPENED THE BOOK, THERE WAS NOTHING WRITTEN IN IT.
AND NEXT, WHEN I OPENED THE BOOK, A WORLD SPREAD OUT BEFORE ME THAT WAS FAR DIFFERENT THAN THE COUNTRY OF RECORT.

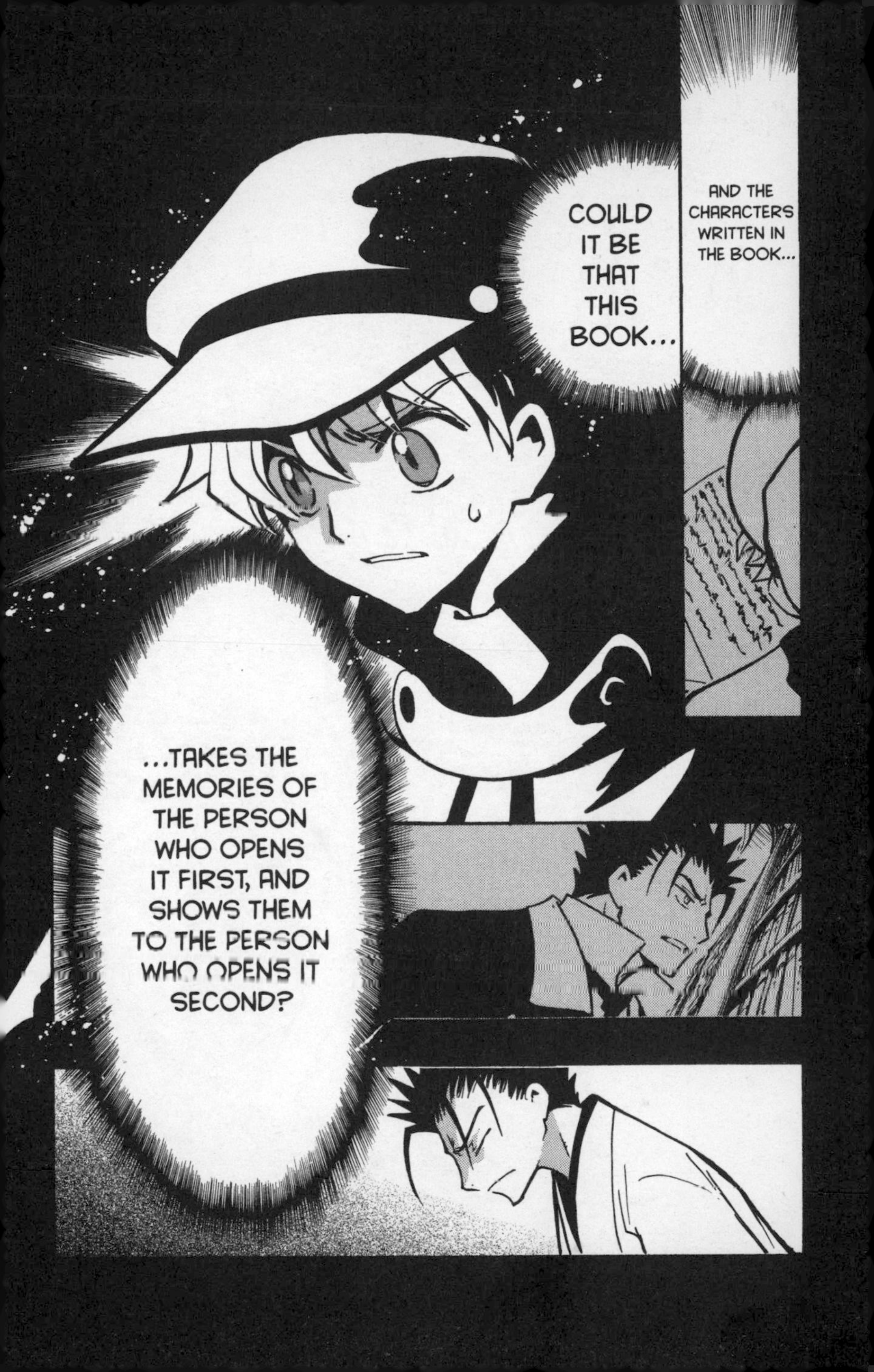
AND THE CHARACTERS WRITTEN IN THE BOOK...
COULD IT BE THAT THIS BOOK...
...TAKES THE MEMORIES OF THE PERSON WHO OPENS IT FIRST, AND SHOWS THEM TO THE PERSON WHO OPENS IT SECOND?

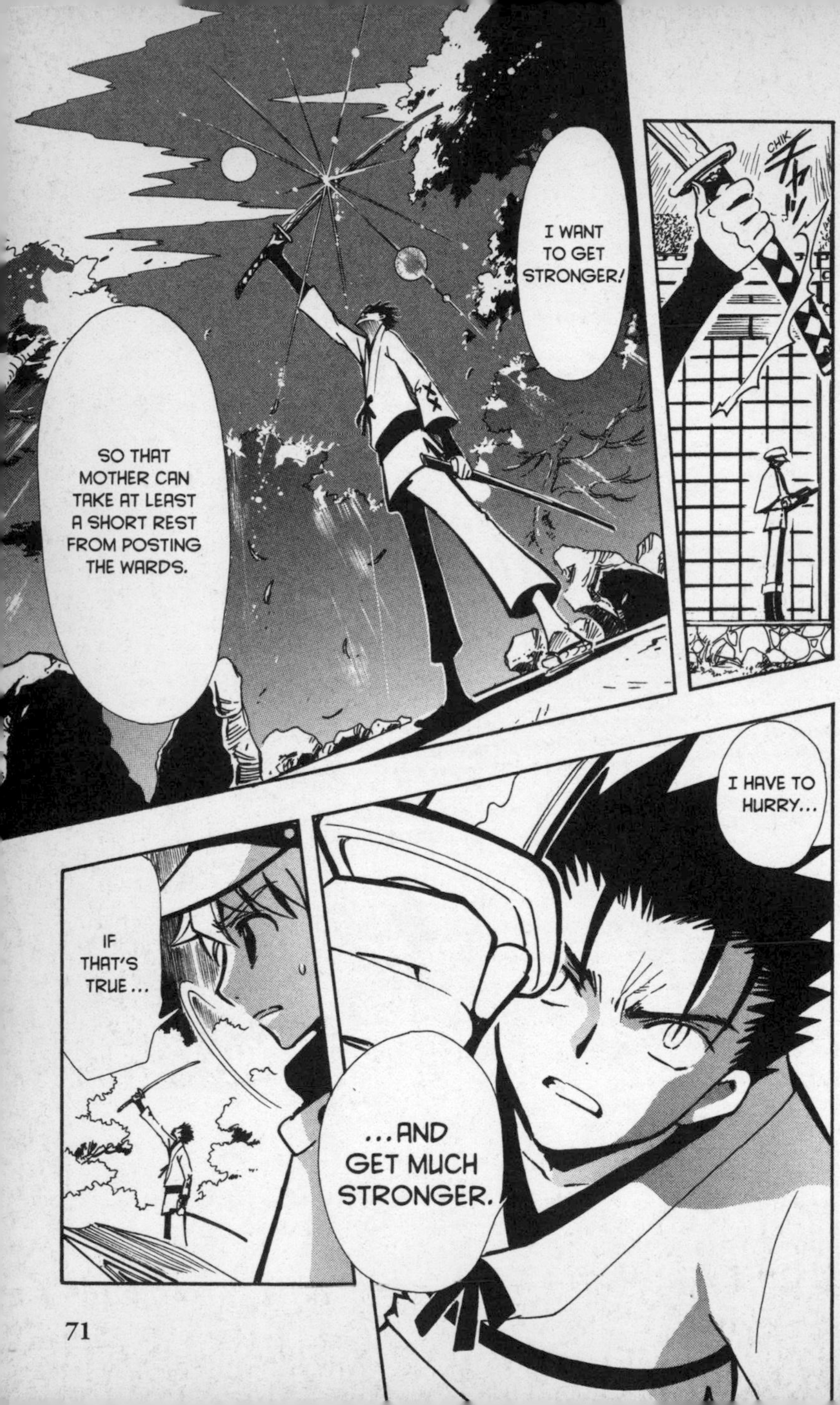
CHIK
I WANT TO GET STRONGER!
SO THAT MOTHER CAN TAKE AT LEAST A SHORT REST FROM POSTING THE WARDS.
I HAVE TO HURRY...
...AND GET MUCH STRONGER.
IF THAT'S TRUE...

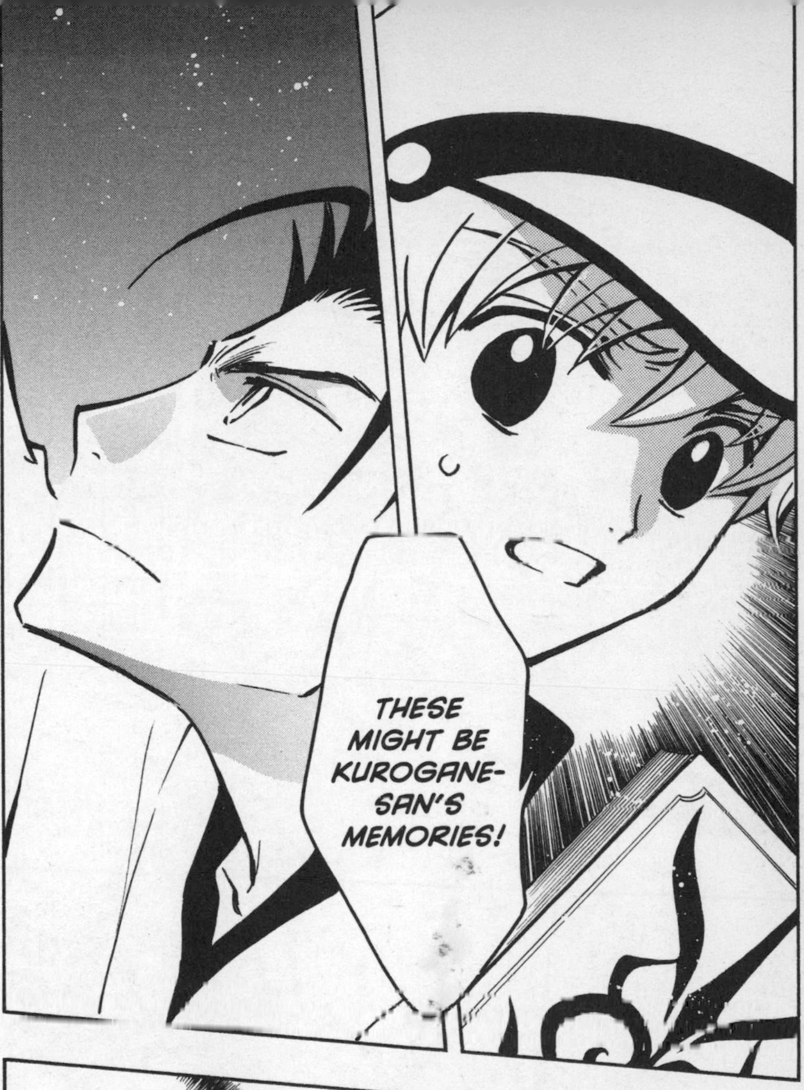
THESE MIGHT BE KUROGANE-SAN'S MEMORIES!
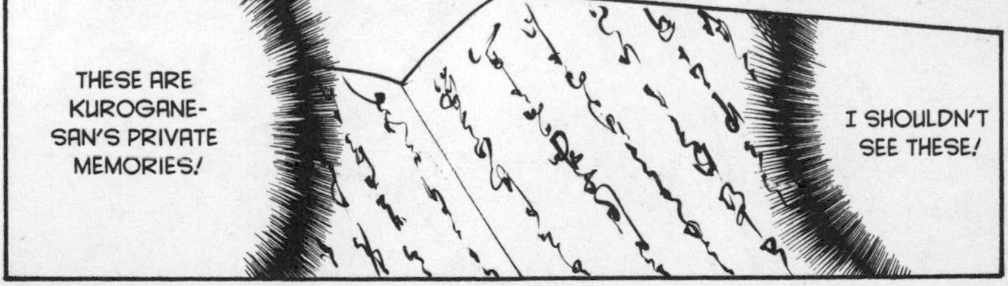
I SHOULDN'T SEE THESE!
THESE ARE KUROGANE-SAN'S PRIVATE MEMORIES!

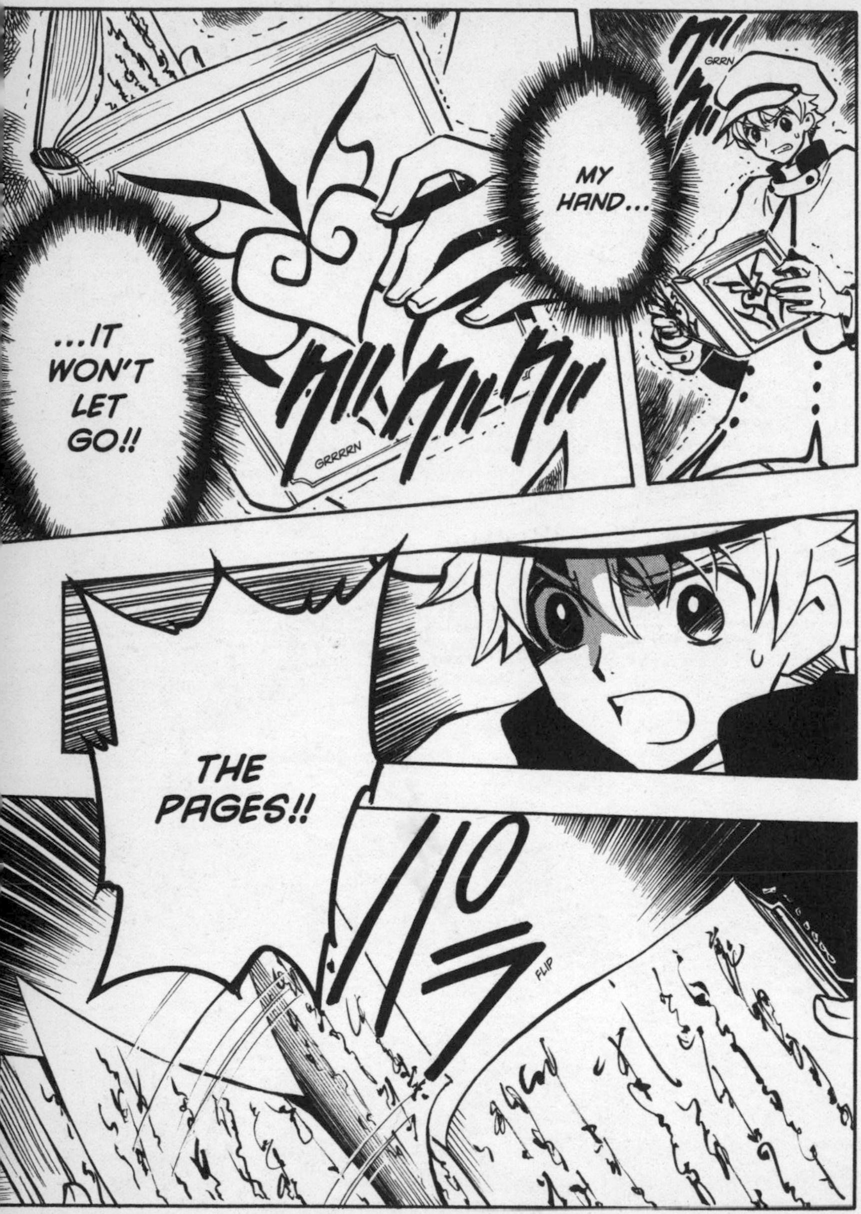
GRRN
MY HAND...
...IT WON'T LET GO!!
GRRRRN
THE PAGES!!
FLIP

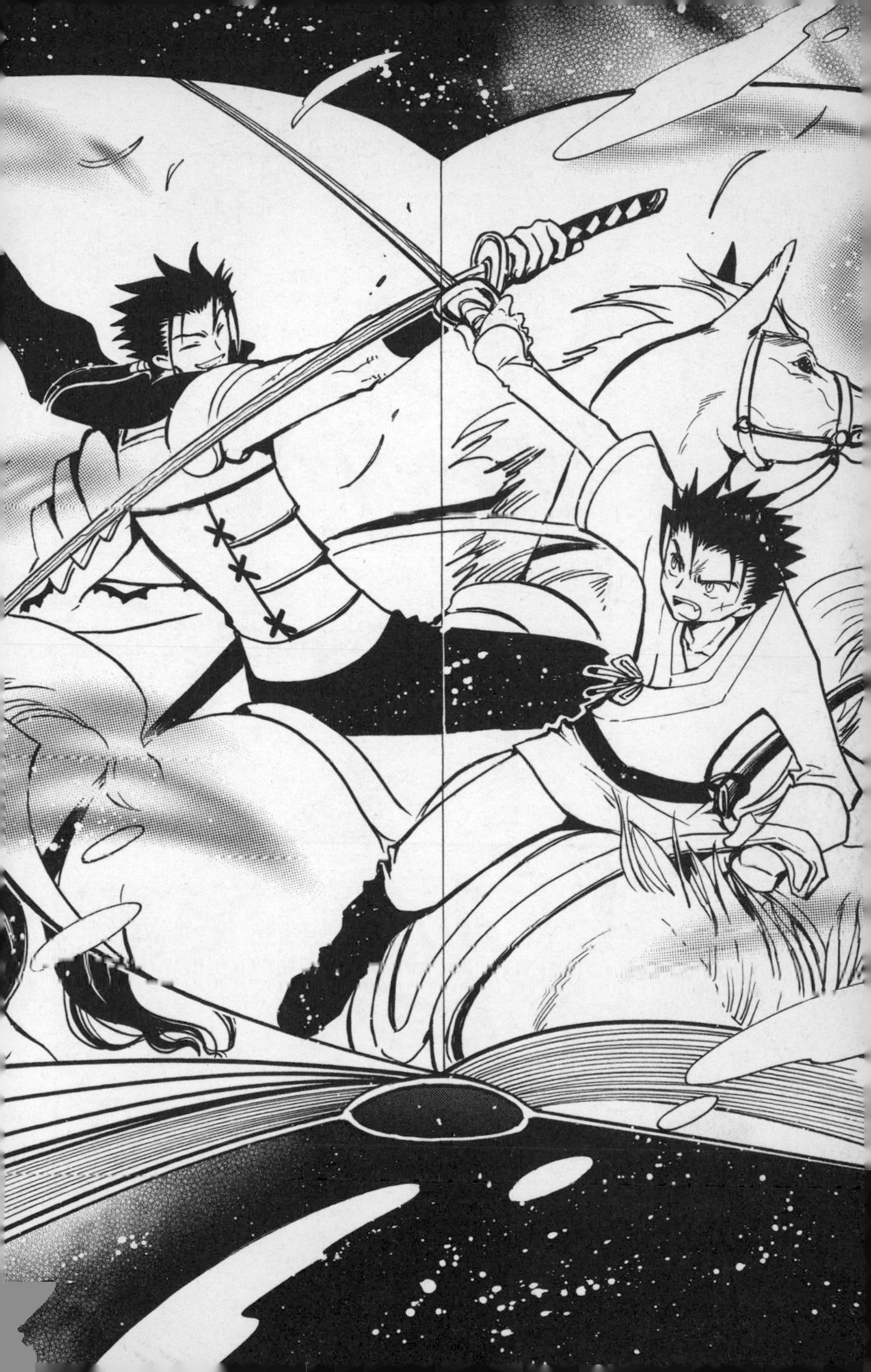

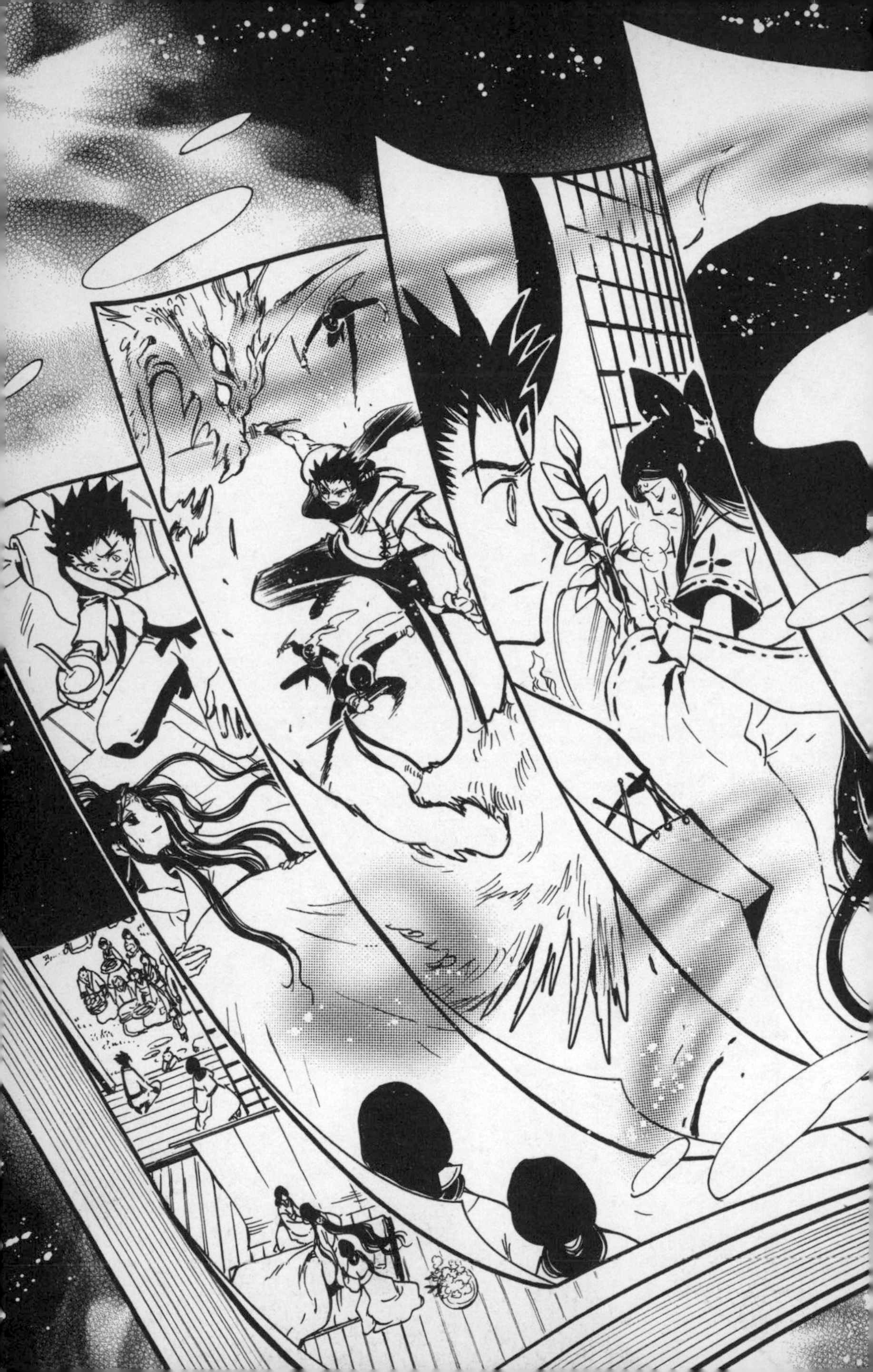

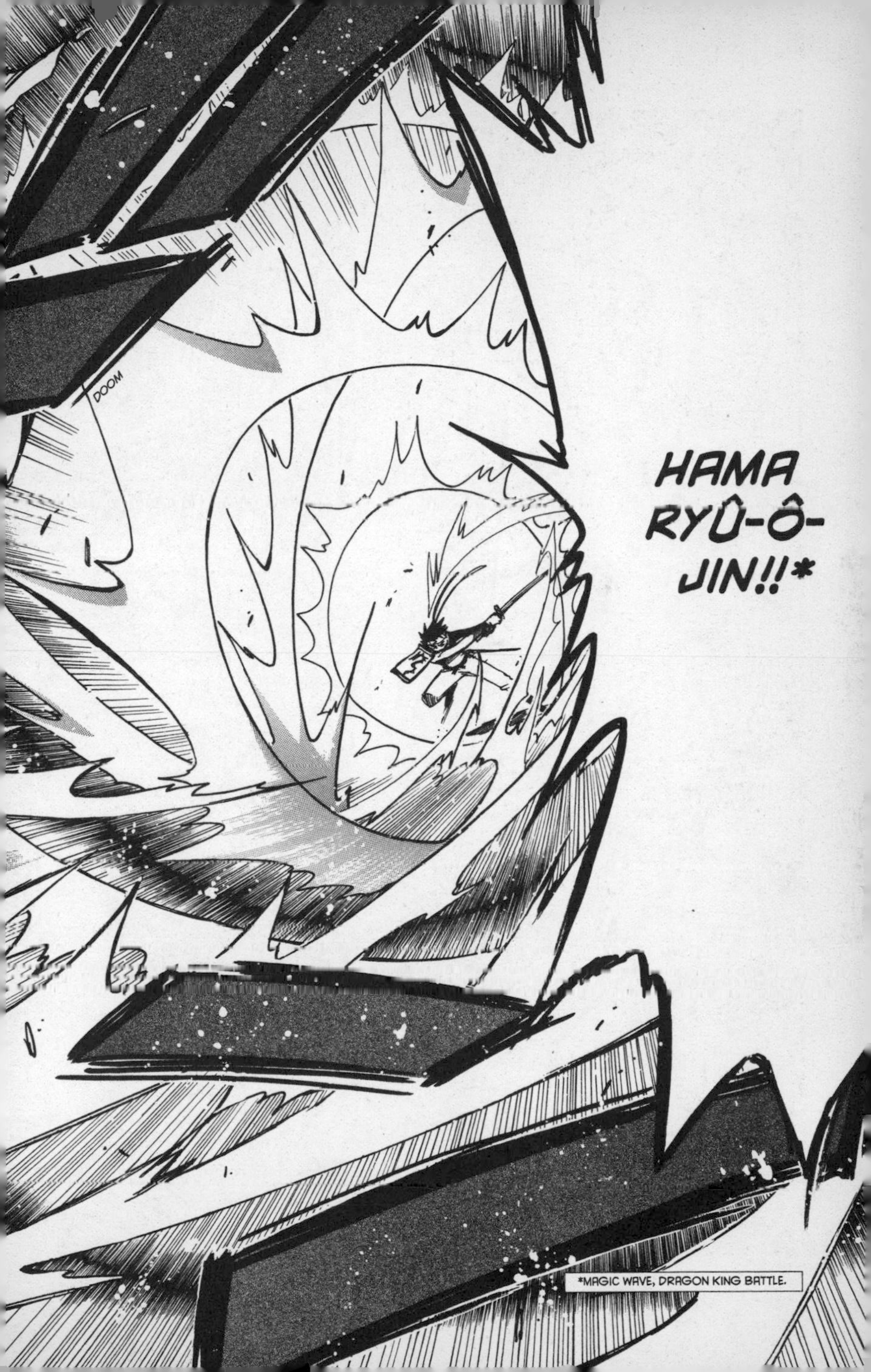
HAMA RYÛ-Ô-JIN!!*
DOOM
*MAGIC WAVE, DRAGON KING BATTLE.

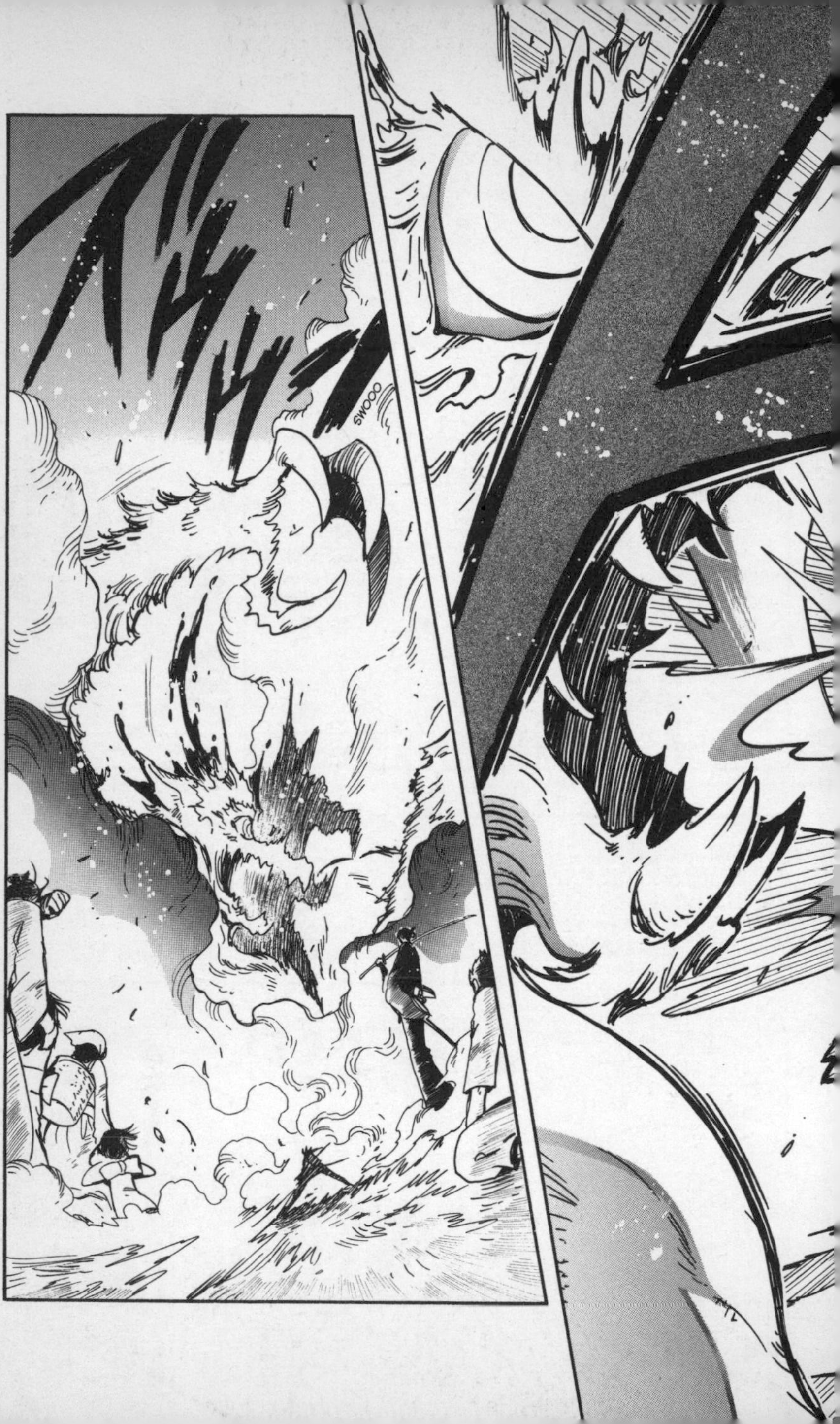
SWOOO

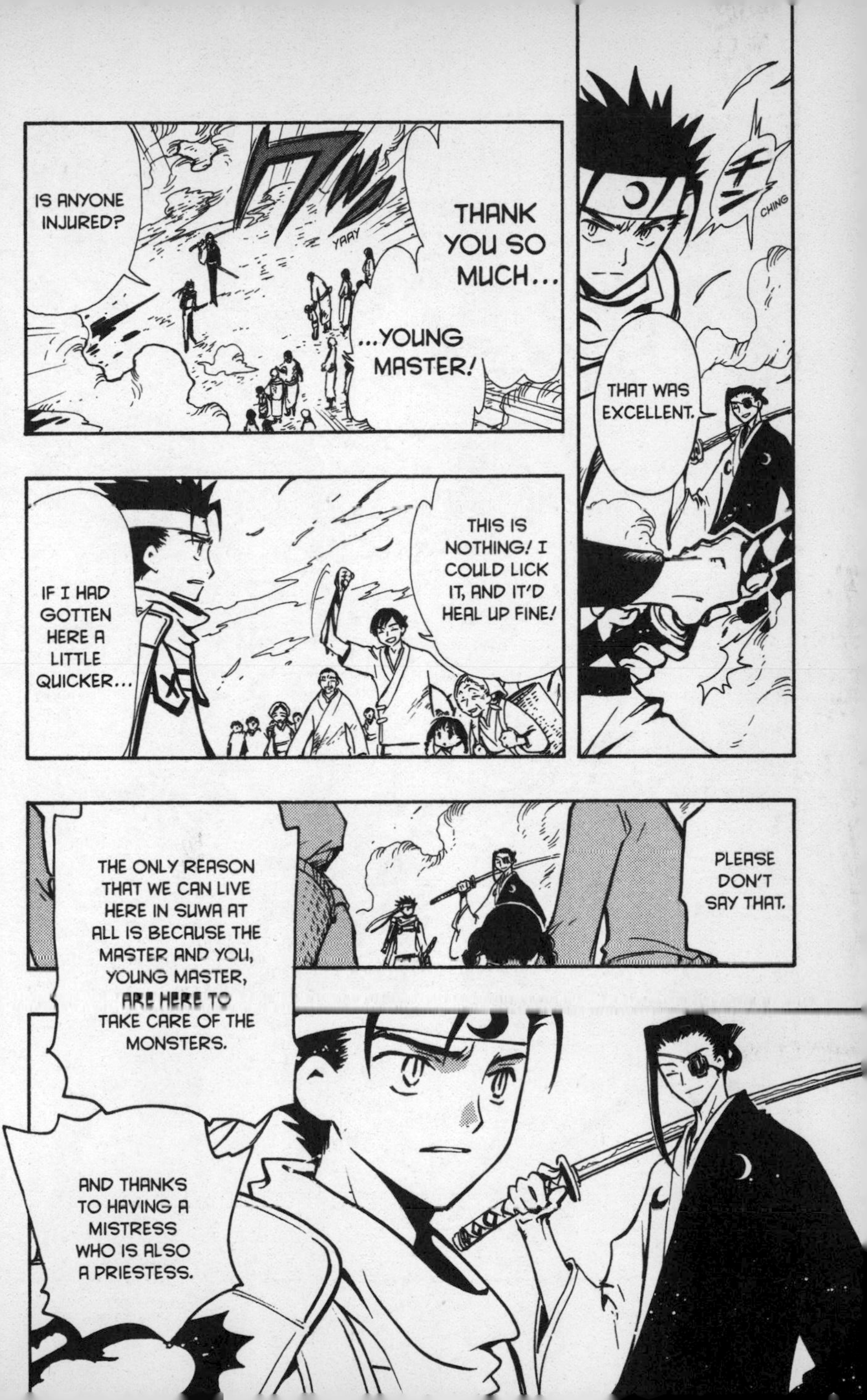
チン
CHING
THAT WAS EXCELLENT.
THANK YOU SO MUCH...
...YOUNG MASTER!
YAAY
IS ANYONE INJURED?
THIS IS NOTHING! I COULD LICK IT, AND IT'D HEAL UP FINE!
IF I HAD GOTTEN HERE A LITTLE QUICKER...
PLEASE DON'T SAY THAT.
THE ONLY REASON THAT WE CAN LIVE HERE IN SUWA AT ALL IS BECAUSE THE MASTER AND YOU, YOUNG MASTER, ARE HERE TO TAKE CARE OF THE MONSTERS.
AND THANKS TO HAVING A MISTRESS WHO IS ALSO A PRIESTESS.

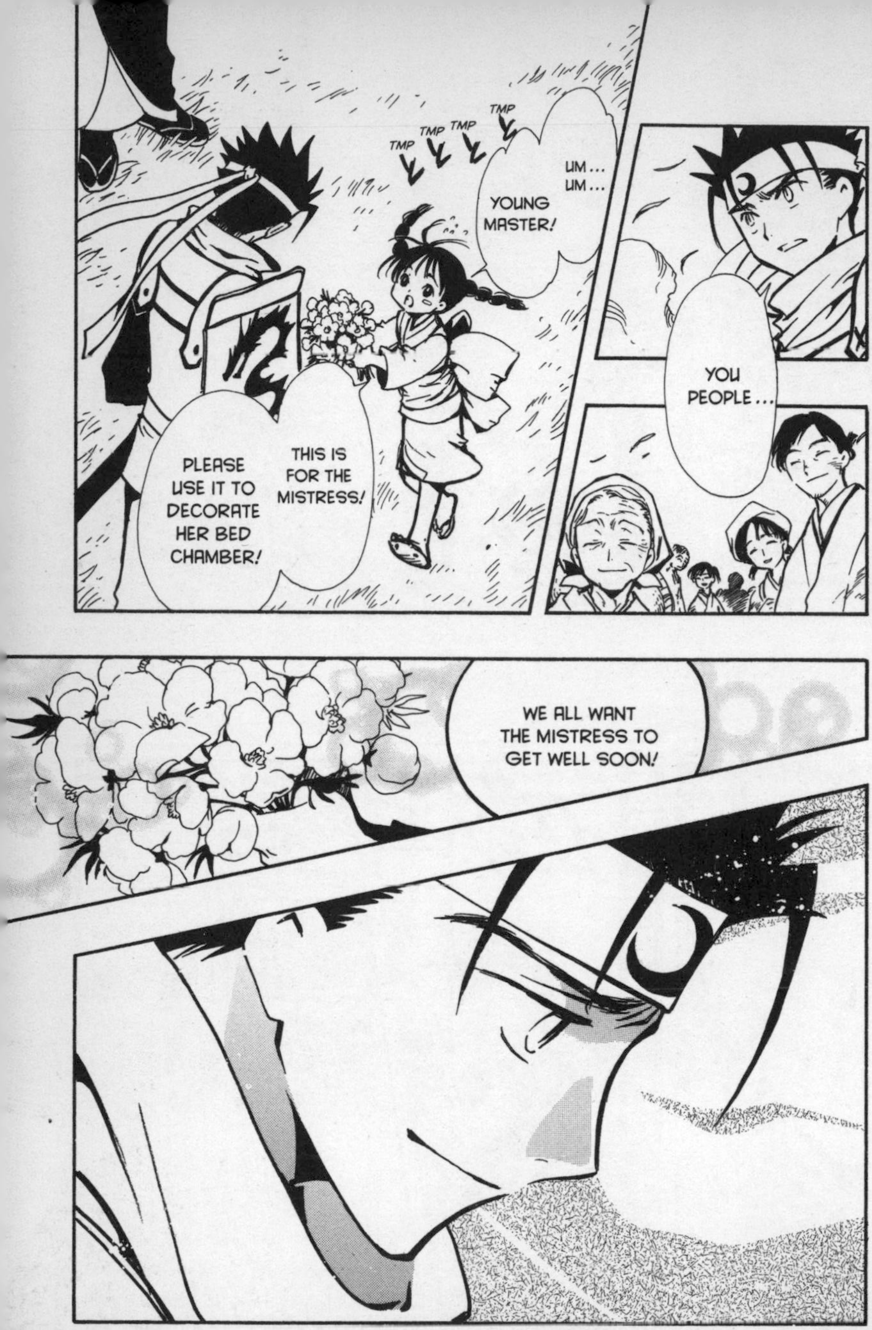
YOU PEOPLE...
TMP TMP TMP TMP
UM... UM...
YOUNG MASTER!
THIS IS FOR THE MISTRESS!
PLEASE USE IT TO DECORATE HER BED CHAMBER!
WE ALL WANT THE MISTRESS TO GET WELL SOON!

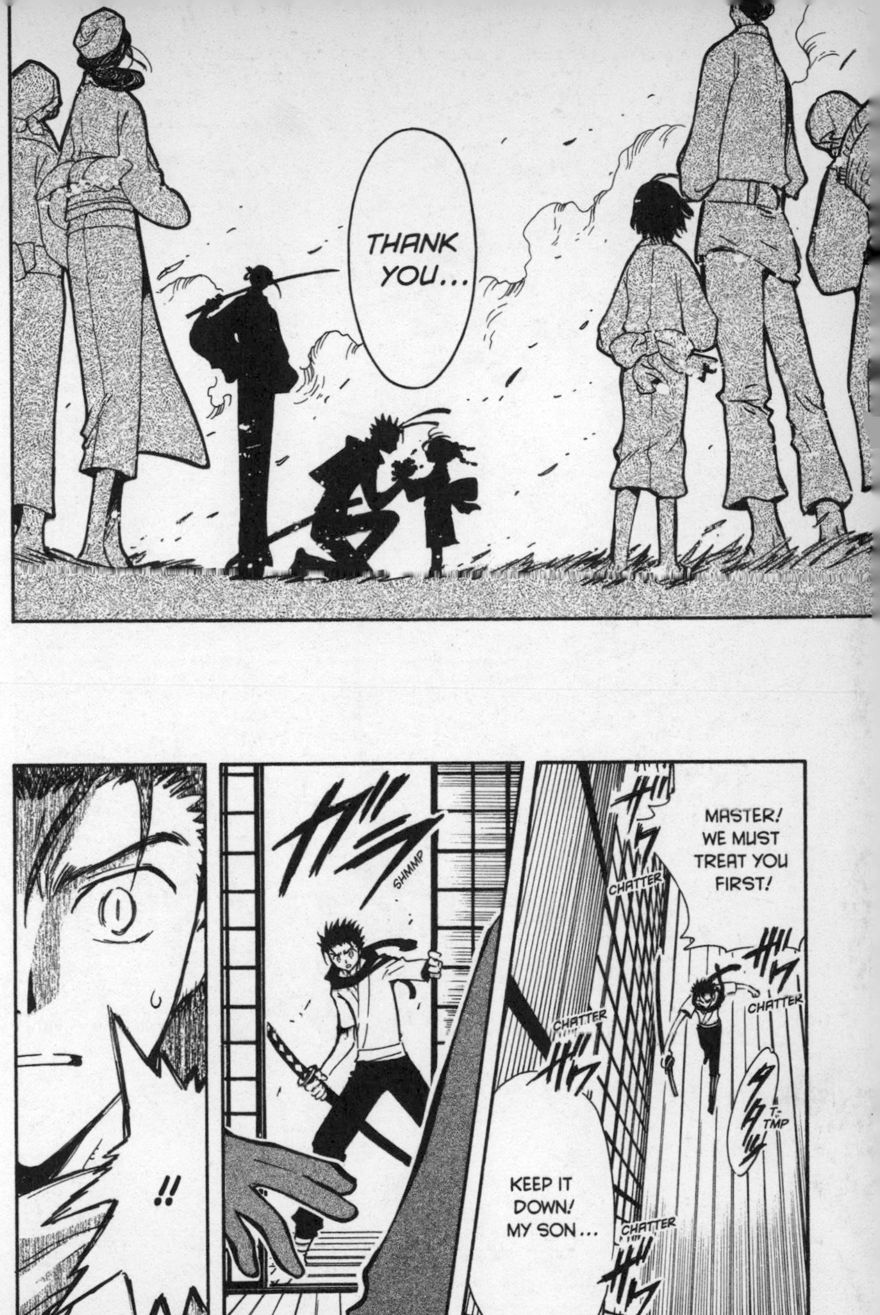
THANK YOU...
MASTER! WE MUST TREAT YOU FIRST!
CHATTER
CHATTER
T-TMP
KEEP IT DOWN! MY SON...
CHATTER
CHATTER
SHMMP
!!

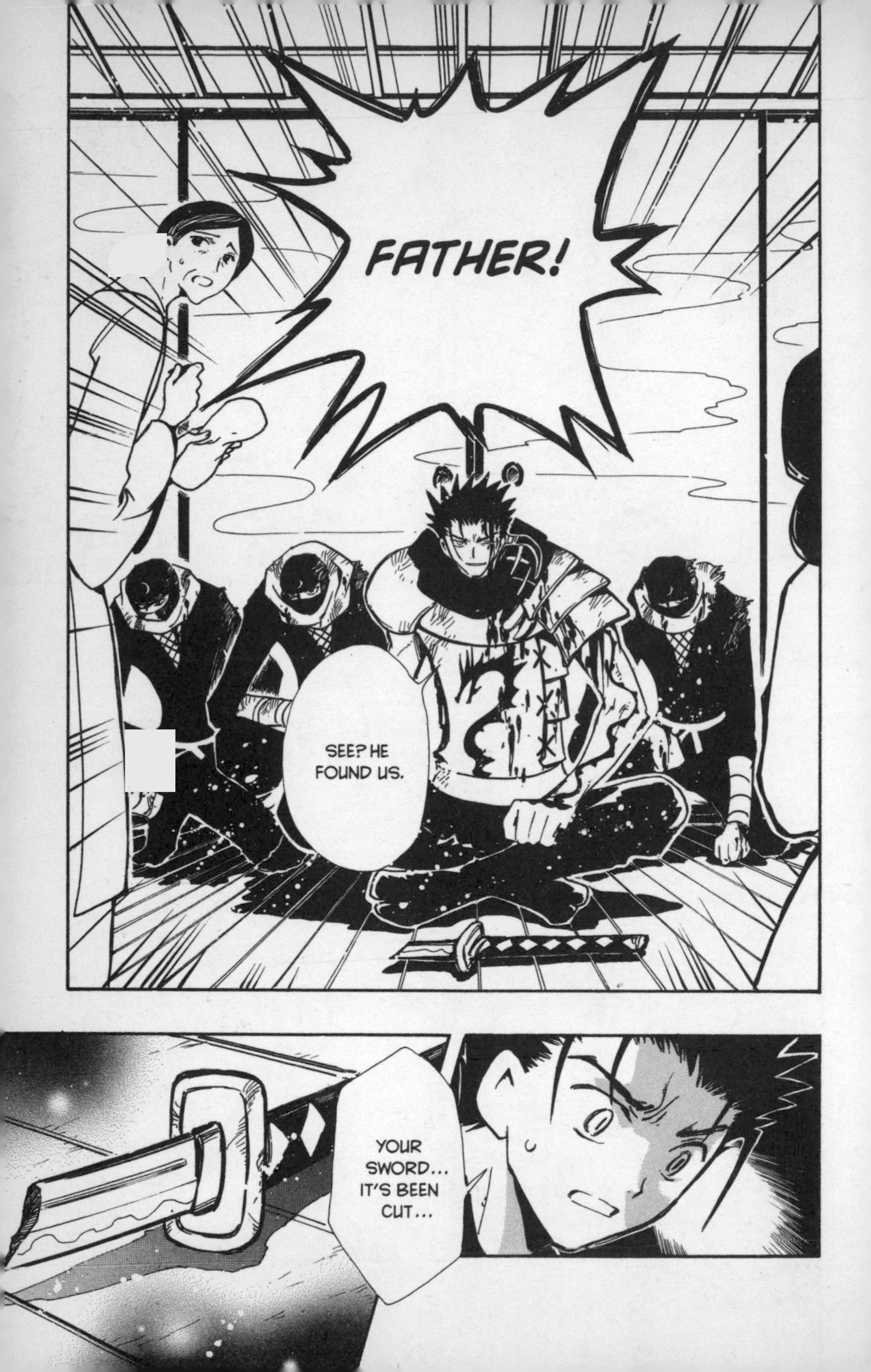
FATHER!
SEE? HE FOUND US.
YOUR SWORD... IT'S BEEN CUT...

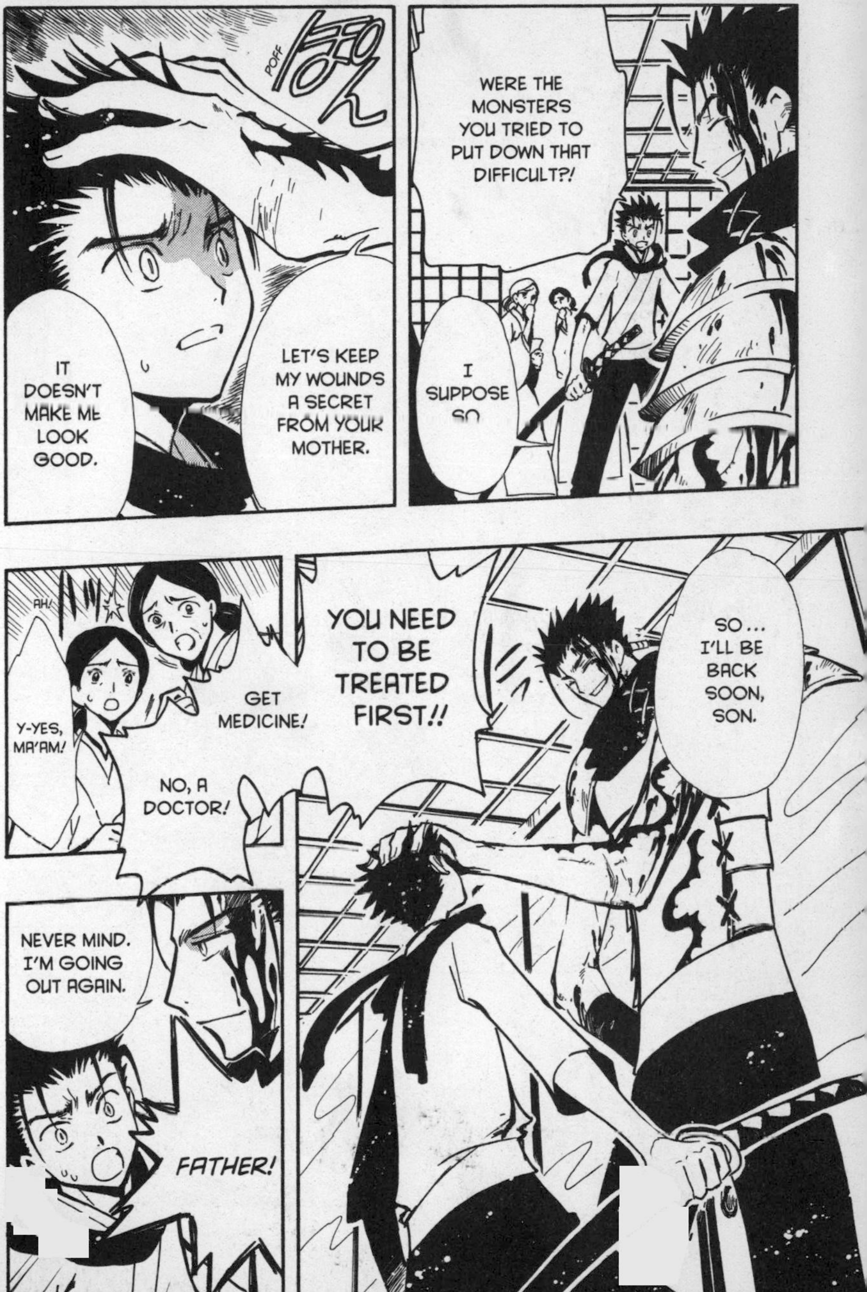
WERE THE MONSTERS YOU TRIED TO PUT DOWN THAT DIFFICULT?!
I SUPPOSE SO.
POFF
LET'S KEEP MY WOUNDS A SECRET FROM YOUR MOTHER.
IT DOESN'T MAKE ME LOOK GOOD.
SO... I'LL BE BACK SOON, SON.
YOU NEED TO BE TREATED FIRST!!
GET MEDICINE!
AH!
Y-YES, MA'AM!
NO, A DOCTOR!
NEVER MIND. I'M GOING OUT AGAIN.
FATHER!

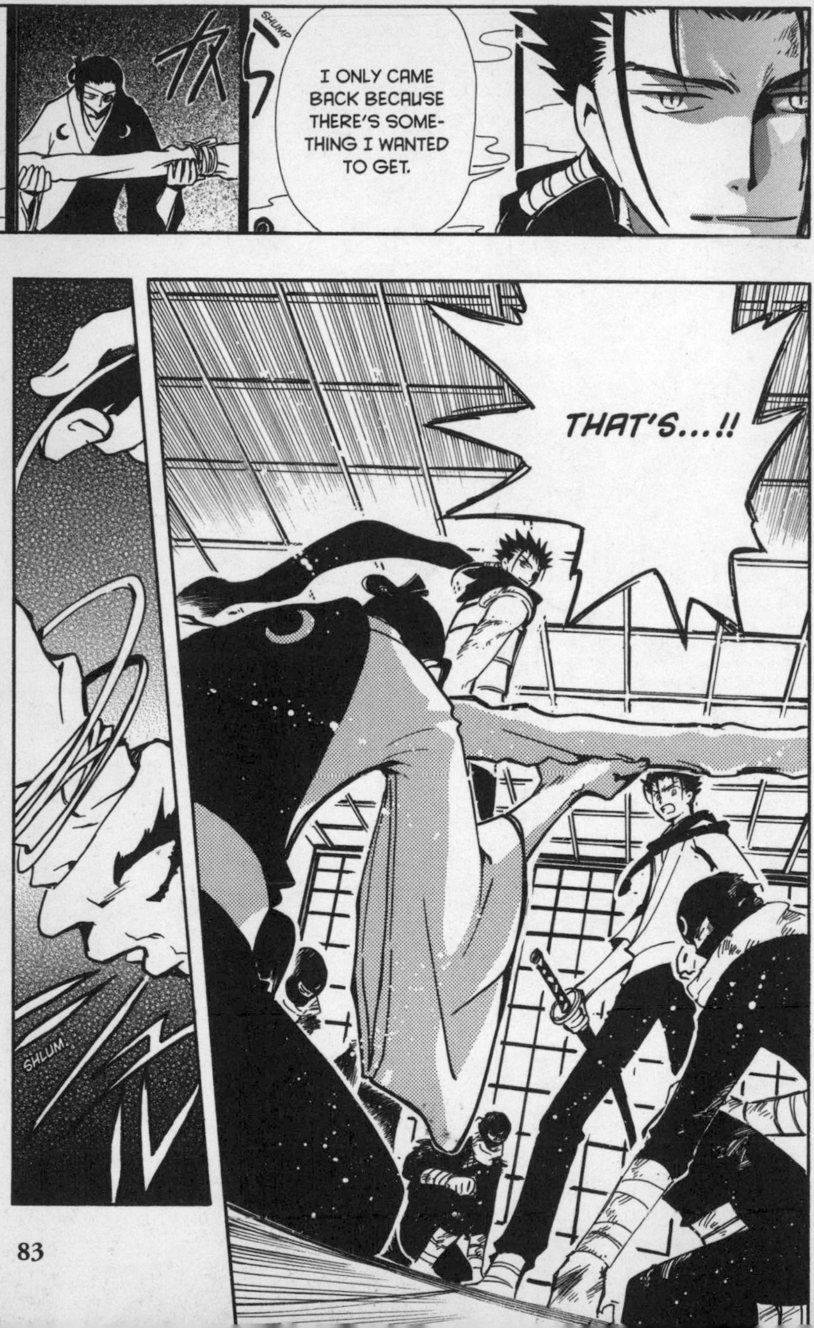
SHUMP
I ONLY CAME BACK BECAUSE THERE'S SOME-THING I WANTED TO GET.
THAT'S...!!
SHLUM.

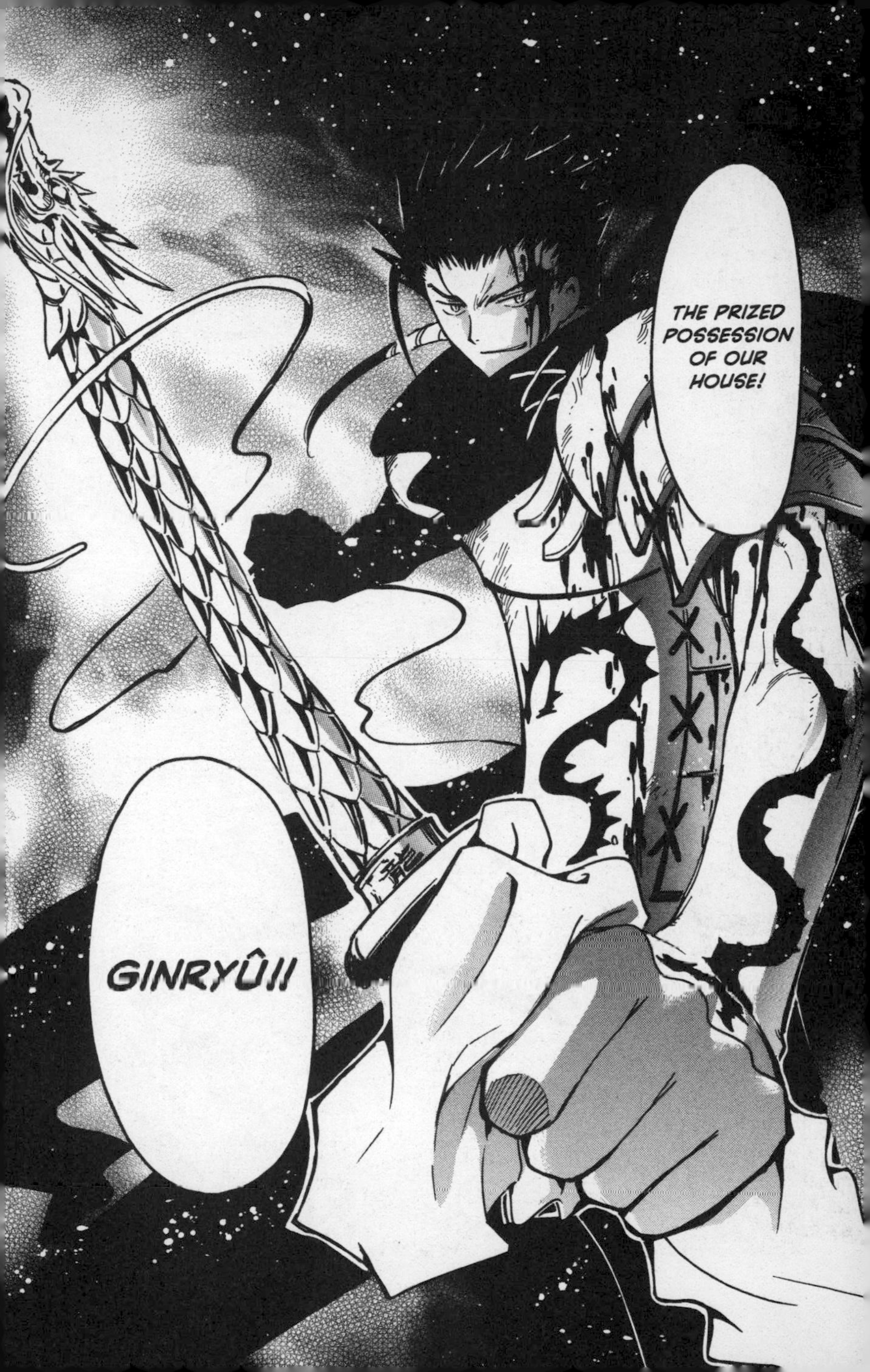
THE PRIZED POSSESSION OF OUR HOUSE!
GINRYÛ!!

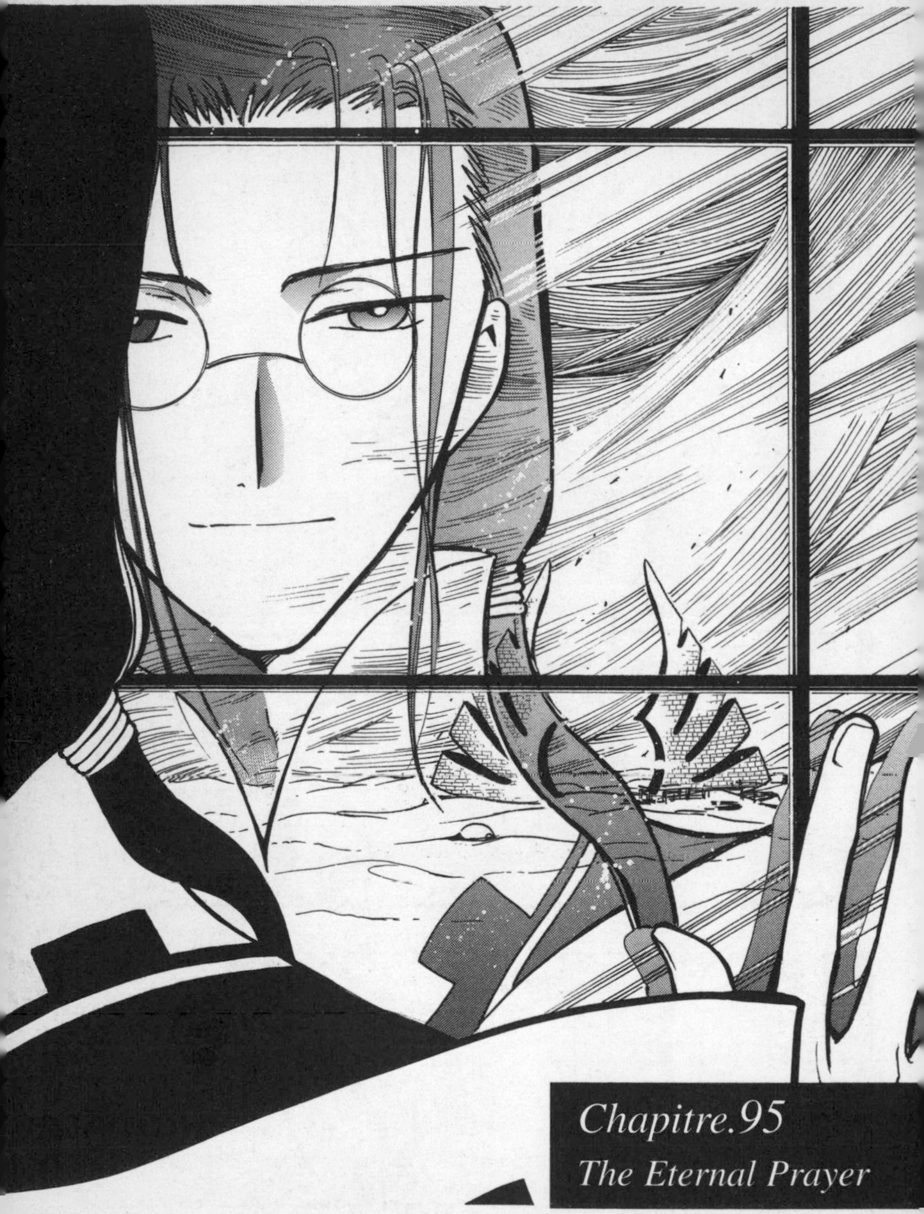
Chapitre.95
The Eternal Prayer

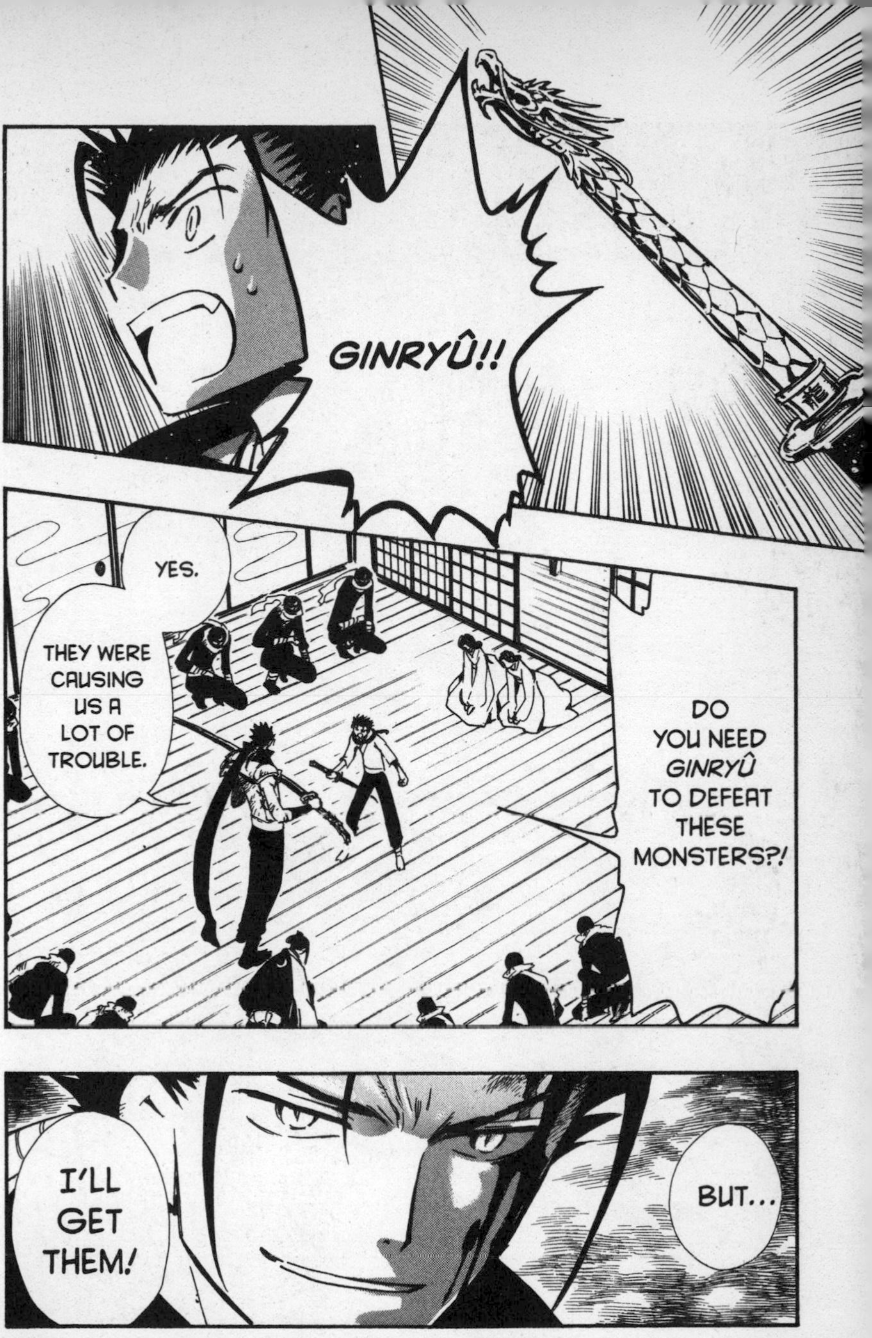
GINRYÛ!!
DO YOU NEED GINRYÛ TO DEFEAT THESE MONSTERS?!
YES.
THEY WERE CAUSING US A LOT OF TROUBLE.
BUT...
I'LL GET THEM!

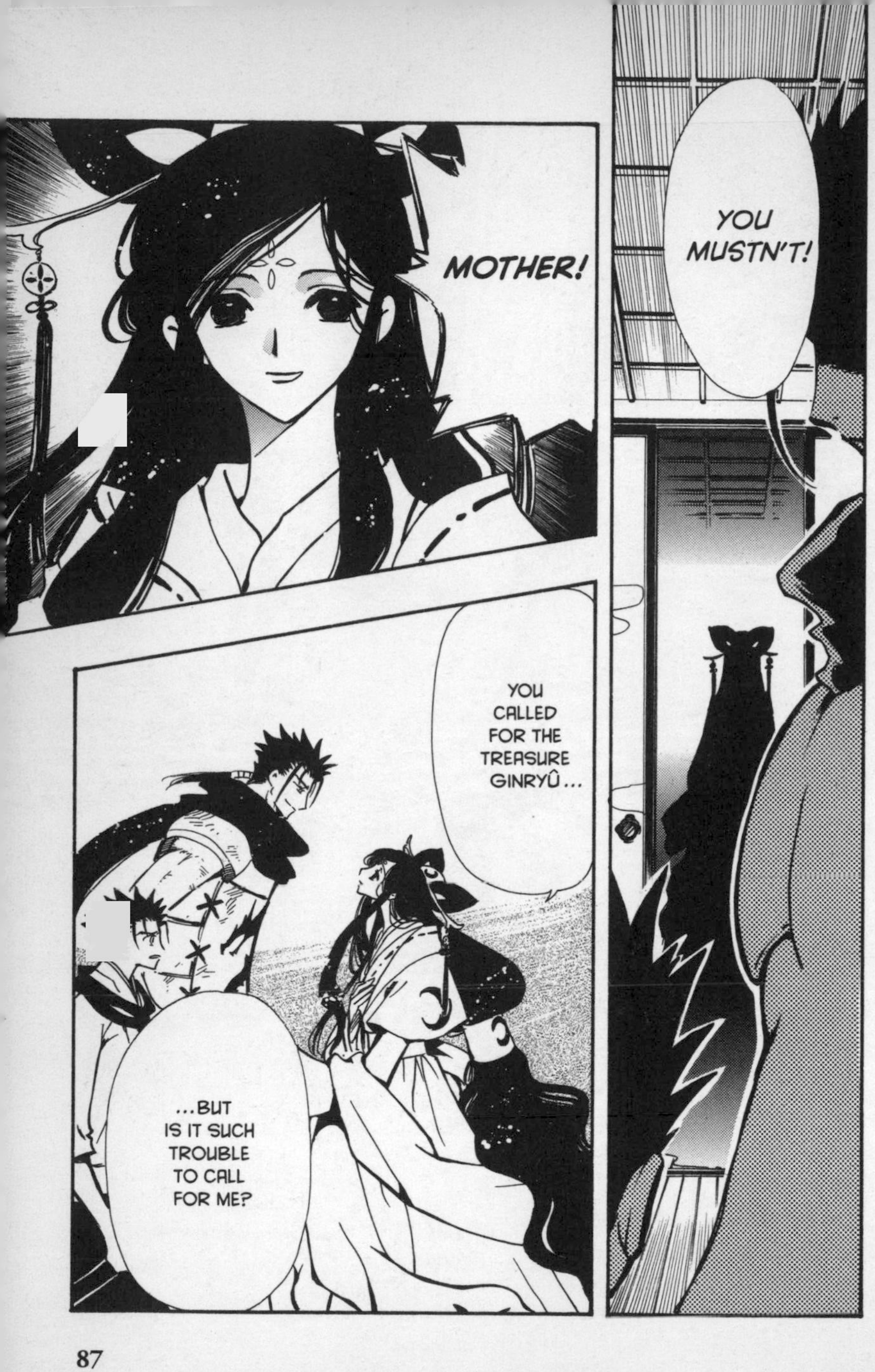
YOU MUSTN'T!
MOTHER!
YOU CALLED FOR THE TREASURE GINRYÛ...
...BUT IS IT SUCH TROUBLE TO CALL FOR ME?

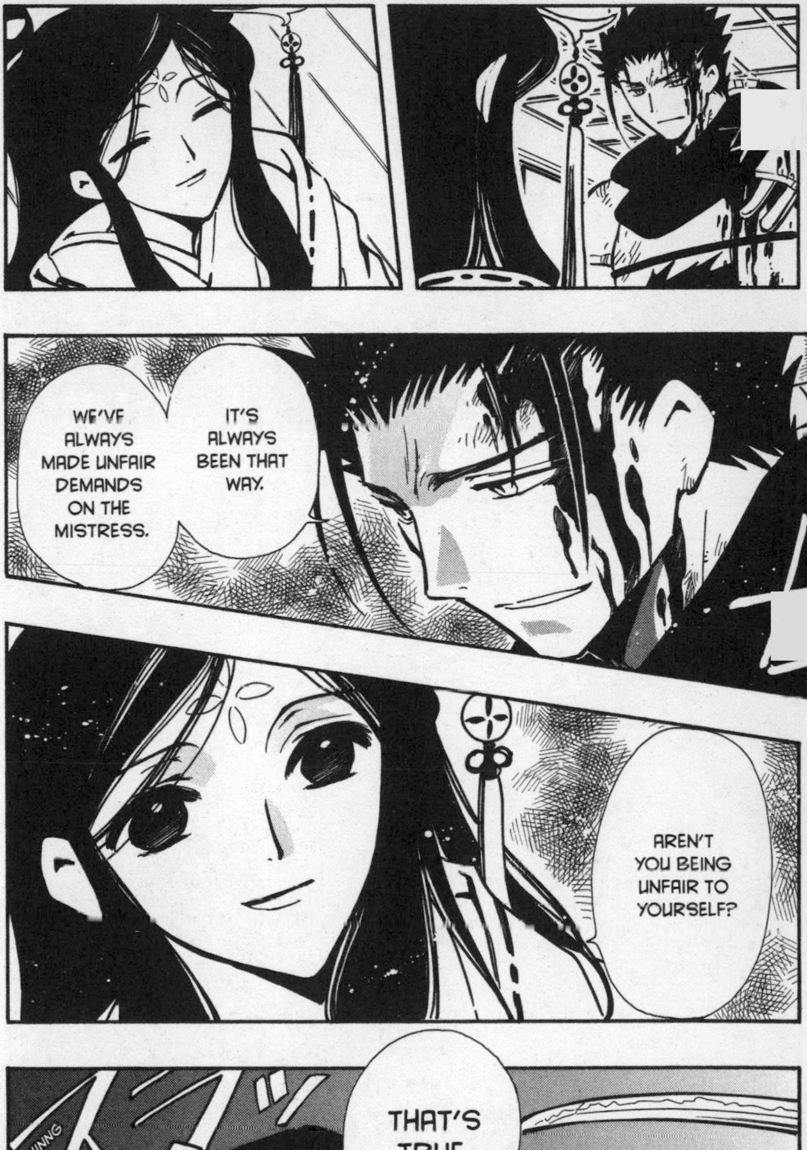
IT'S ALWAYS BEEN THAT WAY.
WE'VE ALWAYS MADE UNFAIR DEMANDS ON THE MISTRESS.
AREN'T YOU BEING UNFAIR TO YOURSELF?
THAT'S TRUE.
SHINNG

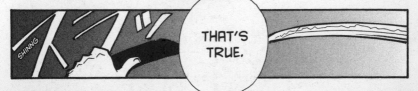

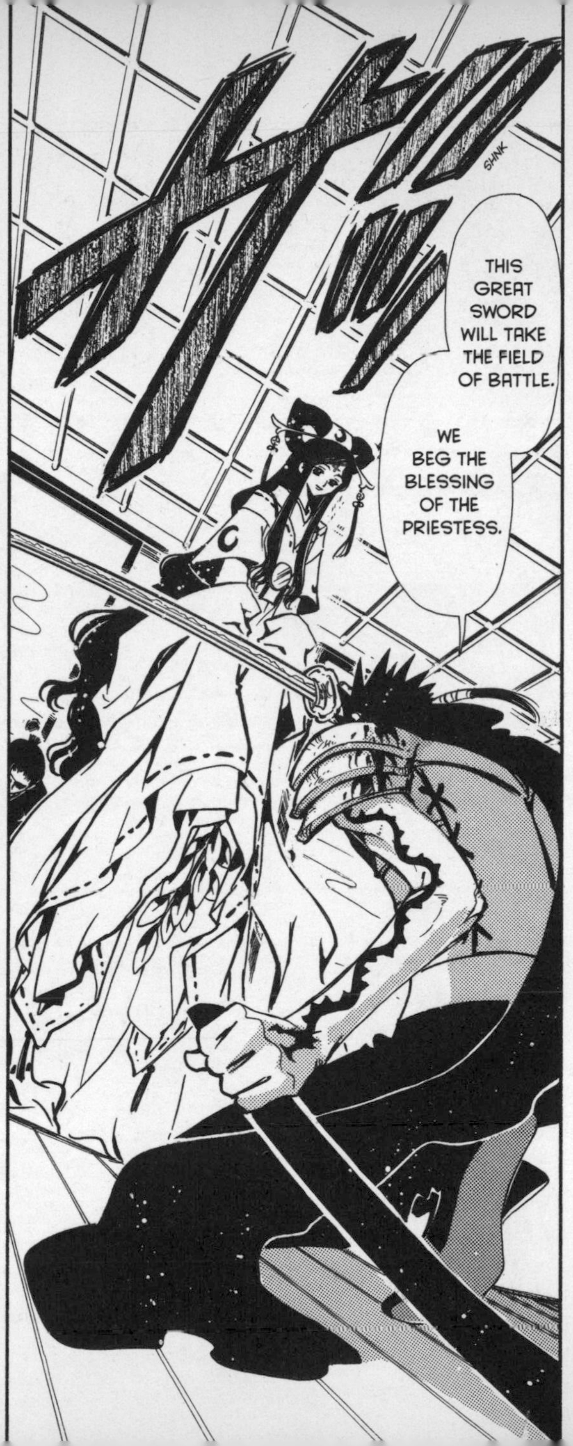
SHNK
THIS GREAT SWORD WILL TAKE THE FIELD OF BATTLE.
WE BEG THE BLESSING OF THE PRIESTESS.
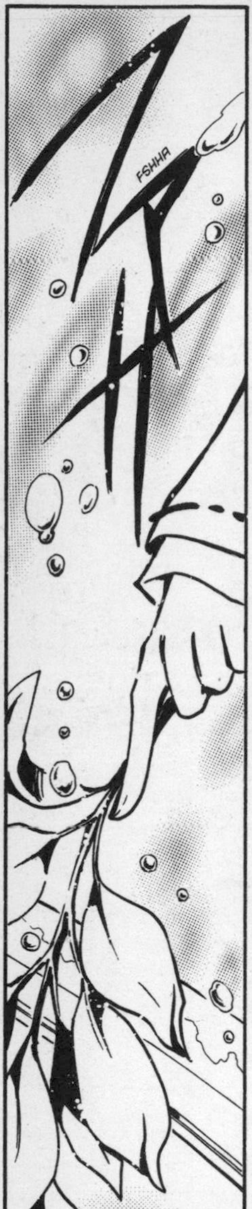
FSHHA

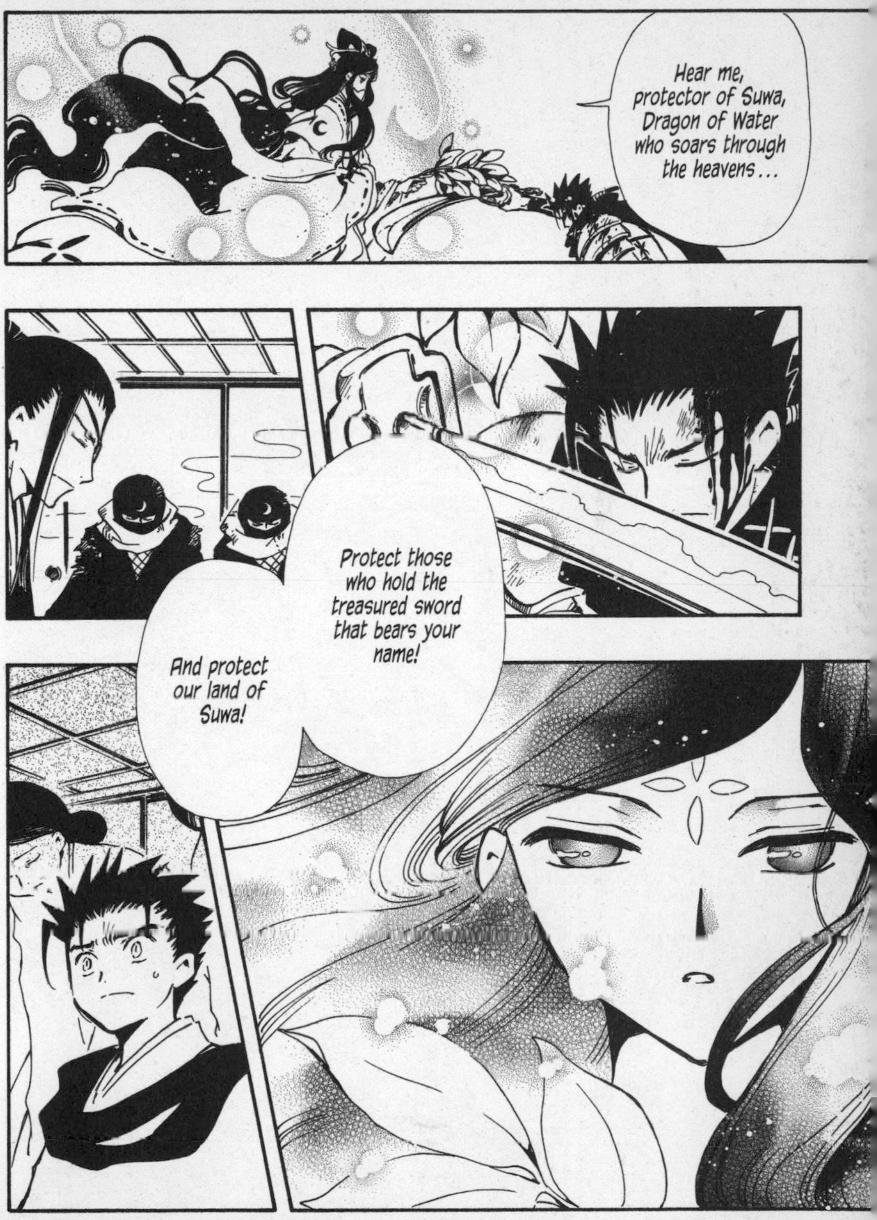
Hear me, protector of Suwa, Dragon of Water who soars through the heavens...
Protect those who hold the treasured sword that bears your name!
And protect our land of Suwa!

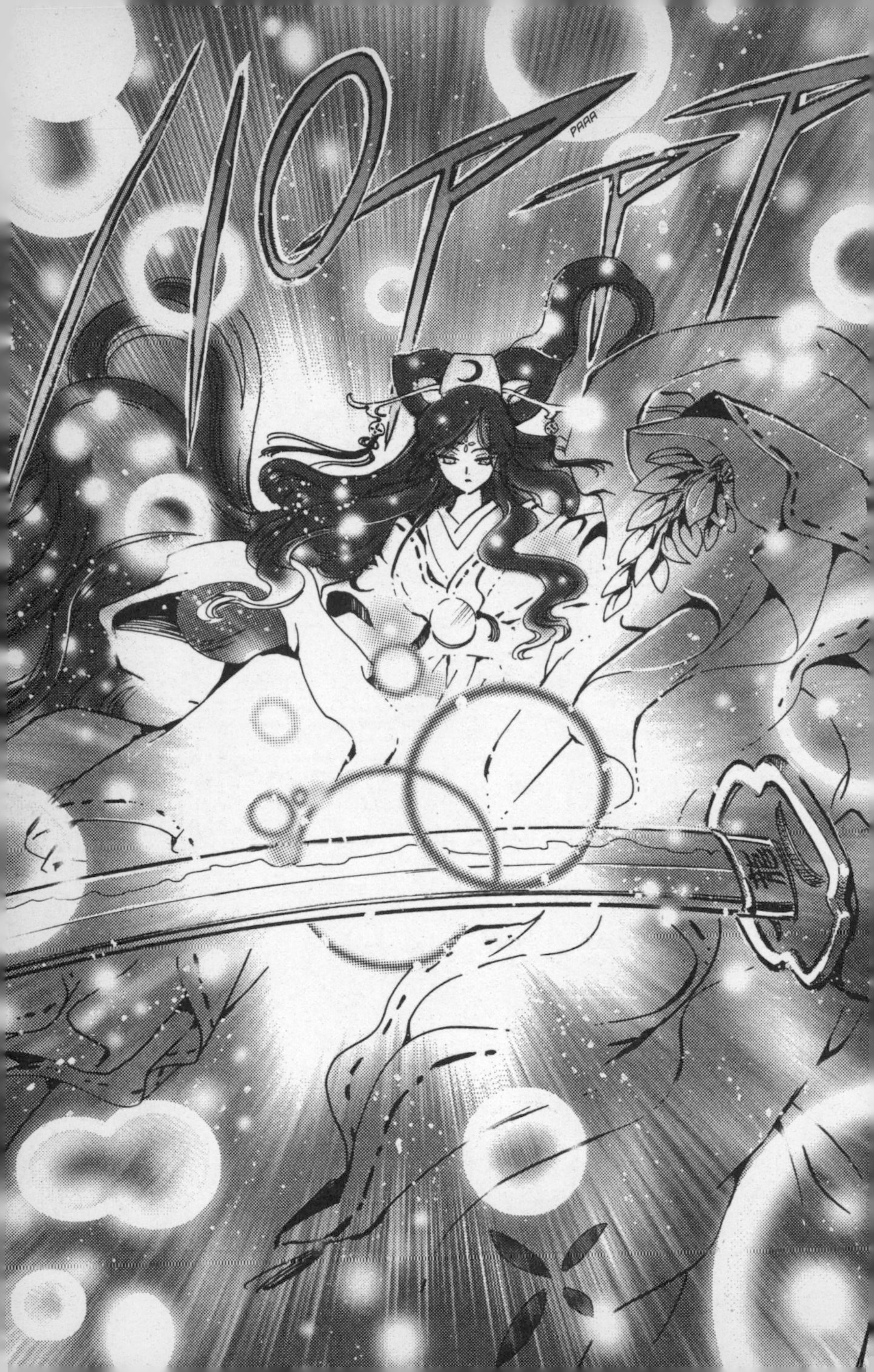
PAAA

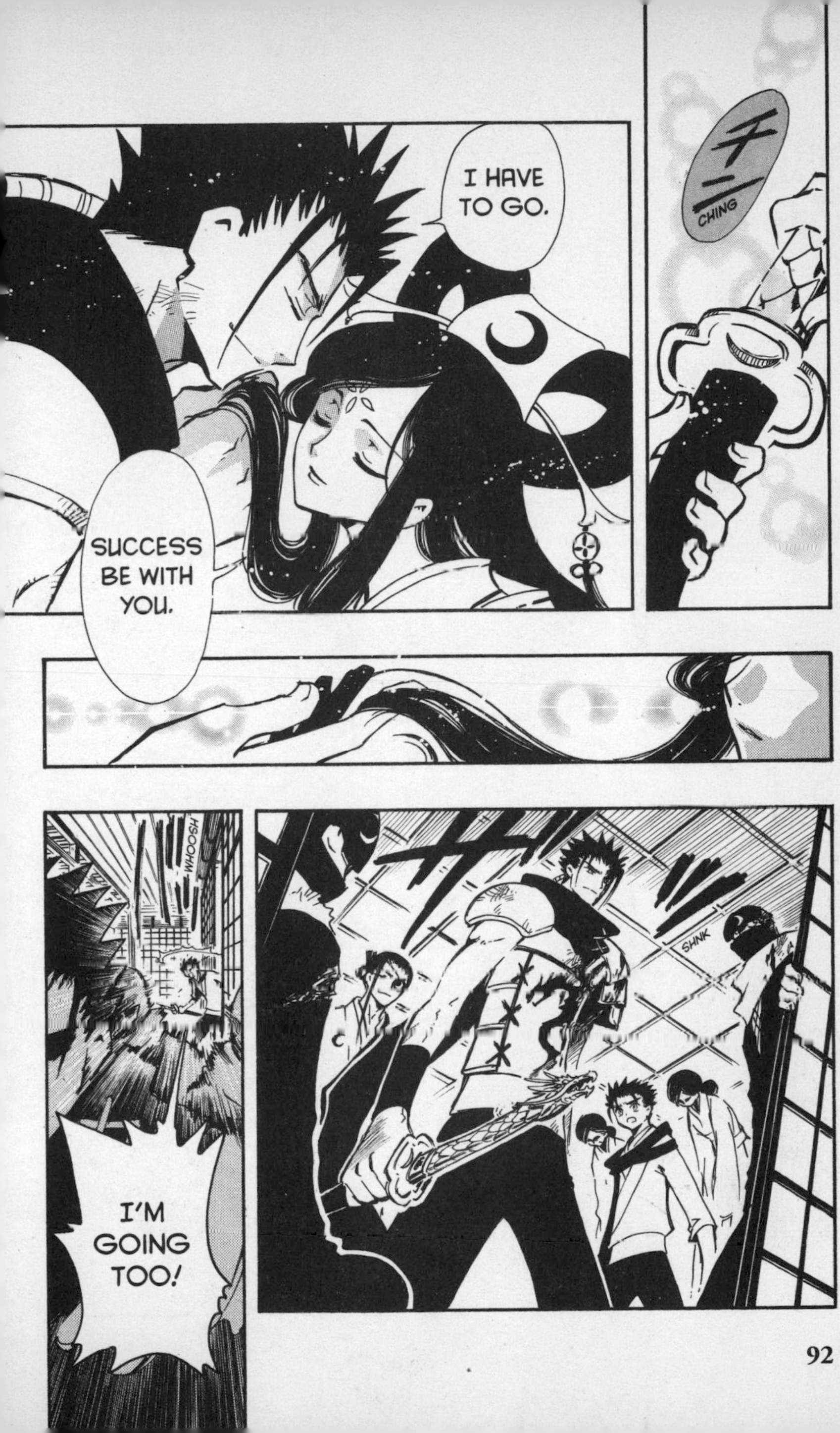
CHING
I HAVE TO GO.
SUCCESS BE WITH YOU.
SHNK
WHOOSH
I'M GOING TOO!

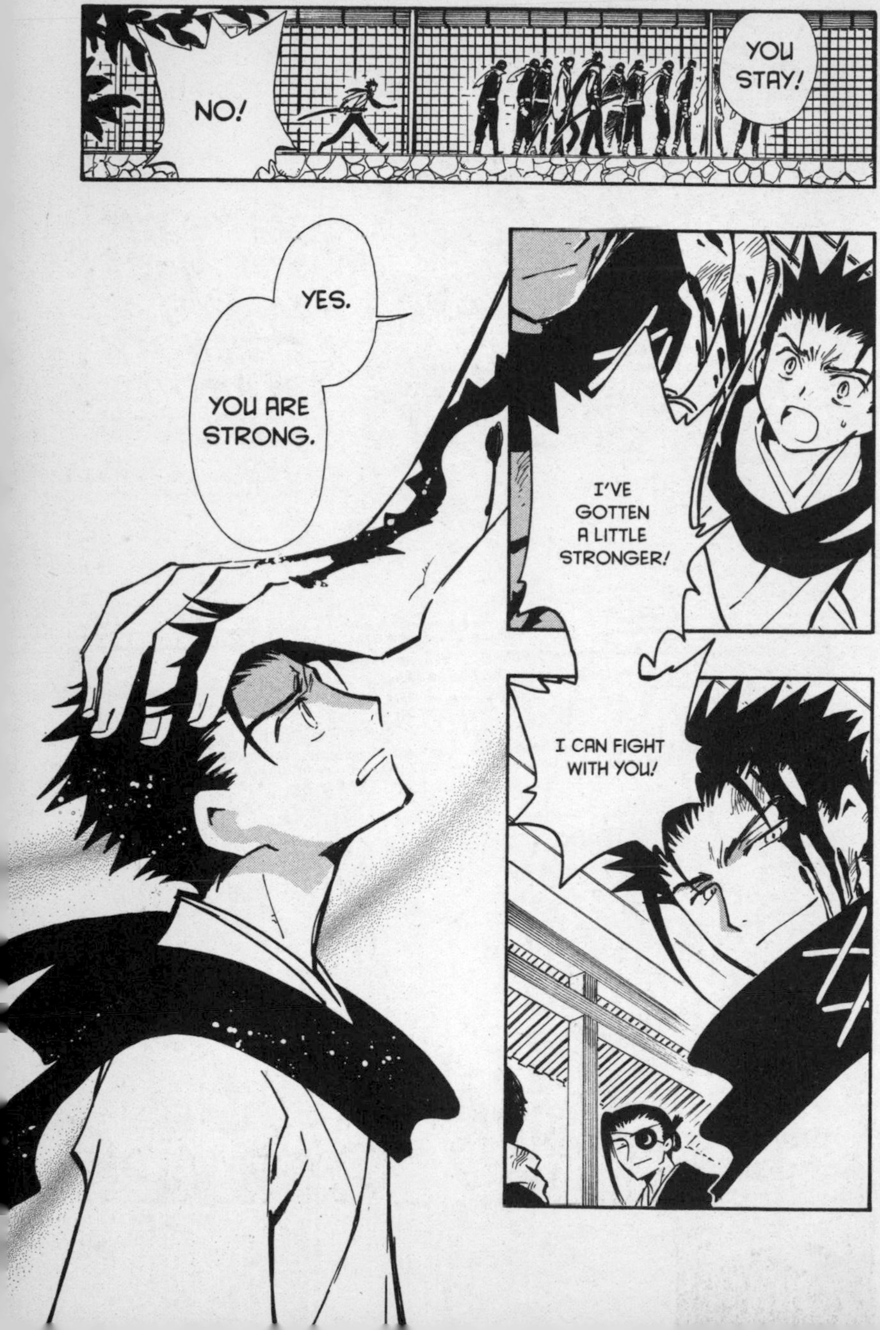
YOU STAY!
NO!
I'VE GOTTEN A LITTLE STRONGER!
I CAN FIGHT WITH YOU!
YES.
YOU ARE STRONG.

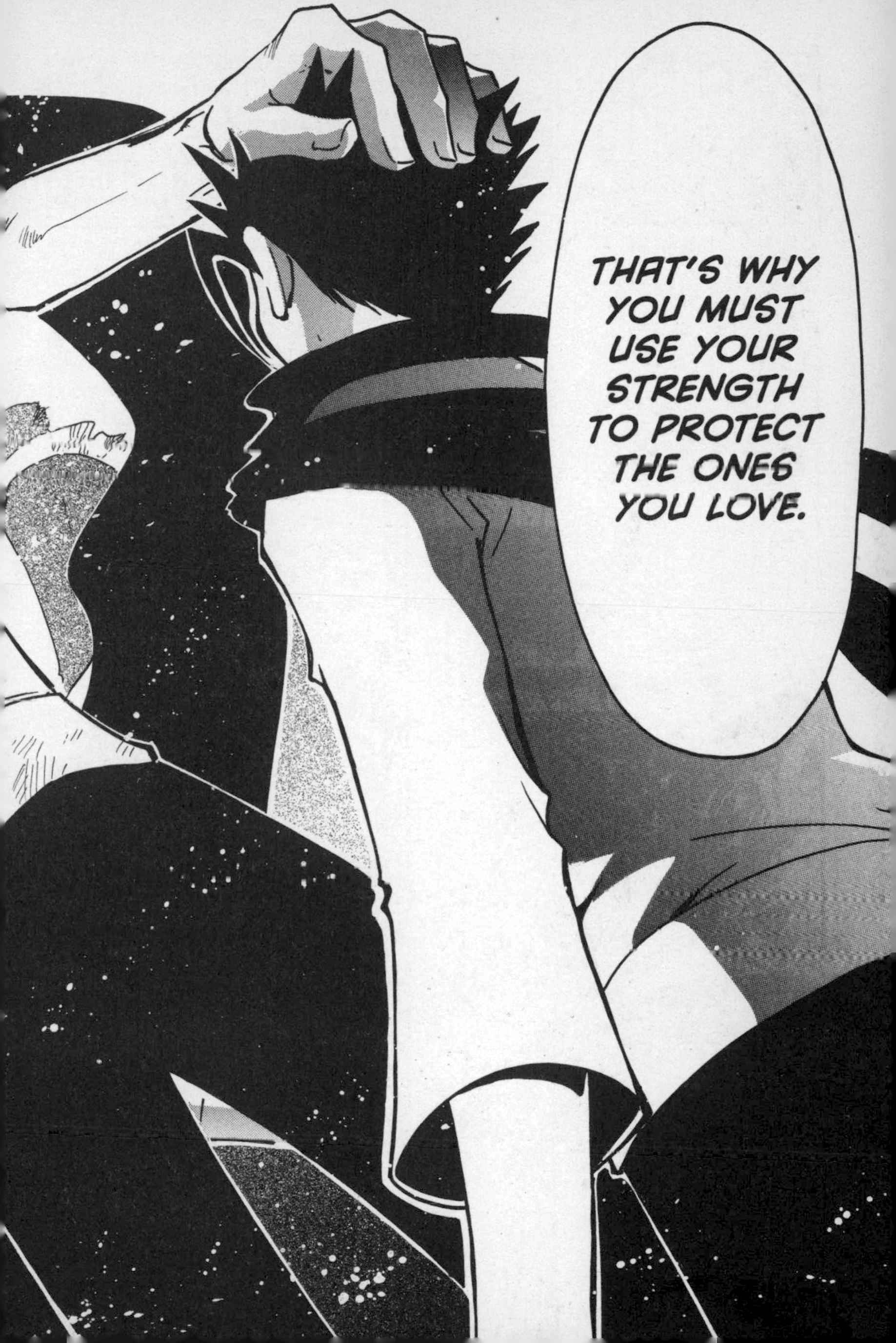
THAT'S WHY YOU MUST USE YOUR STRENGTH TO PROTECT THE ONES YOU LOVE.

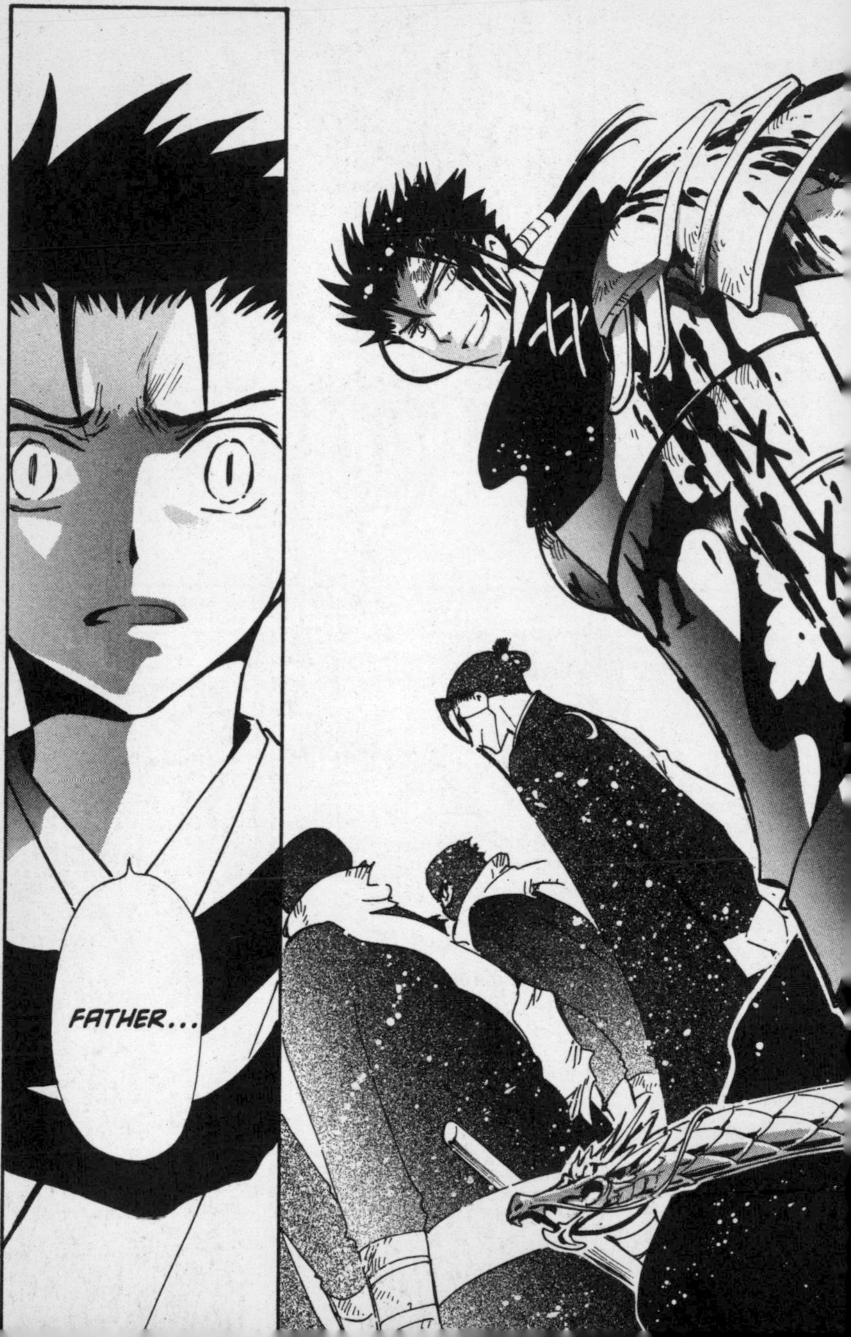
FATHER...

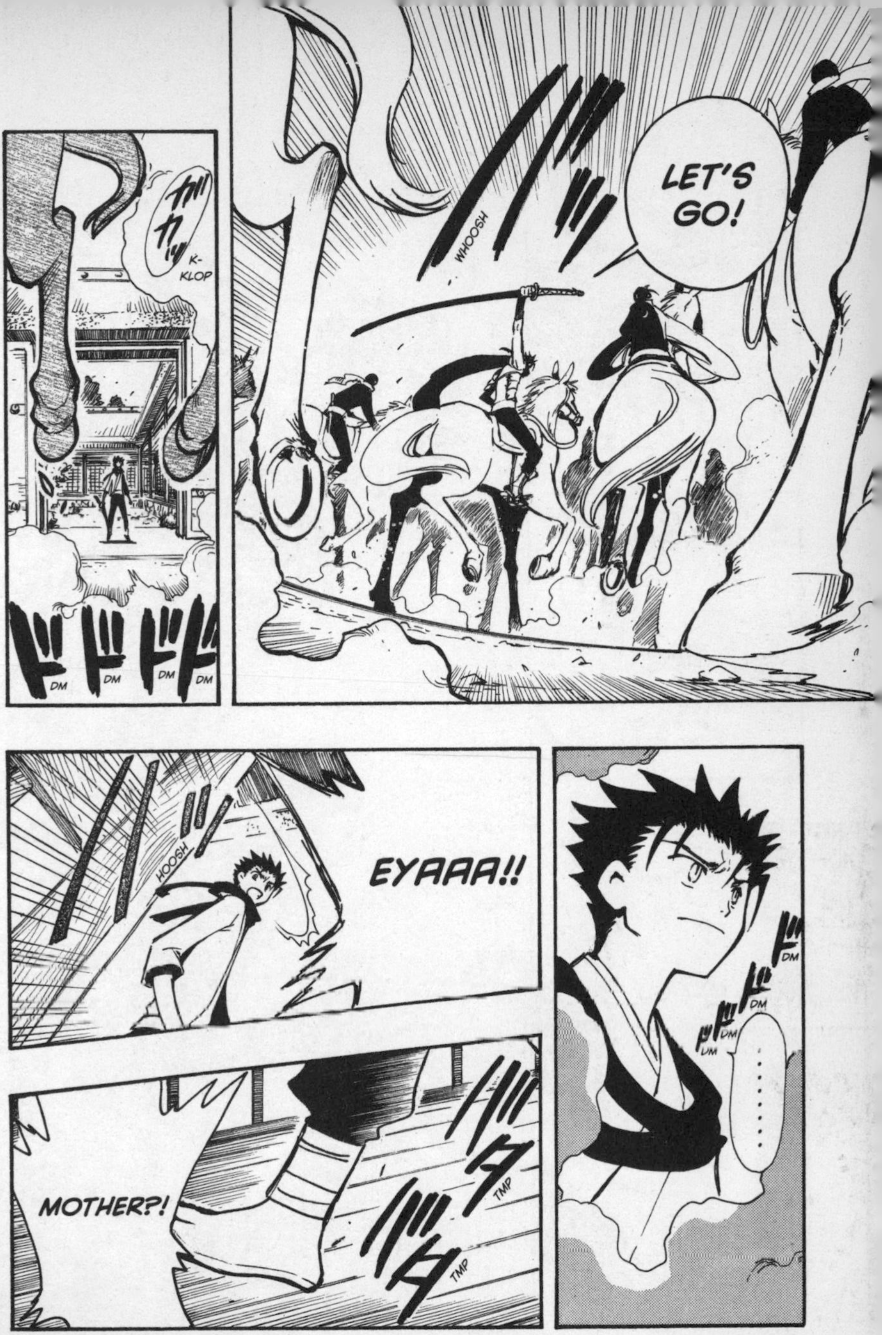
LET'S GO!
WHOOSH
K-KLOP
DM DM DM DM
DM DM DM DM
......
HOOSH
EYAAA!!
MOTHER?!
TMP TMP

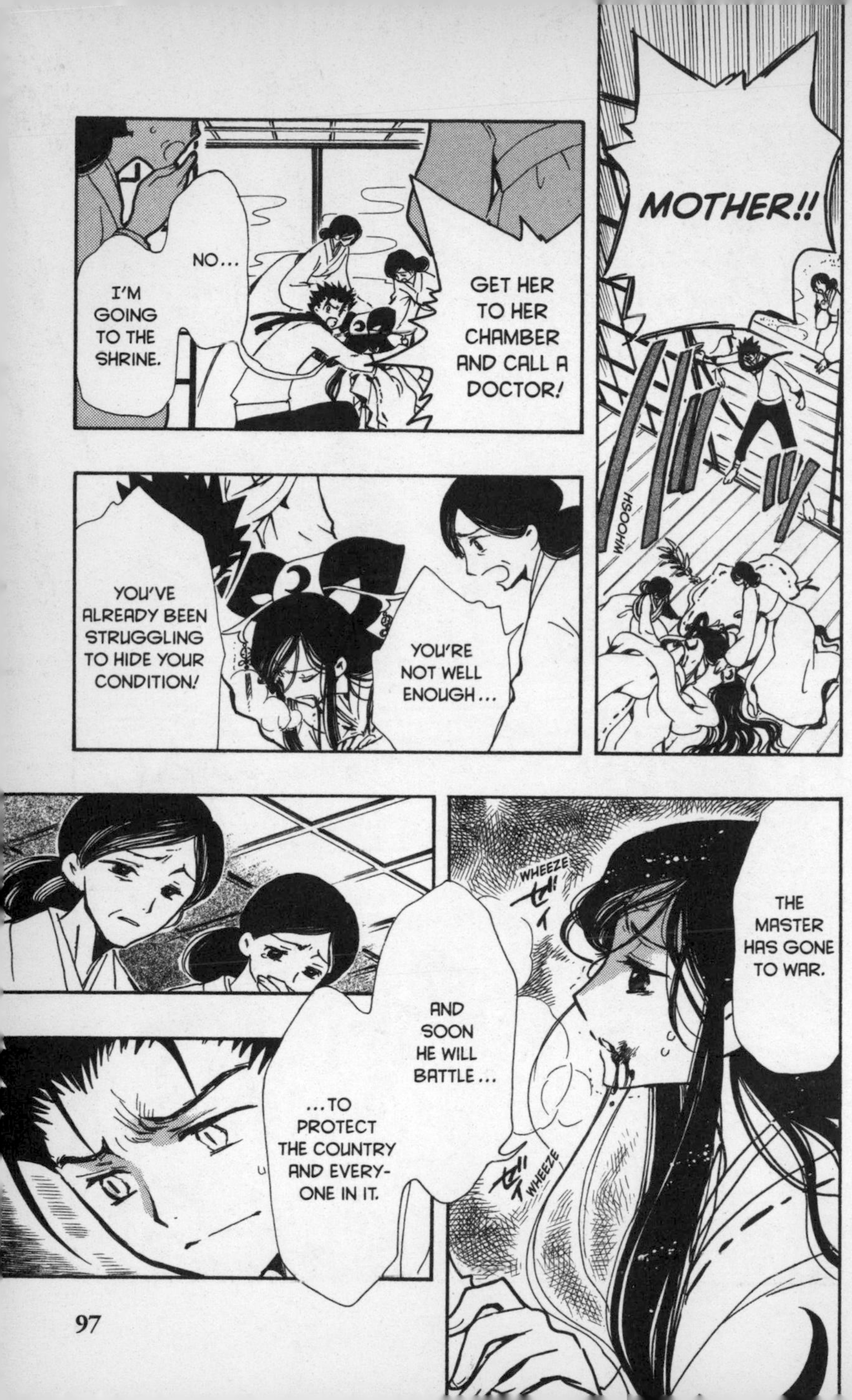
MOTHER!!
WHOOSH
GET HER TO HER CHAMBER AND CALL A DOCTOR!
NO...
I'M GOING TO THE SHRINE.
YOU'RE NOT WELL ENOUGH...
YOU'VE ALREADY BEEN STRUGGLING TO HIDE YOUR CONDITION!
THE MASTER HAS GONE TO WAR.
WHEEZE
AND SOON HE WILL BATTLE...
WHEEZE
...TO PROTECT THE COUNTRY AND EVERY-ONE IN IT.

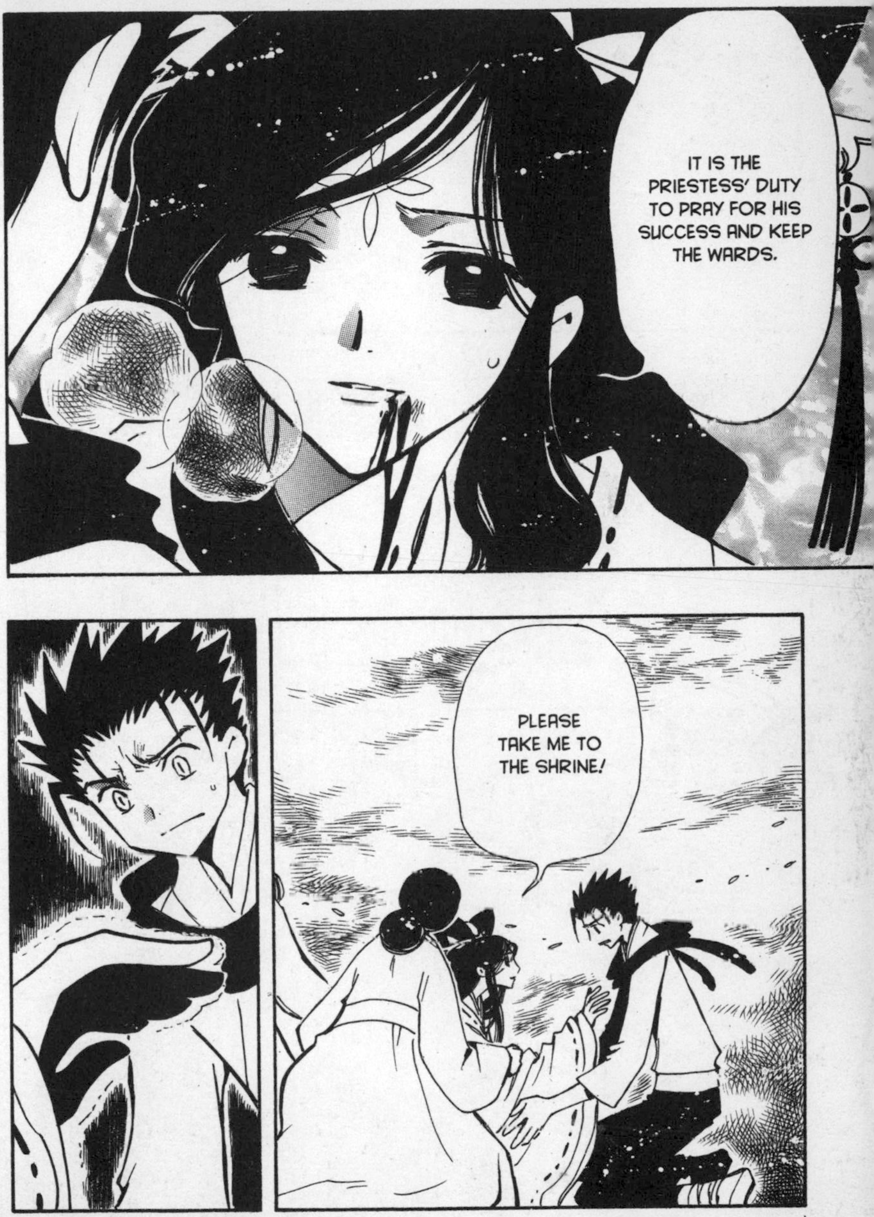
IT IS THE PRIESTESS' DUTY TO PRAY FOR HIS SUCCESS AND KEEP THE WARDS.
PLEASE TAKE ME TO THE SHRINE!

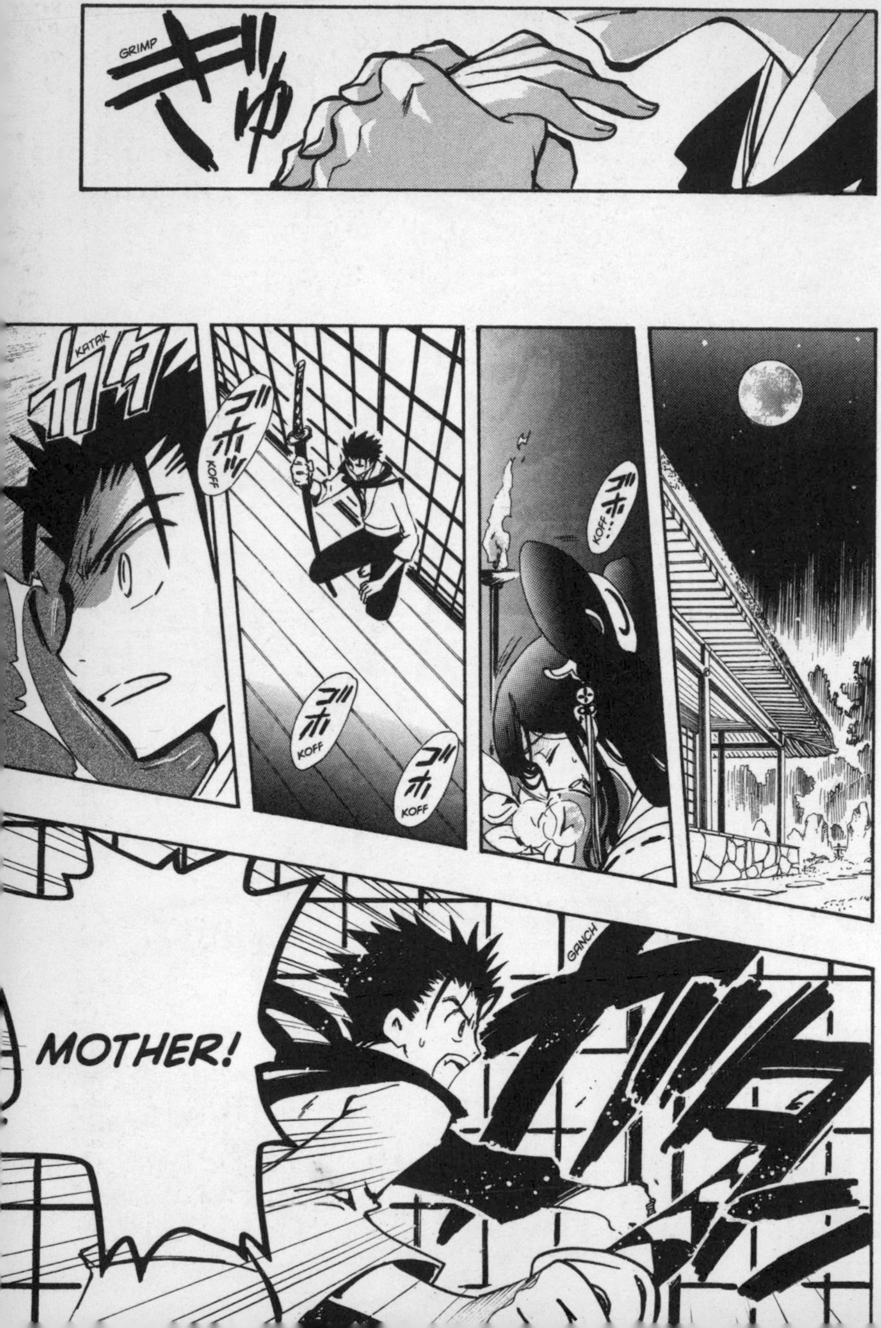
ぎゅ
GRIMP
ゴホ
KOFF...
ゴホッ
KOFF
ゴホ
KOFF
ゴホ
KOFF
カタ
KATAK
ガラ
GANCH
MOTHER!

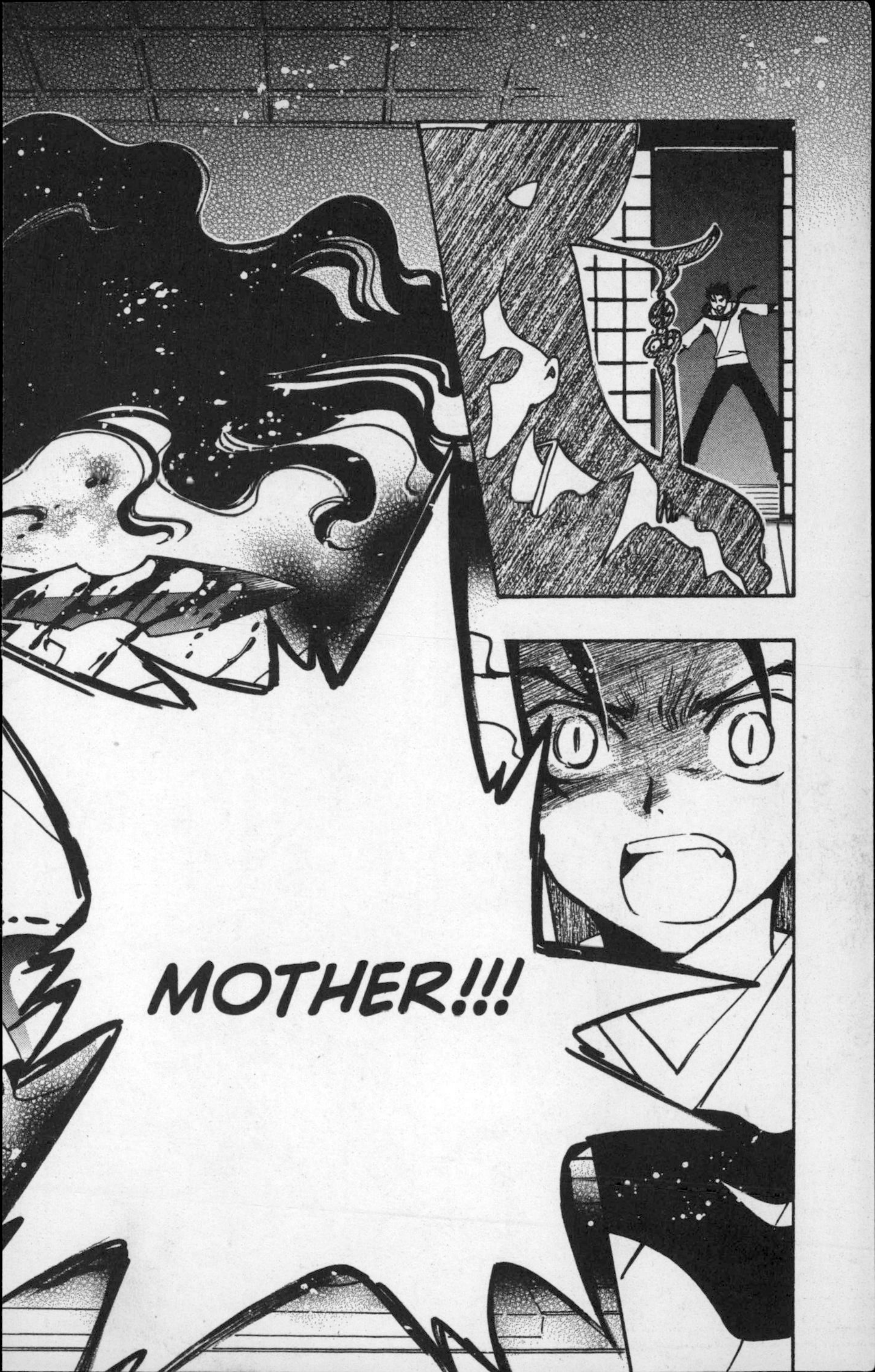
MOTHER!!!

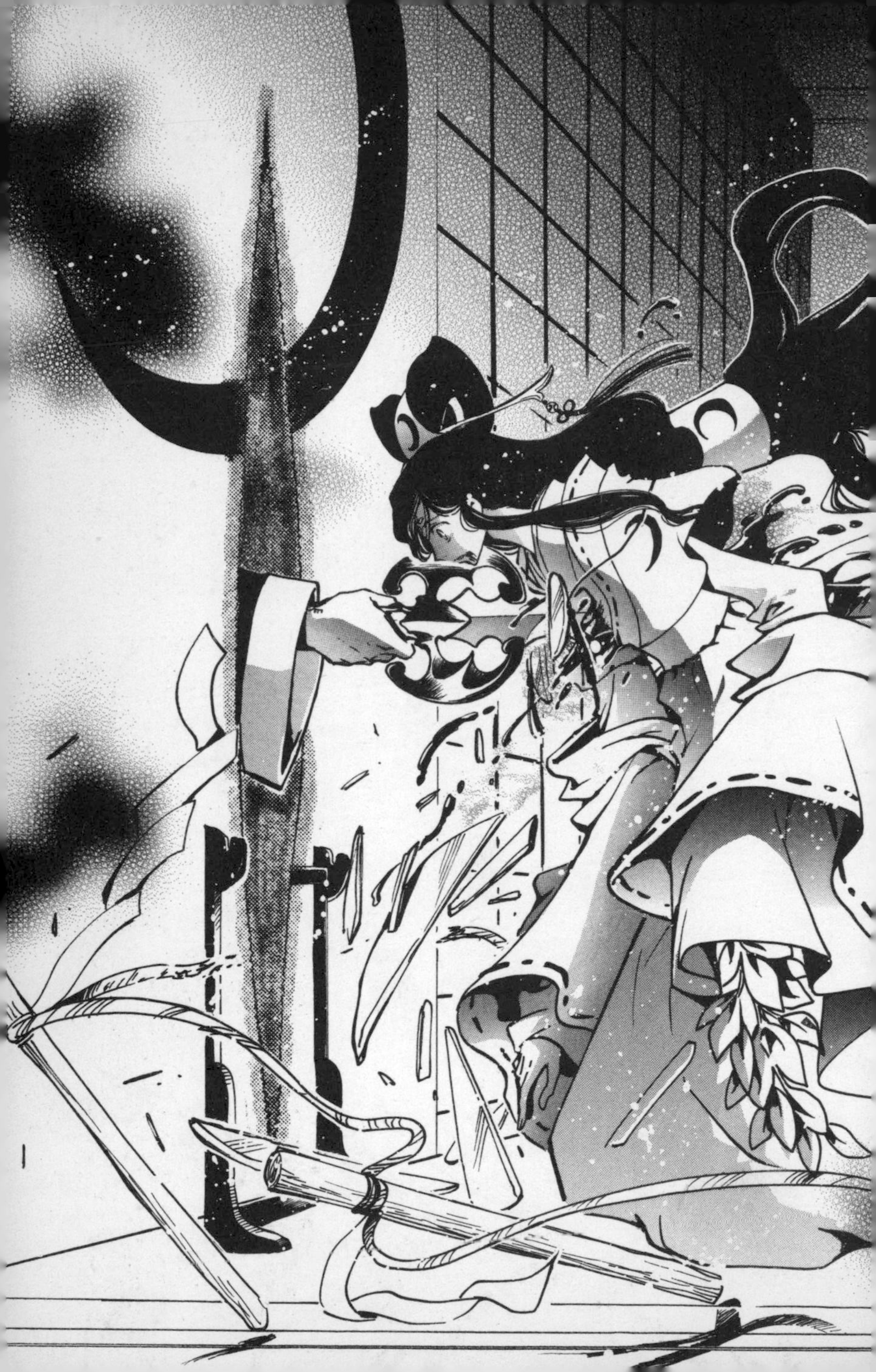

ツバサ

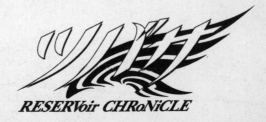

RESERVoir CHRoNiCLE

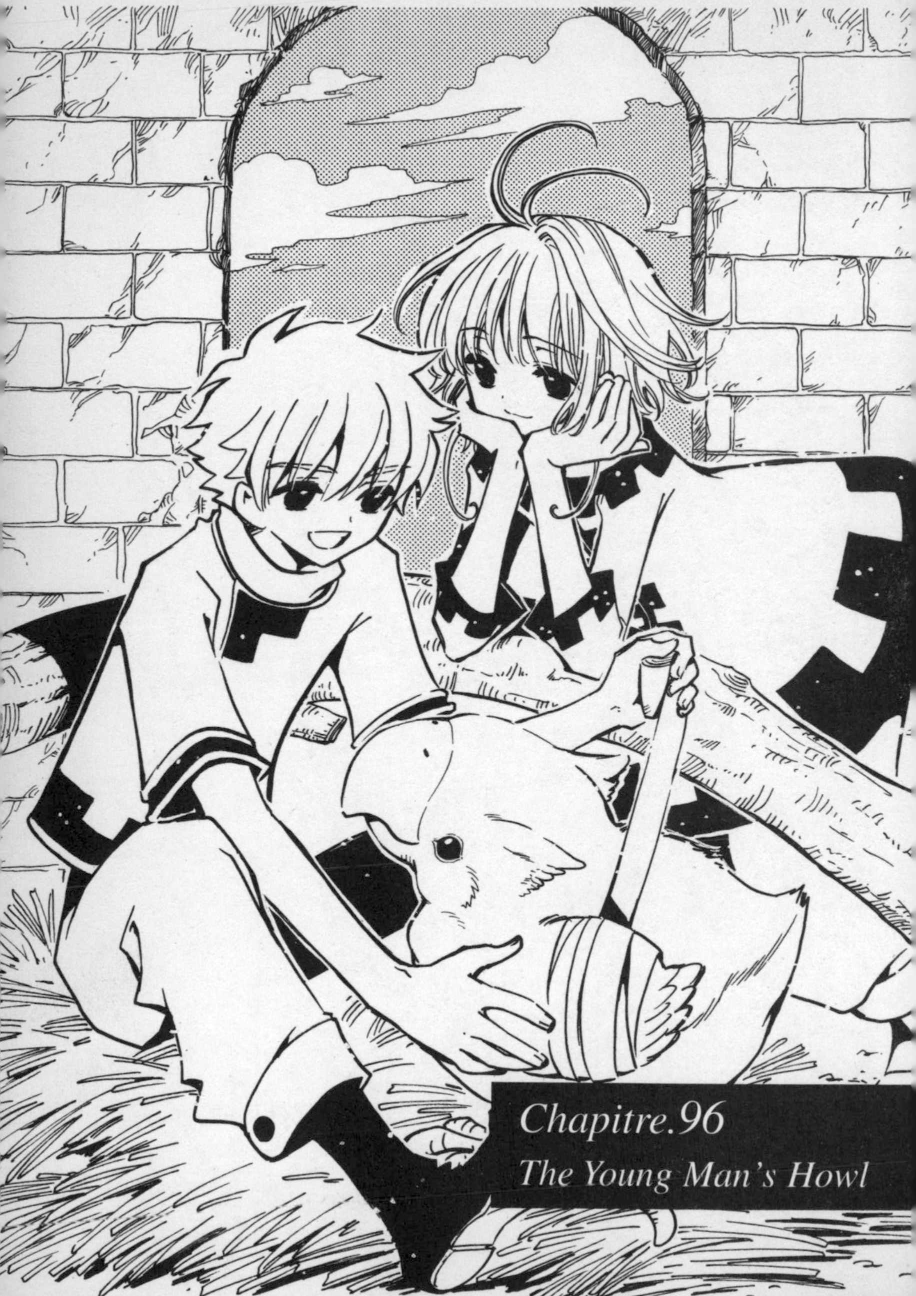
Chapitre.96
The Young Man's Howl

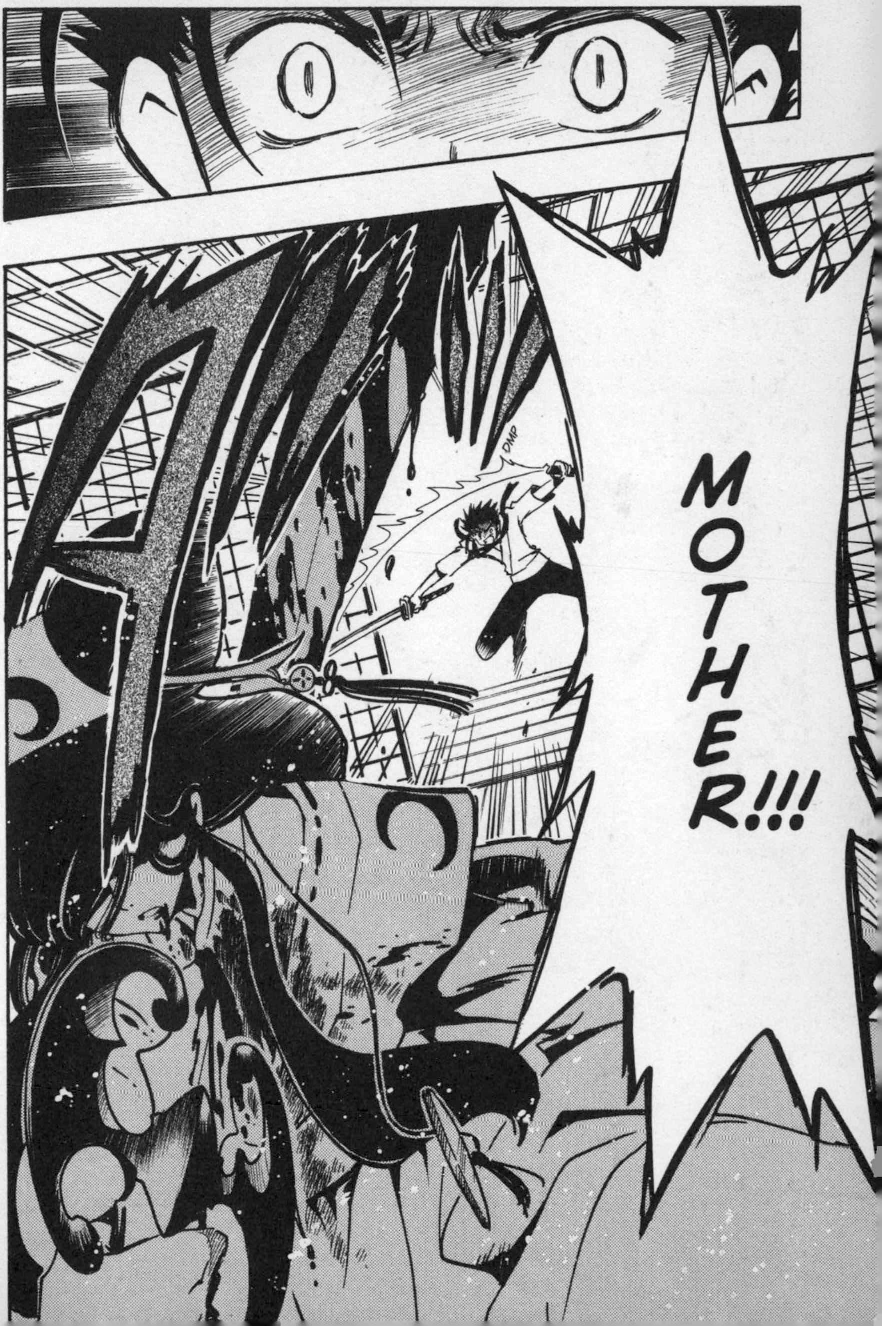
MOTHER!!!
DMP

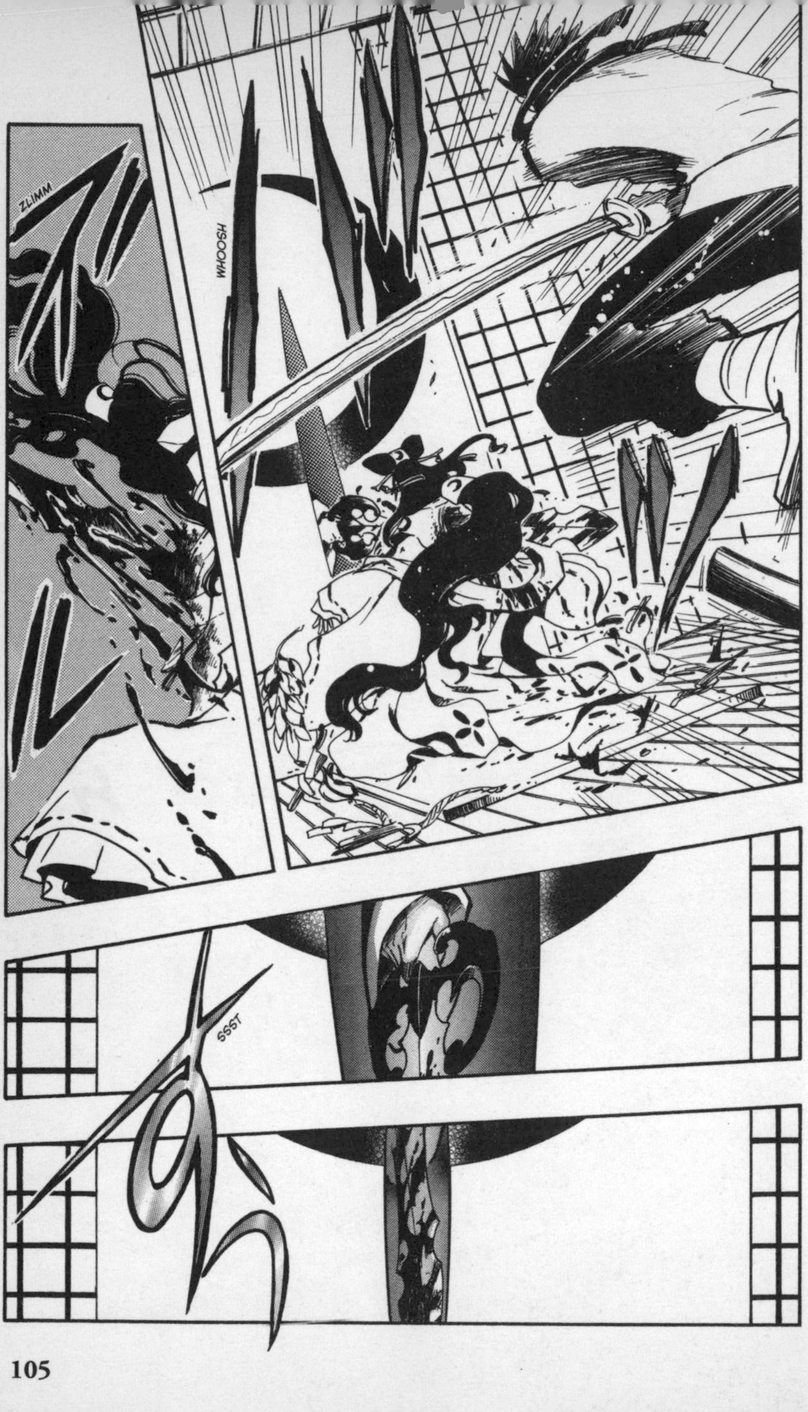
WHOOSH
ZLIMM
SSST

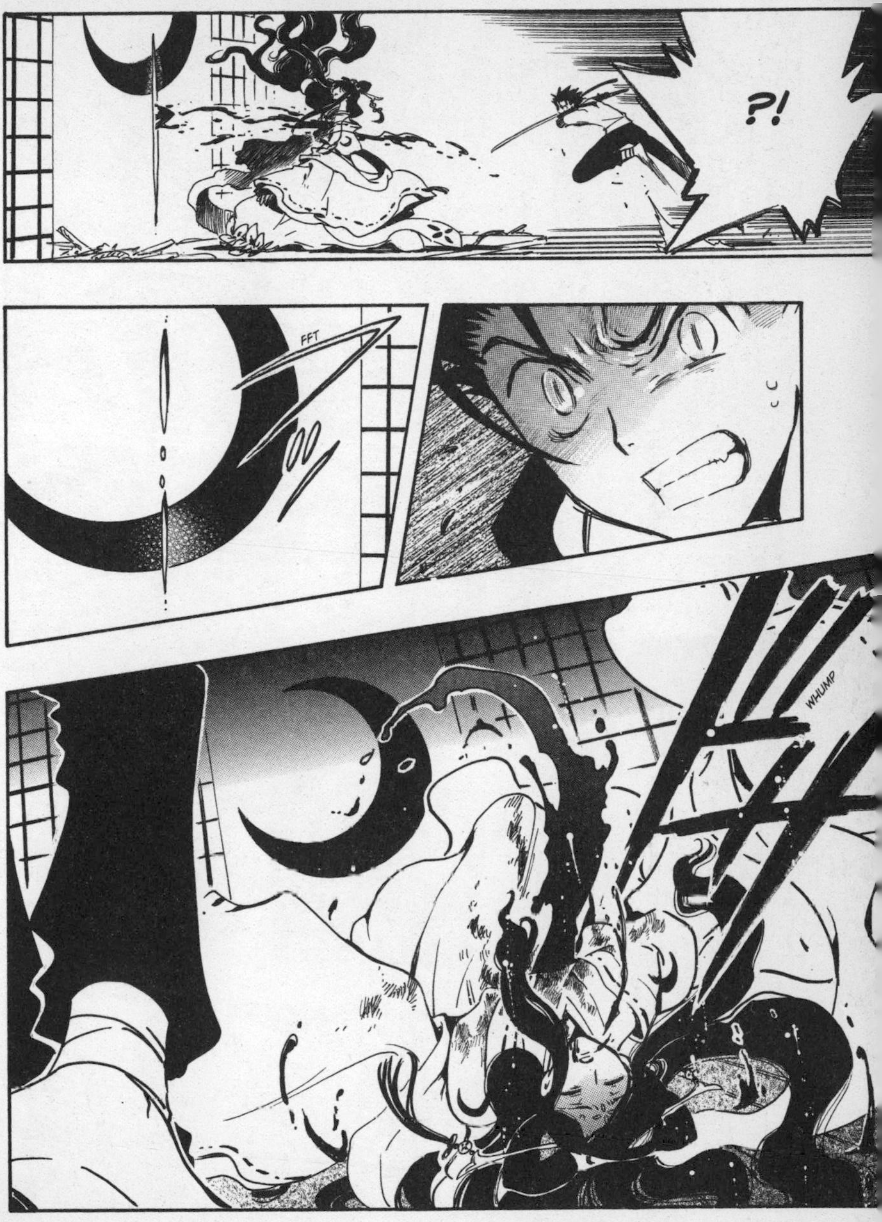
?!
FFT
WHUMP

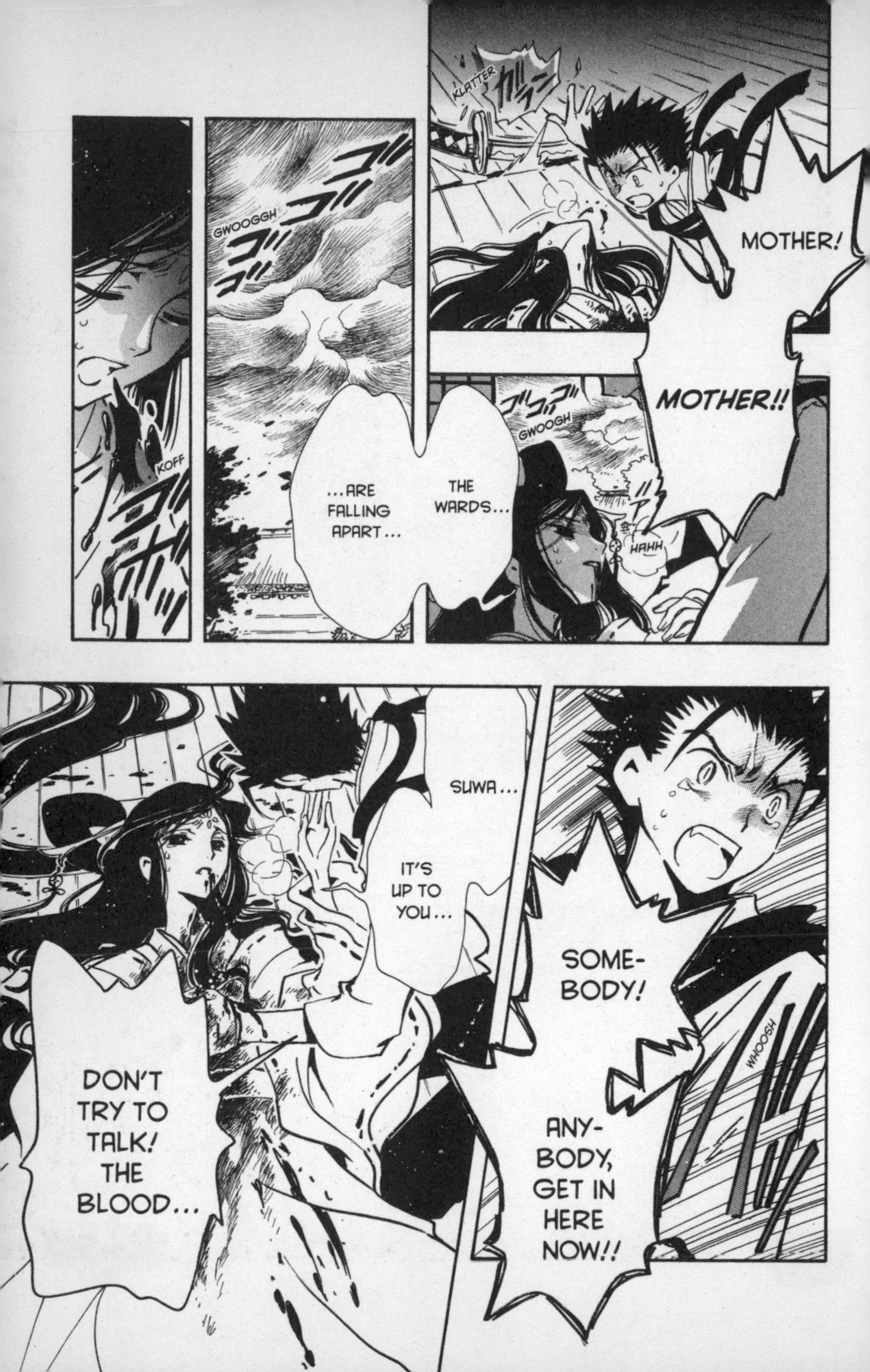
KLATTER
MOTHER!
MOTHER!!
GWOOGH
THE WARDS...
...ARE FALLING APART...
HAHH
GWOOOGGH
KOFF
SOME-BODY!
ANY-BODY, GET IN HERE NOW!!
WHOOSH
SUWA...
IT'S UP TO YOU...
DON'T TRY TO TALK! THE BLOOD...

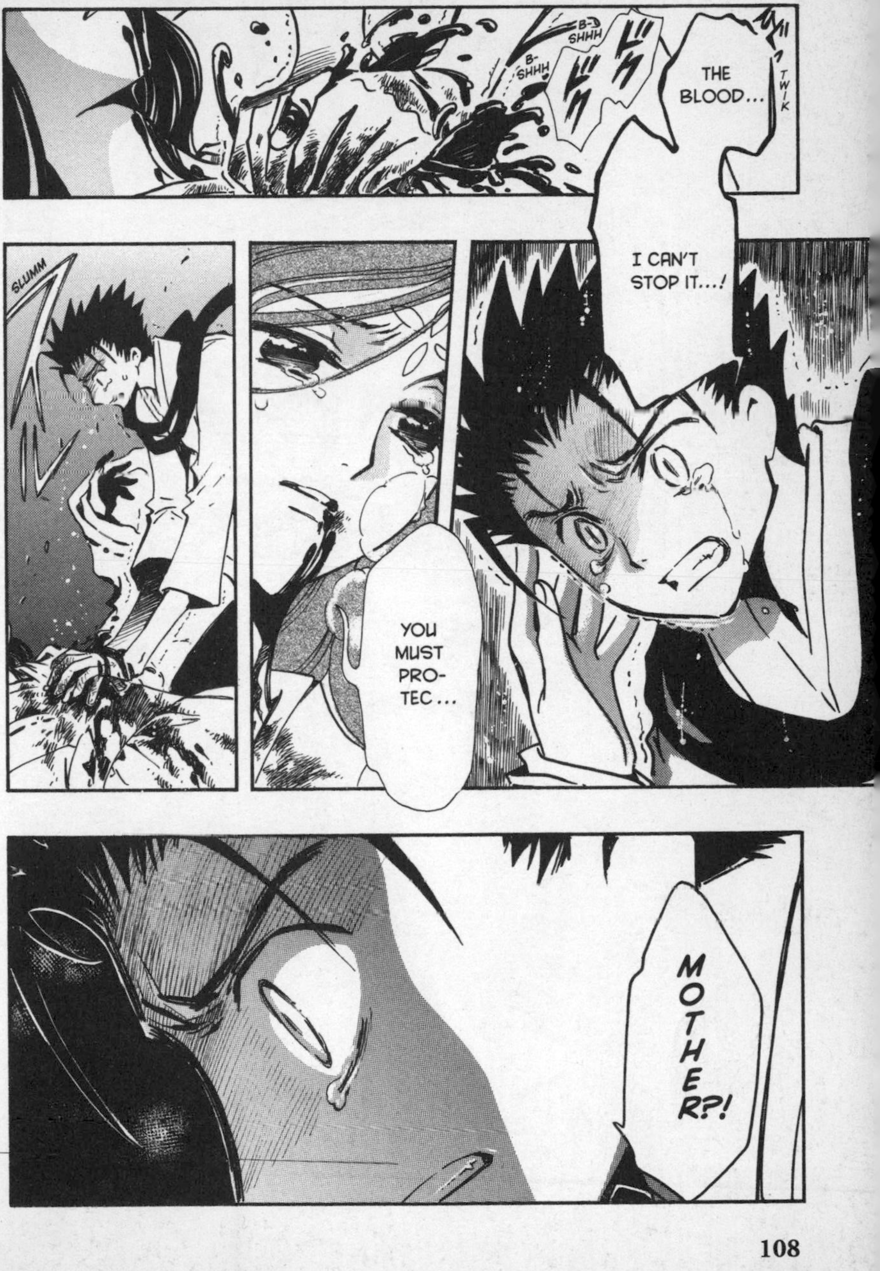
TWIK
THE BLOOD...
B-D SHHH
B-SHHH
I CAN'T STOP IT...!
YOU MUST PRO-TEC...
SLUMM
MOTHER?!

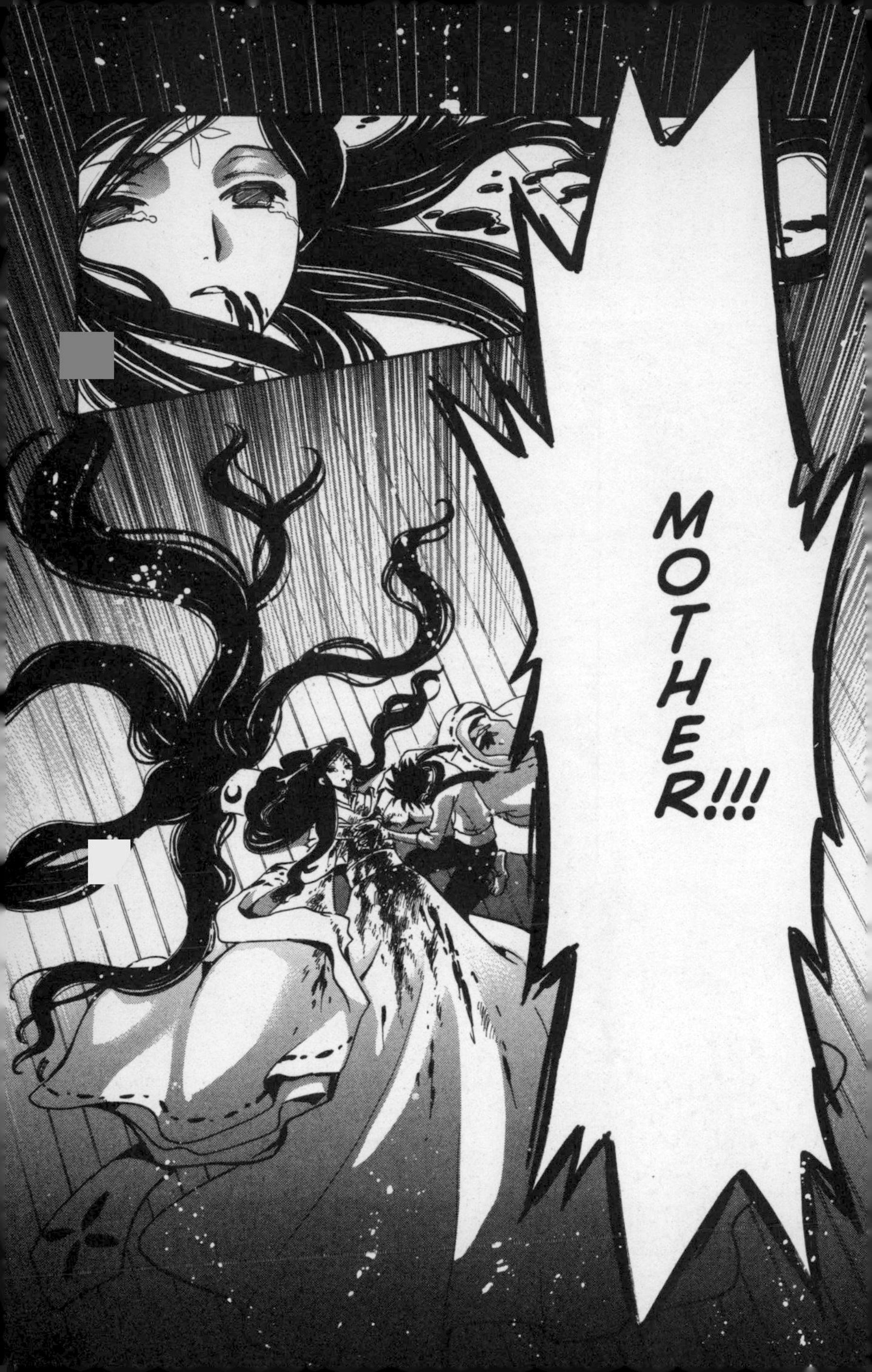
MOTHER!!!

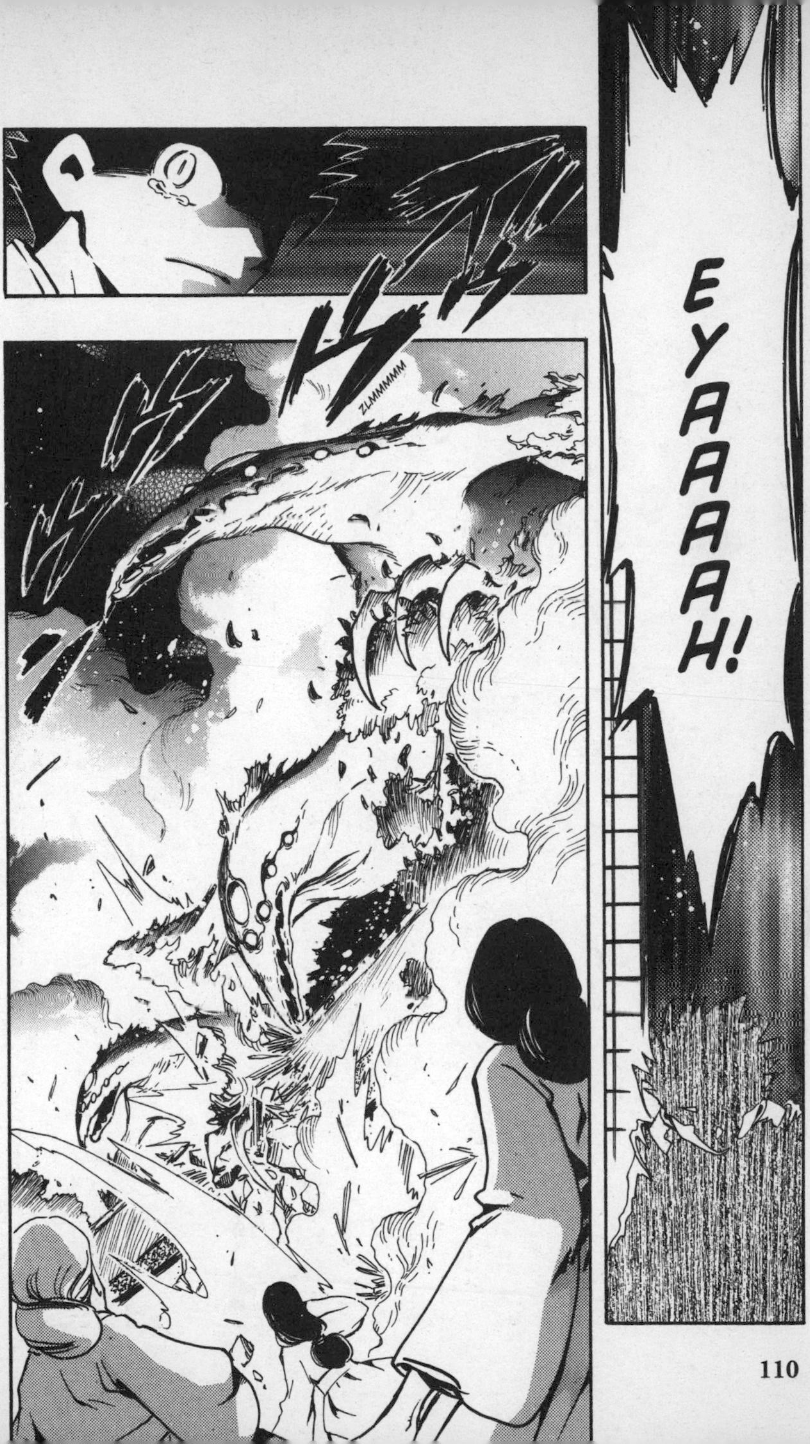
EYAAAAAH!
ZLMMMMM

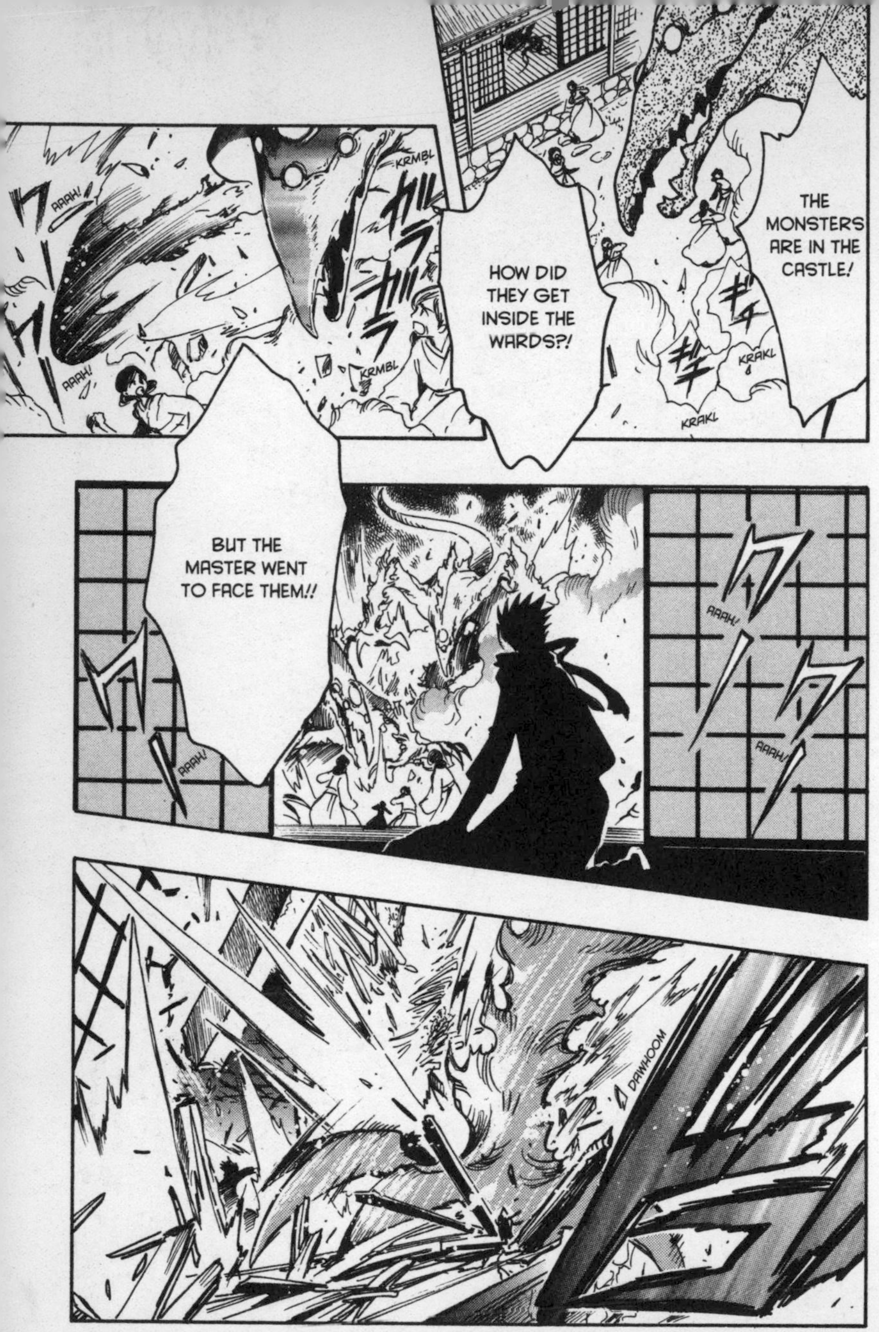
THE MONSTERS ARE IN THE CASTLE!
HOW DID THEY GET INSIDE THE WARDS?!
KRAKL
KRAKL
KRMBL
KRMBL
AAAH!
AAAH!
BUT THE MASTER WENT TO FACE THEM!!
AAAH!
AAAH!
AAAH!
DAWHOOM

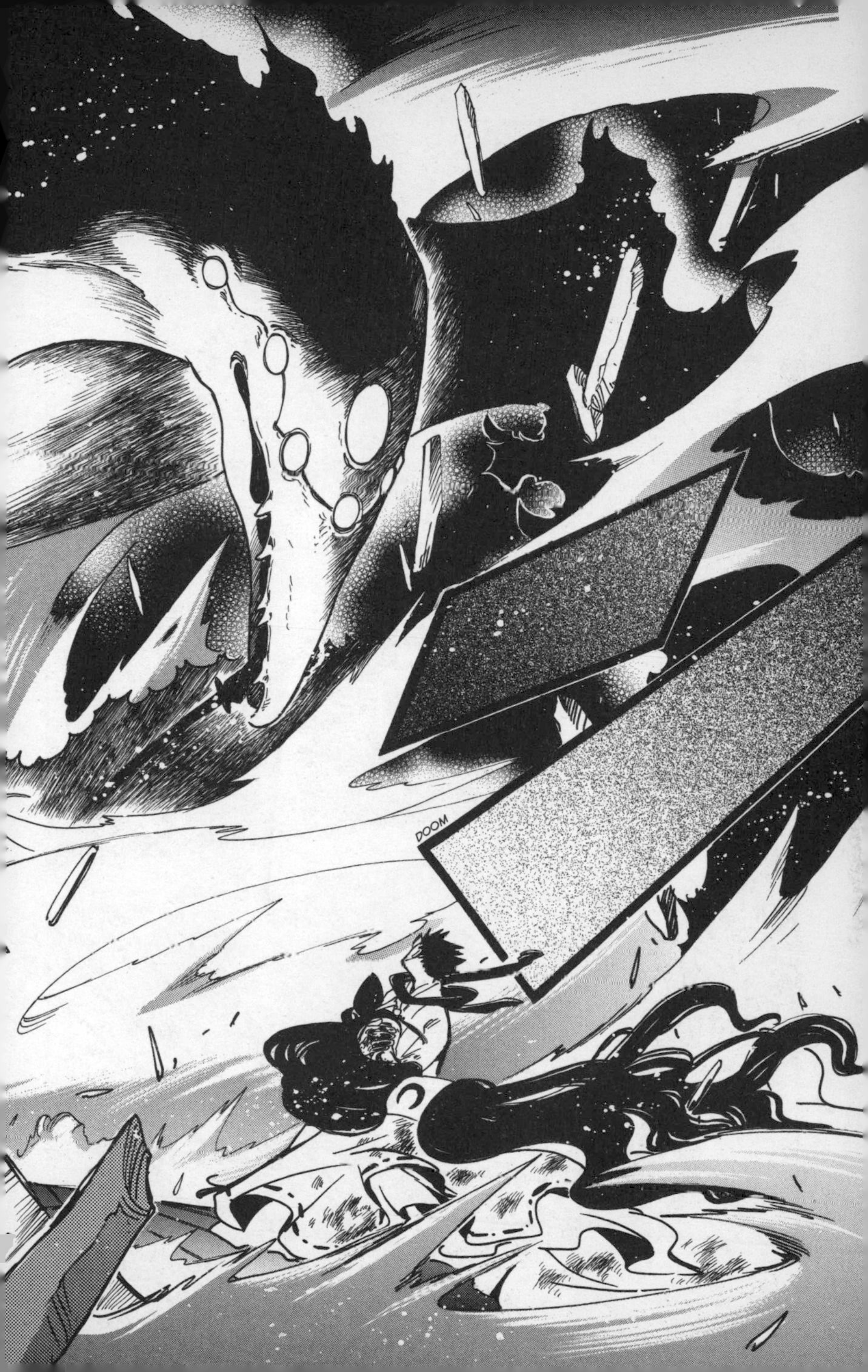
DOOM

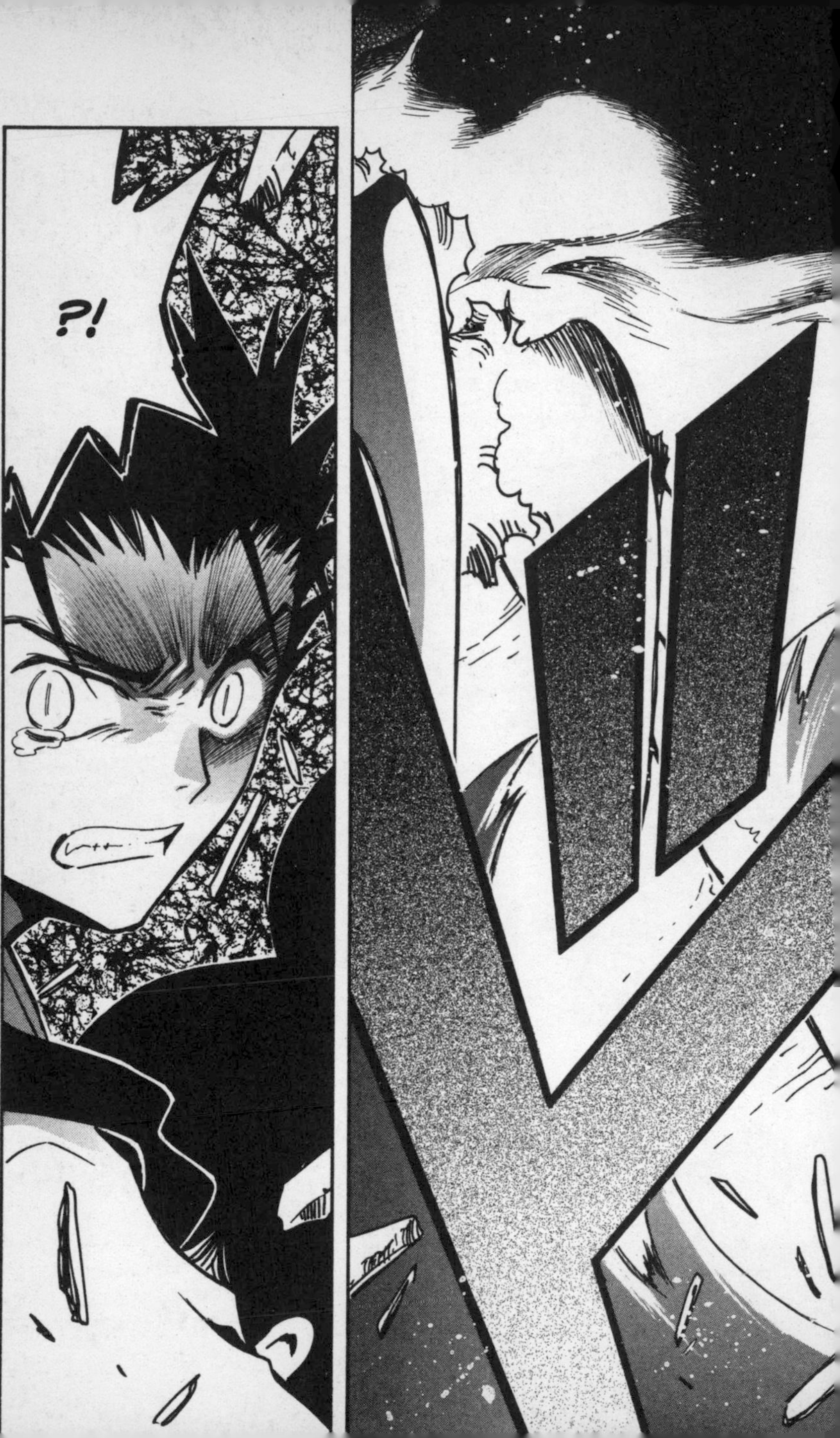
?!

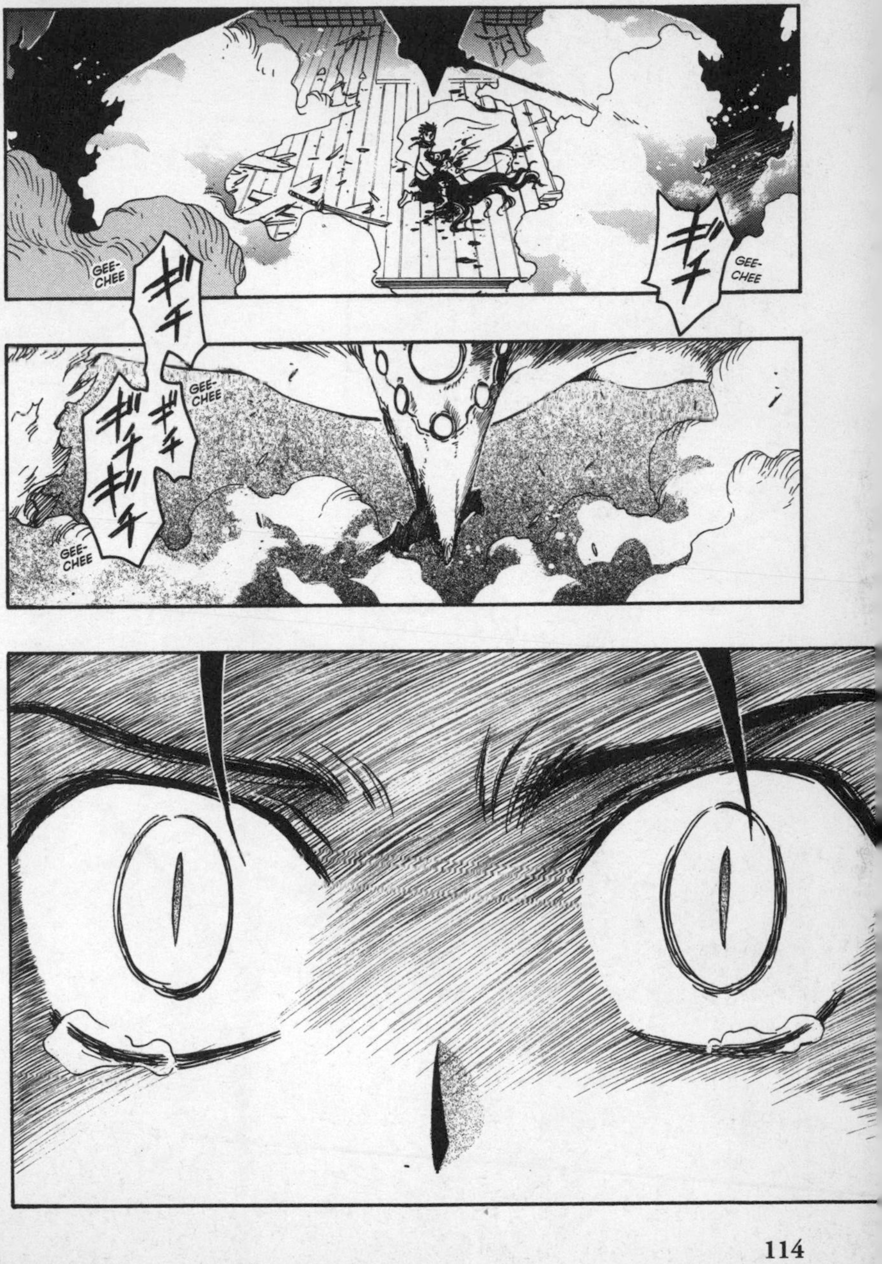
ギチ
GEE-CHEE
ギチ
GEE-CHEE
ギチ
GEE-CHEE
ギチギチ
GEE-CHEE

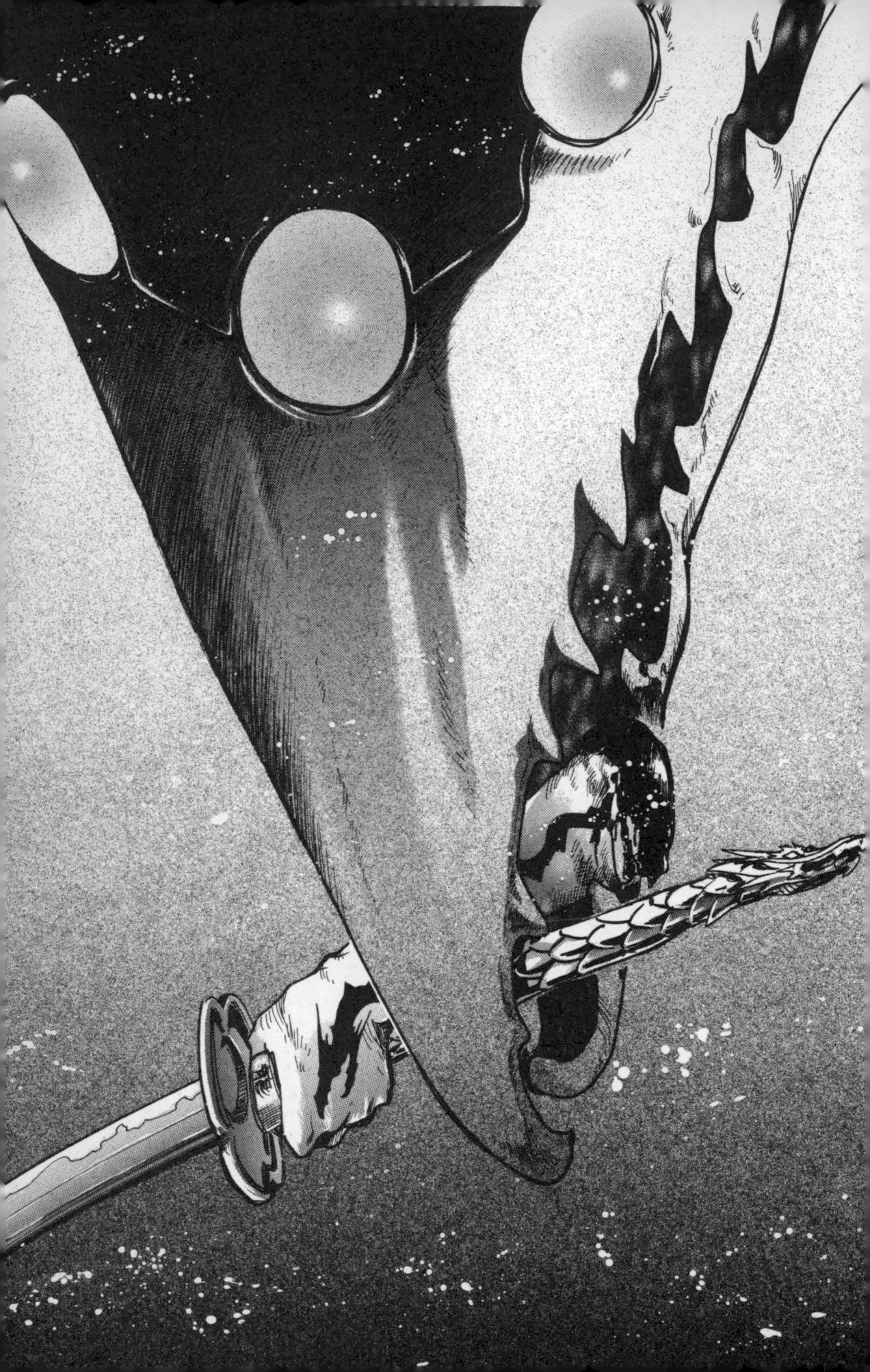

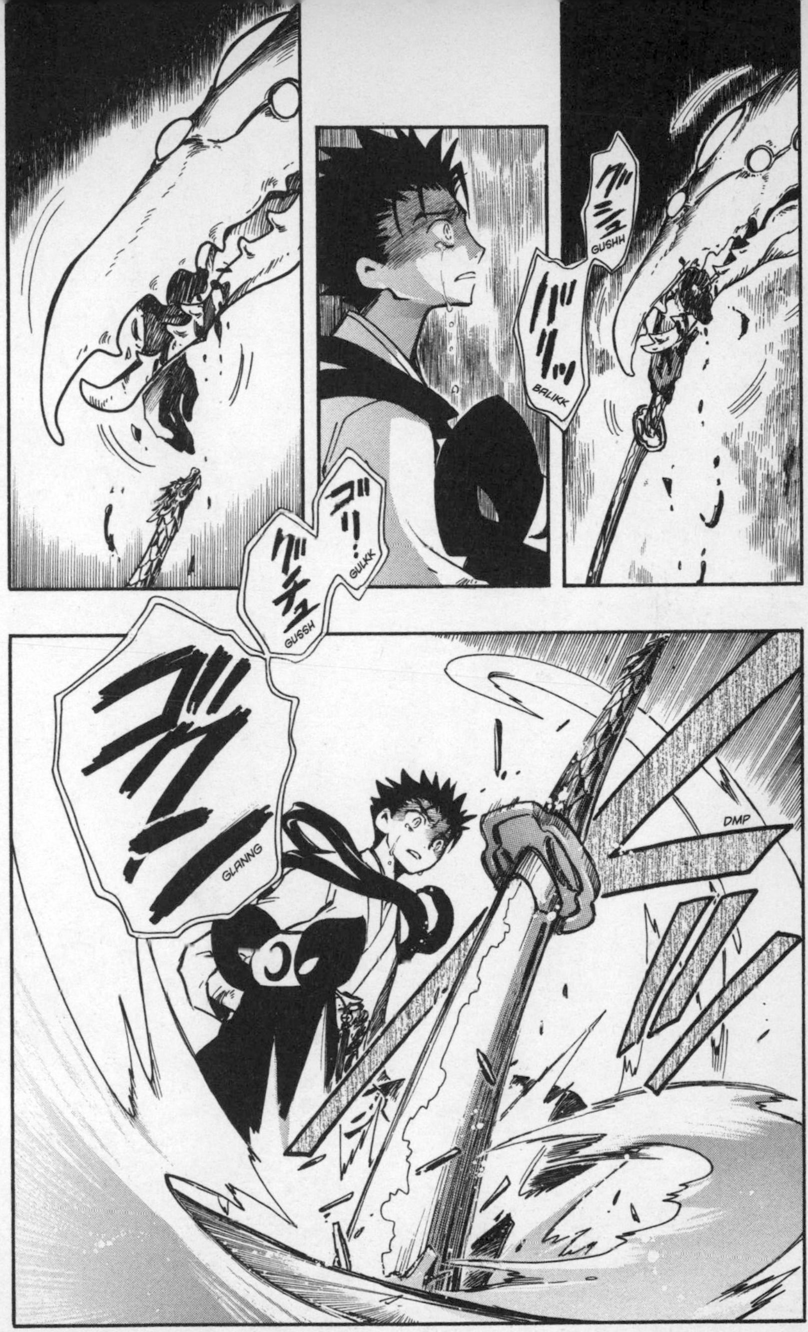
グシュ
GUSHH
バリッ
BALIKK
ゴリ!
GULKK
グチュ
GUSSH
GLANNG
DMP

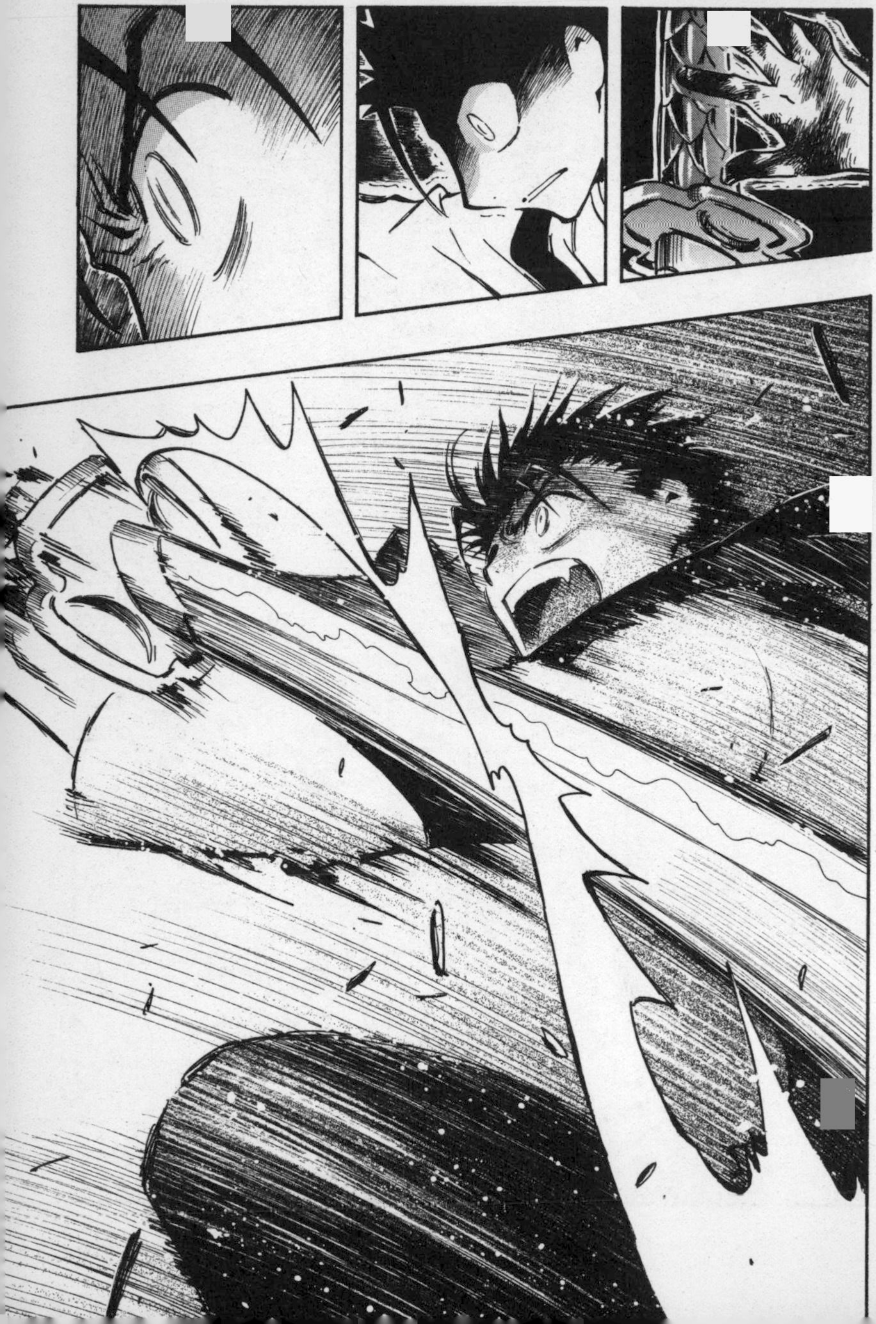

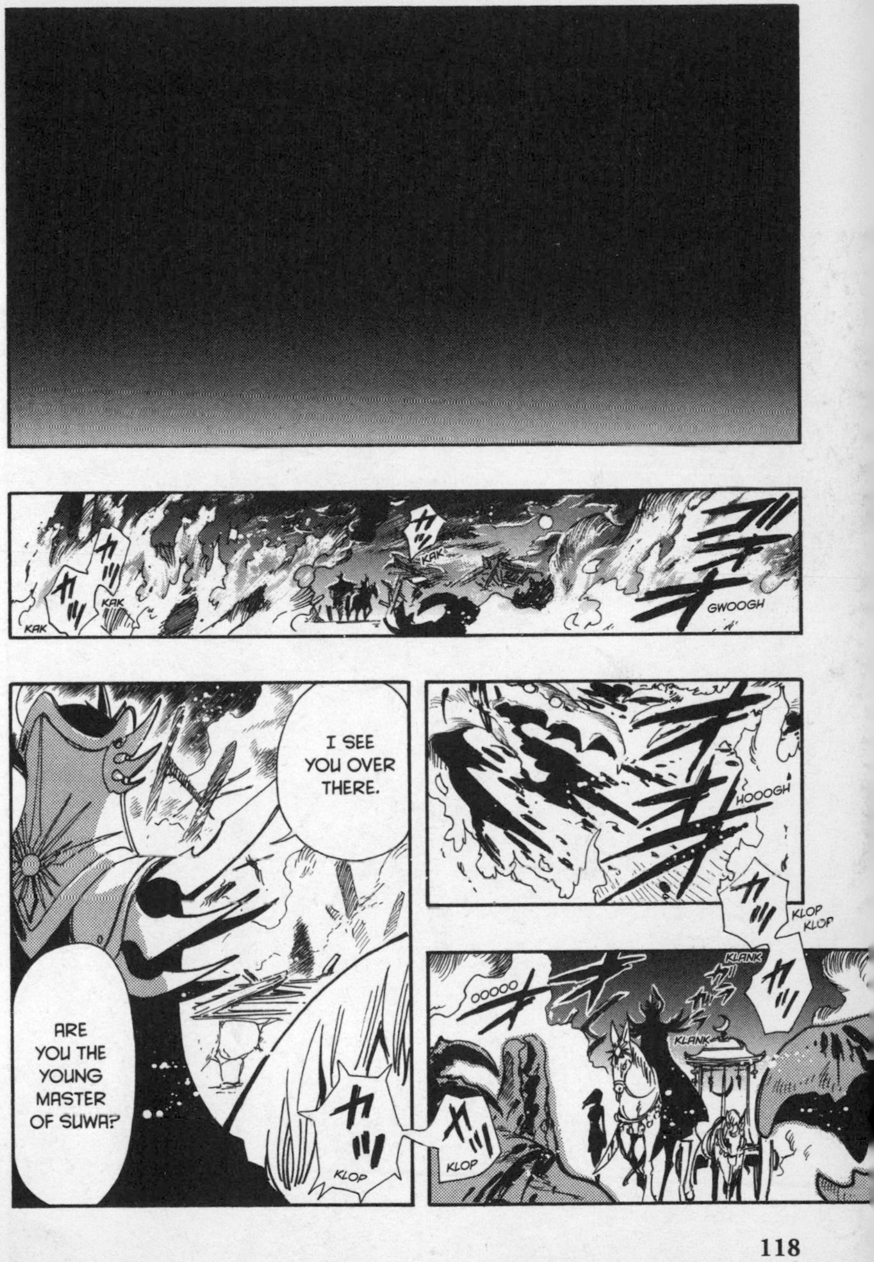
GWOOGH
KAK
KAK
KAK
HOOOGH
KLOP
KLOP
KLANK
KLANK
OOOOO
KLOP
I SEE YOU OVER THERE.
ARE YOU THE YOUNG MASTER OF SUWA?
KLOP

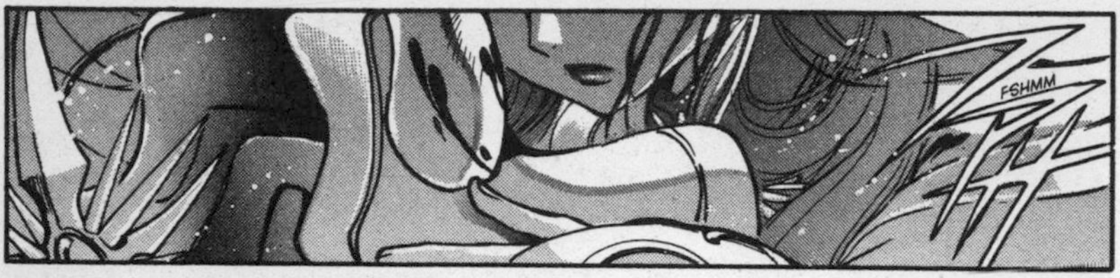
FSHMM

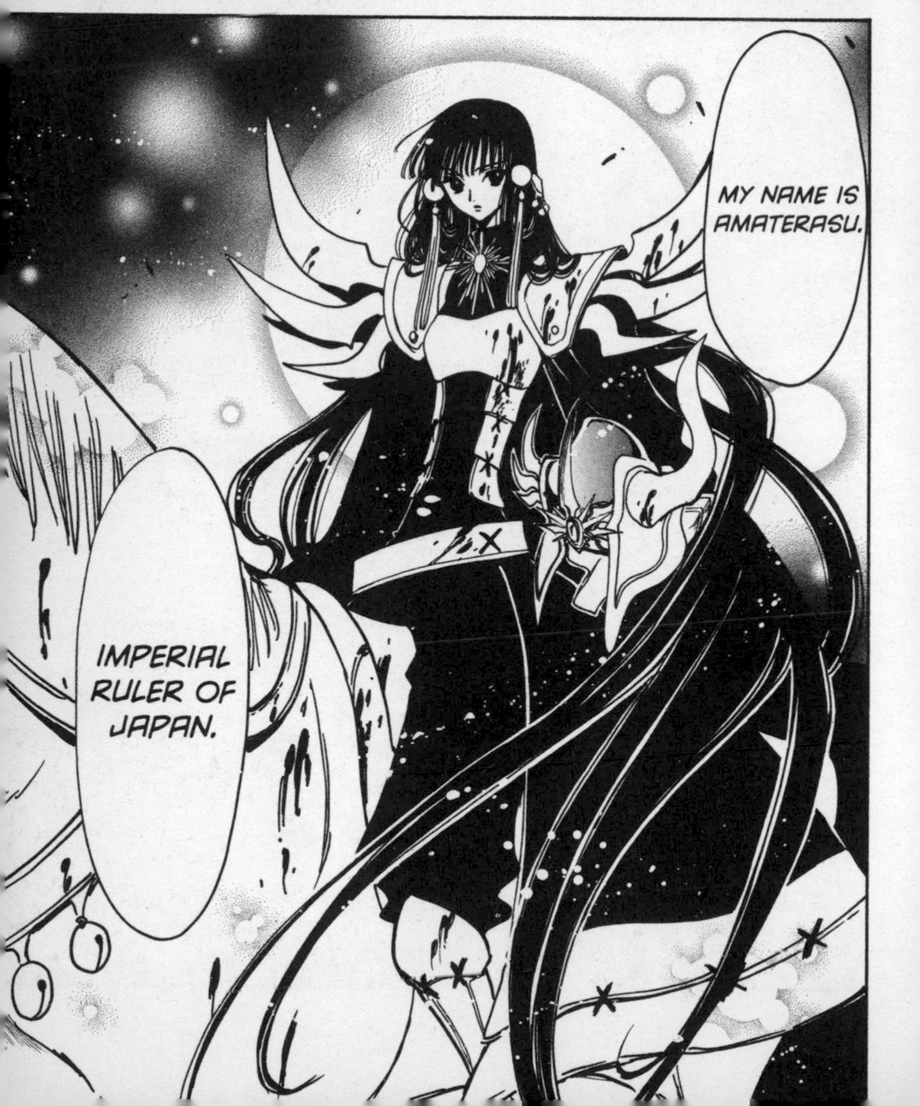
MY NAME IS AMATERASU.
IMPERIAL RULER OF JAPAN.

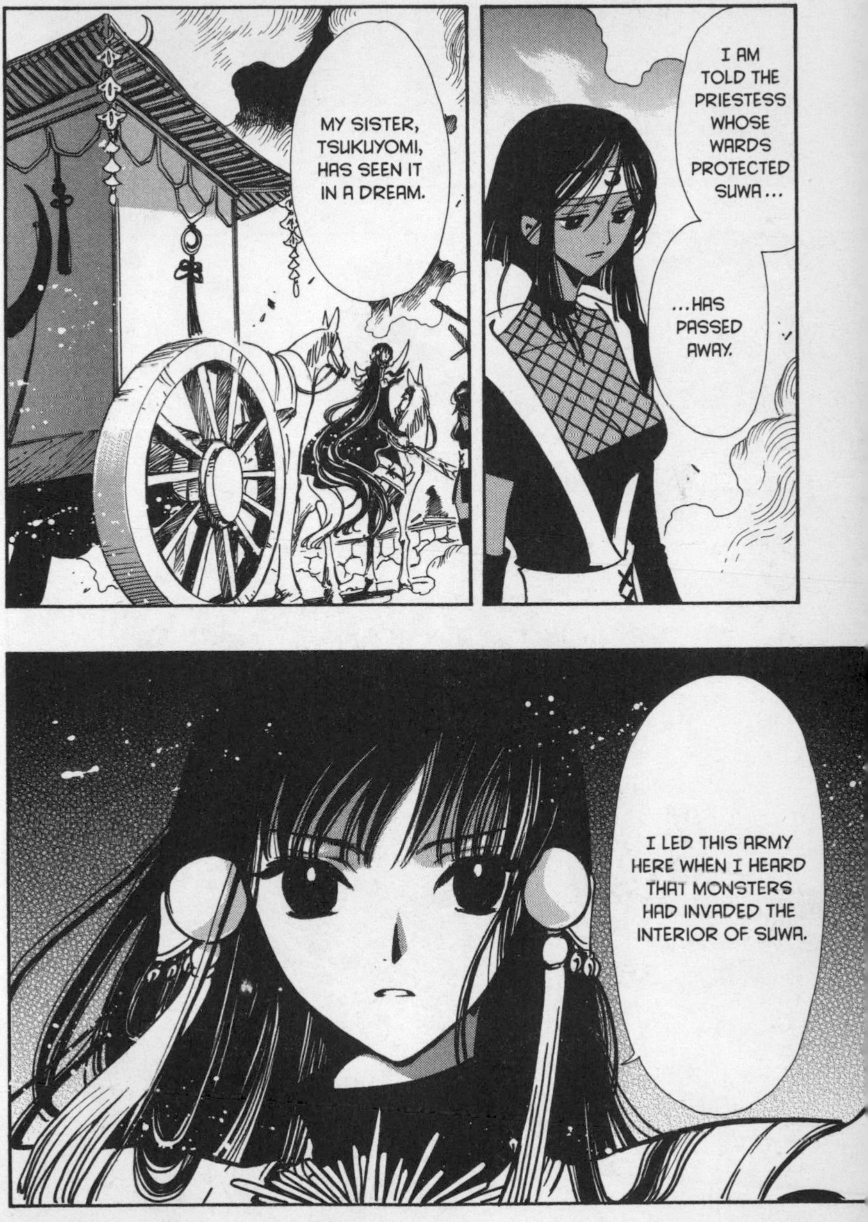
I AM TOLD THE PRIESTESS WHOSE WARDS PROTECTED SUWA...
...HAS PASSED AWAY.
MY SISTER, TSUKUYOMI, HAS SEEN IT IN A DREAM.
I LED THIS ARMY HERE WHEN I HEARD THAT MONSTERS HAD INVADED THE INTERIOR OF SUWA.

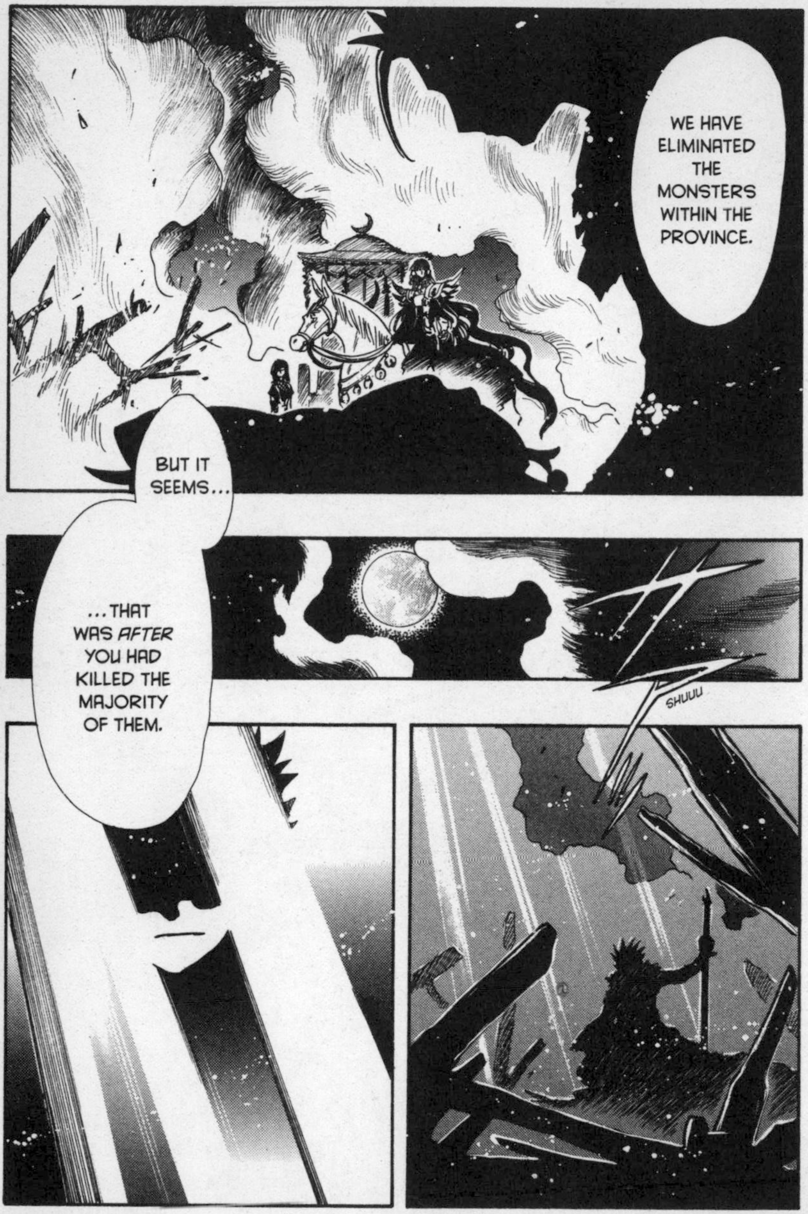
WE HAVE ELIMINATED THE MONSTERS WITHIN THE PROVINCE.
BUT IT SEEMS...
...THAT WAS *AFTER* YOU HAD KILLED THE MAJORITY OF THEM.
SHUUU

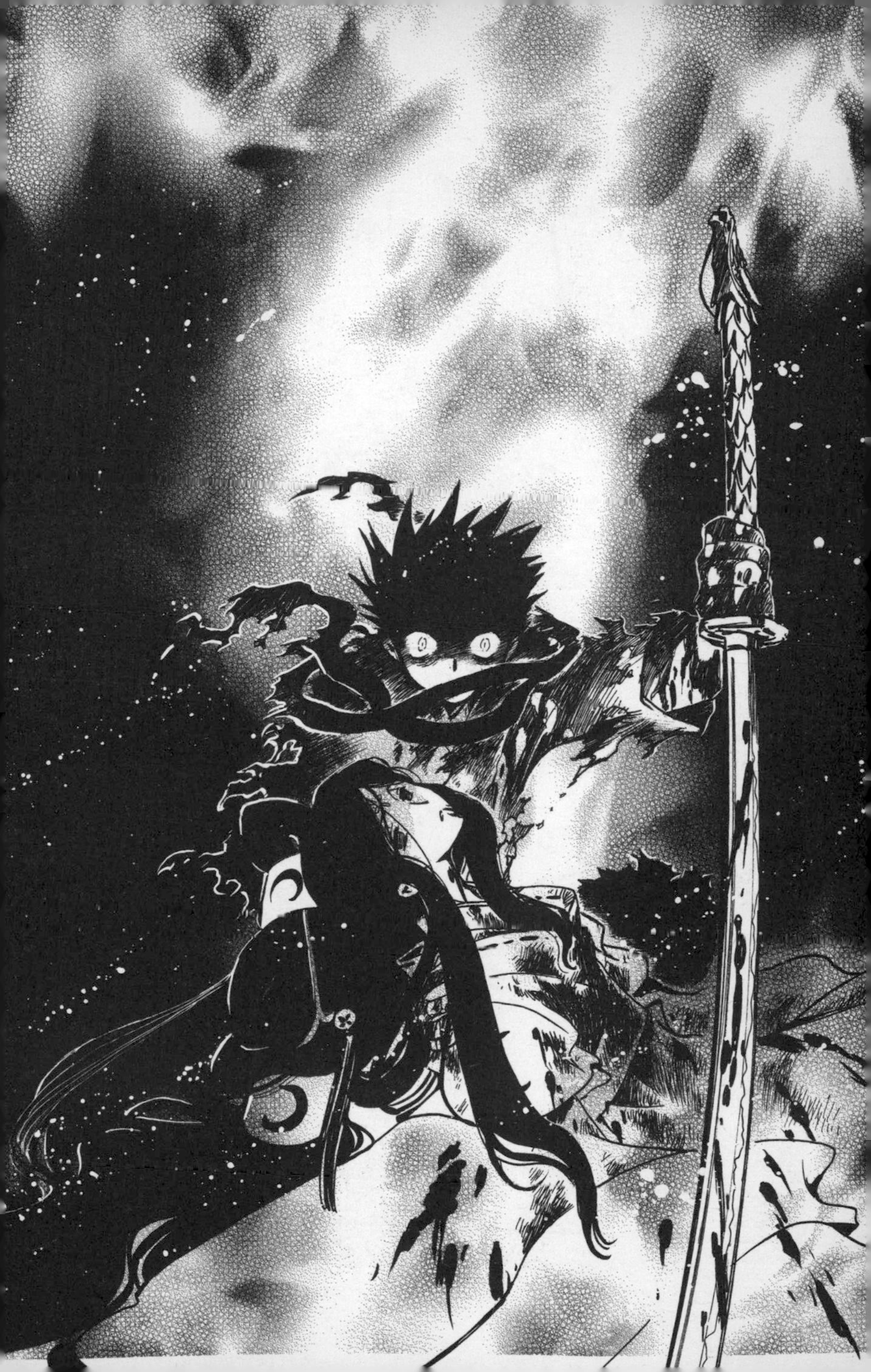

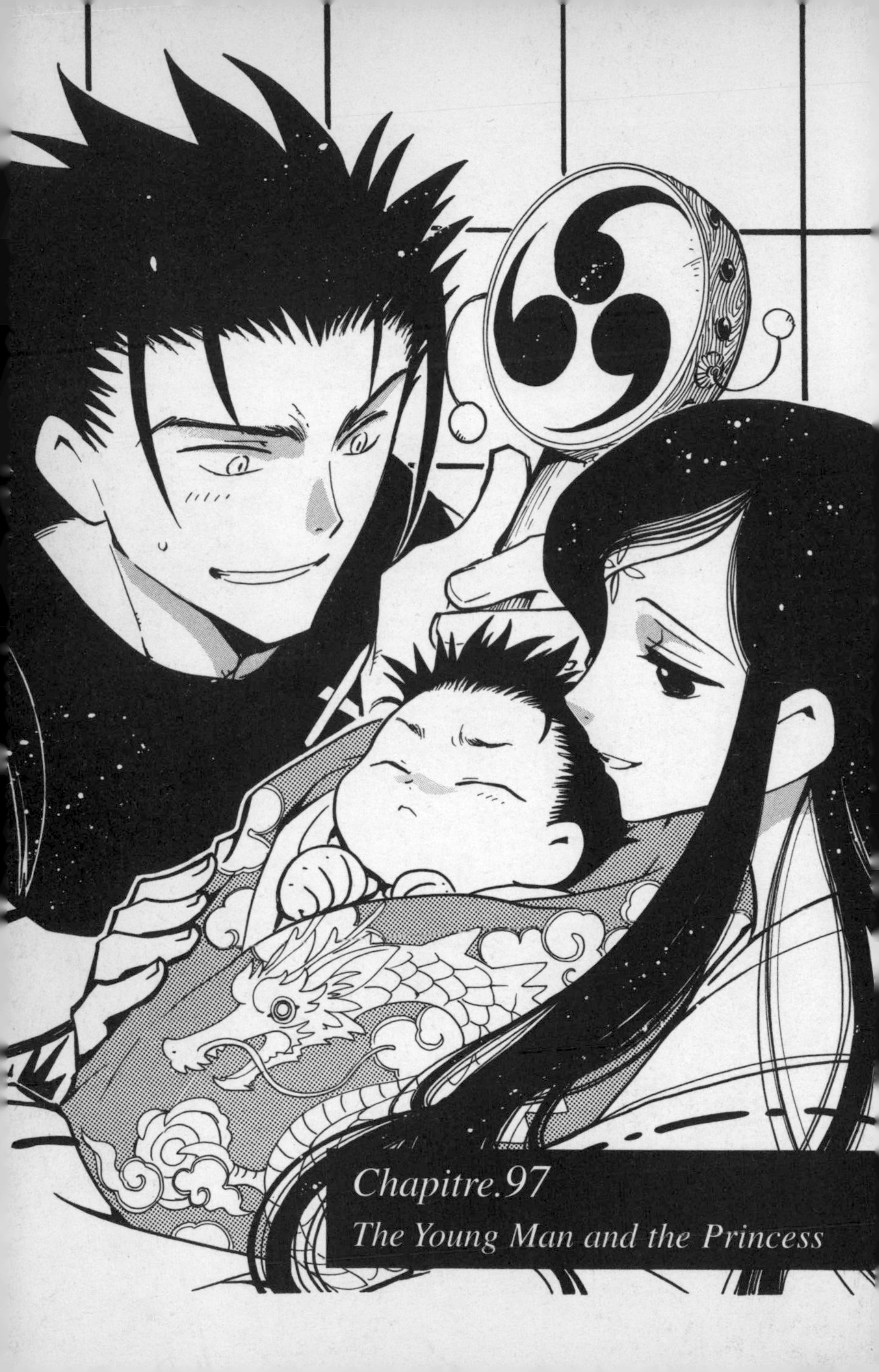

Chapitre.97

The Young Man and the Princess

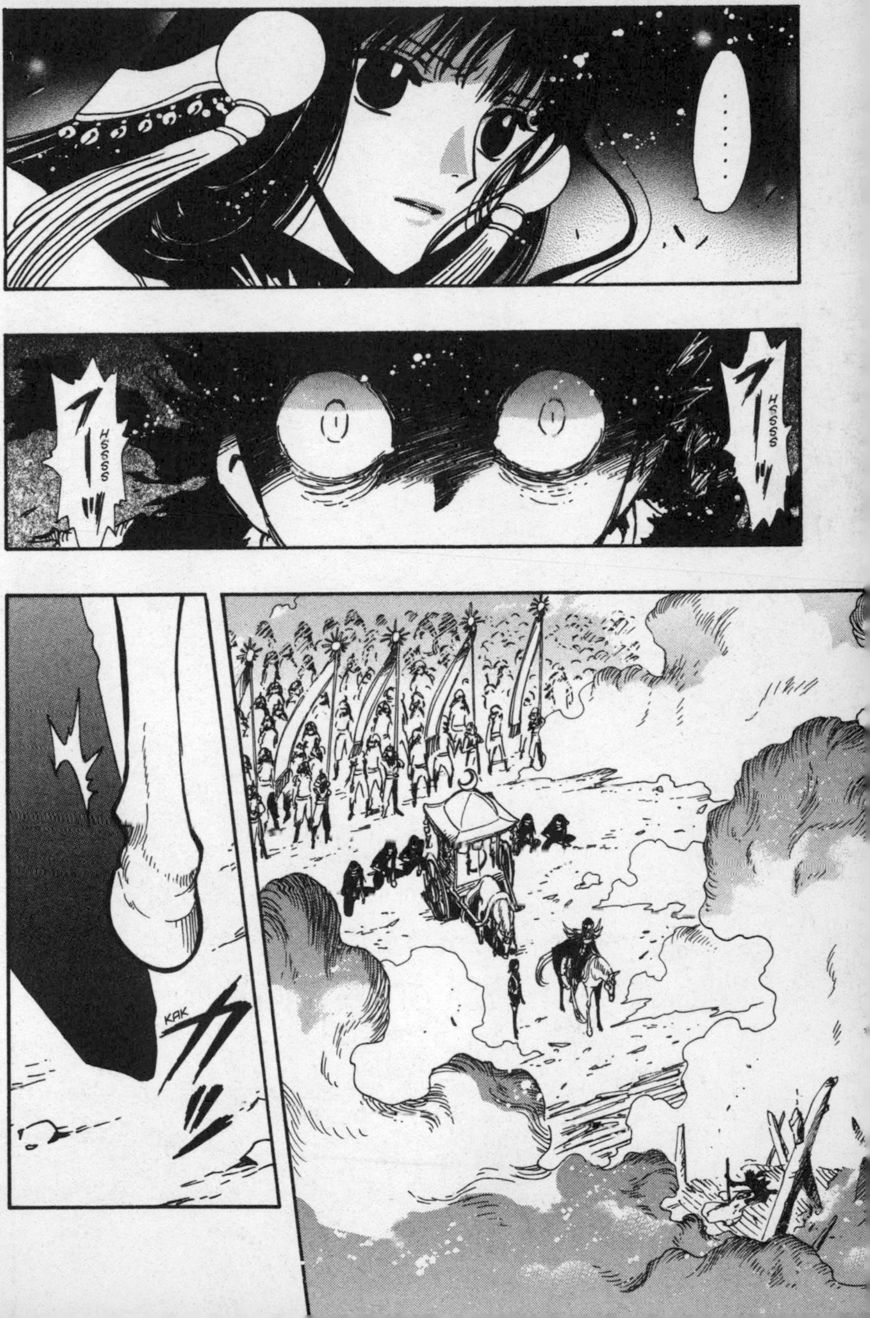
......
HSSSS
HSSSS
KAK

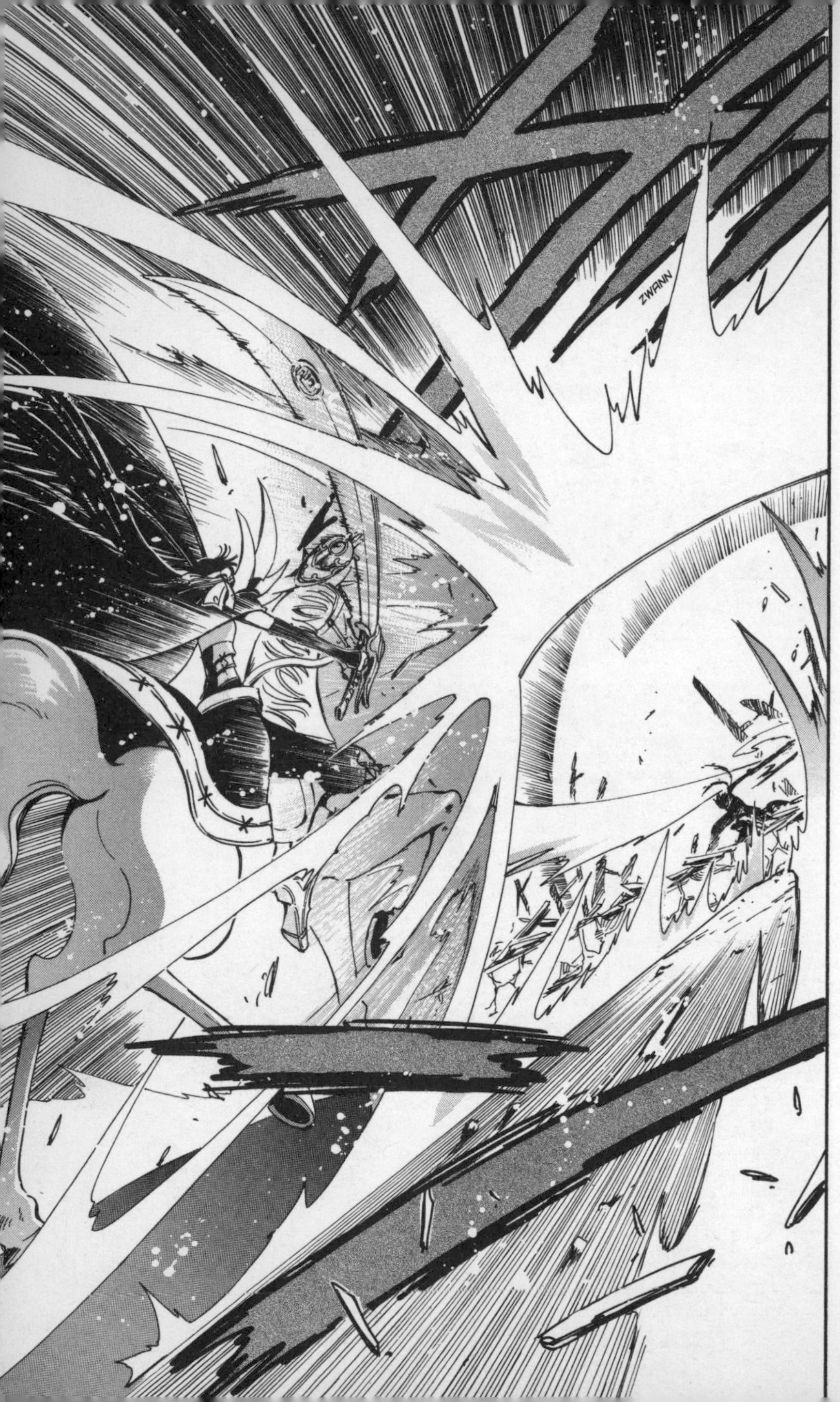
ZWANN

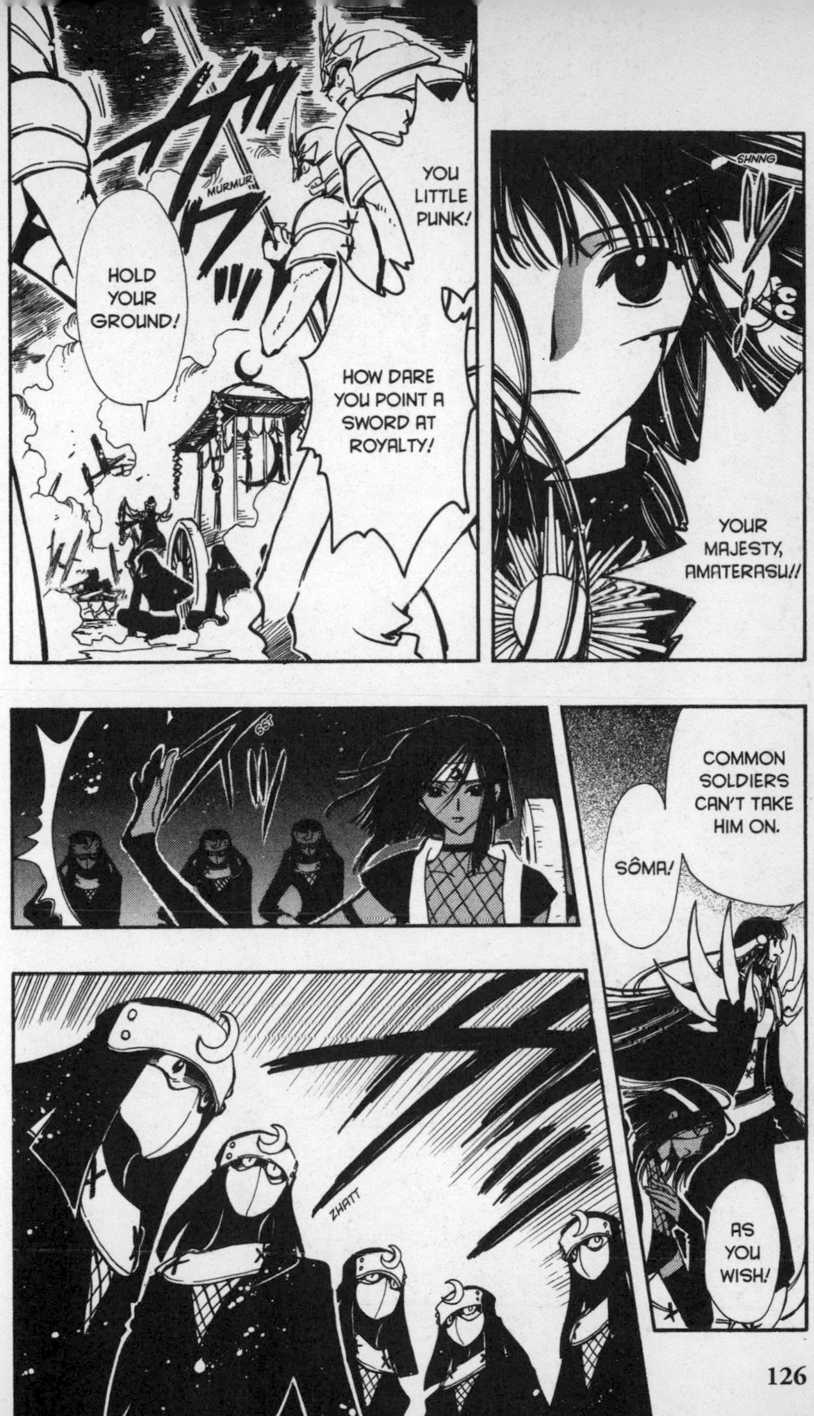
SHNNG
YOUR MAJESTY, AMATERASU!!
YOU LITTLE PUNK!
HOW DARE YOU POINT A SWORD AT ROYALTY!
MURMUR
HOLD YOUR GROUND!
COMMON SOLDIERS CAN'T TAKE HIM ON.
SÔMA!
AS YOU WISH!
SST
ZHATT

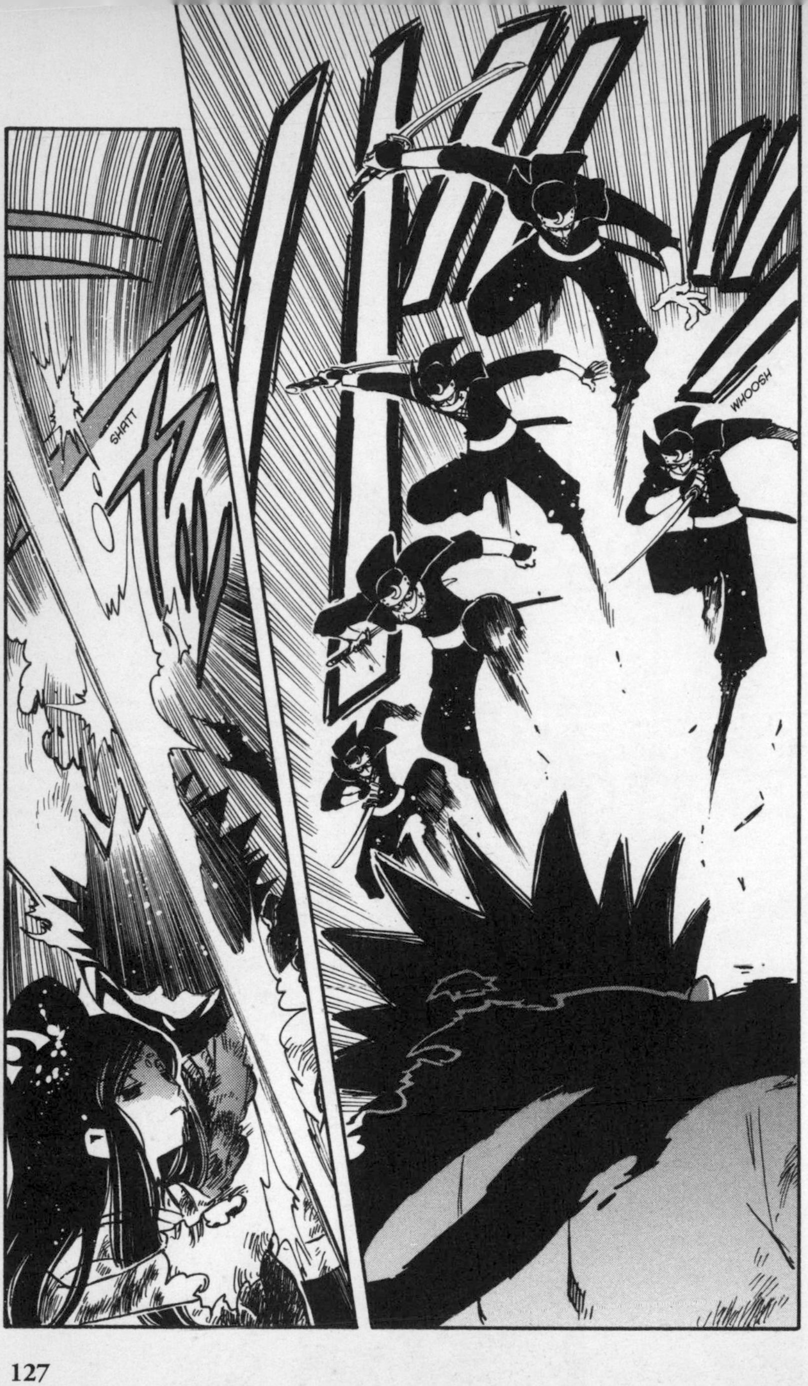
WHOOSH
SHATT

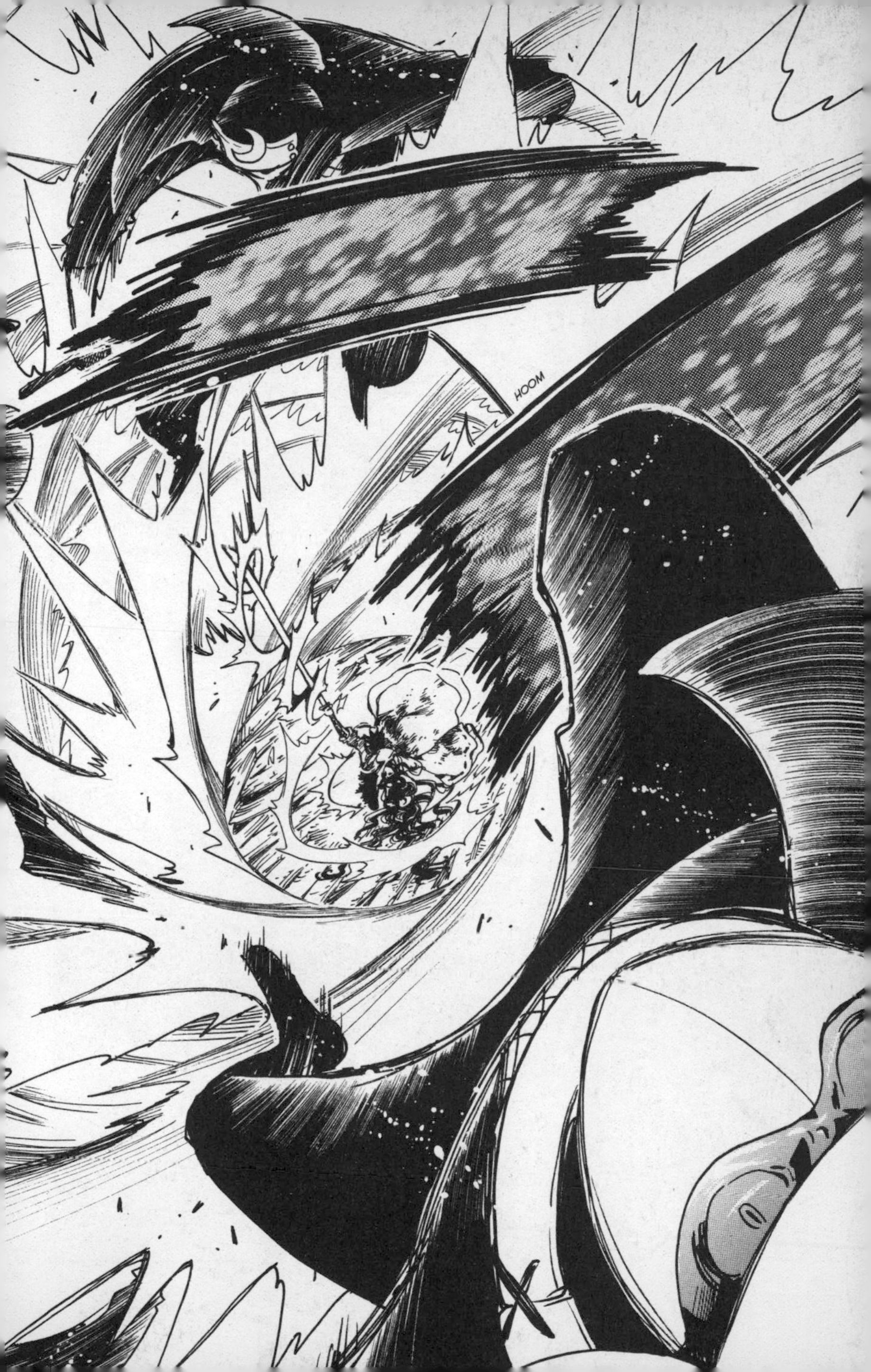
HOOM

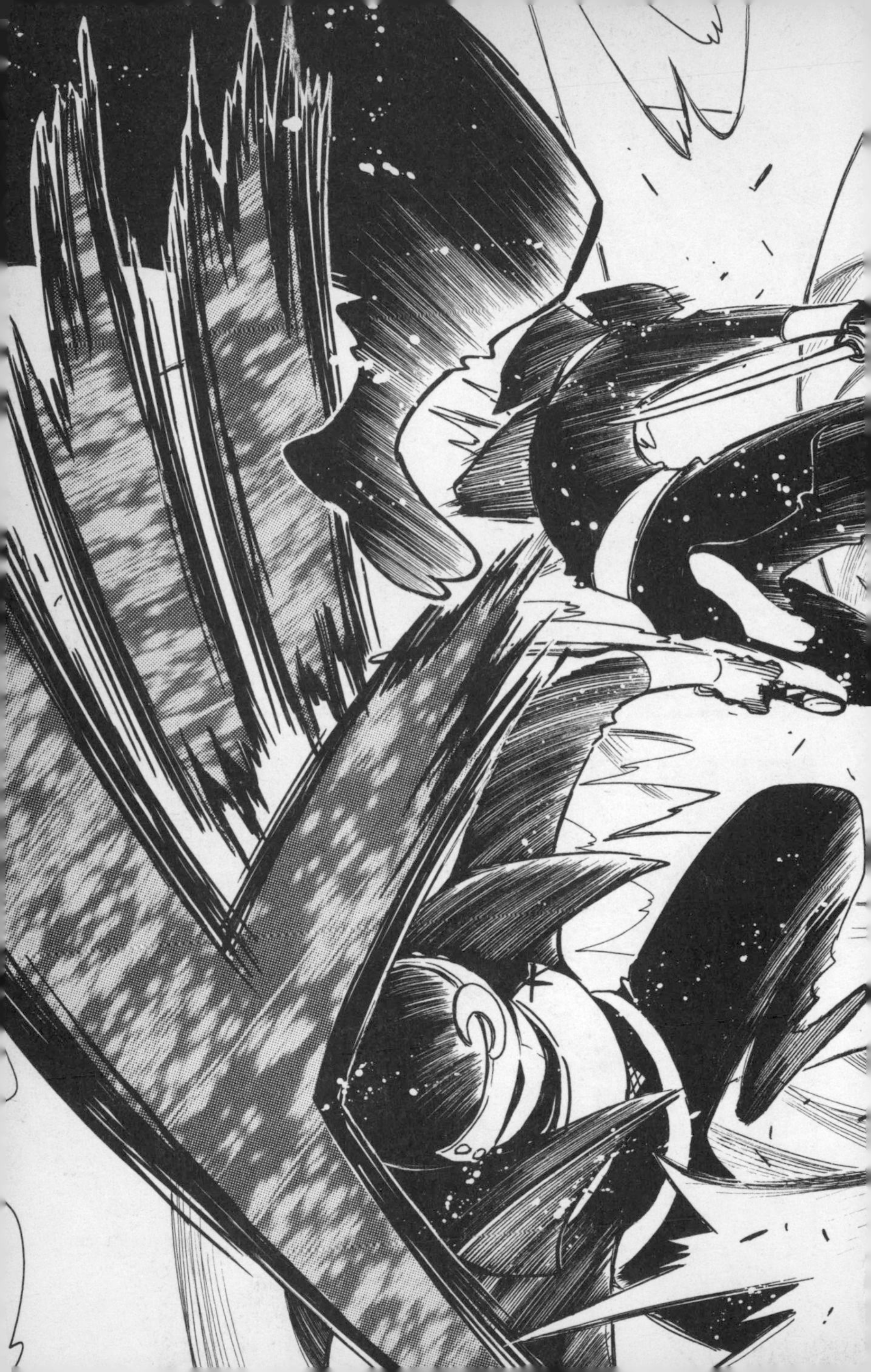

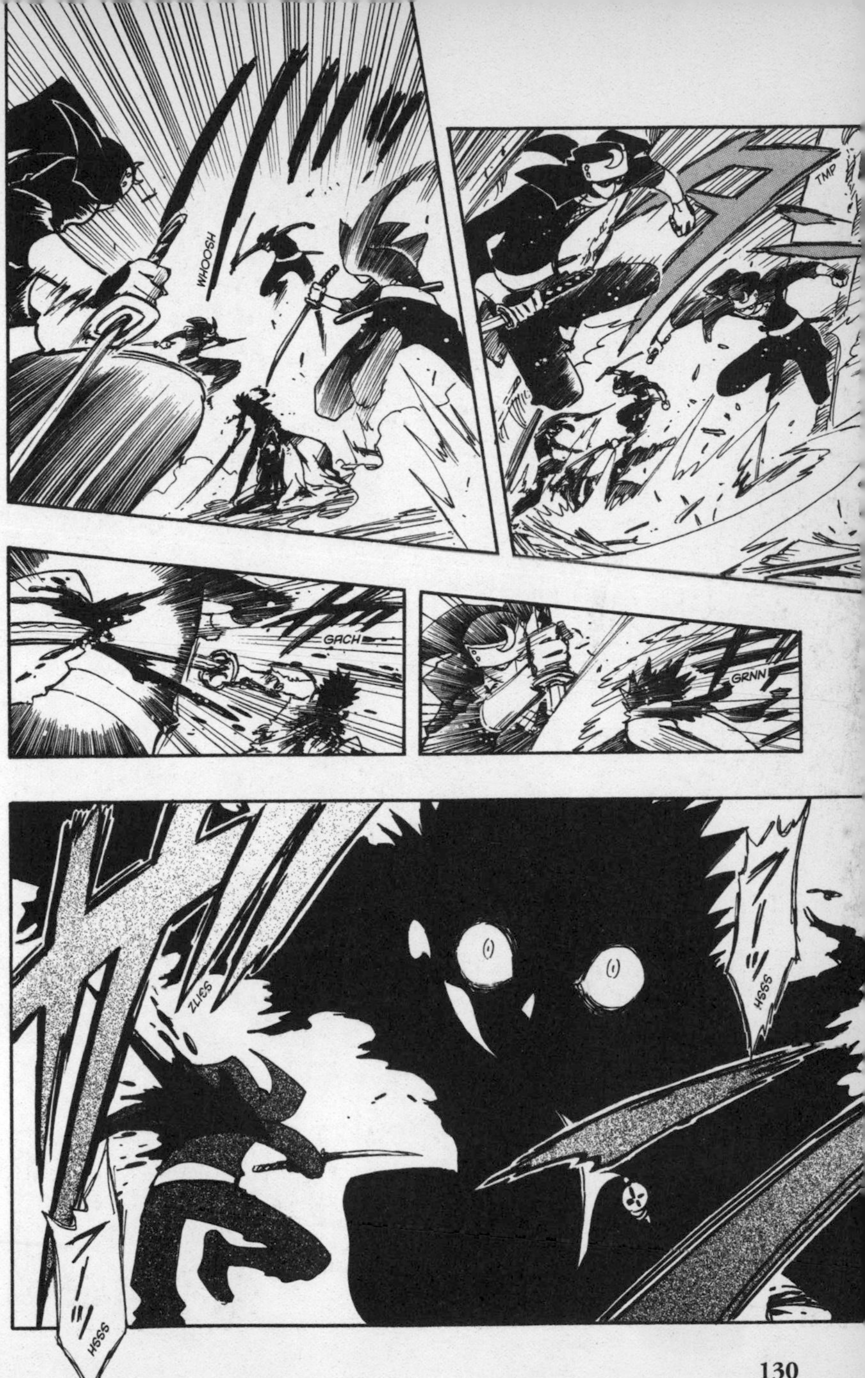
TMP
WHOOSH
GRNN
GACH
HSSS
ZLISS
HSSS

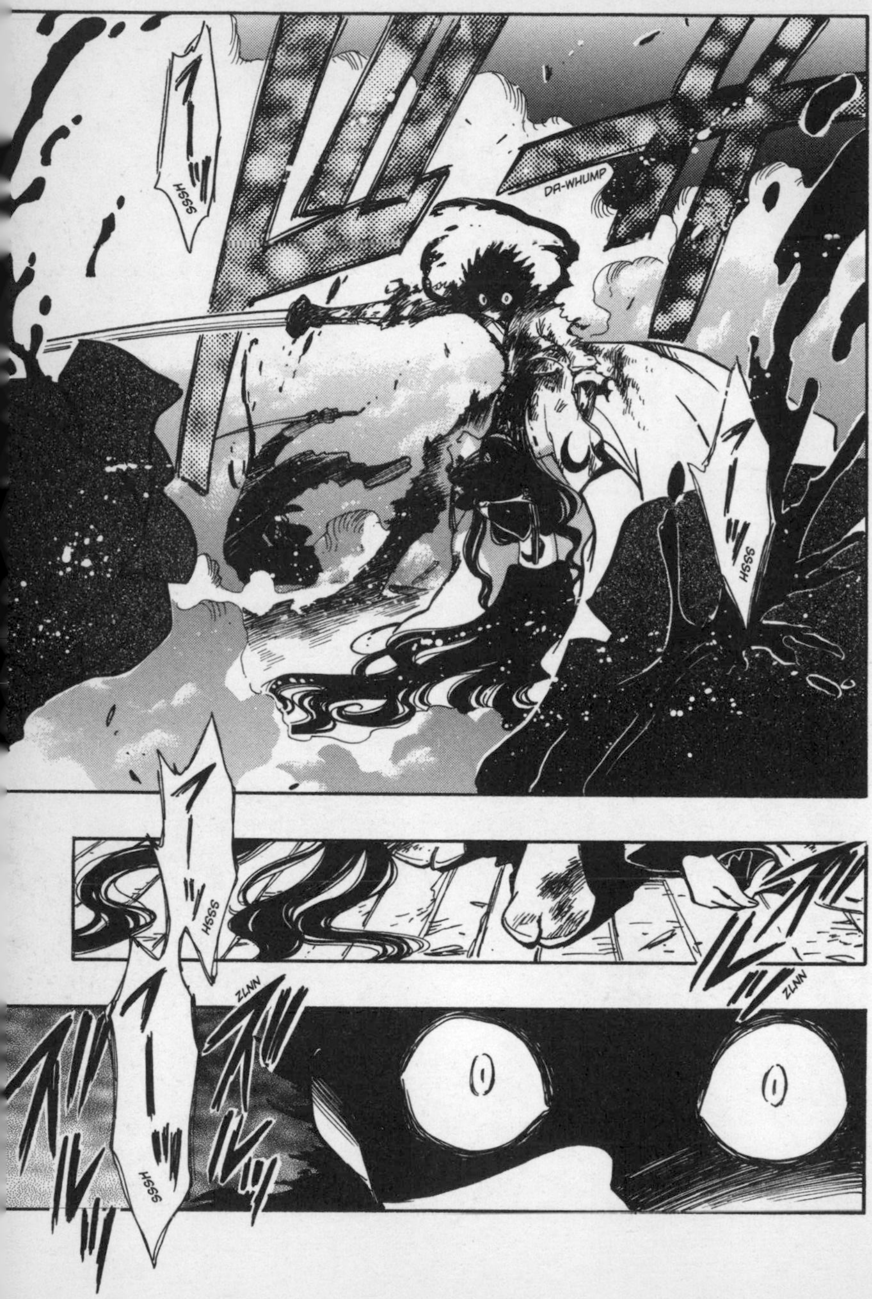
DA-WHUMP
HSSS
SSSH
HSSS
ZLNN
ZLNN
SSSH

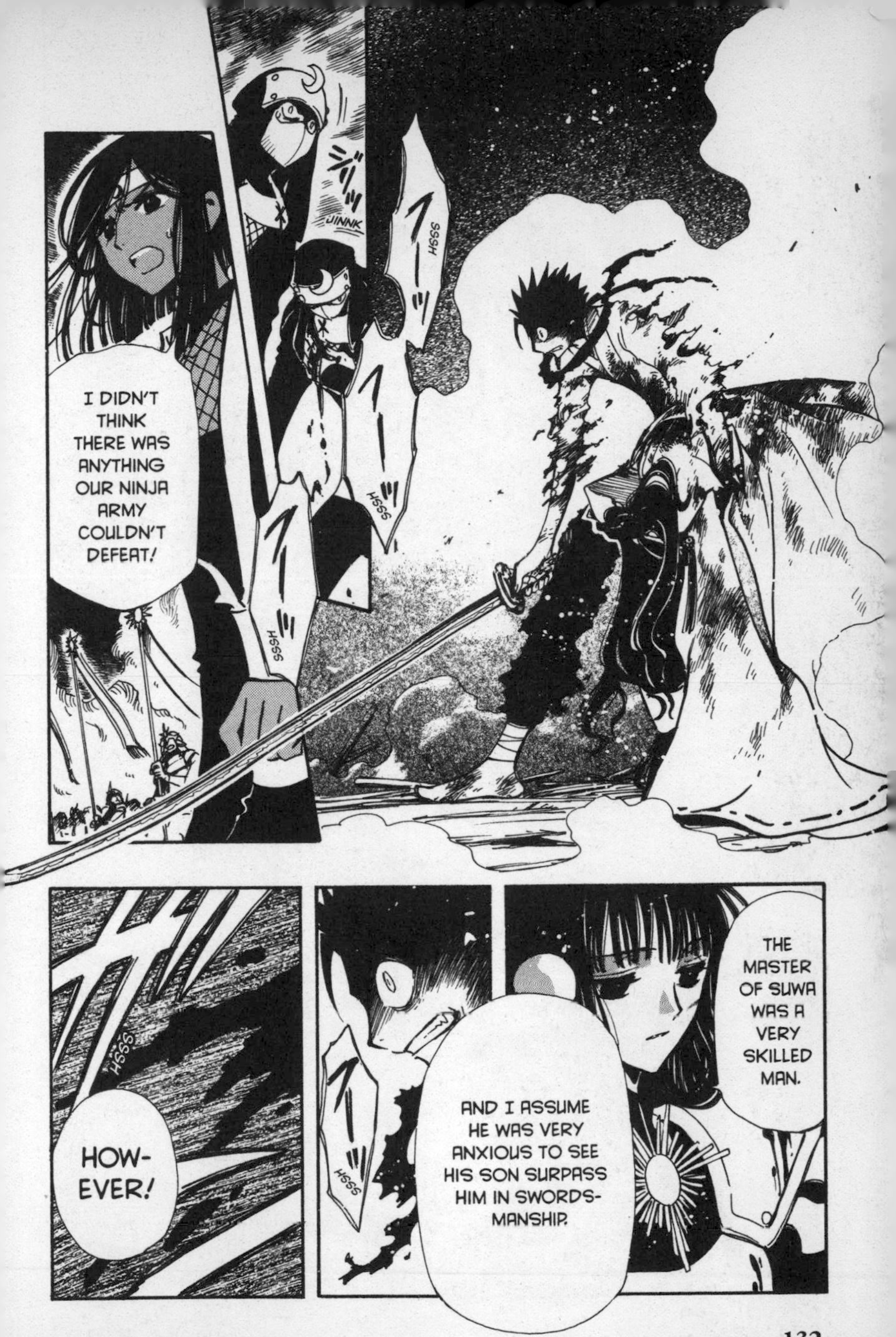
JINNK
HSSS
HSSS
HSSS
I DIDN'T THINK THERE WAS ANYTHING OUR NINJA ARMY COULDN'T DEFEAT!
THE MASTER OF SUWA WAS A VERY SKILLED MAN.
AND I ASSUME HE WAS VERY ANXIOUS TO SEE HIS SON SURPASS HIM IN SWORDS-MANSHIP.
HSSS
HSSS
HOW-EVER!

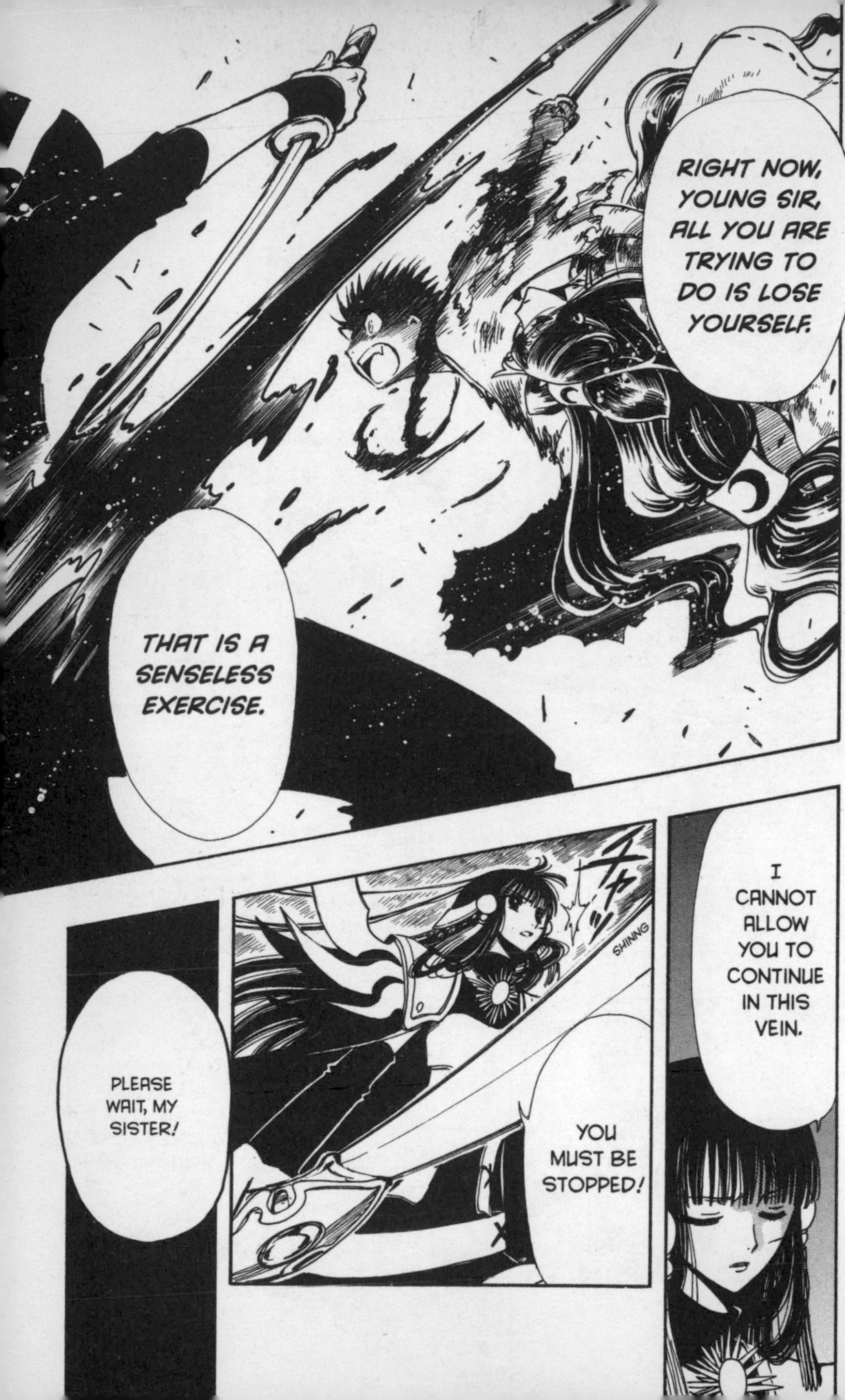
RIGHT NOW, YOUNG SIR, ALL YOU ARE TRYING TO DO IS LOSE YOURSELF.
THAT IS A SENSELESS EXERCISE.
I CANNOT ALLOW YOU TO CONTINUE IN THIS VEIN.
SHINNG
YOU MUST BE STOPPED!
PLEASE WAIT, MY SISTER!

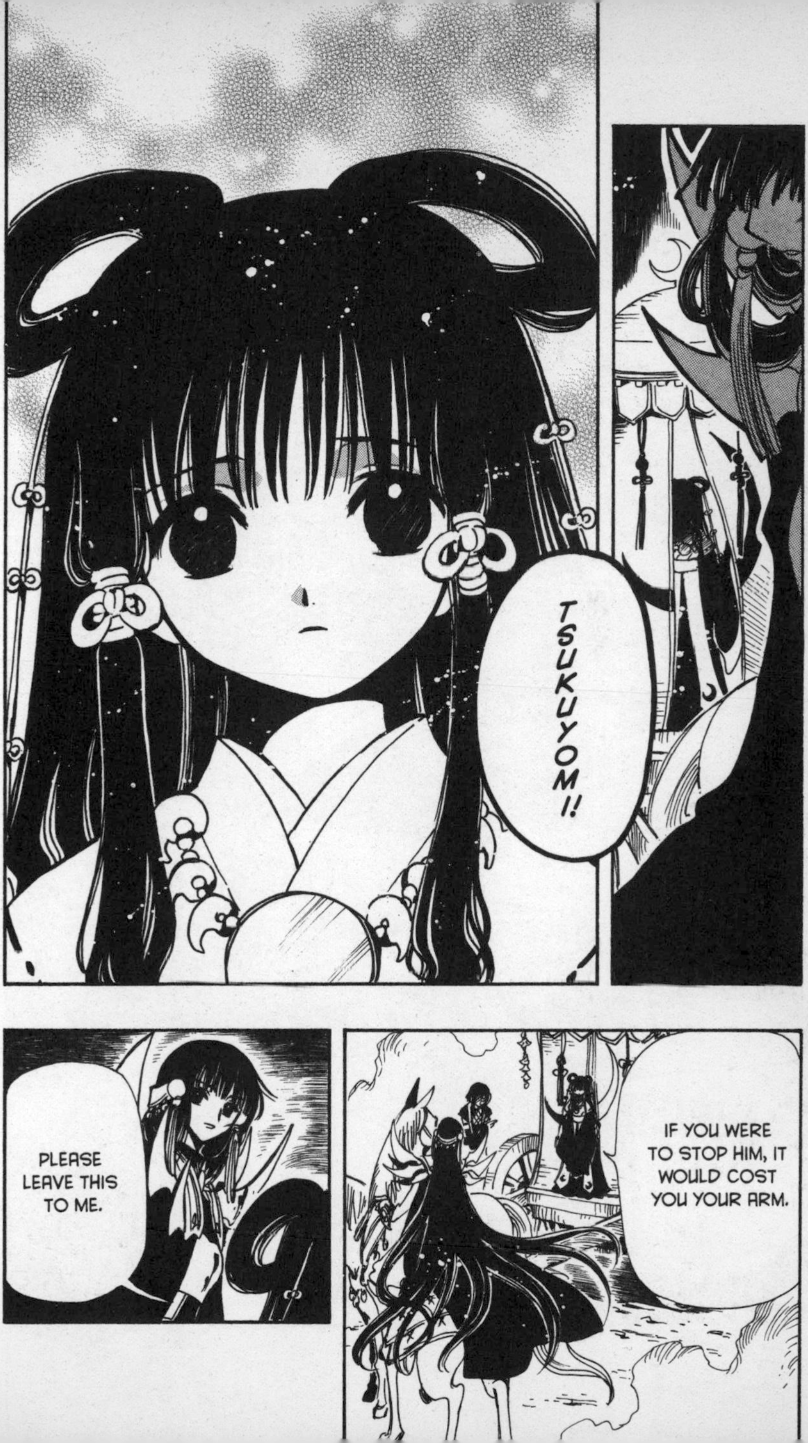
TSUKUYOMI!!
IF YOU WERE TO STOP HIM, IT WOULD COST YOU YOUR ARM.
PLEASE LEAVE THIS TO ME.

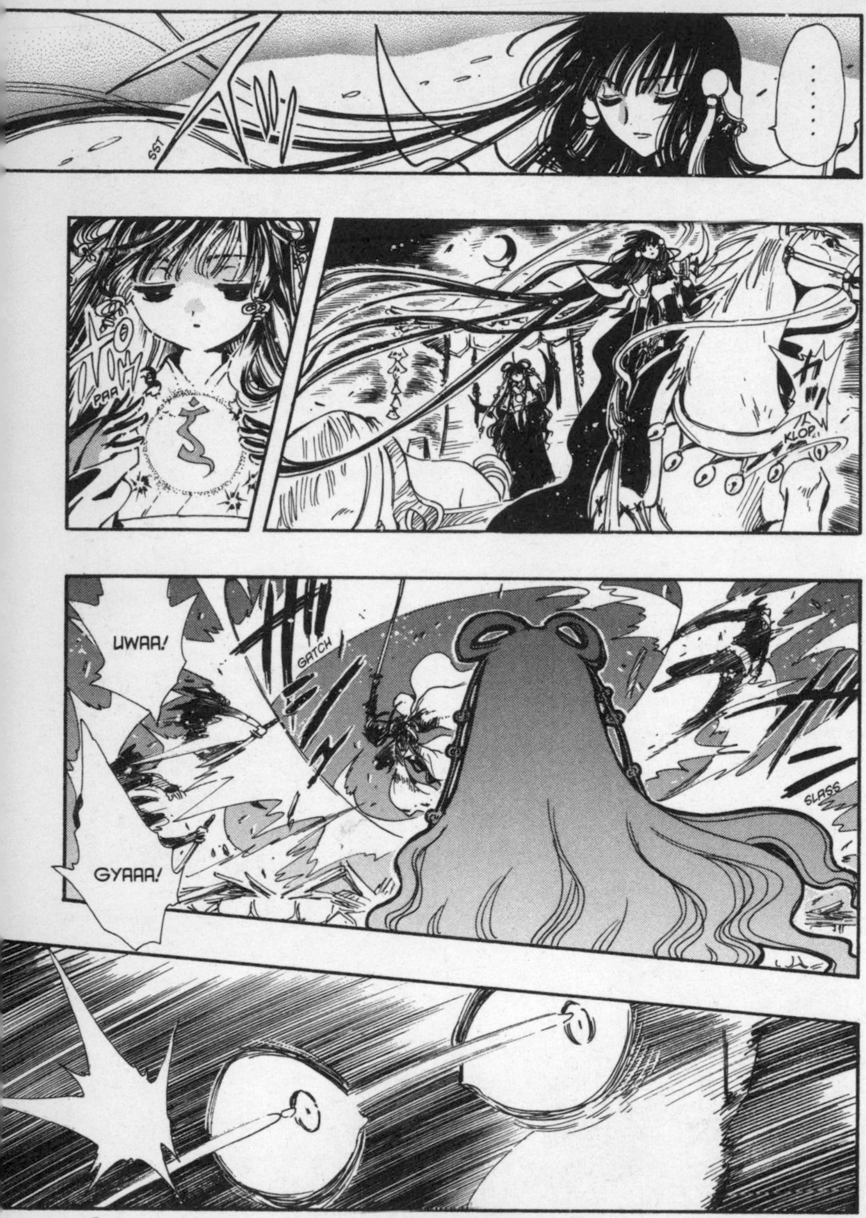
……
SST
KLOP
PAA
SLASS
GATCH
UWAA!
GYAAA!

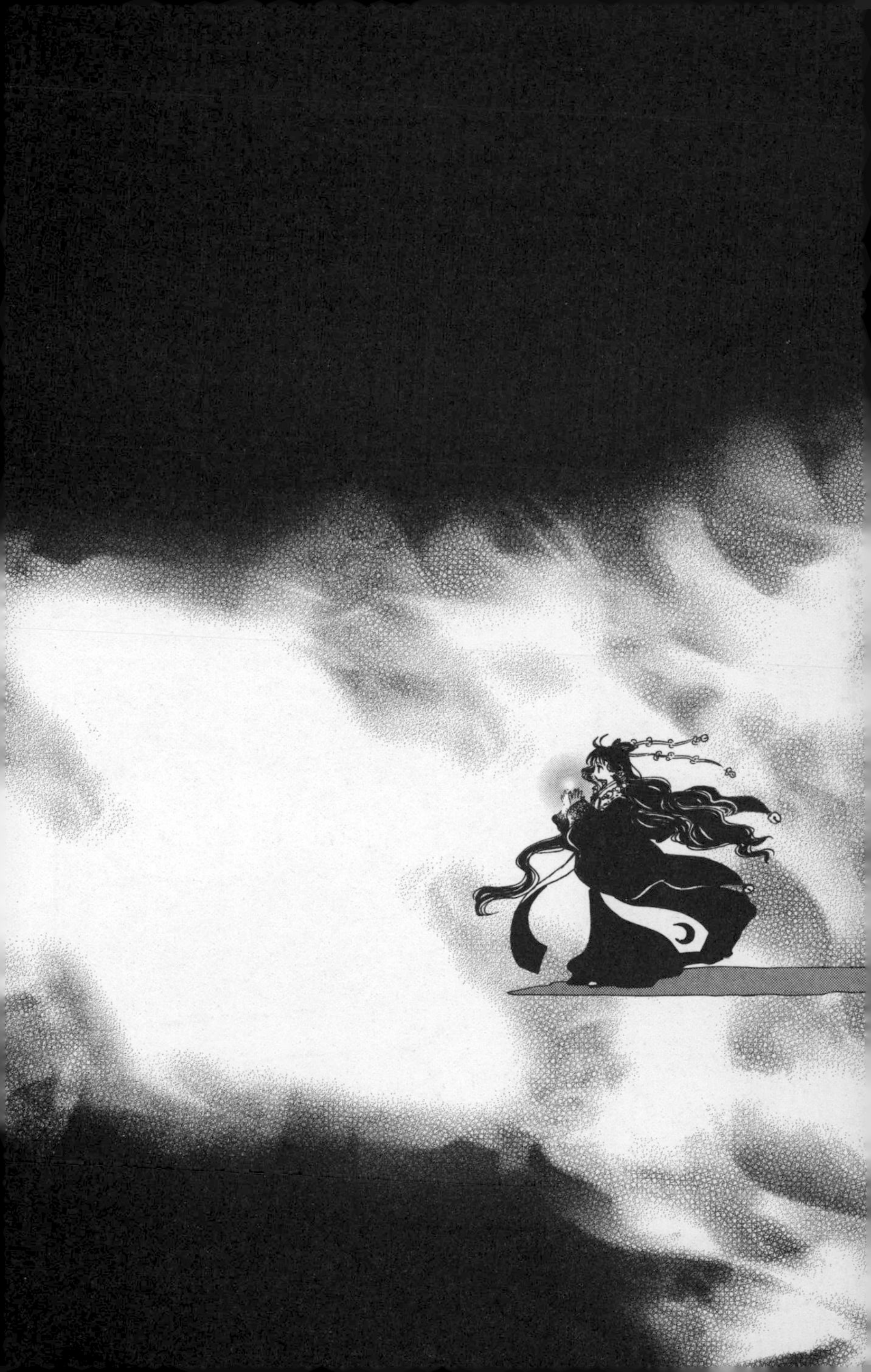

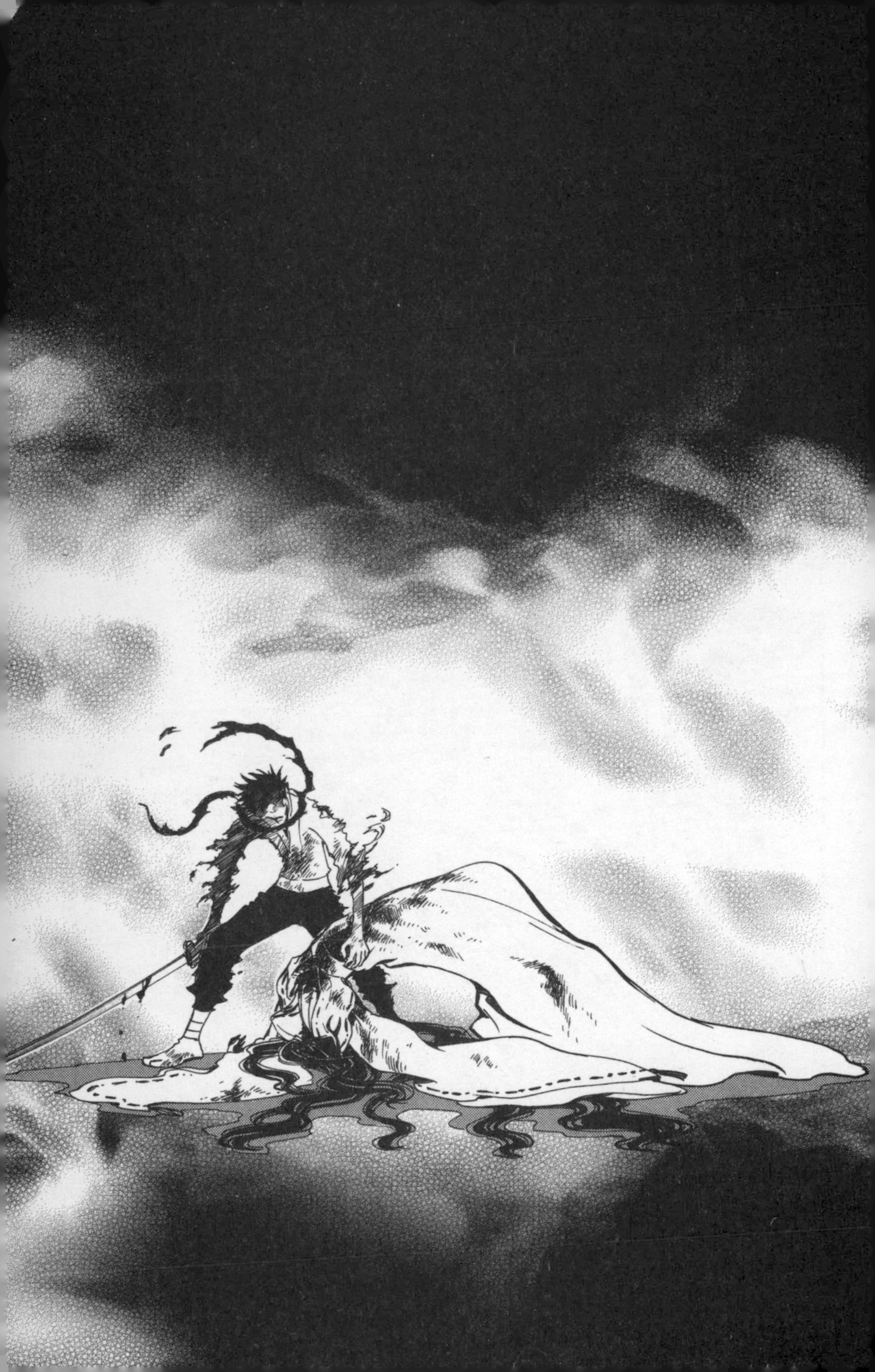

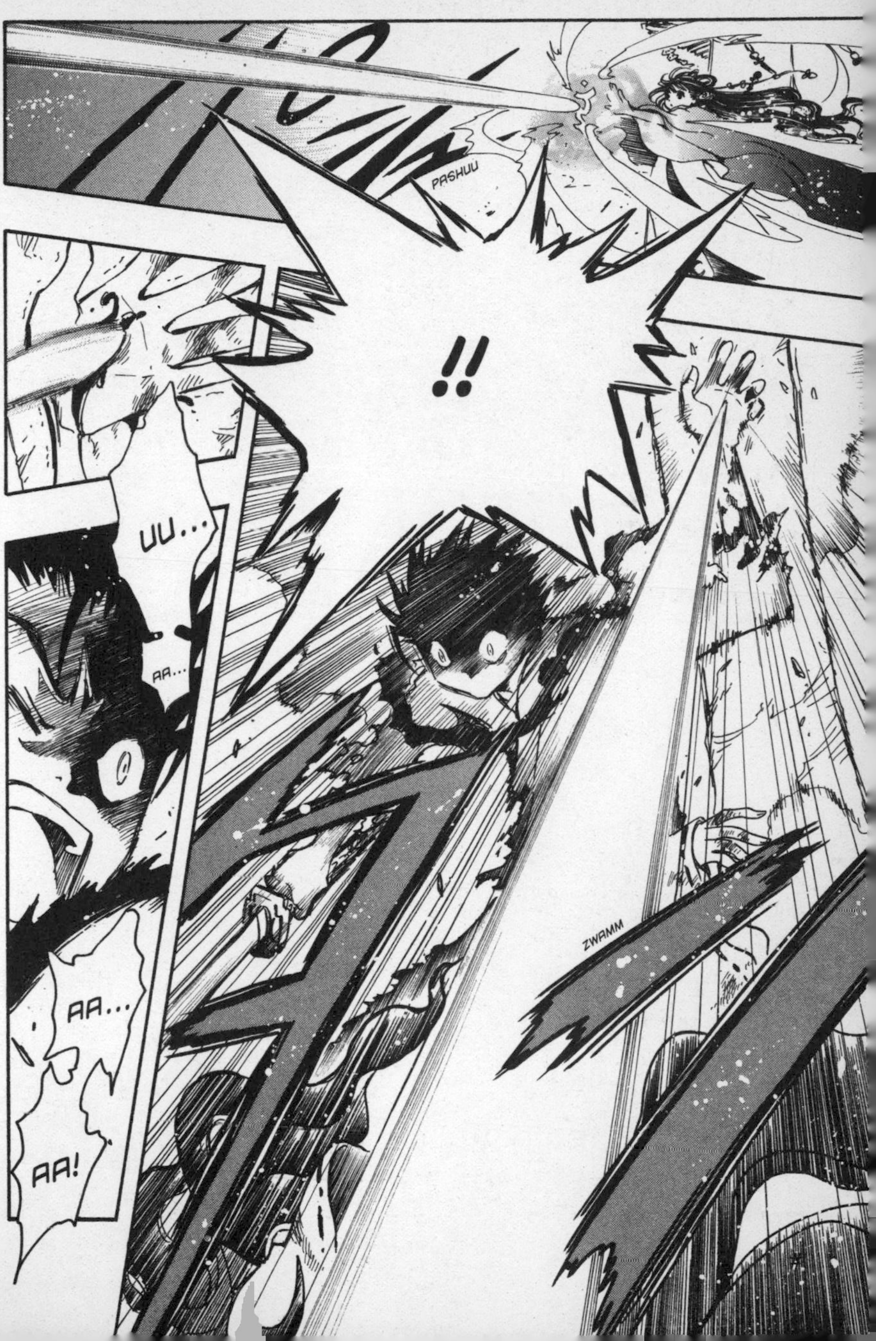
PASHUU
!!
ZWAMM
UU...
AA...
AA...
AA!

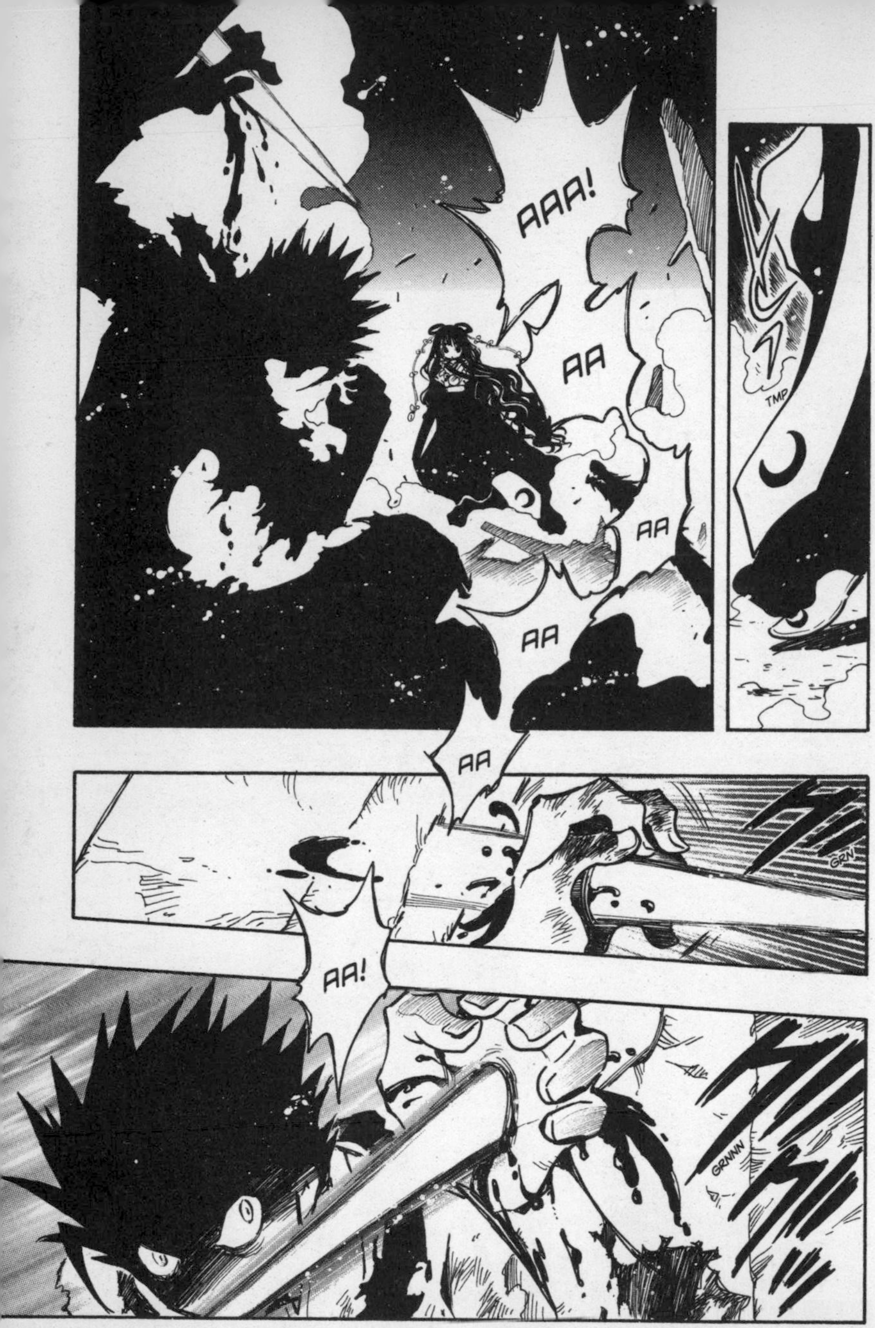
TMP
AAA!
AA
AA
AA
AA
GRN
AA!
GRNNN

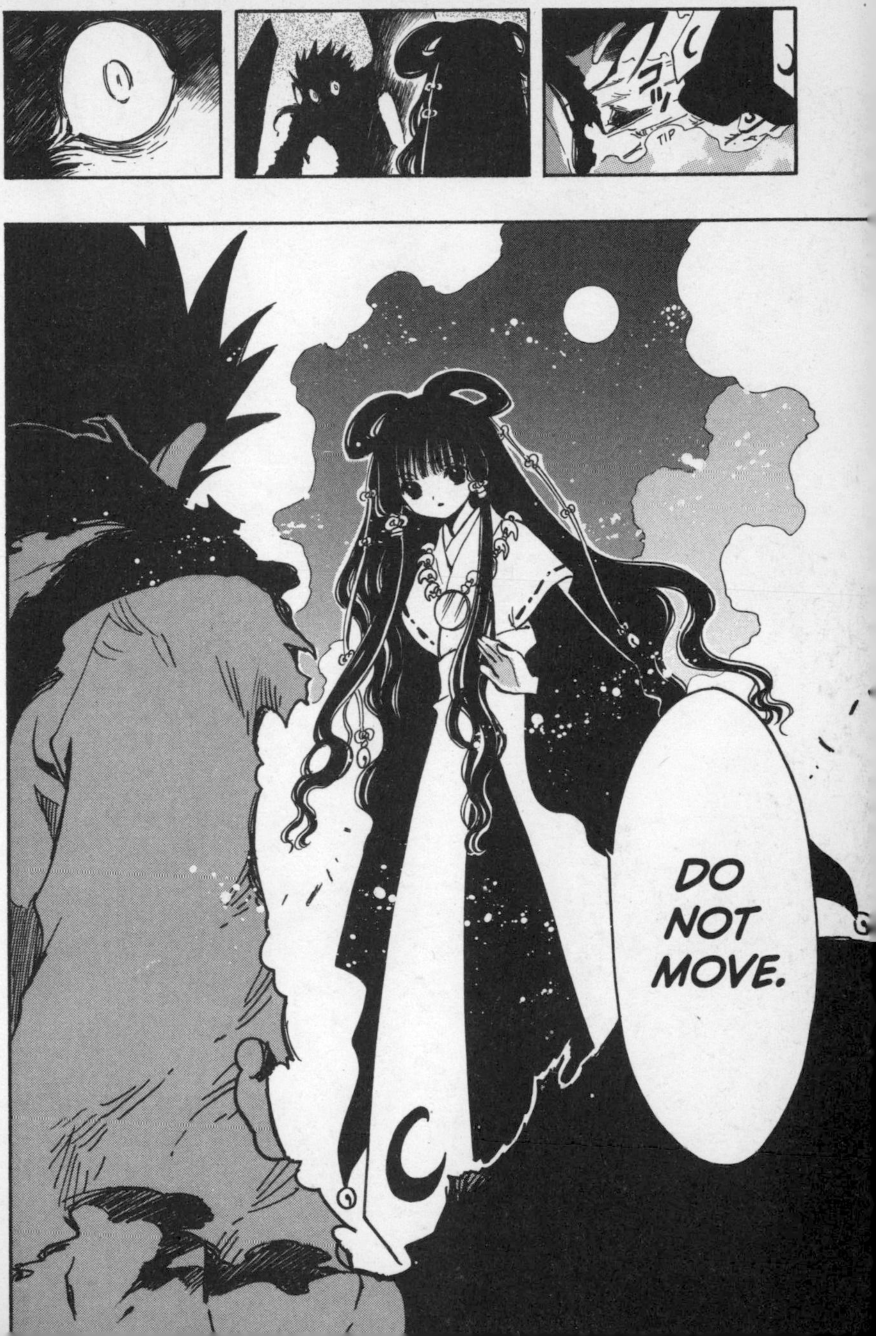
TIP
DO NOT MOVE.

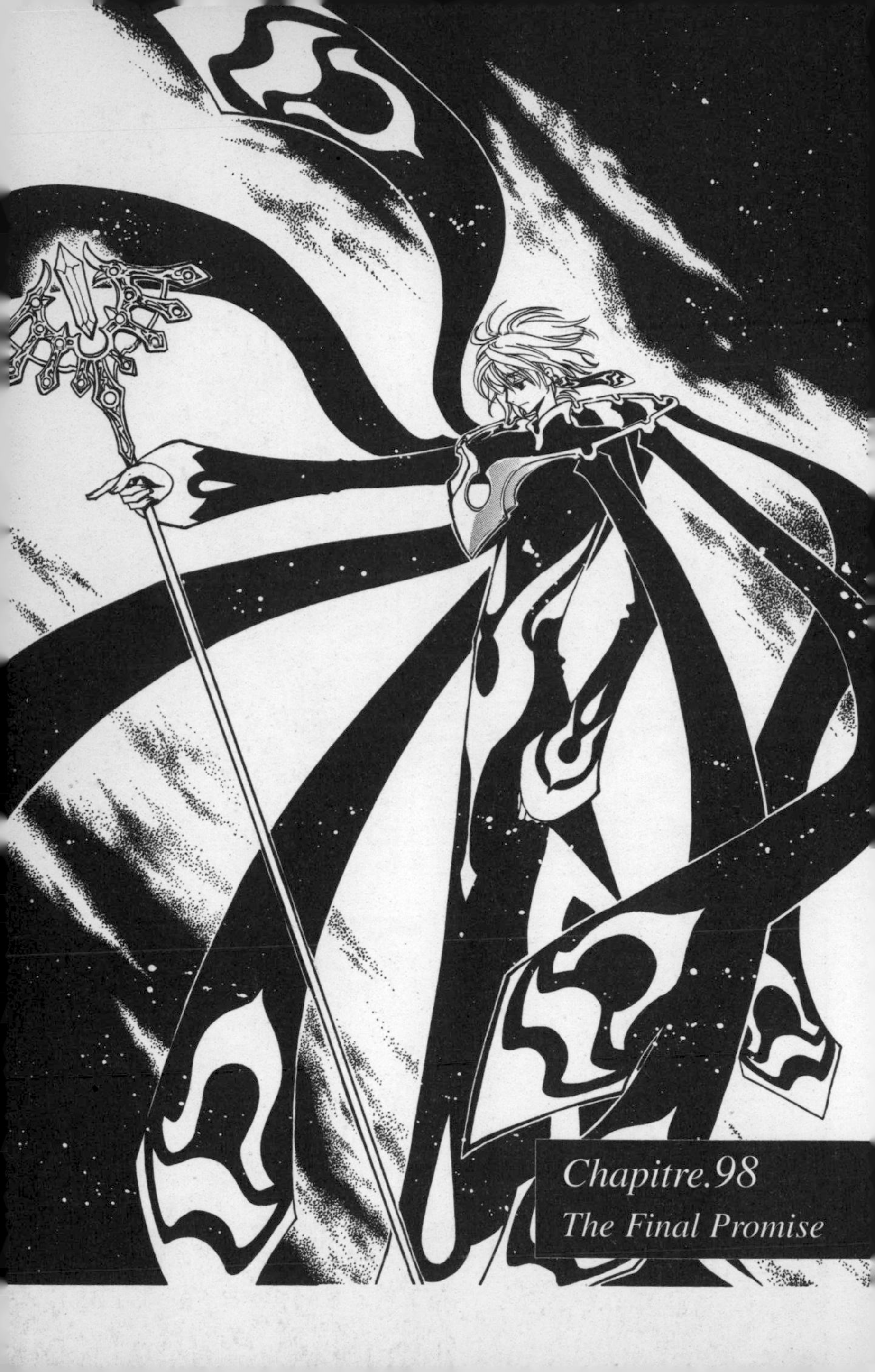
Chapitre.98
The Final Promise

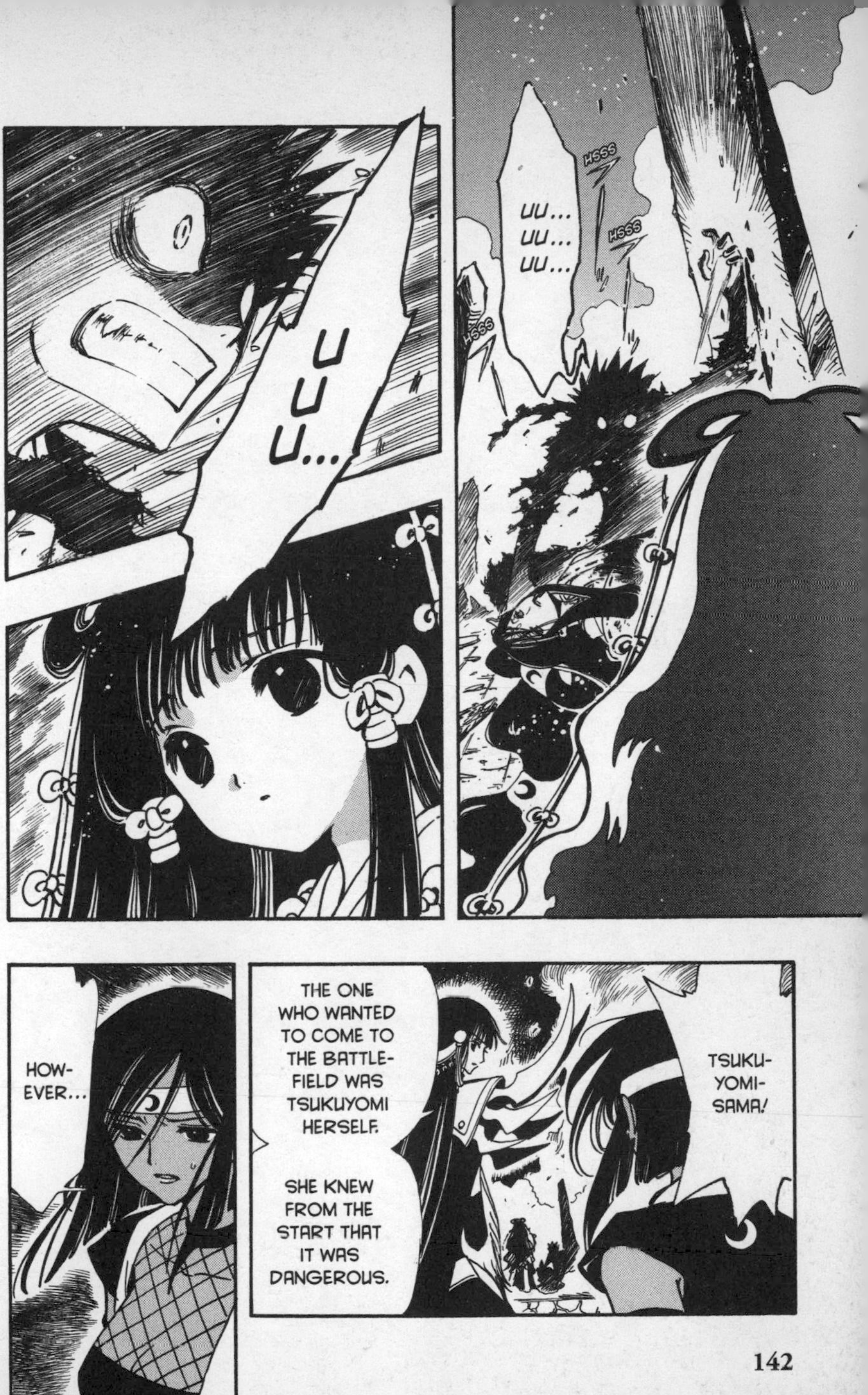
HSSS
UU... UU... UU...
HSSS
HSSS
UUU...
TSUKU-YOMI-SAMA!
THE ONE WHO WANTED TO COME TO THE BATTLE-FIELD WAS TSUKUYOMI HERSELF.
SHE KNEW FROM THE START THAT IT WAS DANGEROUS.
HOW-EVER...

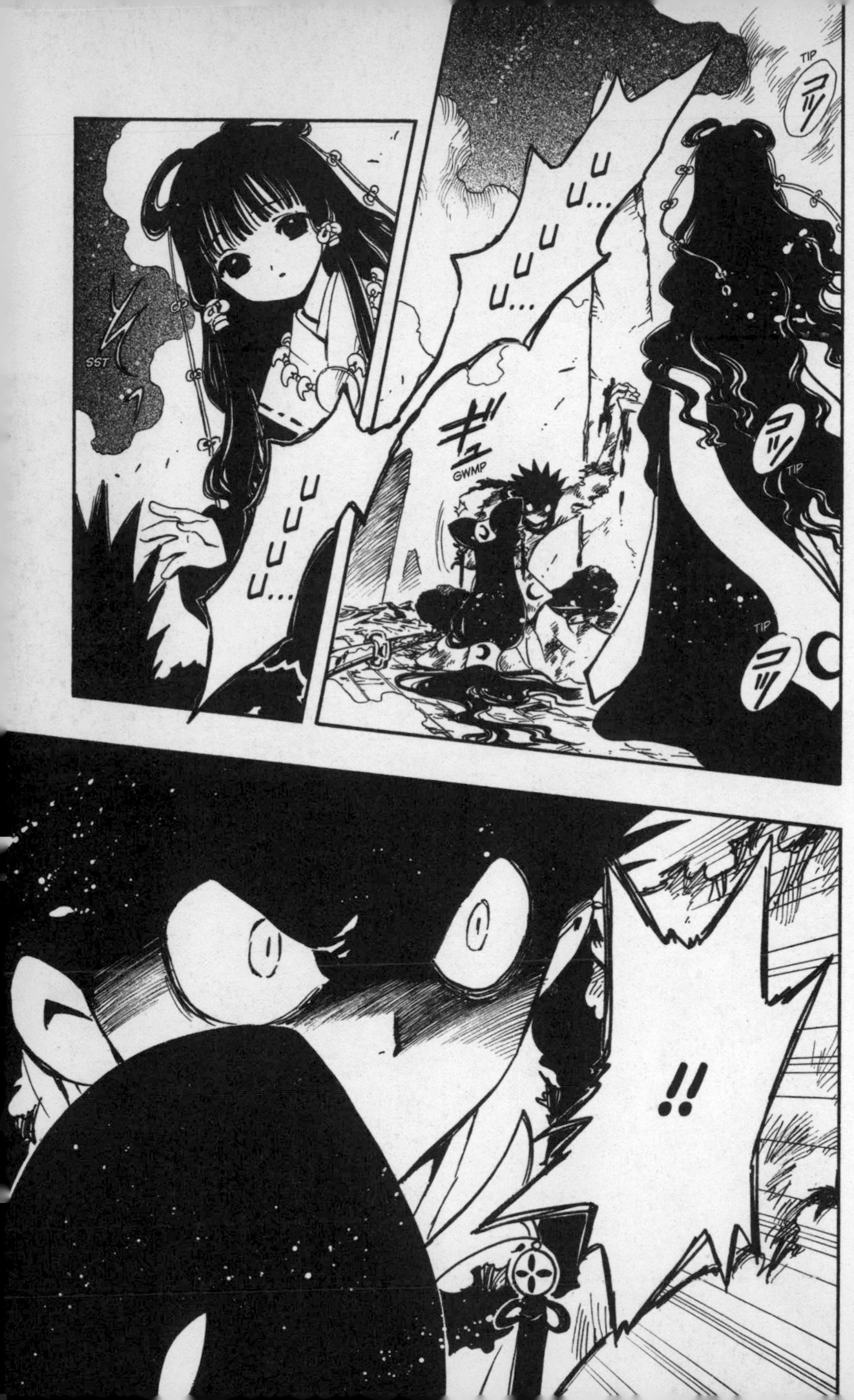
TIP
UU...
UUU...
GWMP
TIP
TIP
SST
UUUUU...
!!

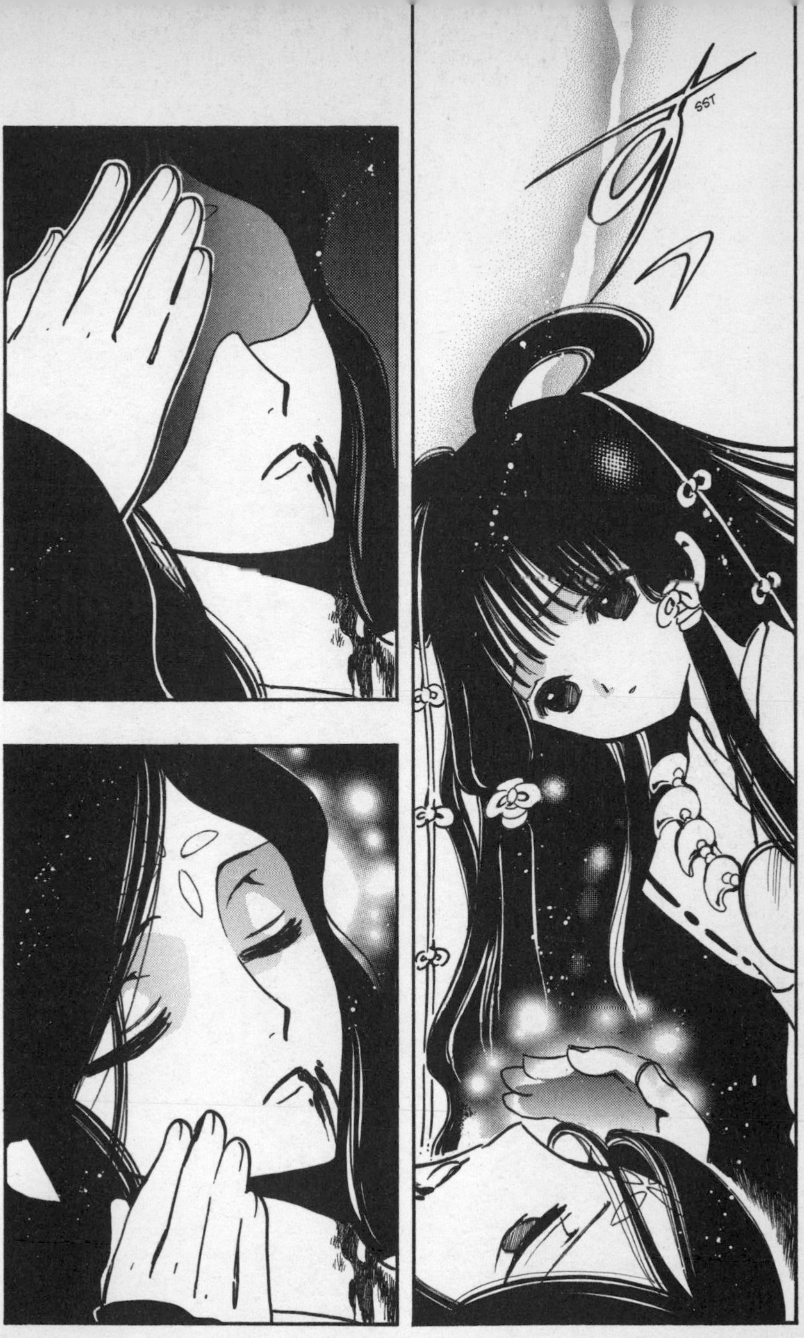
SST

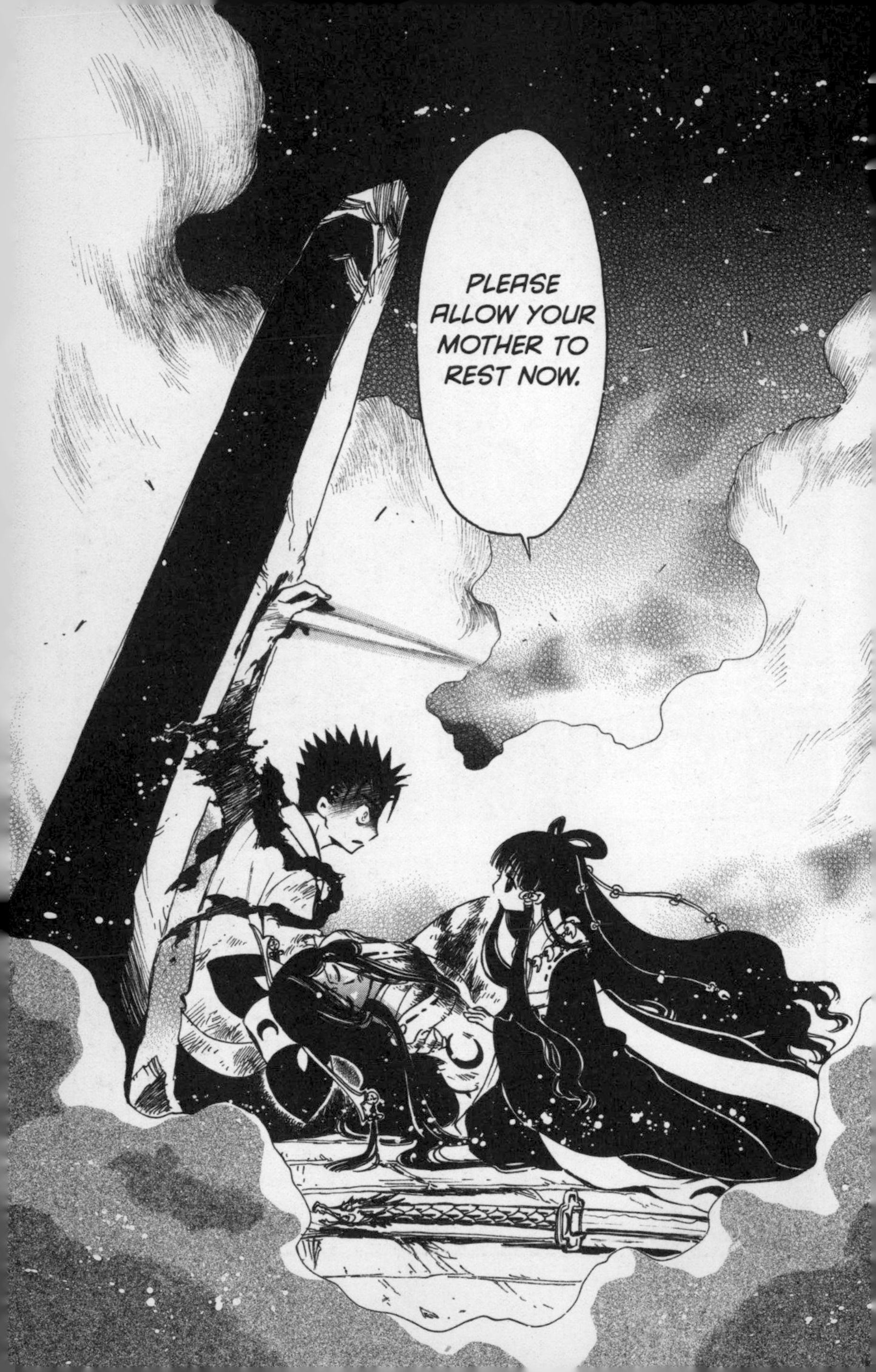
PLEASE ALLOW YOUR MOTHER TO REST NOW.

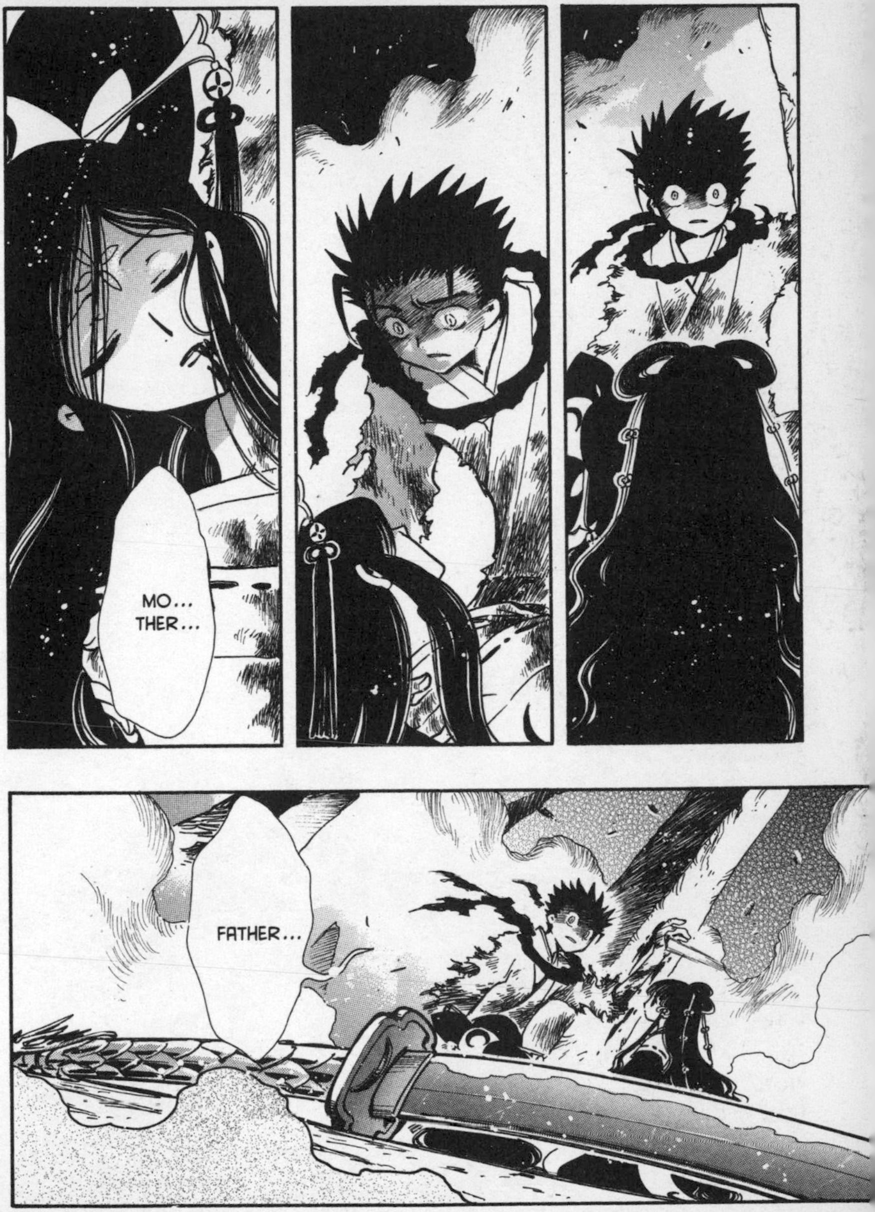
MO... THER...
FATHER...

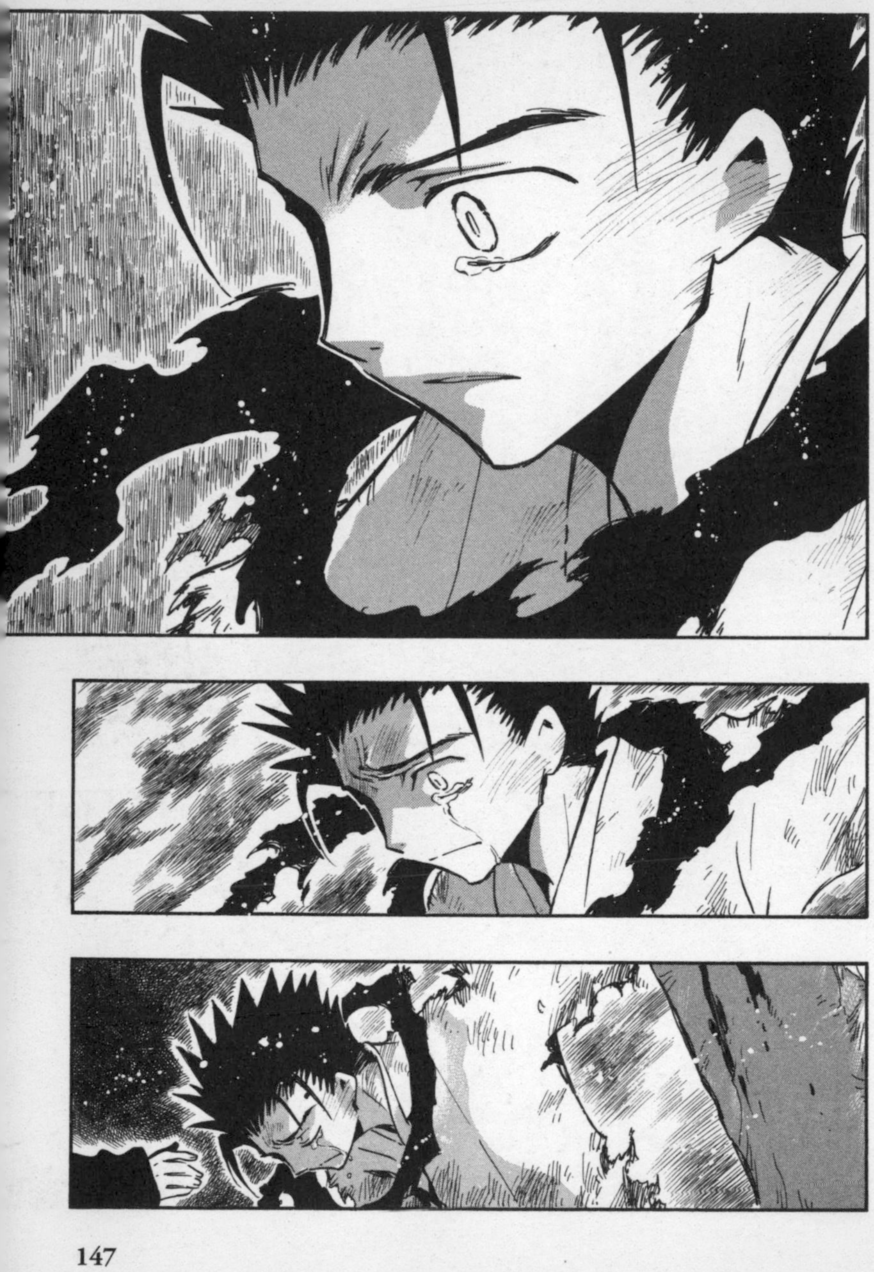

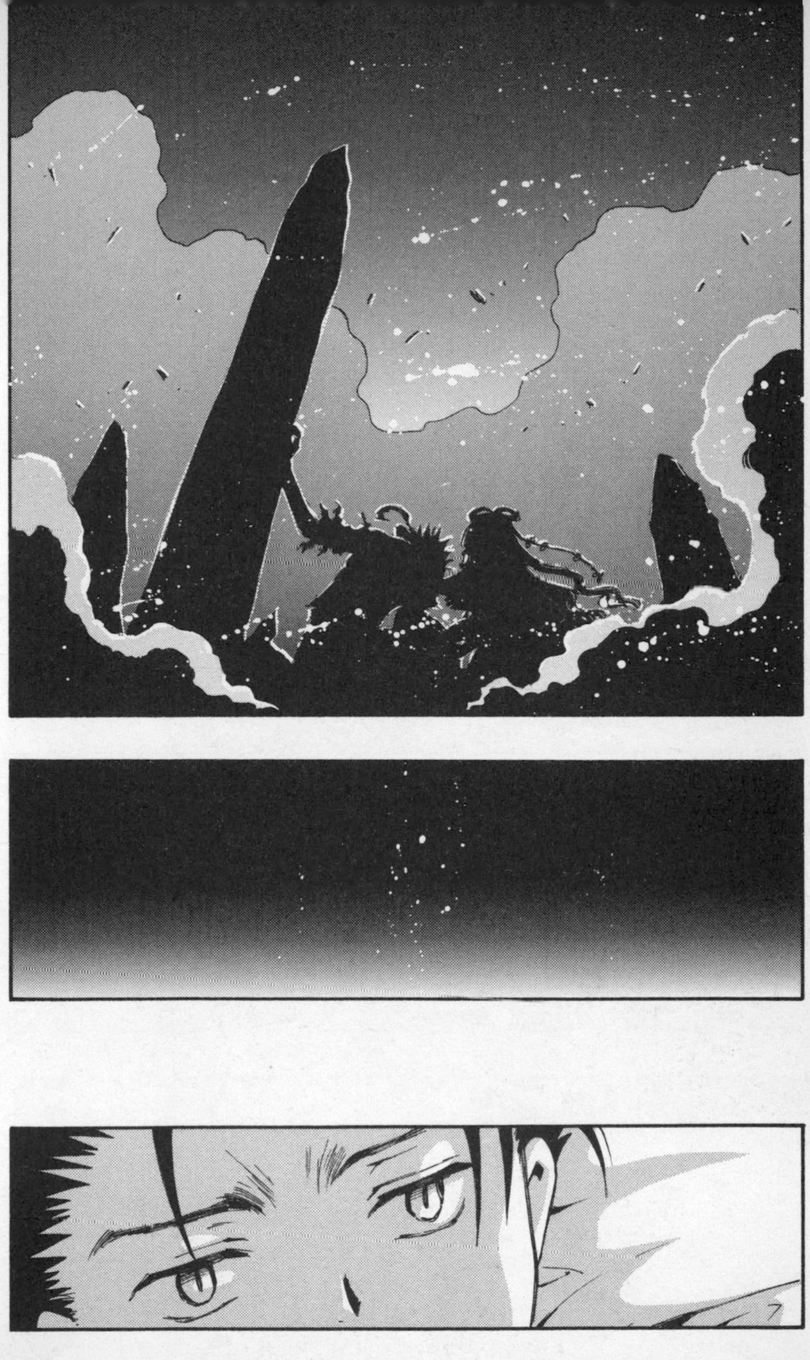

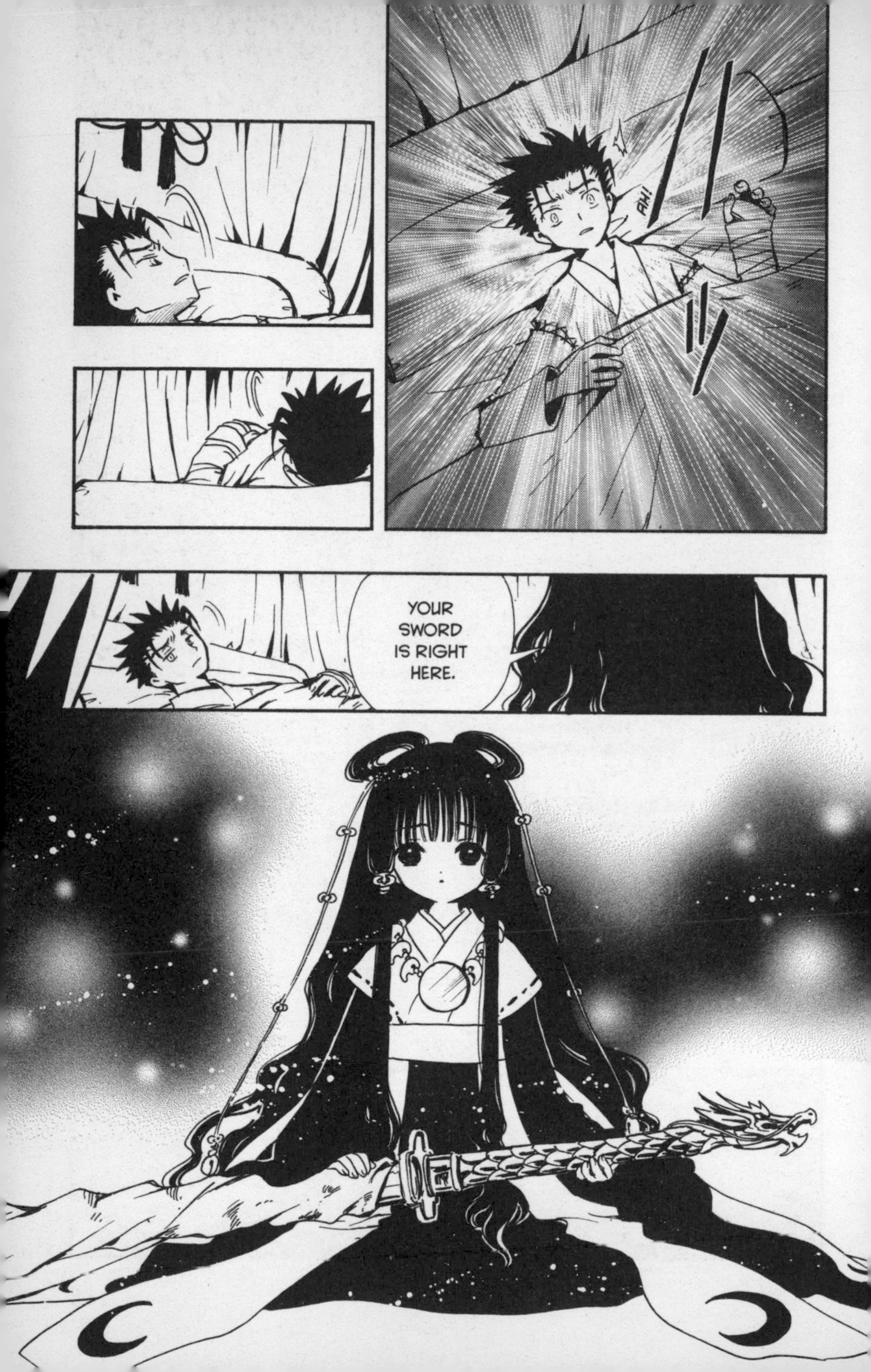
AH!
YOUR SWORD IS RIGHT HERE.

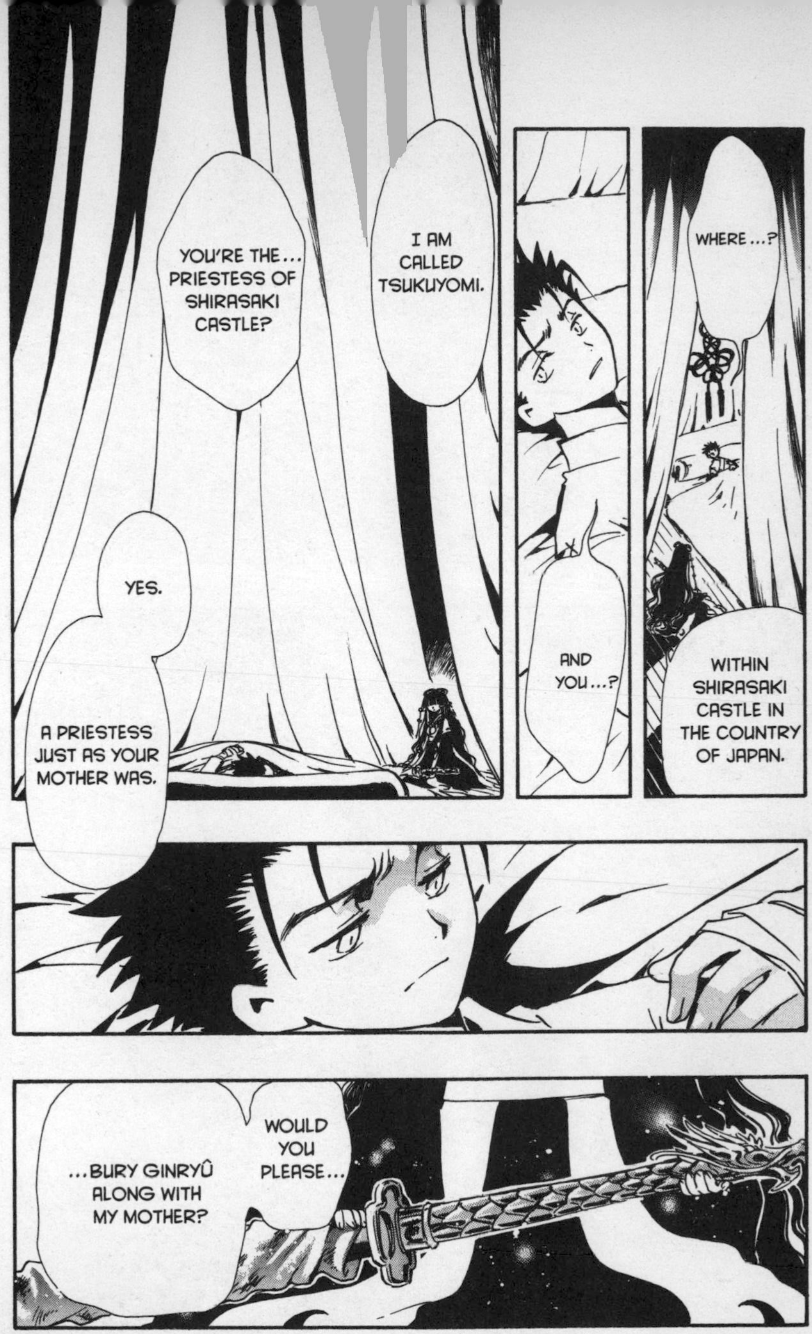
WHERE...?
WITHIN SHIRASAKI CASTLE IN THE COUNTRY OF JAPAN.
AND YOU...?
I AM CALLED TSUKUYOMI.
YOU'RE THE... PRIESTESS OF SHIRASAKI CASTLE?
YES.
A PRIESTESS JUST AS YOUR MOTHER WAS.
WOULD YOU PLEASE...
...BURY GINRYÛ ALONG WITH MY MOTHER?

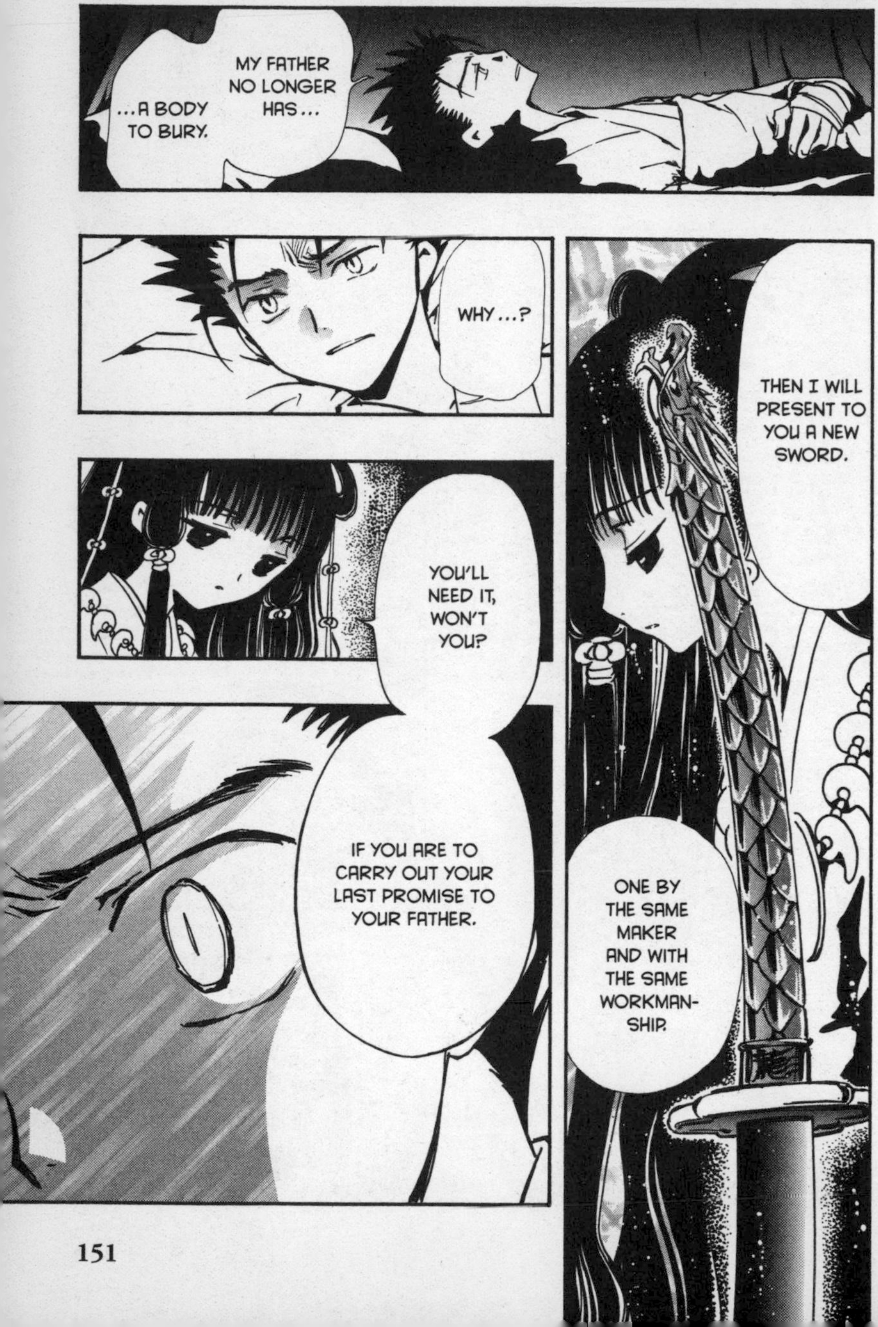
MY FATHER NO LONGER HAS...
...A BODY TO BURY.
THEN I WILL PRESENT TO YOU A NEW SWORD.
ONE BY THE SAME MAKER AND WITH THE SAME WORKMAN-SHIP.
WHY...?
YOU'LL NEED IT, WON'T YOU?
IF YOU ARE TO CARRY OUT YOUR LAST PROMISE TO YOUR FATHER.

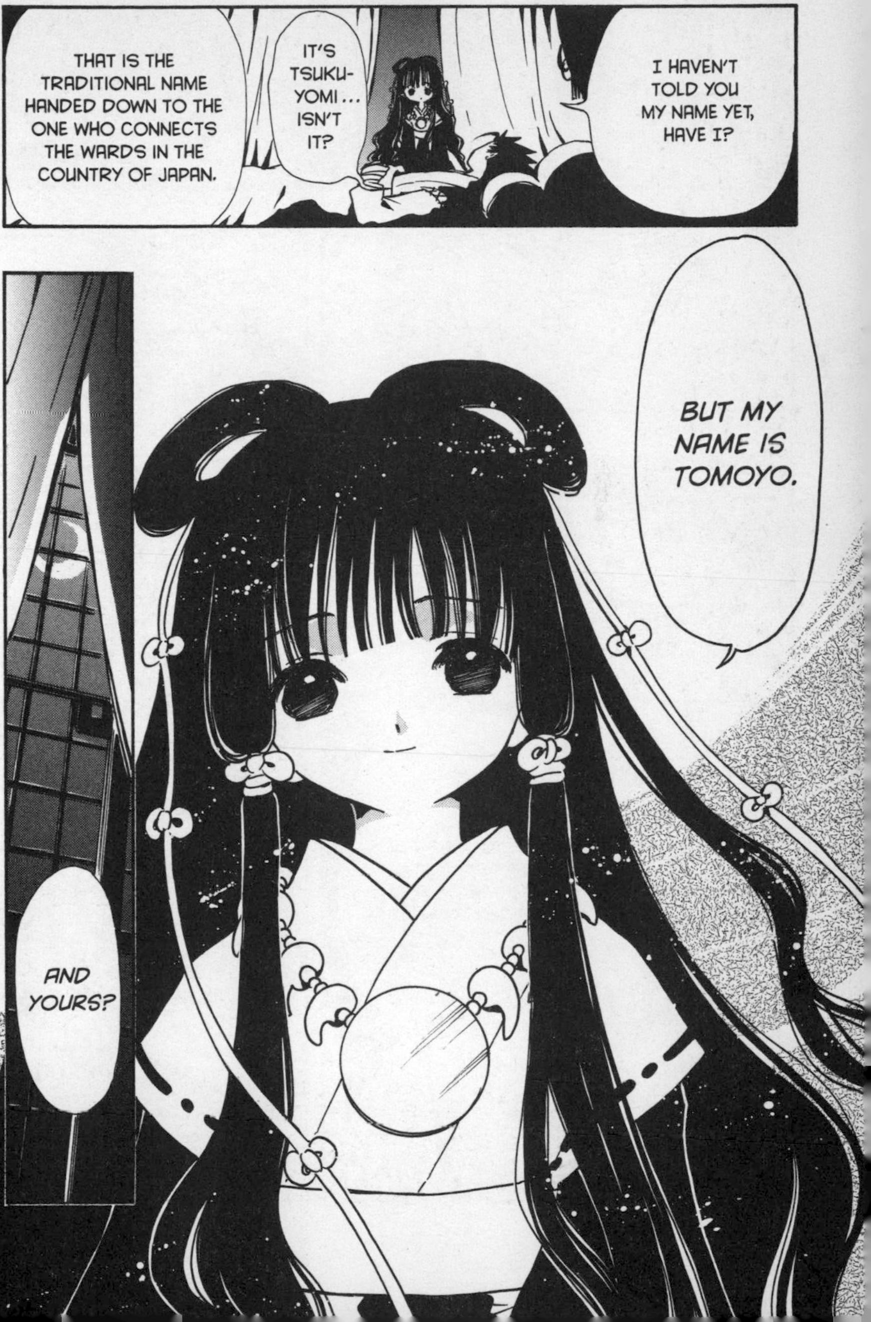
I HAVEN'T TOLD YOU MY NAME YET, HAVE I?
IT'S TSUKU-YOMI… ISN'T IT?
THAT IS THE TRADITIONAL NAME HANDED DOWN TO THE ONE WHO CONNECTS THE WARDS IN THE COUNTRY OF JAPAN.
BUT MY NAME IS TOMOYO.
AND YOURS?

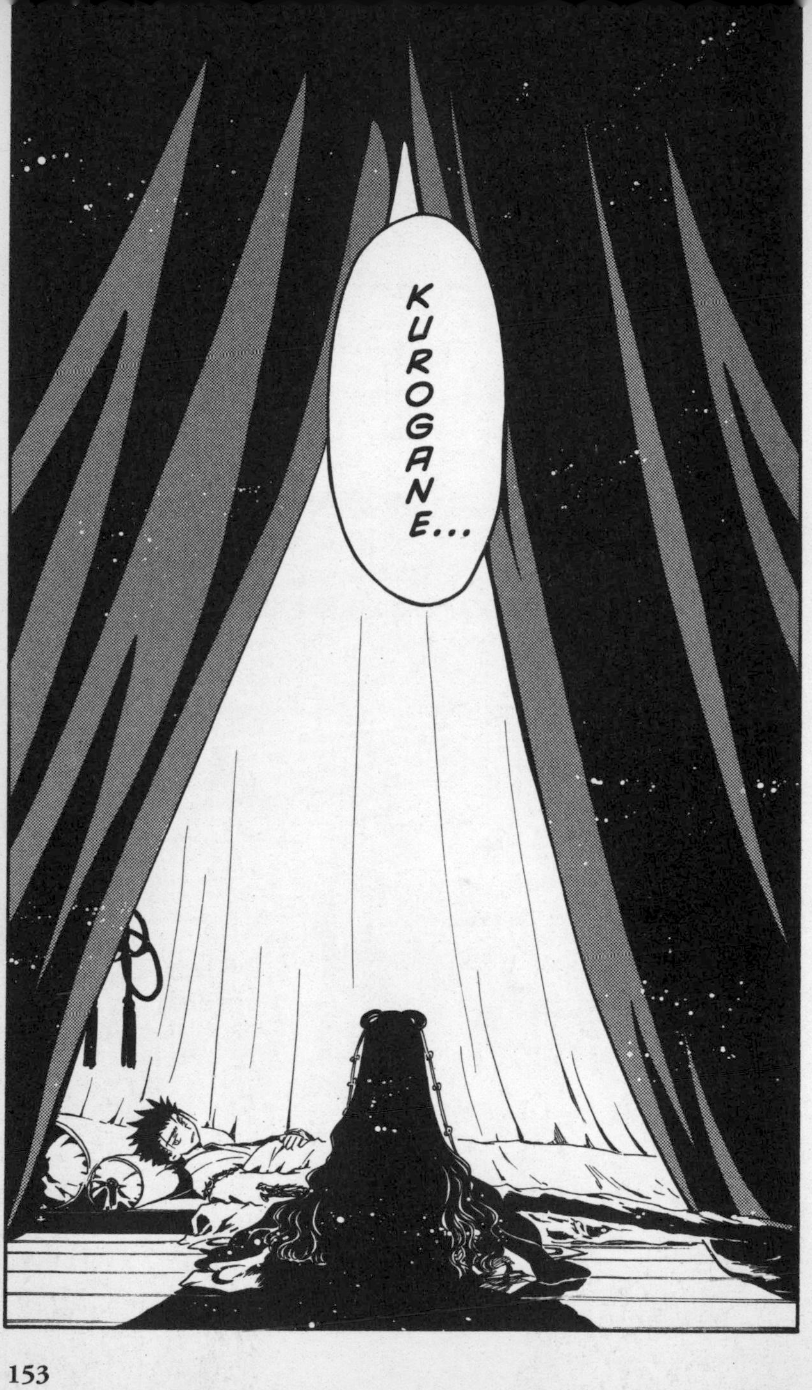
KUROGANE...

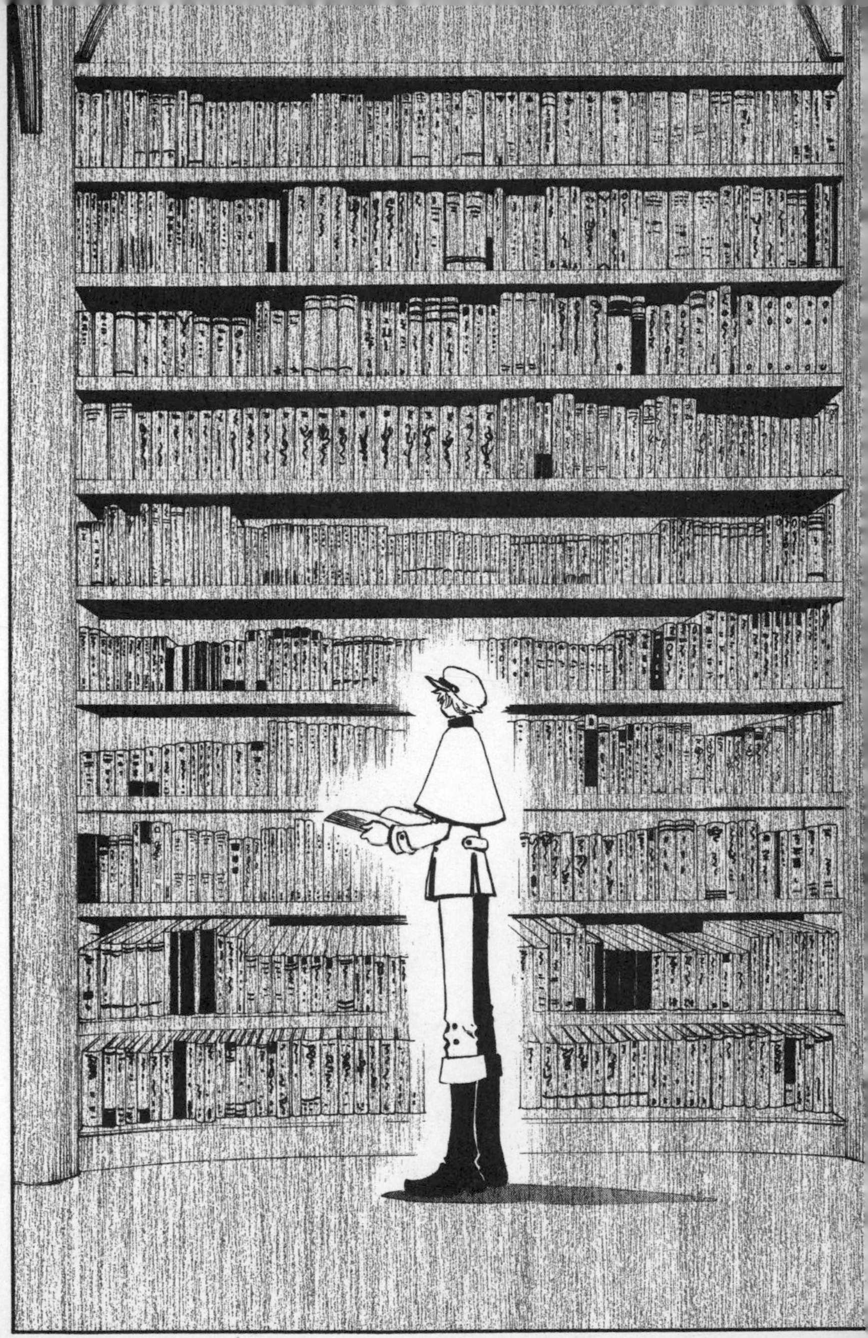

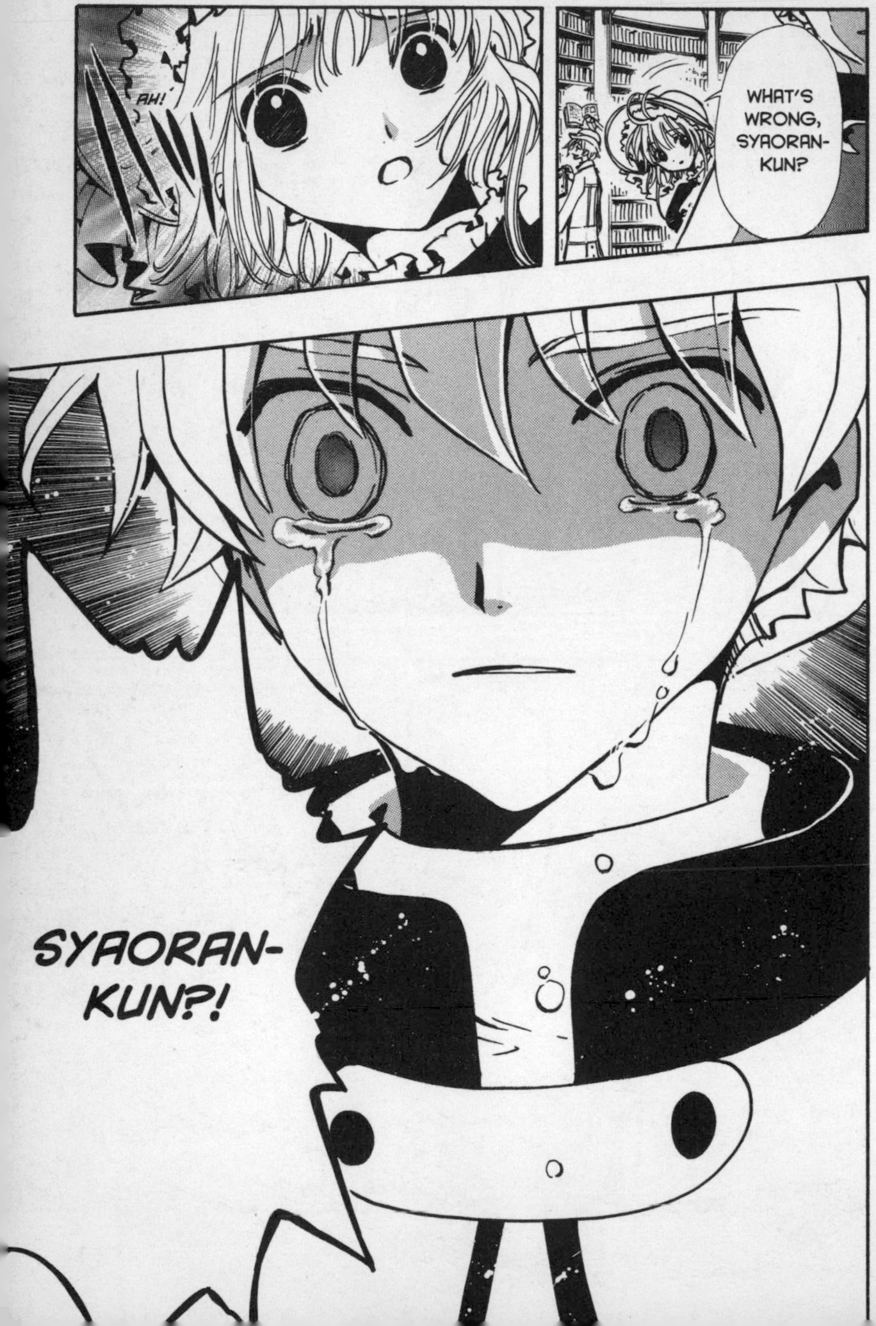
WHAT'S WRONG, SYAORAN-KUN?
AH!
SYAORAN-KUN?!

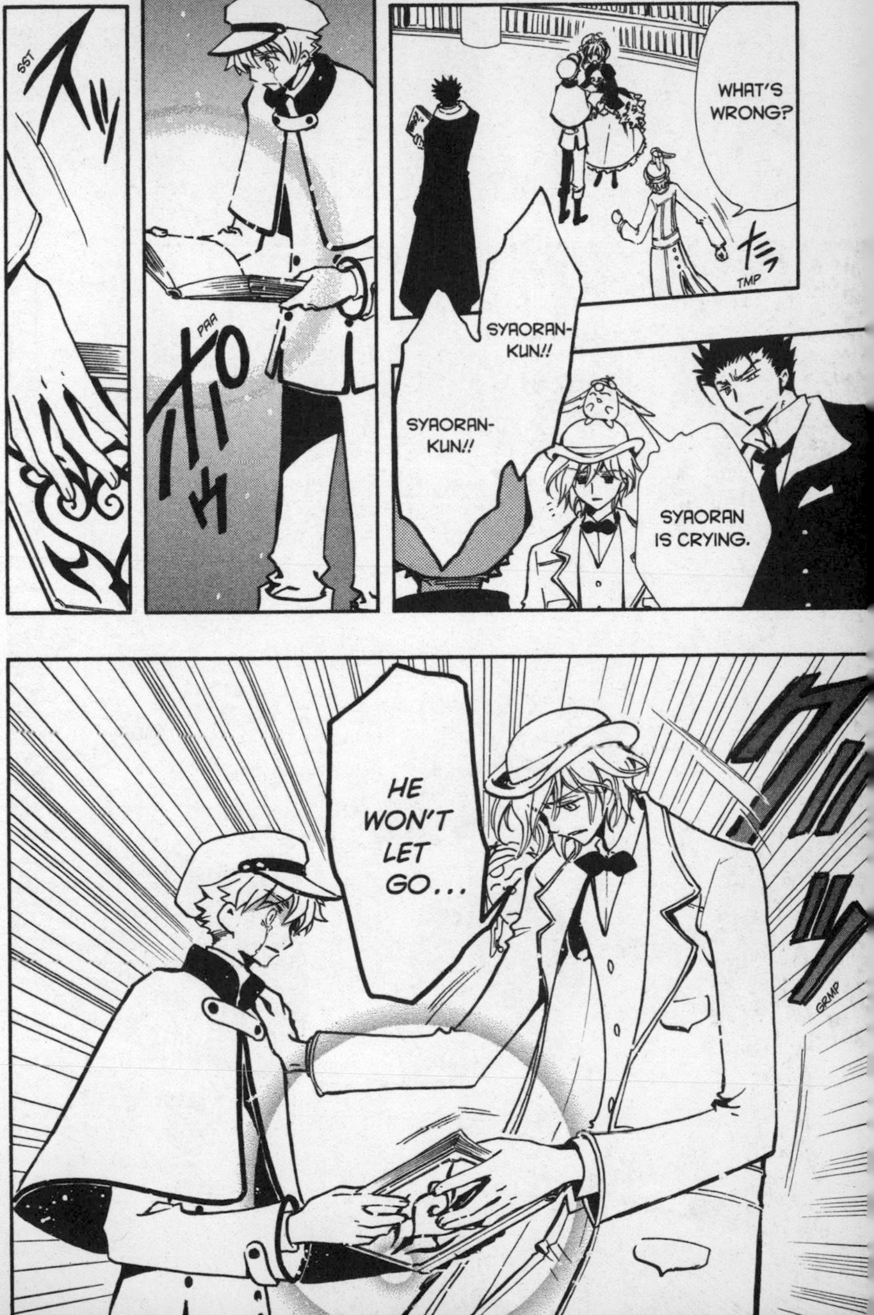
WHAT'S WRONG?
TMP
SYAORAN-KUN!!
SYAORAN IS CRYING.
SYAORAN-KUN!!
PAA
SST
GRMP
HE WON'T LET GO...

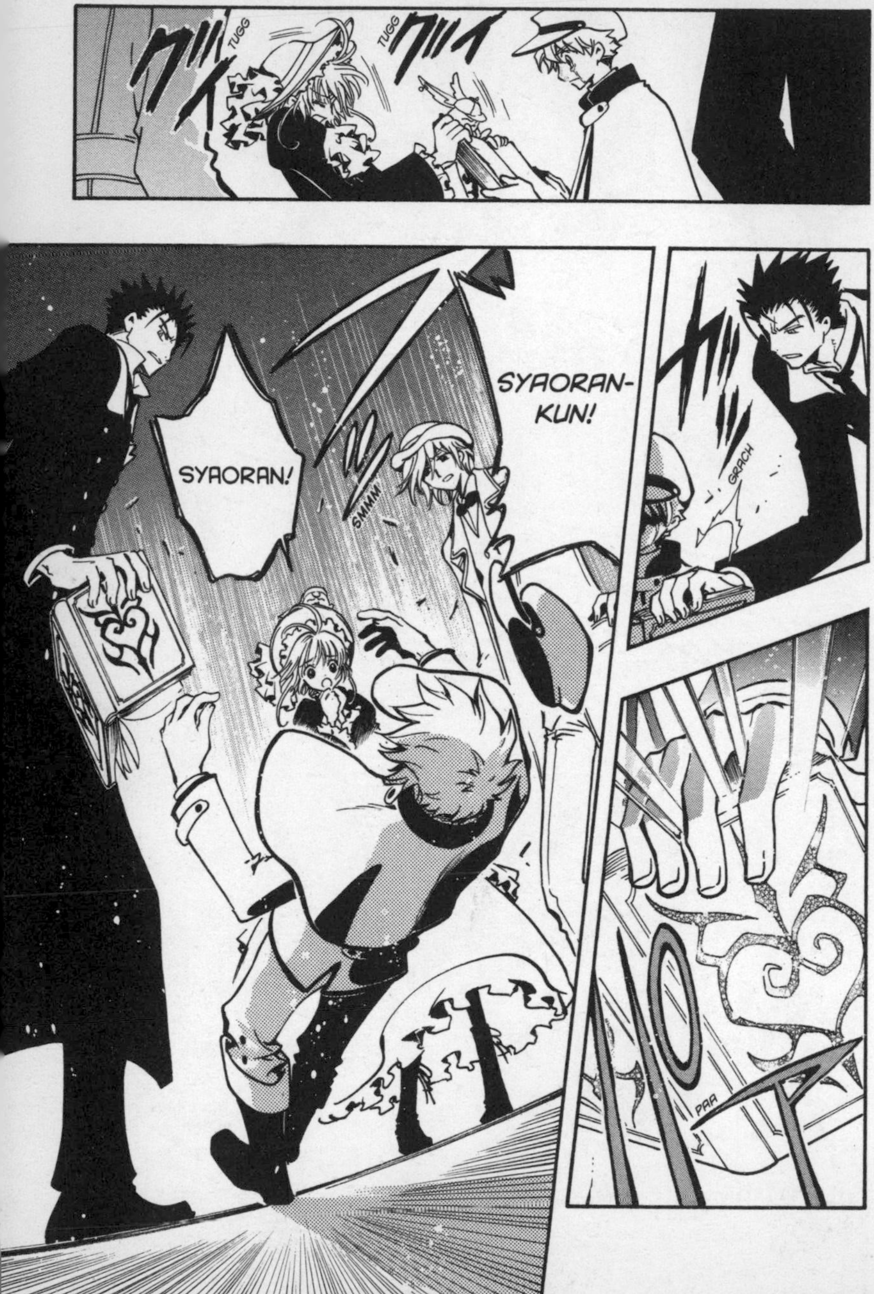

TUGG
TUGG
GRACH
PAA
SYAORAN-KUN!
SYAORAN!
SMMM

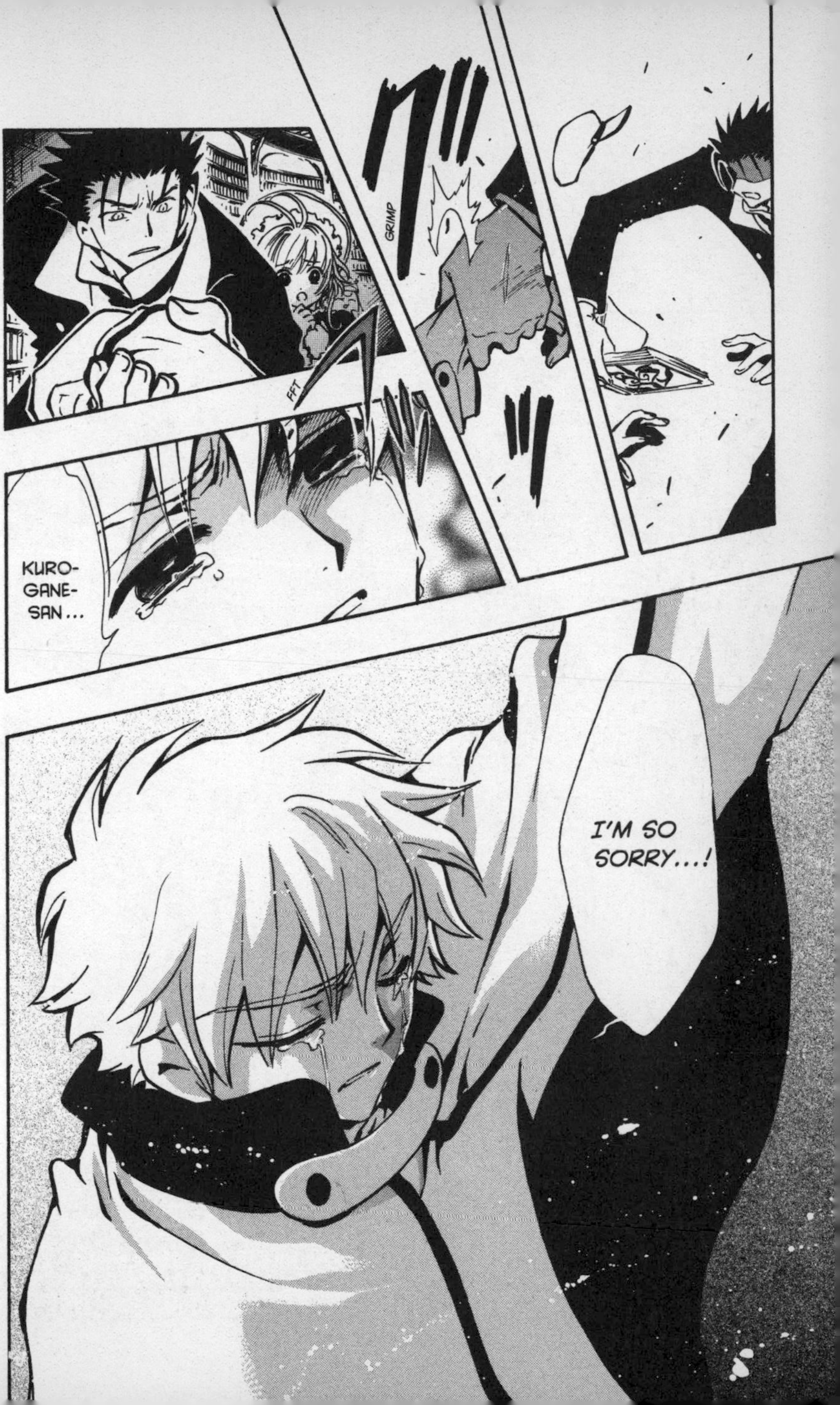
GRIMP
FFT
KURO-GANE-SAN...
I'M SO SORRY...!

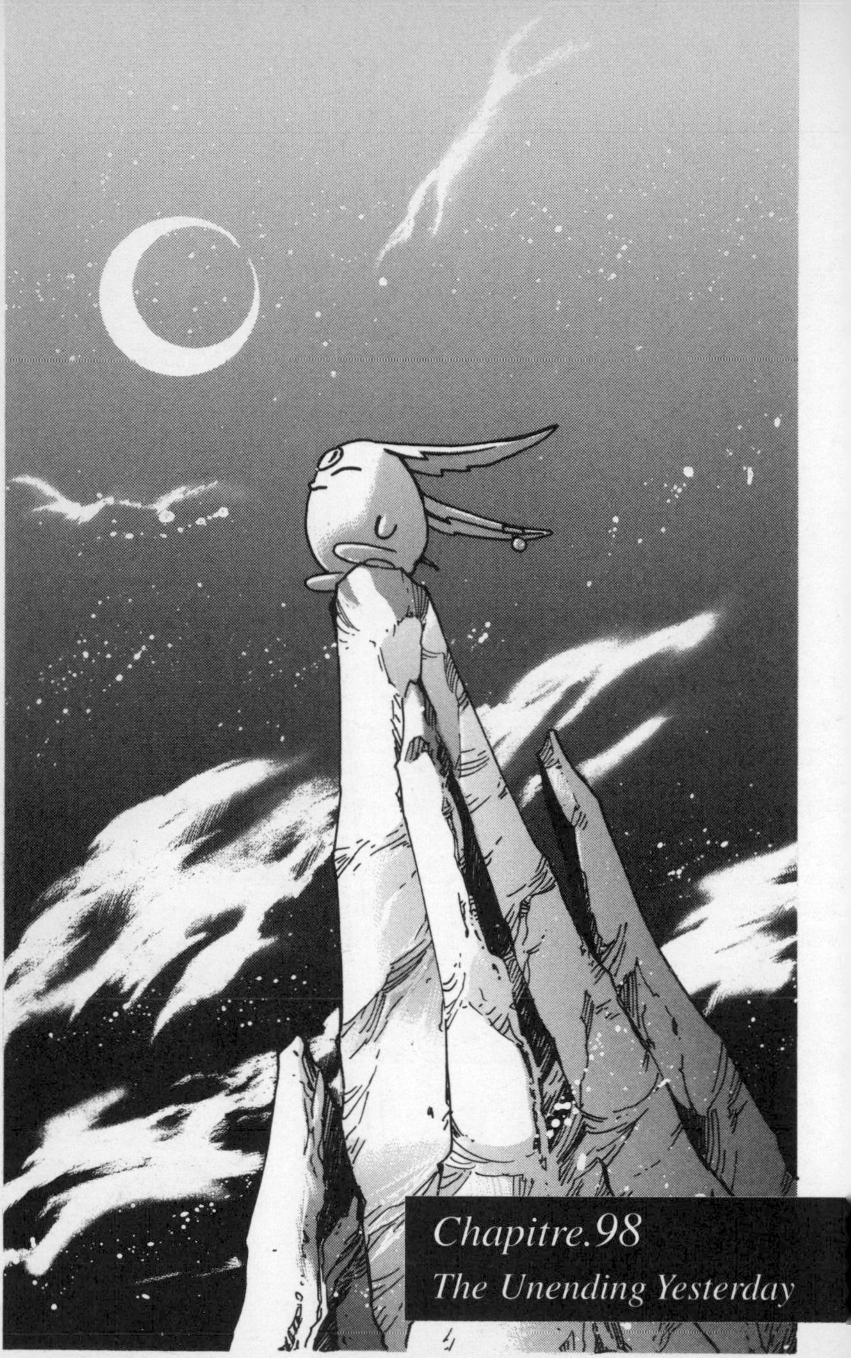
Chapitre.98
The Unending Yesterday

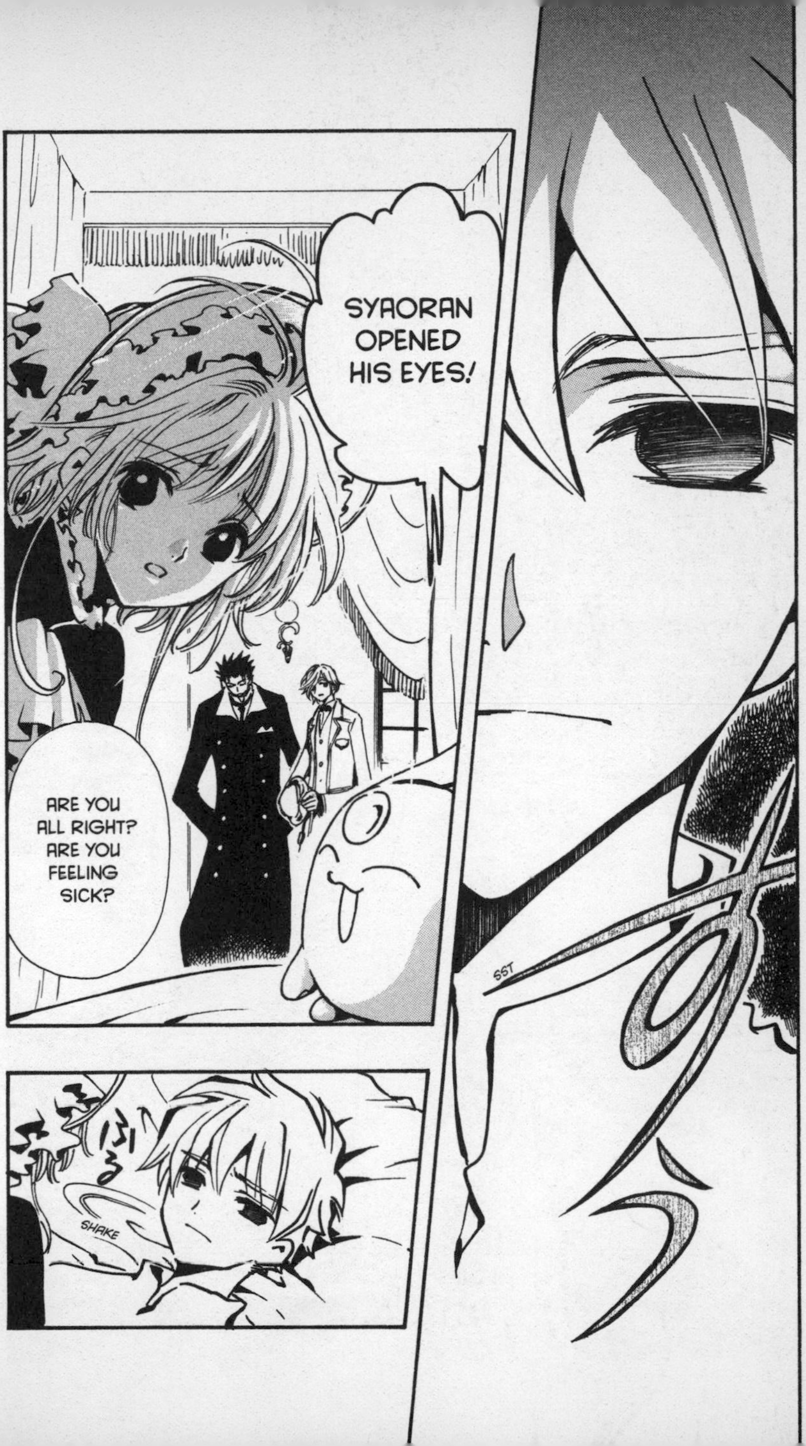
SST
SYAORAN OPENED HIS EYES!
ARE YOU ALL RIGHT? ARE YOU FEELING SICK?
SHAKE

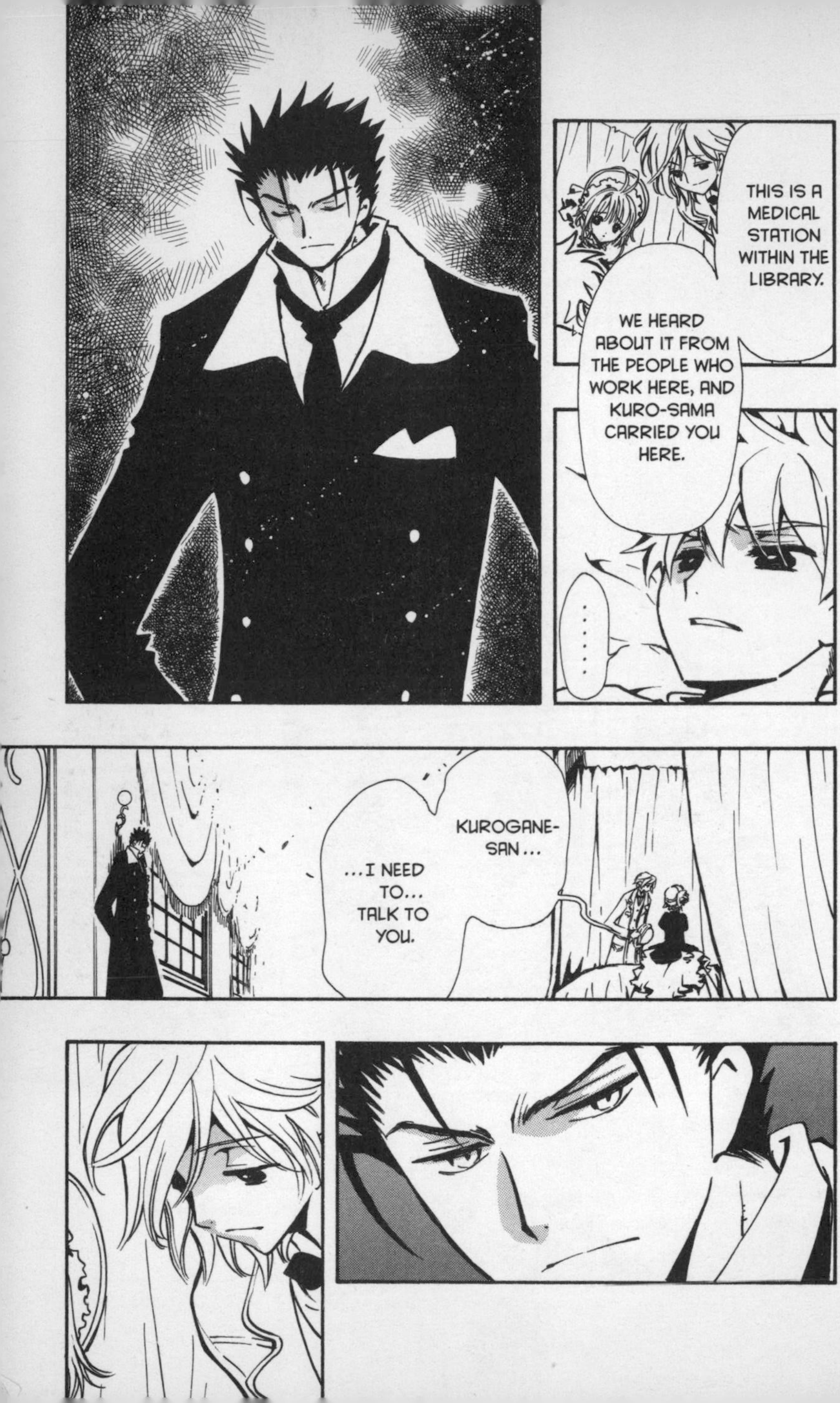
THIS IS A MEDICAL STATION WITHIN THE LIBRARY.
WE HEARD ABOUT IT FROM THE PEOPLE WHO WORK HERE, AND KURO-SAMA CARRIED YOU HERE.
......
KUROGANE-SAN...
...I NEED TO... TALK TO YOU.

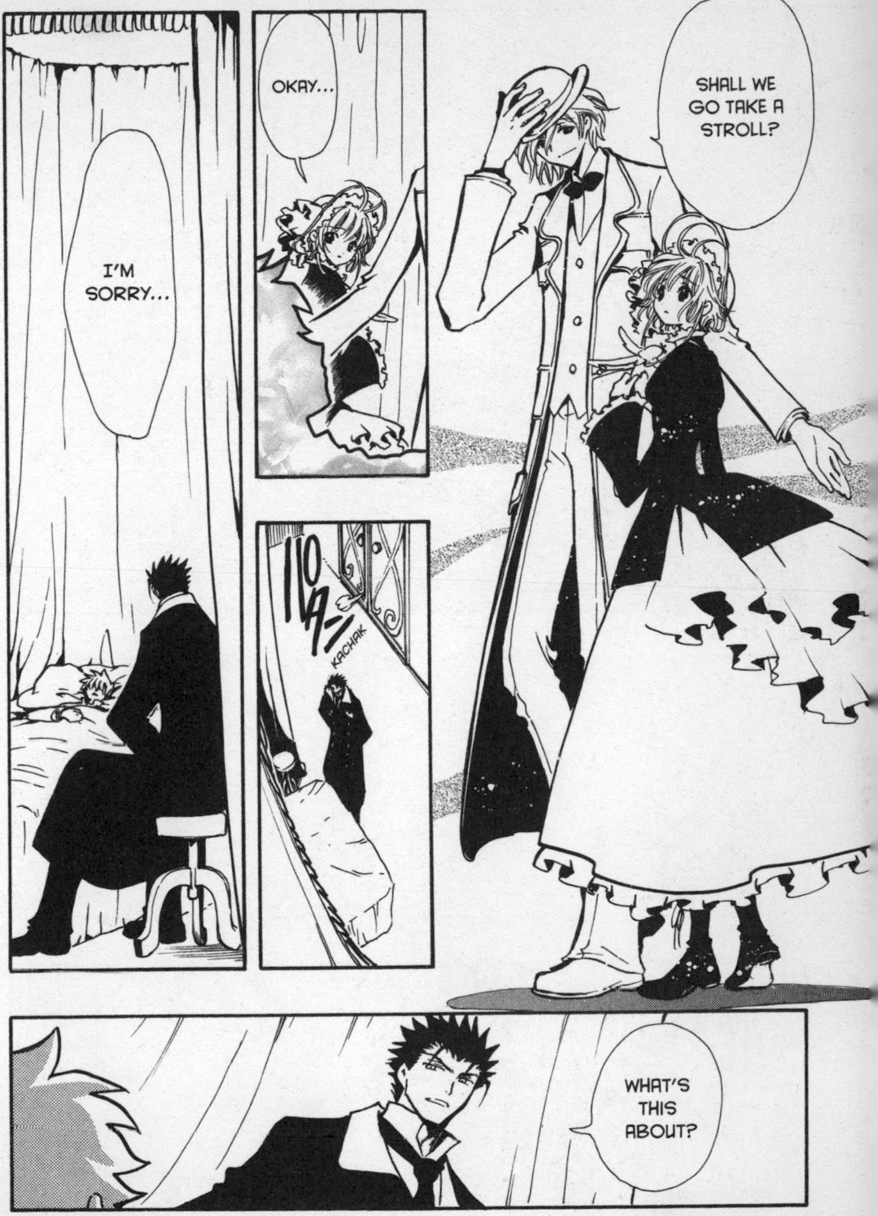
SHALL WE GO TAKE A STROLL?
OKAY...
KACHAK
I'M SORRY...
WHAT'S THIS ABOUT?

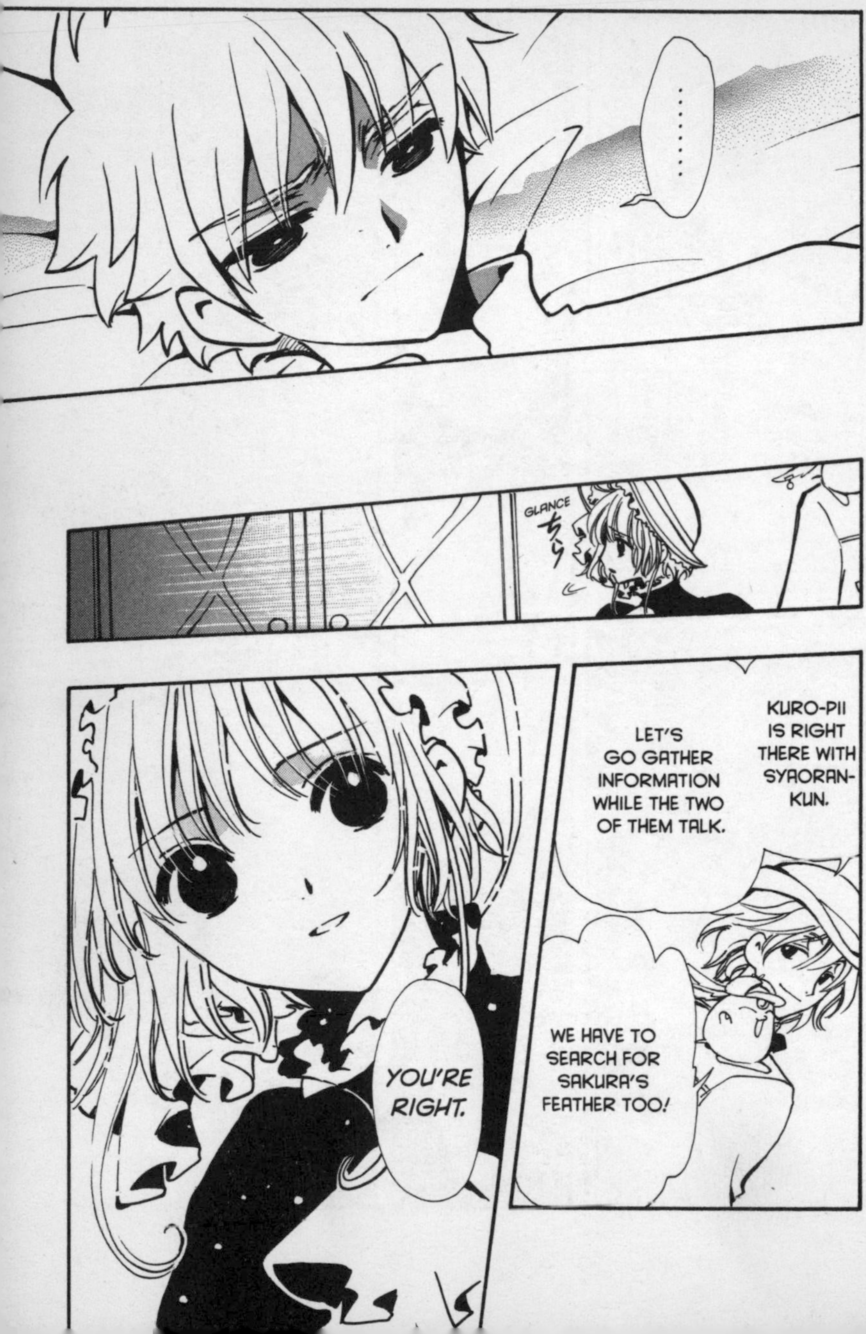
……
GLANCE
ちら
KURO-PII IS RIGHT THERE WITH SYAORAN-KUN.
LET'S GO GATHER INFORMATION WHILE THE TWO OF THEM TALK.
WE HAVE TO SEARCH FOR SAKURA'S FEATHER TOO!
YOU'RE RIGHT.

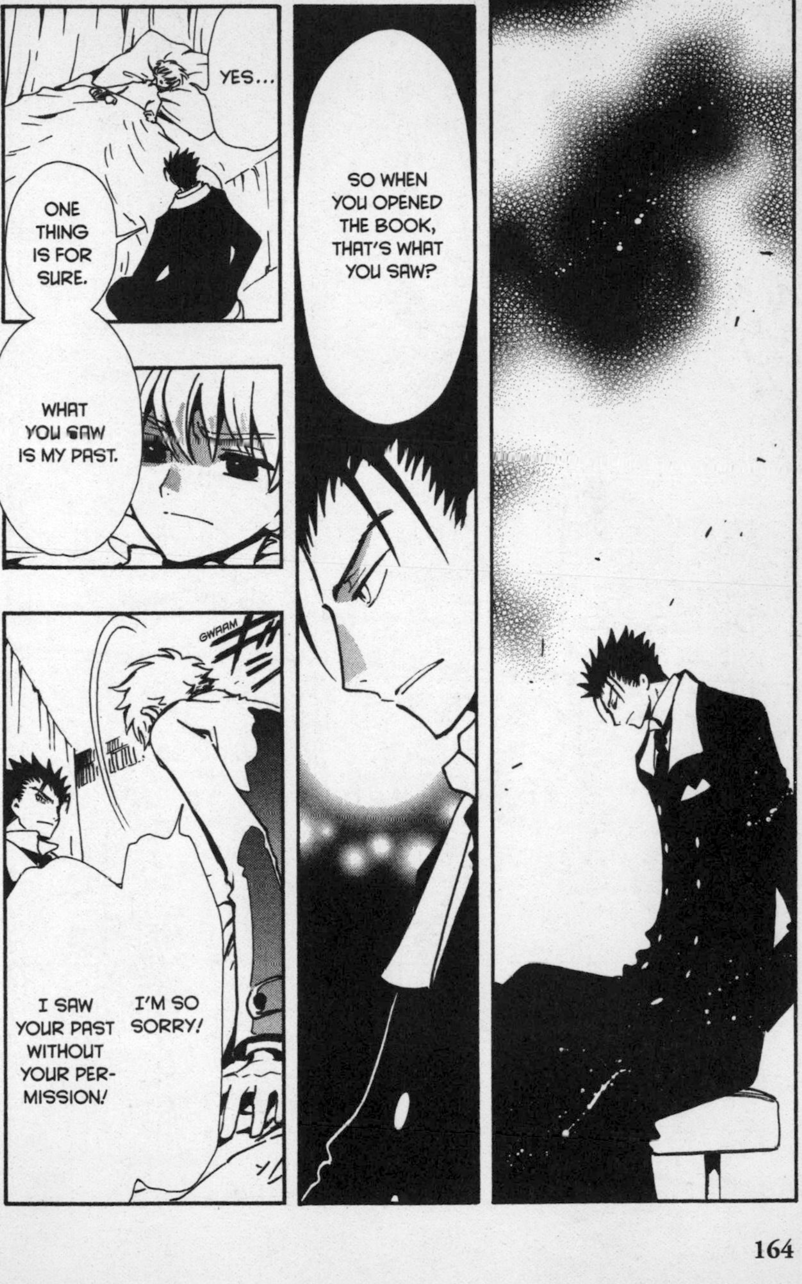
SO WHEN YOU OPENED THE BOOK, THAT'S WHAT YOU SAW?
YES...
ONE THING IS FOR SURE.
WHAT YOU SAW IS MY PAST.
GWAAM
I'M SO SORRY!
I SAW YOUR PAST WITHOUT YOUR PER-MISSION!

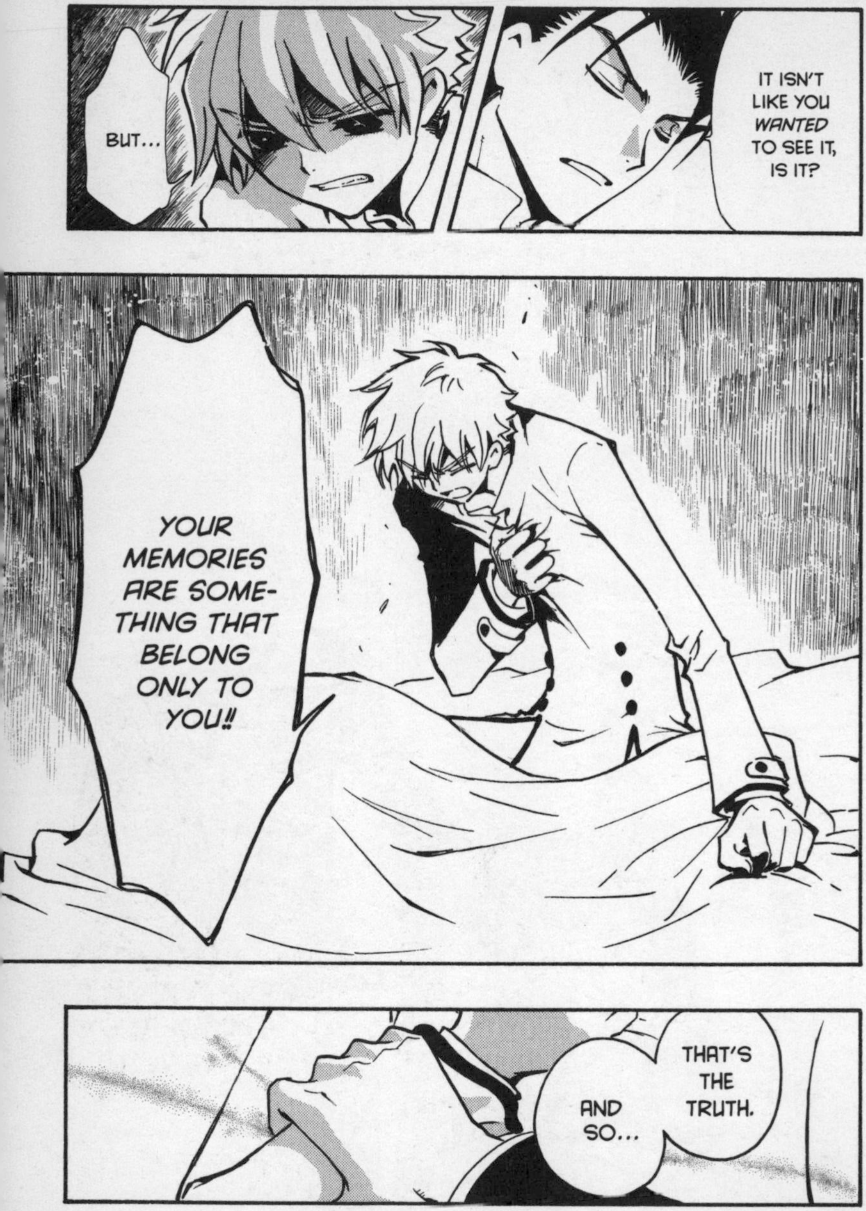
IT ISN'T LIKE YOU *WANTED* TO SEE IT, IS IT?
BUT...
YOUR MEMORIES ARE SOMETHING THAT BELONG ONLY TO YOU!!
THAT'S THE TRUTH.
AND SO...

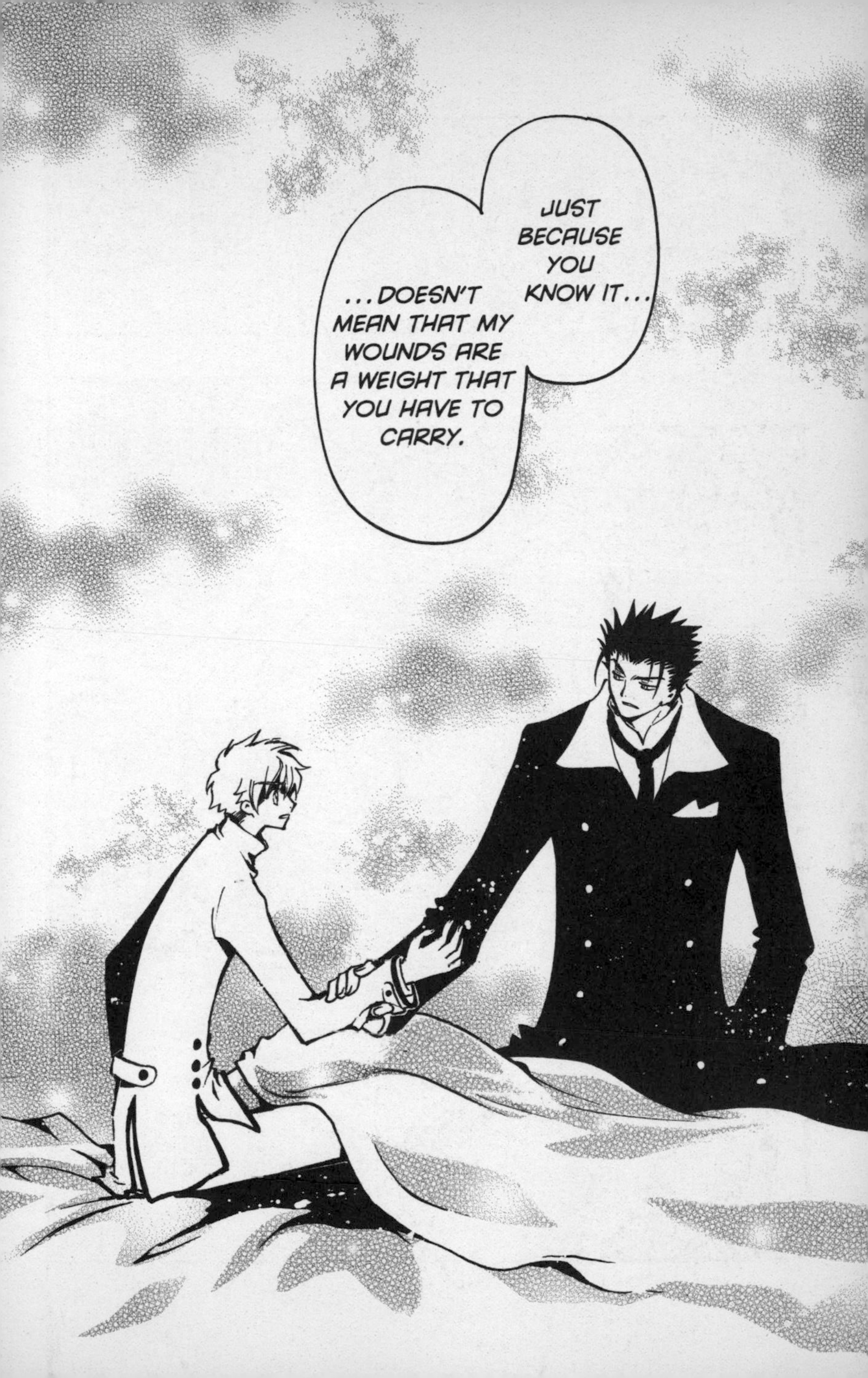
JUST BECAUSE YOU KNOW IT...
...DOESN'T MEAN THAT MY WOUNDS ARE A WEIGHT THAT YOU HAVE TO CARRY.

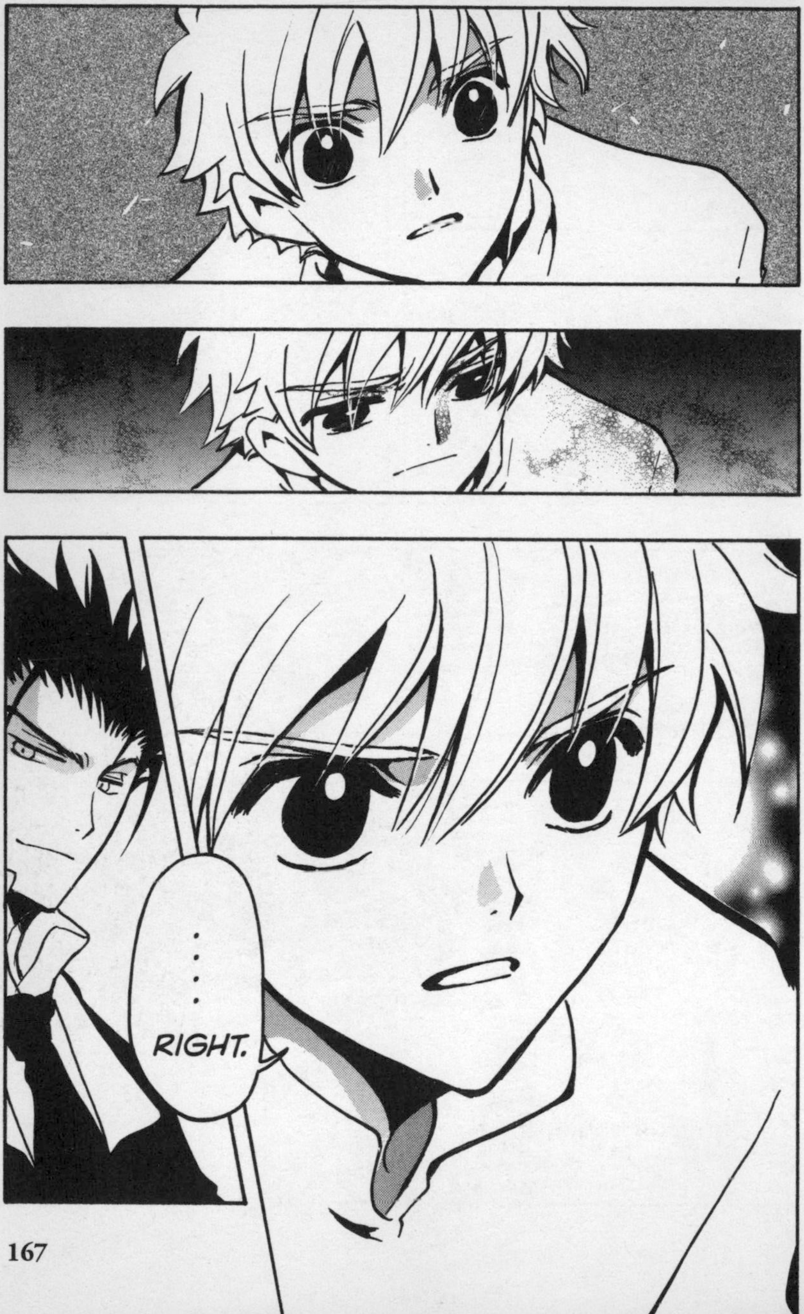

....
RIGHT.

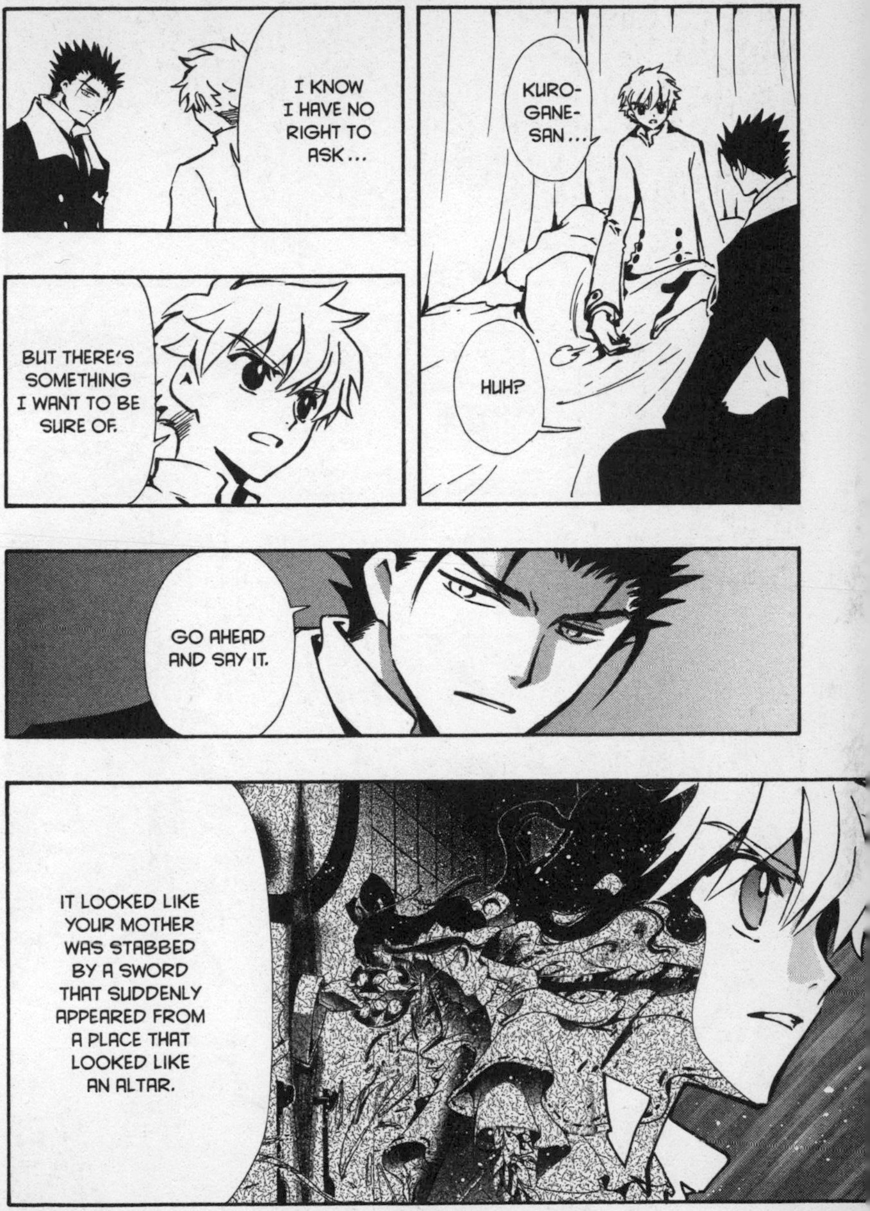
KURO-GANE-SAN...
HUH?
I KNOW I HAVE NO RIGHT TO ASK...
BUT THERE'S SOMETHING I WANT TO BE SURE OF.
GO AHEAD AND SAY IT.
IT LOOKED LIKE YOUR MOTHER WAS STABBED BY A SWORD THAT SUDDENLY APPEARED FROM A PLACE THAT LOOKED LIKE AN ALTAR.

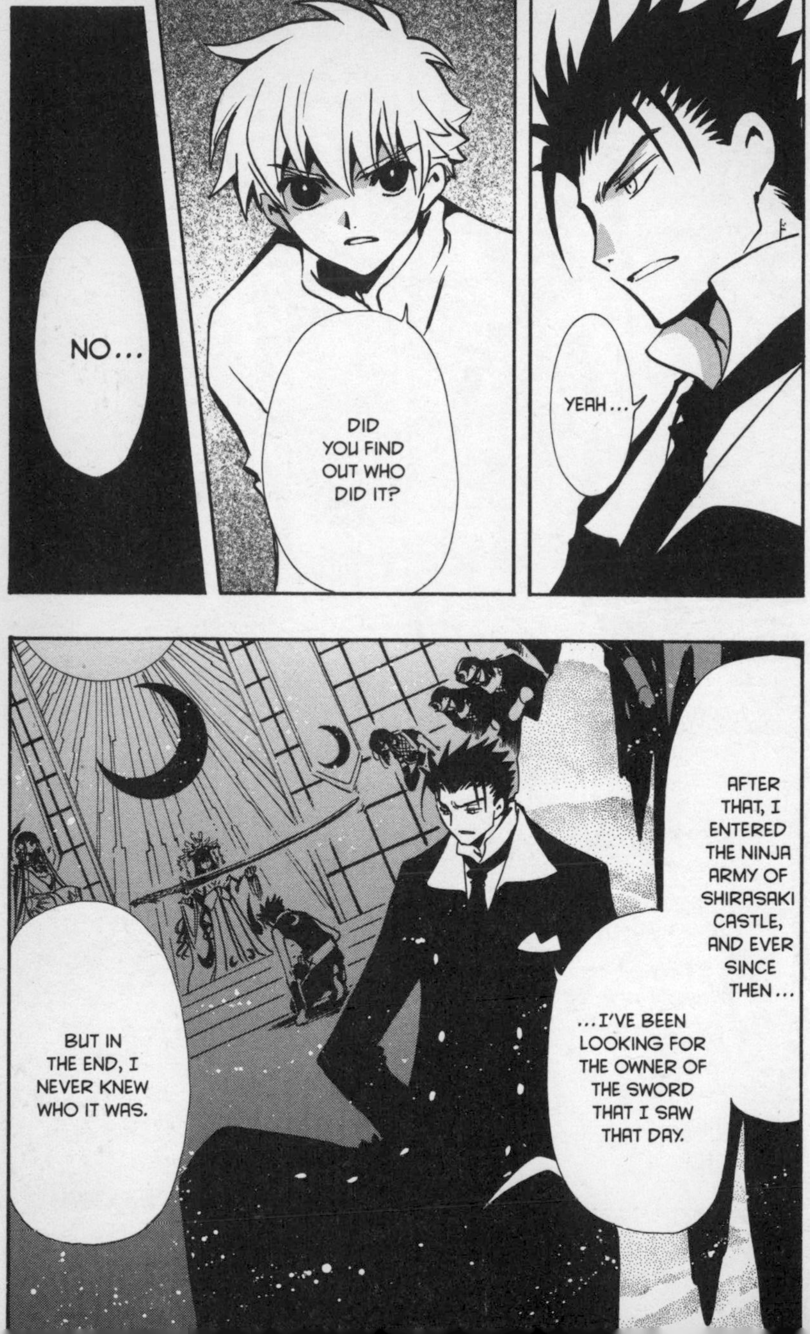
YEAH...
DID YOU FIND OUT WHO DID IT?
NO...
AFTER THAT, I ENTERED THE NINJA ARMY OF SHIRASAKI CASTLE, AND EVER SINCE THEN...
...I'VE BEEN LOOKING FOR THE OWNER OF THE SWORD THAT I SAW THAT DAY.
BUT IN THE END, I NEVER KNEW WHO IT WAS.

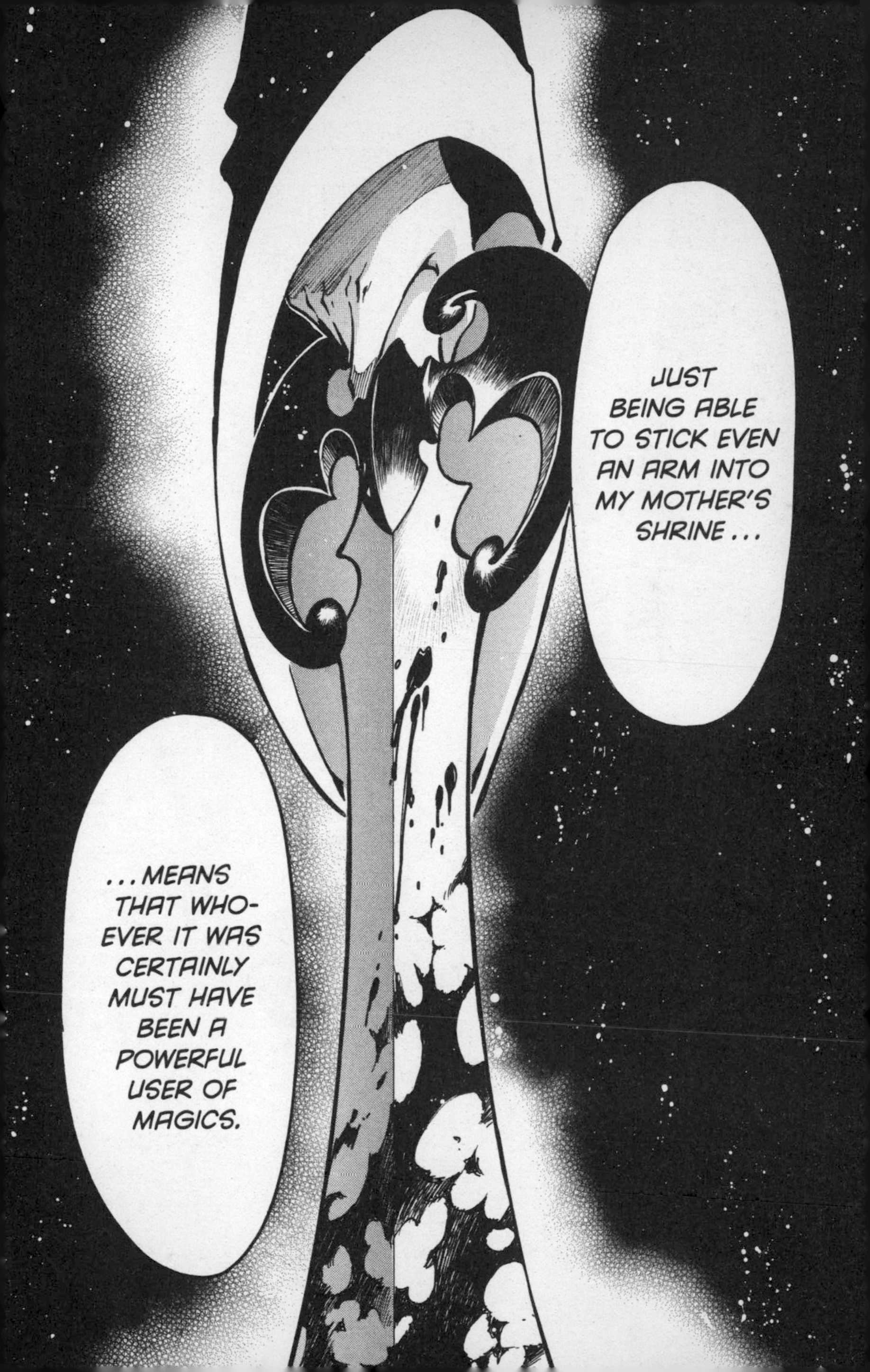
JUST BEING ABLE TO STICK EVEN AN ARM INTO MY MOTHER'S SHRINE . . .
. . . MEANS THAT WHO-EVER IT WAS CERTAINLY MUST HAVE BEEN A POWERFUL USER OF MAGICS.

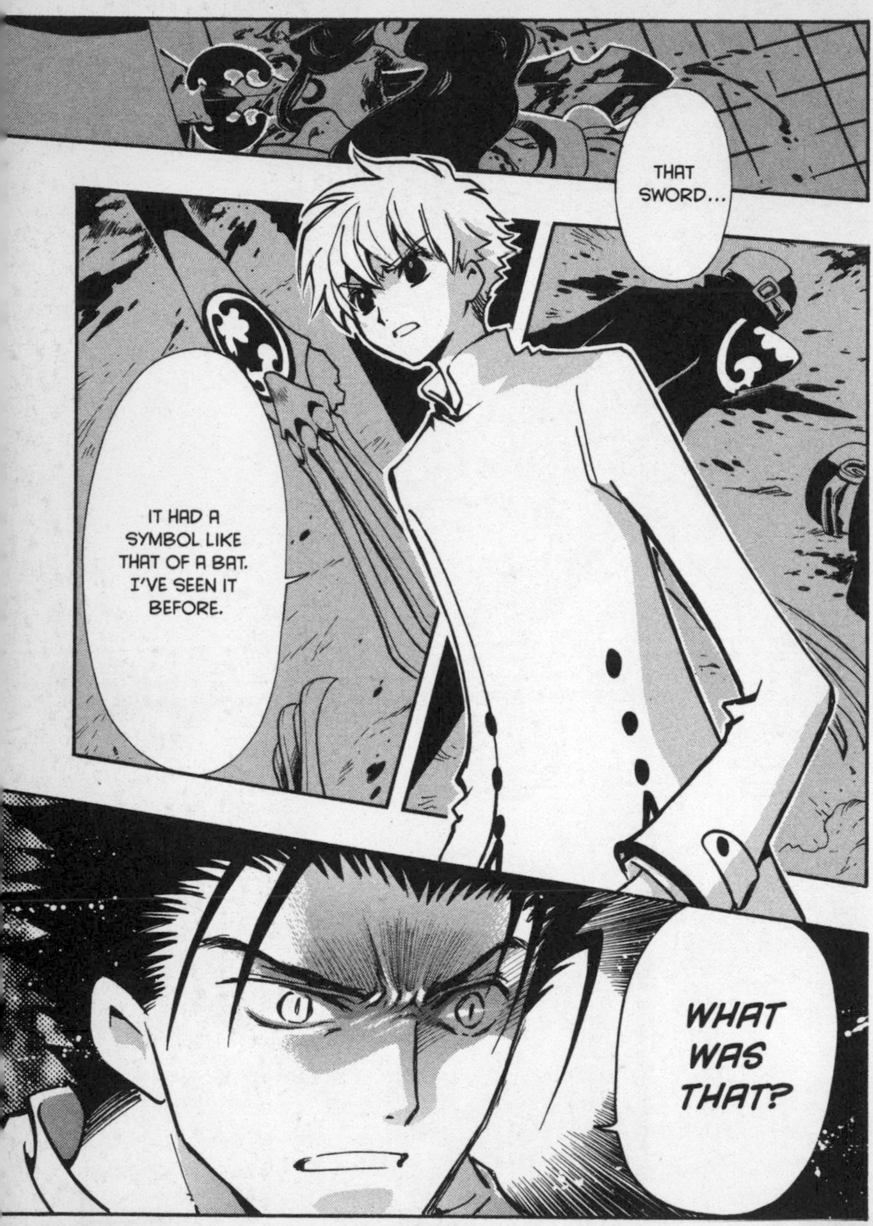
THAT SWORD...
IT HAD A SYMBOL LIKE THAT OF A BAT. I'VE SEEN IT BEFORE.
WHAT WAS THAT?

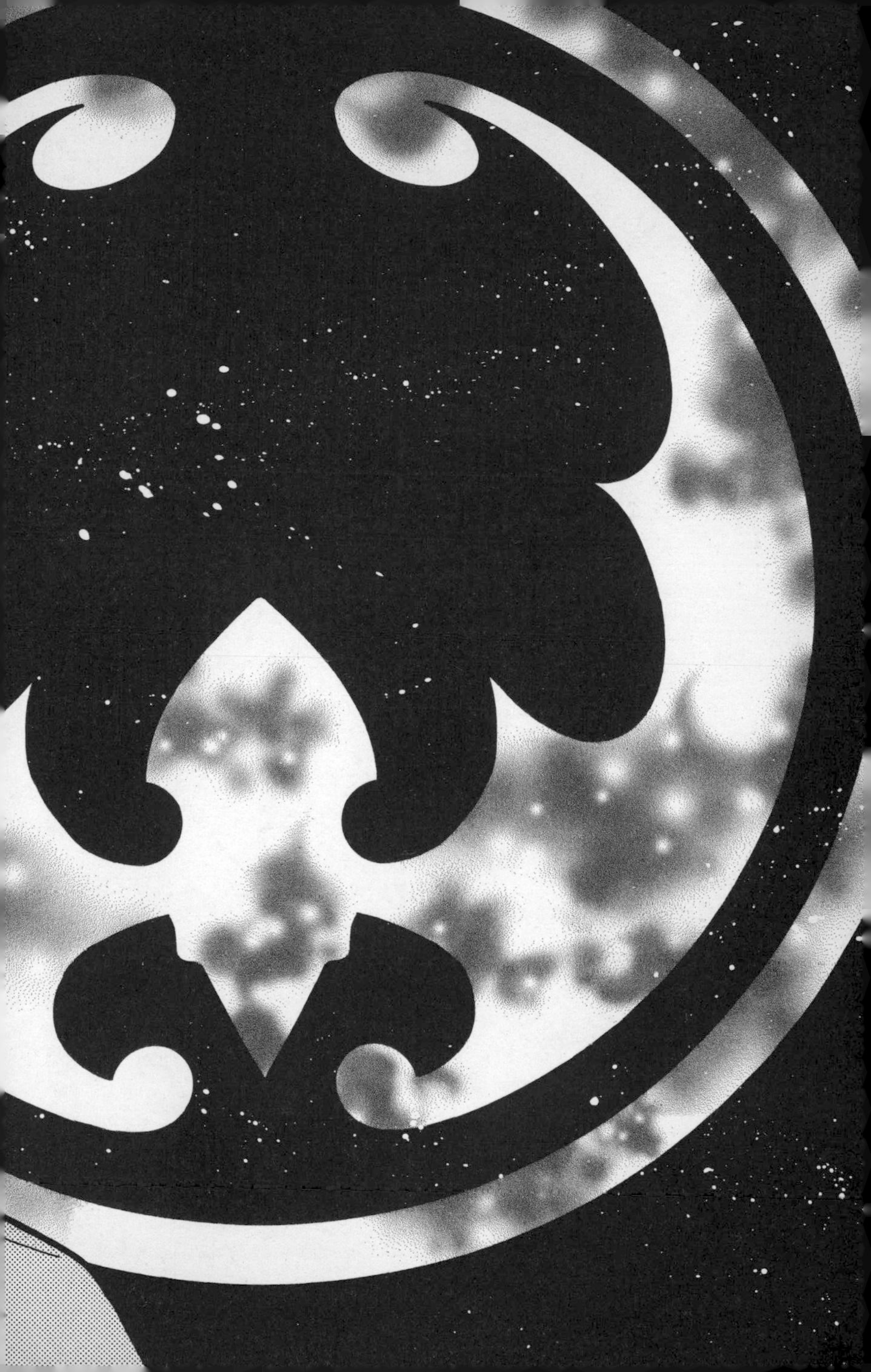

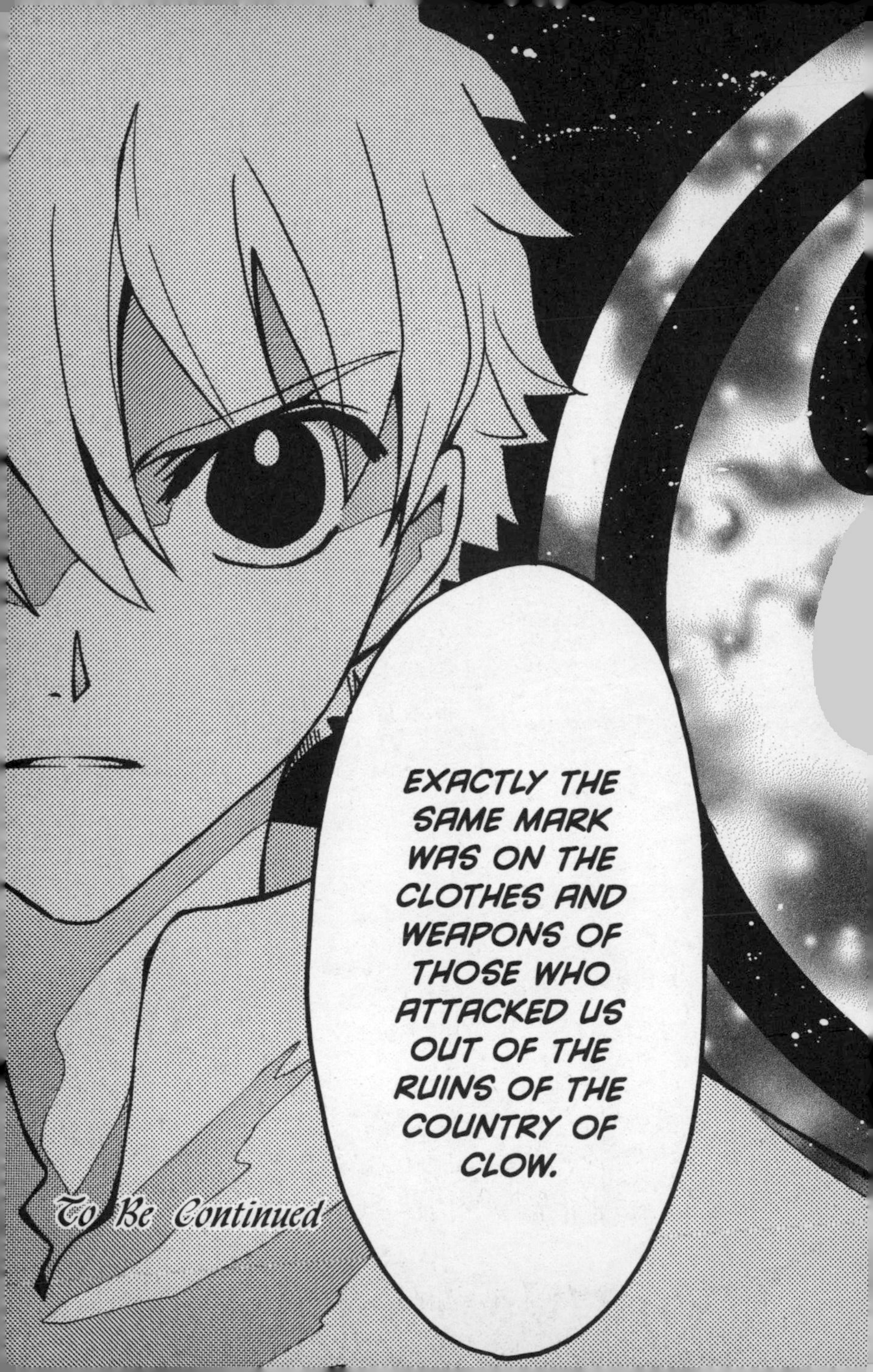
EXACTLY THE SAME MARK WAS ON THE CLOTHES AND WEAPONS OF THOSE WHO ATTACKED US OUT OF THE RUINS OF THE COUNTRY OF CLOW.
To Be Continued

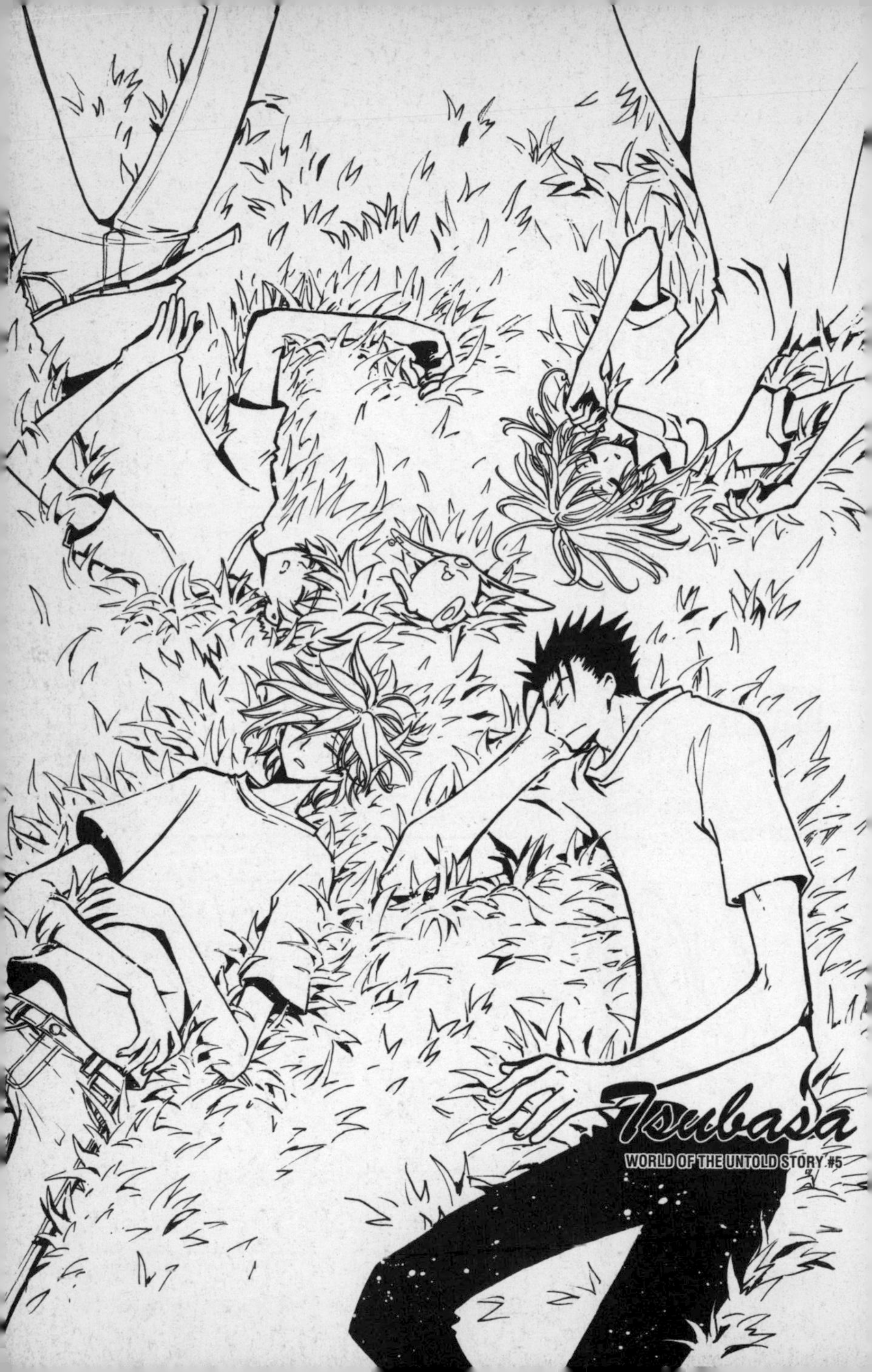
Tsubasa
WORLD OF THE UNTOLD STORY #5

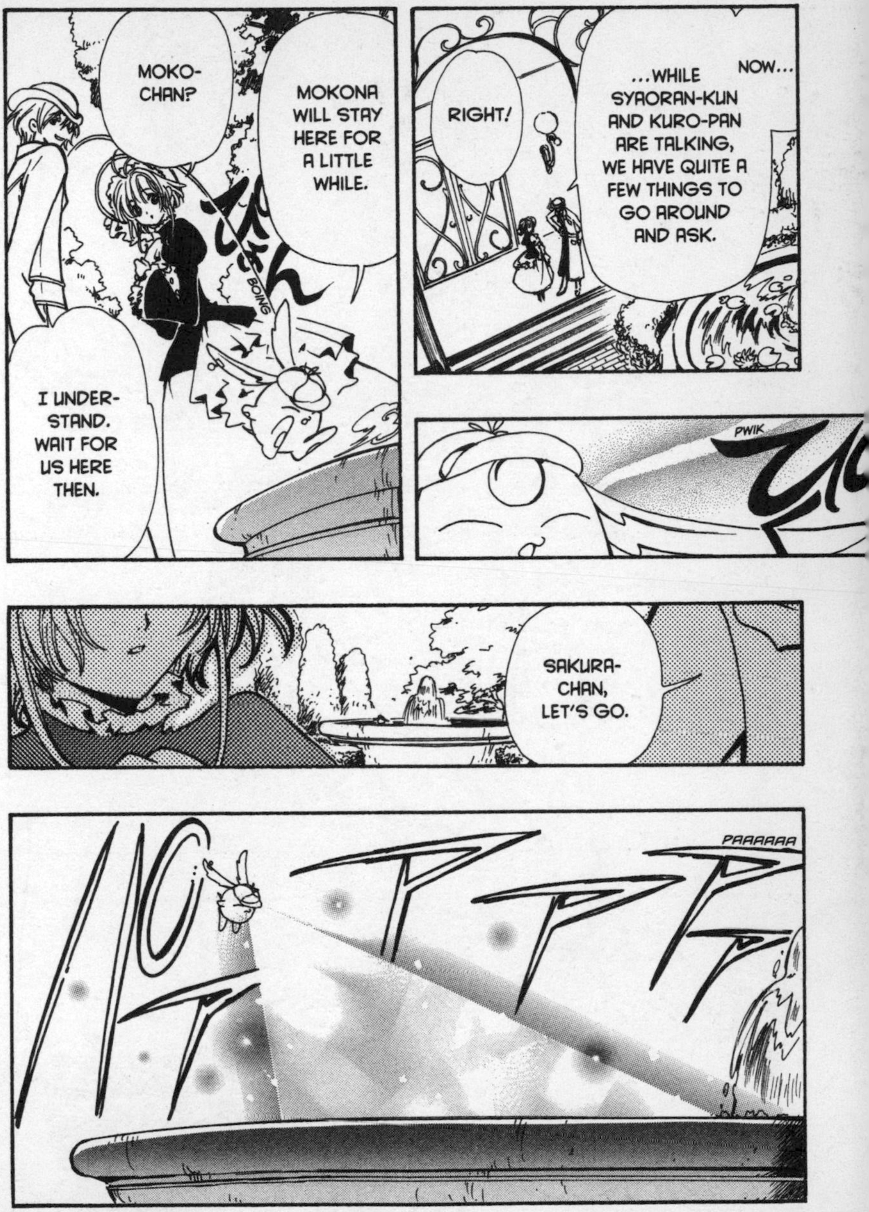
NOW...
...WHILE SYAORAN-KUN AND KURO-PAN ARE TALKING, WE HAVE QUITE A FEW THINGS TO GO AROUND AND ASK.
RIGHT!
PWIK
MOKONA WILL STAY HERE FOR A LITTLE WHILE.
MOKO-CHAN?
BOING
I UNDER-STAND. WAIT FOR US HERE THEN.
SAKURA-CHAN, LET'S GO.
PAAAAAA

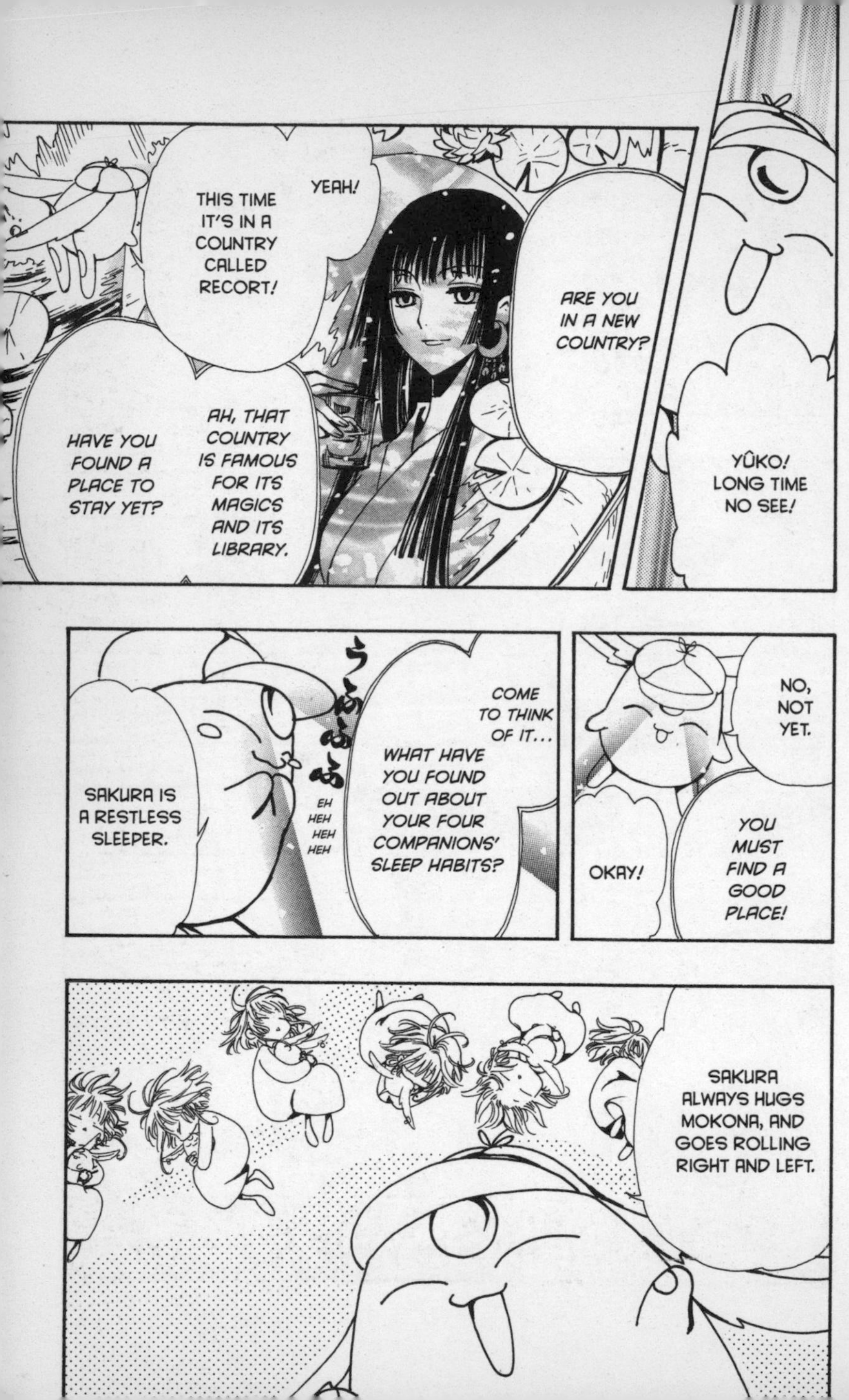
YÛKO! LONG TIME NO SEE!
ARE YOU IN A NEW COUNTRY?
YEAH!
THIS TIME IT'S IN A COUNTRY CALLED RECORT!
AH, THAT COUNTRY IS FAMOUS FOR ITS MAGICS AND ITS LIBRARY.
HAVE YOU FOUND A PLACE TO STAY YET?
NO, NOT YET.
YOU MUST FIND A GOOD PLACE!
OKAY!
COME TO THINK OF IT...
WHAT HAVE YOU FOUND OUT ABOUT YOUR FOUR COMPANIONS' SLEEP HABITS?
うふふふ
EH HEH HEH HEH
SAKURA IS A RESTLESS SLEEPER.
SAKURA ALWAYS HUGS MOKONA, AND GOES ROLLING RIGHT AND LEFT.

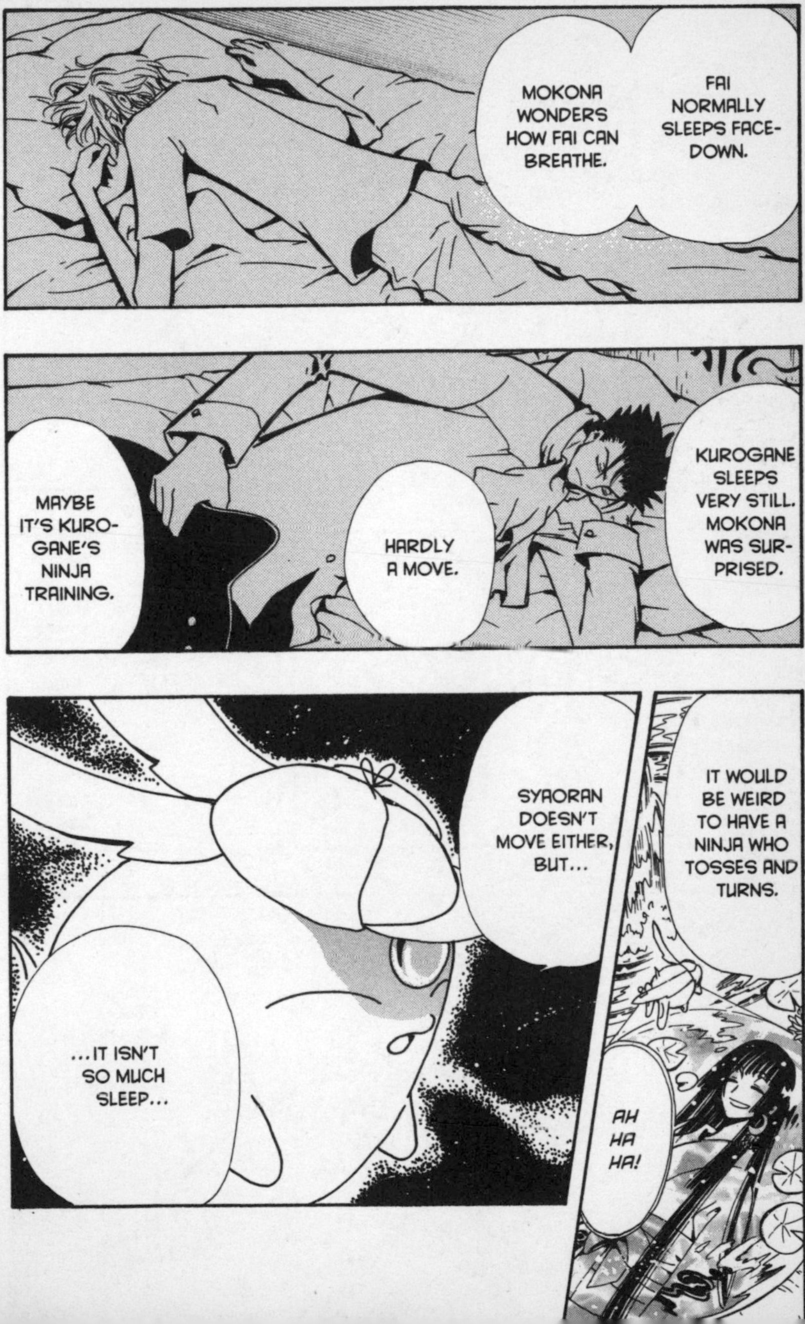
FAI NORMALLY SLEEPS FACE-DOWN.
MOKONA WONDERS HOW FAI CAN BREATHE.
KUROGANE SLEEPS VERY STILL. MOKONA WAS SURPRISED.
HARDLY A MOVE.
MAYBE IT'S KURO-GANE'S NINJA TRAINING.
IT WOULD BE WEIRD TO HAVE A NINJA WHO TOSSES AND TURNS.
AH HA HA!
SYAORAN DOESN'T MOVE EITHER, BUT...
...IT ISN'T SO MUCH SLEEP...

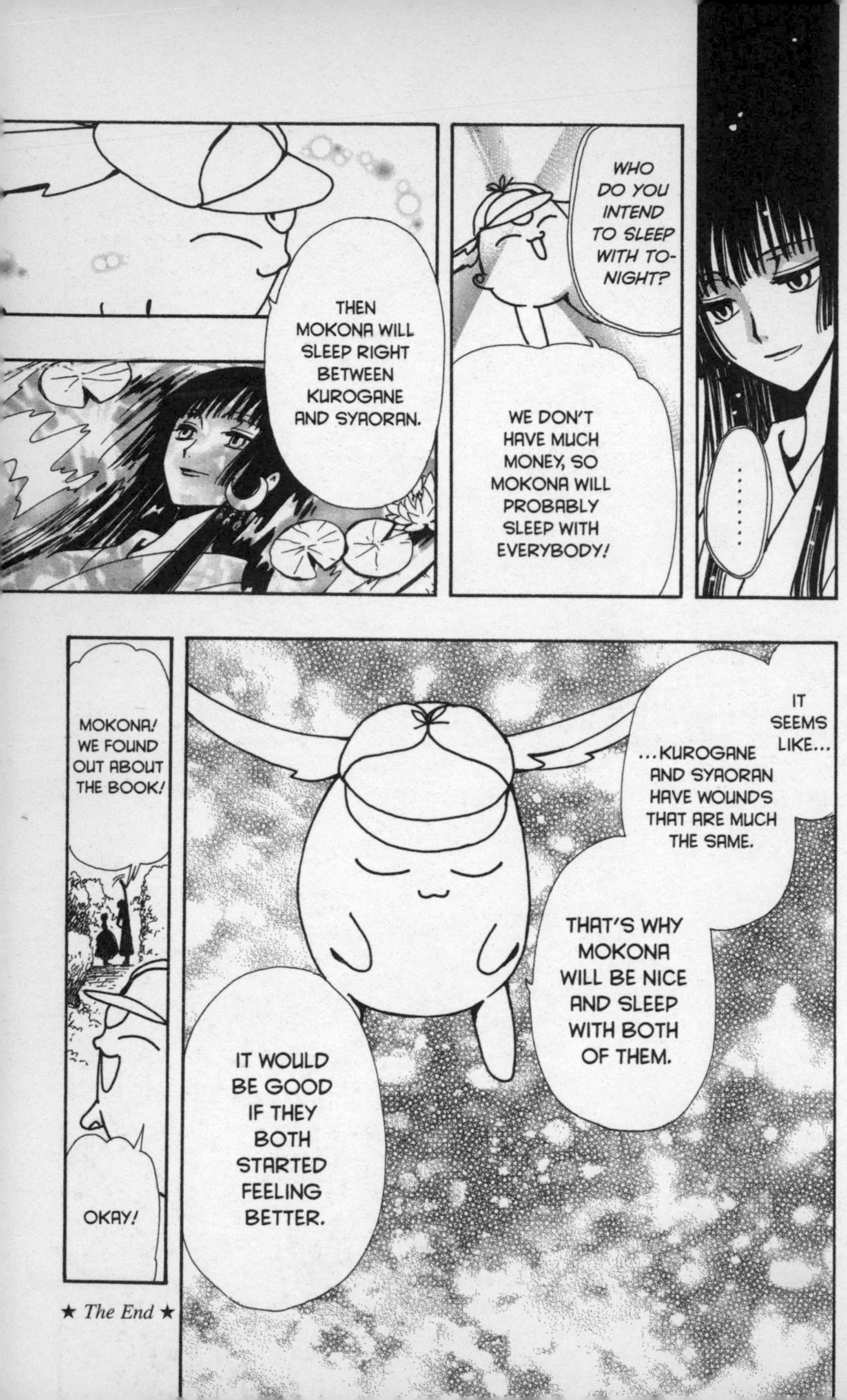
......
WHO DO YOU INTEND TO SLEEP WITH TO-NIGHT?
WE DON'T HAVE MUCH MONEY, SO MOKONA WILL PROBABLY SLEEP WITH EVERYBODY!
THEN MOKONA WILL SLEEP RIGHT BETWEEN KUROGANE AND SYAORAN.
IT SEEMS LIKE...
...KUROGANE AND SYAORAN HAVE WOUNDS THAT ARE MUCH THE SAME.
THAT'S WHY MOKONA WILL BE NICE AND SLEEP WITH BOTH OF THEM.
IT WOULD BE GOOD IF THEY BOTH STARTED FEELING BETTER.
MOKONA! WE FOUND OUT ABOUT THE BOOK!
OKAY!

★ *The End* ★

About the Creators

CLAMP is a group of four women who have become the most popular manga artists in America—Ageha Ohkawa, Mokona, Satsuki Igarashi, and Tsubaki Nekoi. They started out as *doujinshi* (fan comics) creators, but their skill and craft brought them to the attention of publishers very quickly. Their first work from a major publisher was *RG Veda*, but their first mass success was with *Magic Knight Rayearth*. From there, they went on to write many series, including Cardcaptor Sakura and Chobits, two of the most popular manga in the United States. Like many Japanese manga artists, they prefer to avoid the spotlight, and little is known about them personally.

CLAMP is currently publishing three series in Japan: Tsubasa and xxxHOLiC with Kodansha and Gohou Drug with Kadokawa.

Translation Notes

Japanese is a tricky language for most Westerners, and translation is often more art than science. For your edification and reading pleasure, here are notes on some of the places where we could have gone in a different direction in our translation of the work, or where a Japanese cultural reference is used.

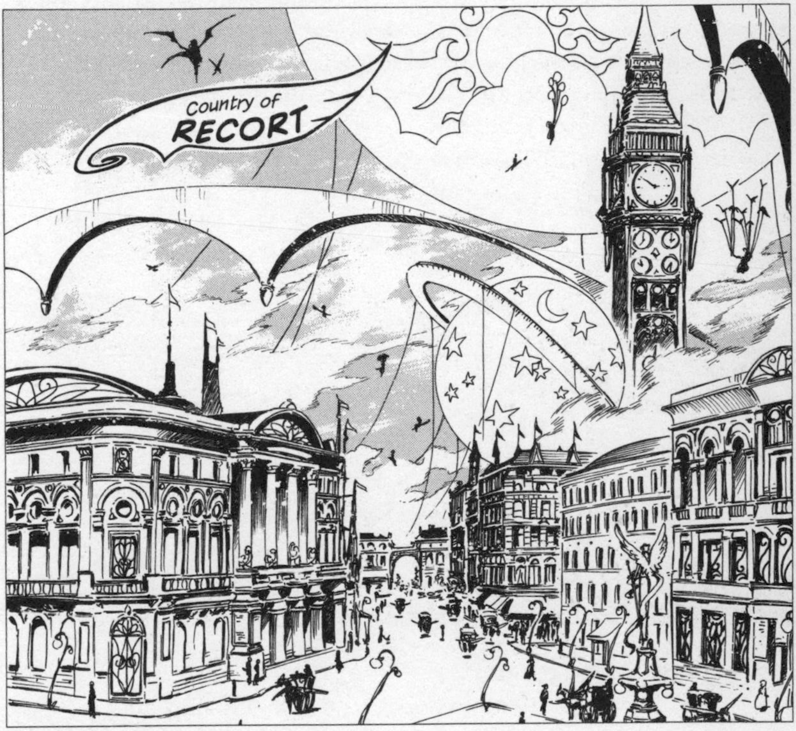
Country of
RECORT

Recort, page 15

Until we receive official Roman alphabet (our alphabet) spellings, the best I can do as a translator is try to figure out what CLAMP was shooting for when there is a name given in *katakana* (the

Japanese syllabary usually used for foreign words). In this case, CLAMP seems to be basing the world on a magical version of Europe during the Victorian or Edwardian eras. The safe route is to simply transliterate the letters into roman letters, which would give us Rekoruto, but that doesn't seem to match the setting. An alternate spelling of LeCourt certainly captures the European setting, but considering the story line, a variation of the word "record" seems to be what CLAMP was aiming for (without making it obvious). I considered Recourt, but Recort seems to match the world well enough, and it's very close to the word "record." In any case, both you the reader and I will wait anxiously until an official spelling is provided.

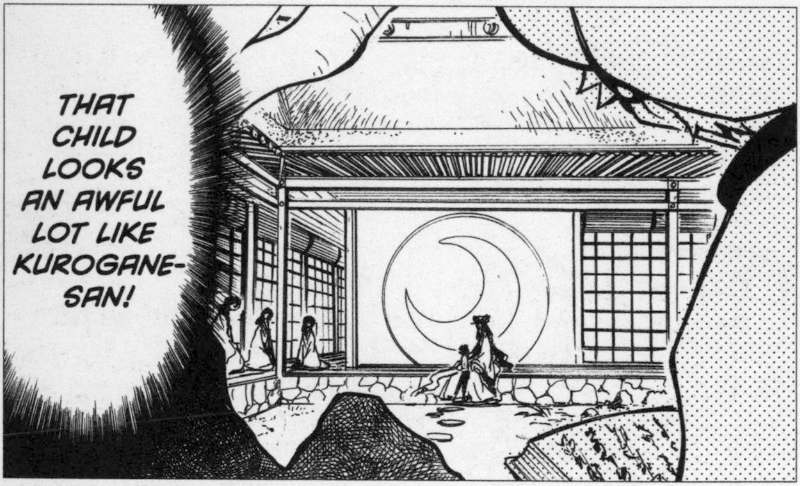
THAT CHILD LOOKS AN AWFUL LOT LIKE KUROGANE-SAN!

Aristocracy, page 30

The young family that Syaoran sees is the image that the Japanese hold for aristocracy during the *Sengoku* (warring states) period. This period started in the late 1400s and continued until the early 1600s when Ieyasu Tokugawa united the country under his shogunate, which is considered the beginning of the Edo period. Although there was both an emperor and shogun during the *Sengoku* period, the

central government was weak, and the provinces were mainly left to fend for themselves. Therefore it was a time where most of the feudal lords were laws unto themselves, and conflicts between provinces were common.

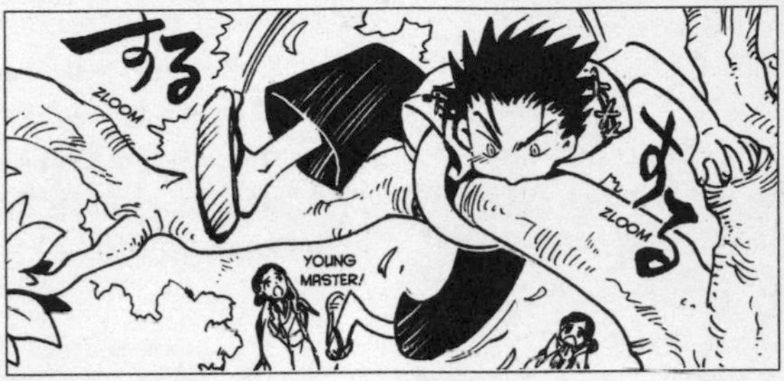
する
ZLOOM
YOUNG MASTER!
する
ZLOOM

Young Master, page 37

The heir to a still-living lord was normally called *Waka* in Japanese by all those serving the lord (military, domestic servants, peasants, etc.). The word *Waka* simply means "young," and it distinguishes between the reigning lord and the heir.

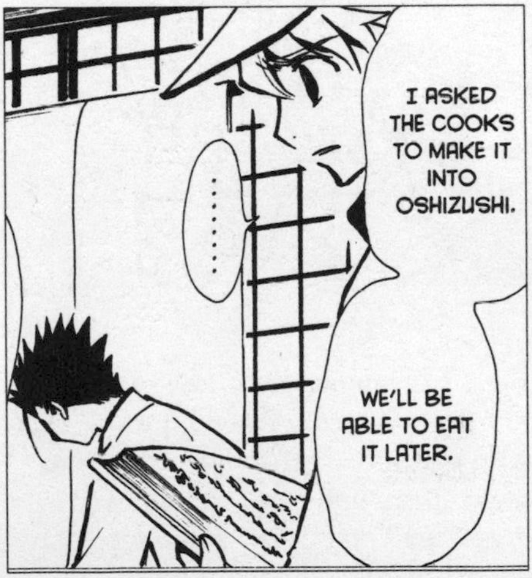
I ASKED THE COOKS TO MAKE IT INTO OSHIZUSHI.
WE'LL BE ABLE TO EAT IT LATER.
......

***Oshizushi*, page 66**

Pressed sushi. Toppings such as fish, vegetables, or other delicacies are placed into a rectangular wooden box, then it is covered with rice and pressed with a wooden board to form a long, rectangular sushi cake. The cake is then cut into bite-sized squares for eating.

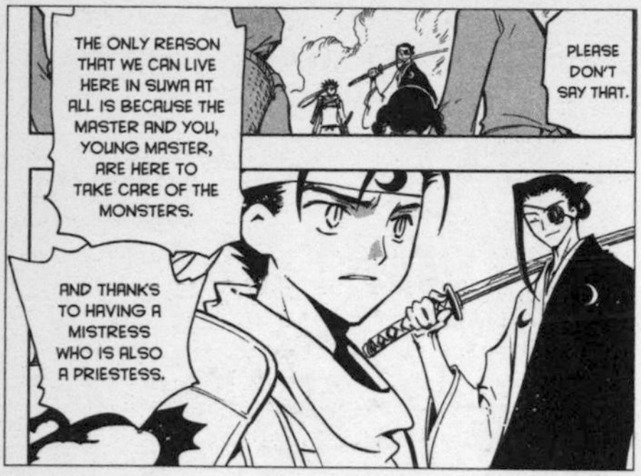
PLEASE DON'T SAY THAT.
THE ONLY REASON THAT WE CAN LIVE HERE IN SUWA AT ALL IS BECAUSE THE MASTER AND YOU, YOUNG MASTER, ARE HERE TO TAKE CARE OF THE MONSTERS.
AND THANKS TO HAVING A MISTRESS WHO IS ALSO A PRIESTESS.

Enthusiastic peasants, page 78

It may sound a little odd for the peasants to be enthusiastic about their lot in their feudal life, but this could also be a part of the autocratic nature of Japanese provincial life during the *Sengoku* period. A bad lord could slaughter the peasants at will, so it paid to be enthusiastic, and a good, just lord was a rare thing and could actually engender some real enthusiasm.

Gentle chiding, page 87

Everyone, even the lord's wife, is considered subservient to the provincial lord. Although some wives in feudal Japan were able to claim the power in their relationships, generally the wife had to work within the same constraints as the lord's military commanders. Everyone had to disagree with the lord very carefully. So, as the dutiful wife, the priestess in this situation cannot show anger at the lord especially in front of his other subjects, so the only way to let him know that she disapproves of his failure to call for her is gentle chiding.

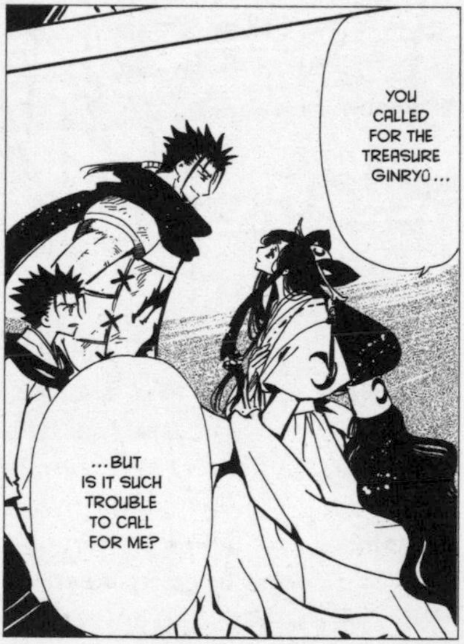
YOU CALLED FOR THE TREASURE GINRYŪ...
...BUT IS IT SUCH TROUBLE TO CALL FOR ME?

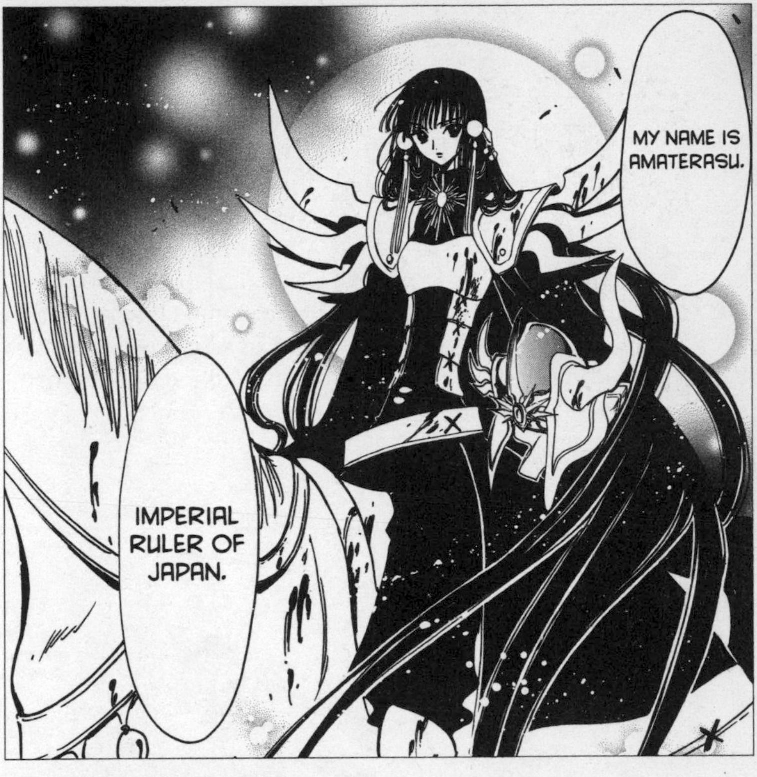
MY NAME IS AMATERASU.
IMPERIAL RULER OF JAPAN.

Amaterasu, page 119

Amaterasu is the name of one of the sun goddesses in Japanese mythology. Prior to 1945, she was considered the ultimate ancestor of the Japanese imperial line. The emperors were thought to be descended in a direct line from her and considered *kami* (gods) themselves. Following World War II in 1945, the imperial line renounced this belief. Kurogane's Country of Japan differs from the *Sengoku* period in many ways. In our world, the monsters didn't exist (we assume), the emperors were male, and for most of history, the emperors had no real political power themselves. Amaterasu, as a female emperor with real political power, would have been inconceivable in the real Japan.

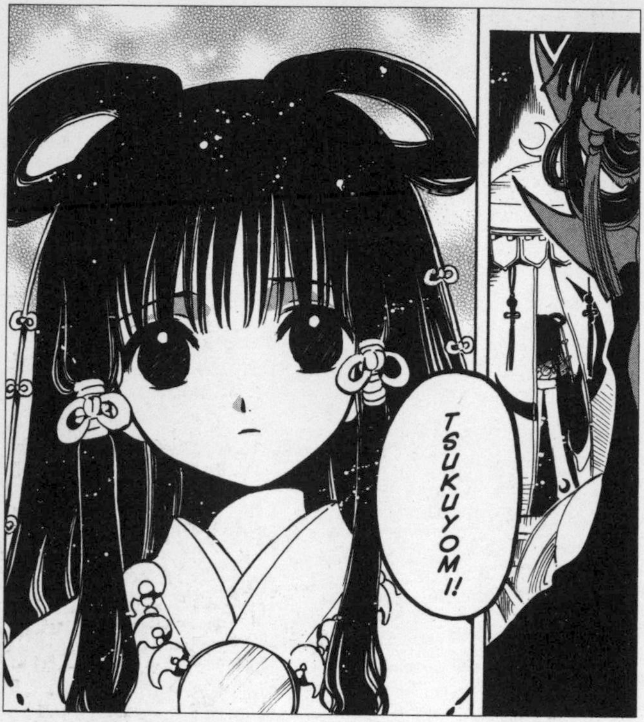
TSUKUYOMI!!

Tsukuyomi, page 134

Although Japanese mythology disagrees on how Amaterasu and Tsukiyomi were born, all myths agree that Izanagi, the male of the twin deities who created the world, was their father, and that Amaterasu is the older sister while Tsukiyomi is the younger brother. Amaterasu represents the sun and Tsukiyomi represents the moon (*tsuki* means "the moon"). In CLAMP's version, Tsukiyomi becomes Tsukuyomi, and for *yomi,* they use an alternate *kanji* that means "to read" rather than the *kanji* for "darkness" as is found in most Japanese legends. So as the "moon reader," Tomoyo is not only a priestess, but can read the future at night with her precognitive dreams.

Preview of volume 14

We're pleased to present you a preview of volume 14. This volume will be available in English July 31, 2007, but for now you'll have to make do with Japanese!

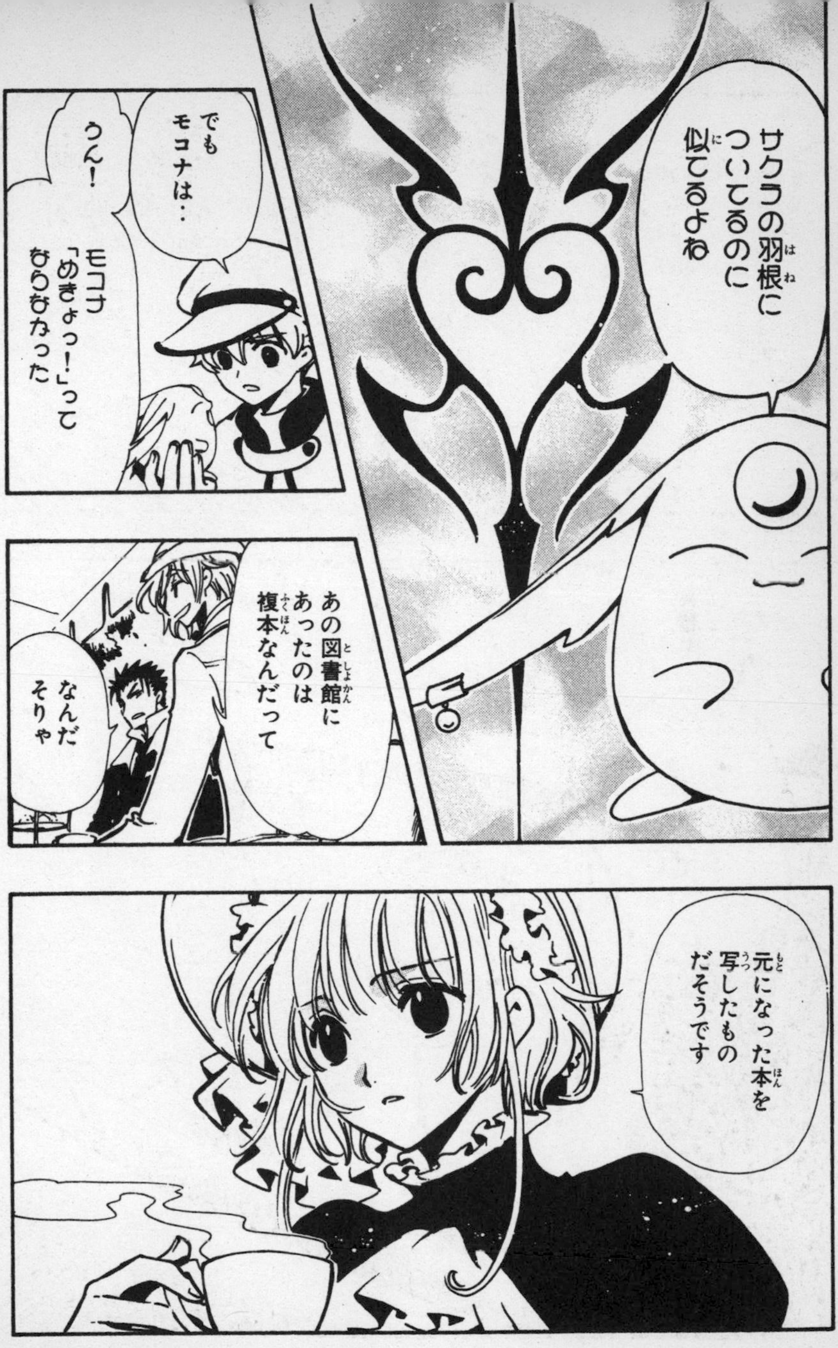
サクラの羽根についてるのに似てるよね
でもモコナは・・
うん!
モコナ「めきょっ!」ってならなかった
あの図書館にあったのは複本なんだって
なんだそりゃ
元になった本を写したものだそうです

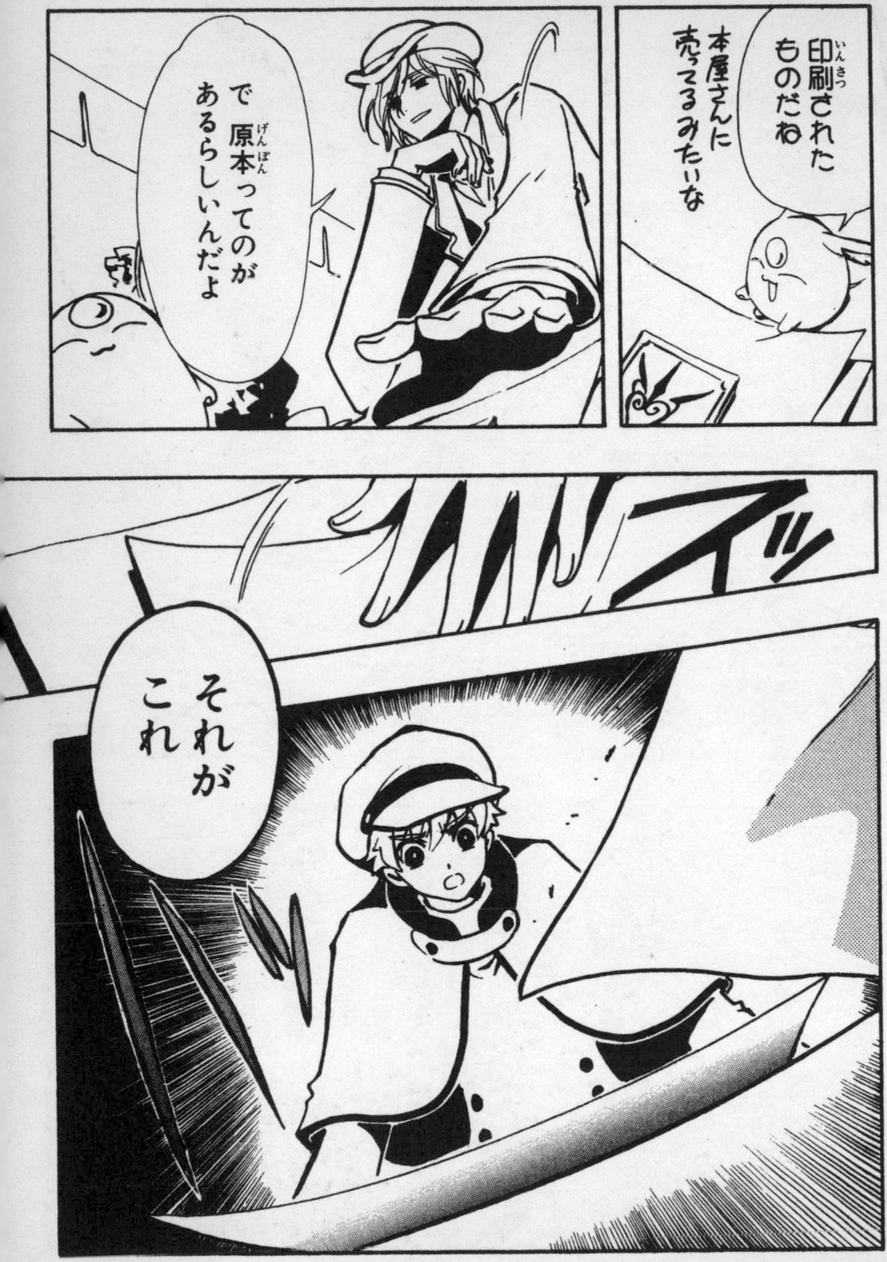
印刷されたものだね
本屋さんに売ってるみたいな
で 原本ってのがあるらしいんだよ
ズッ
それがこれ

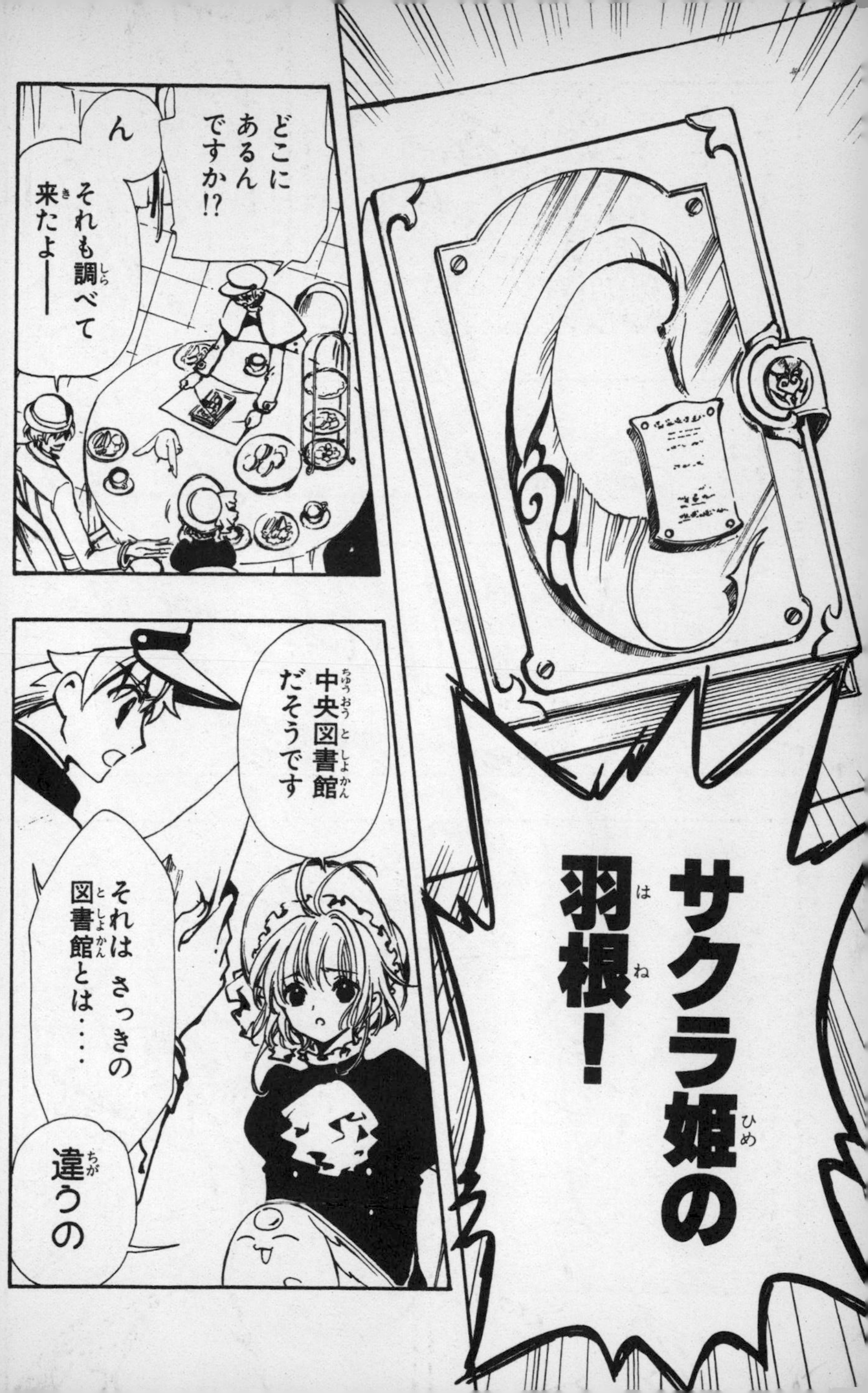
サクラ姫の羽根!
どこにあるんですか!?
ん
それも調べて来たよ——
中央図書館だそうです
それは さっきの図書館とは・・・・
違うの

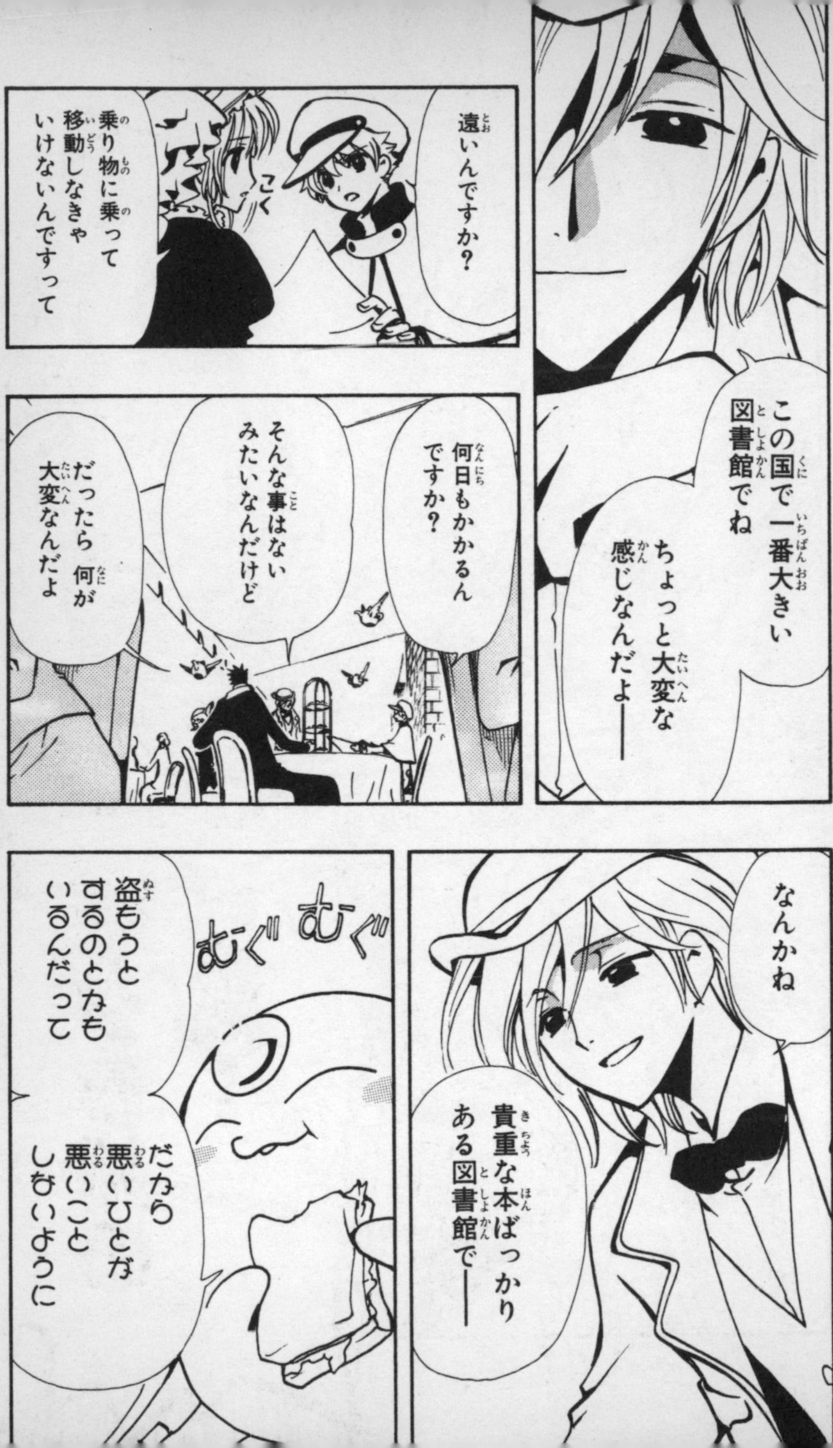

この国で一番大きい図書館でね
ちょっと大変な感じなんだよ——
遠いんですか？
こく
乗り物に乗って移動しなきゃいけないんですって
何日もかかるんですか？
そんな事はないみたいなんだけど
だったら 何が大変なんだよ
なんかね
貴重な本ばっかりある図書館で——
むぐ むぐ
盗もうとするのとかもいるんだって
だから悪いひとが悪いことしないように

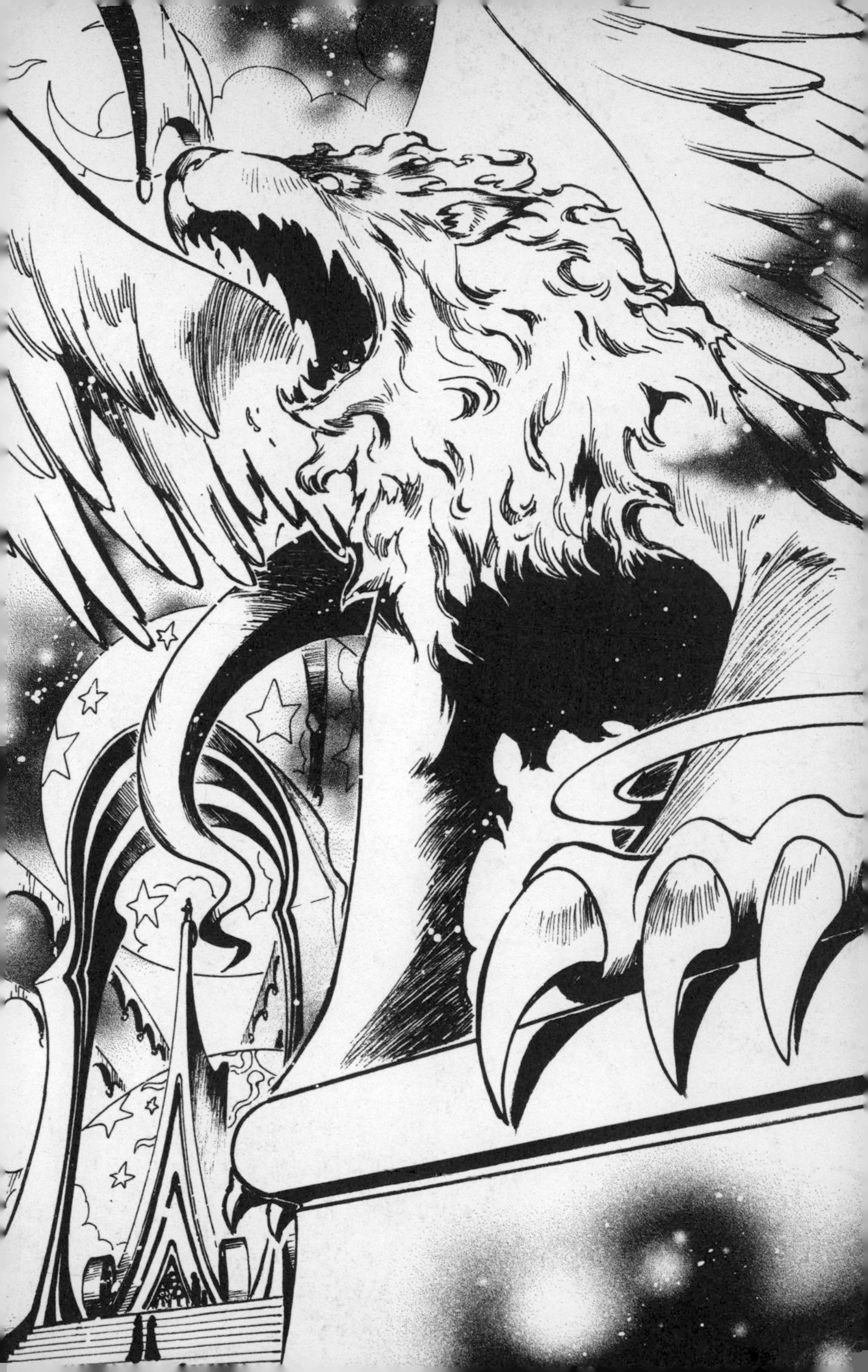

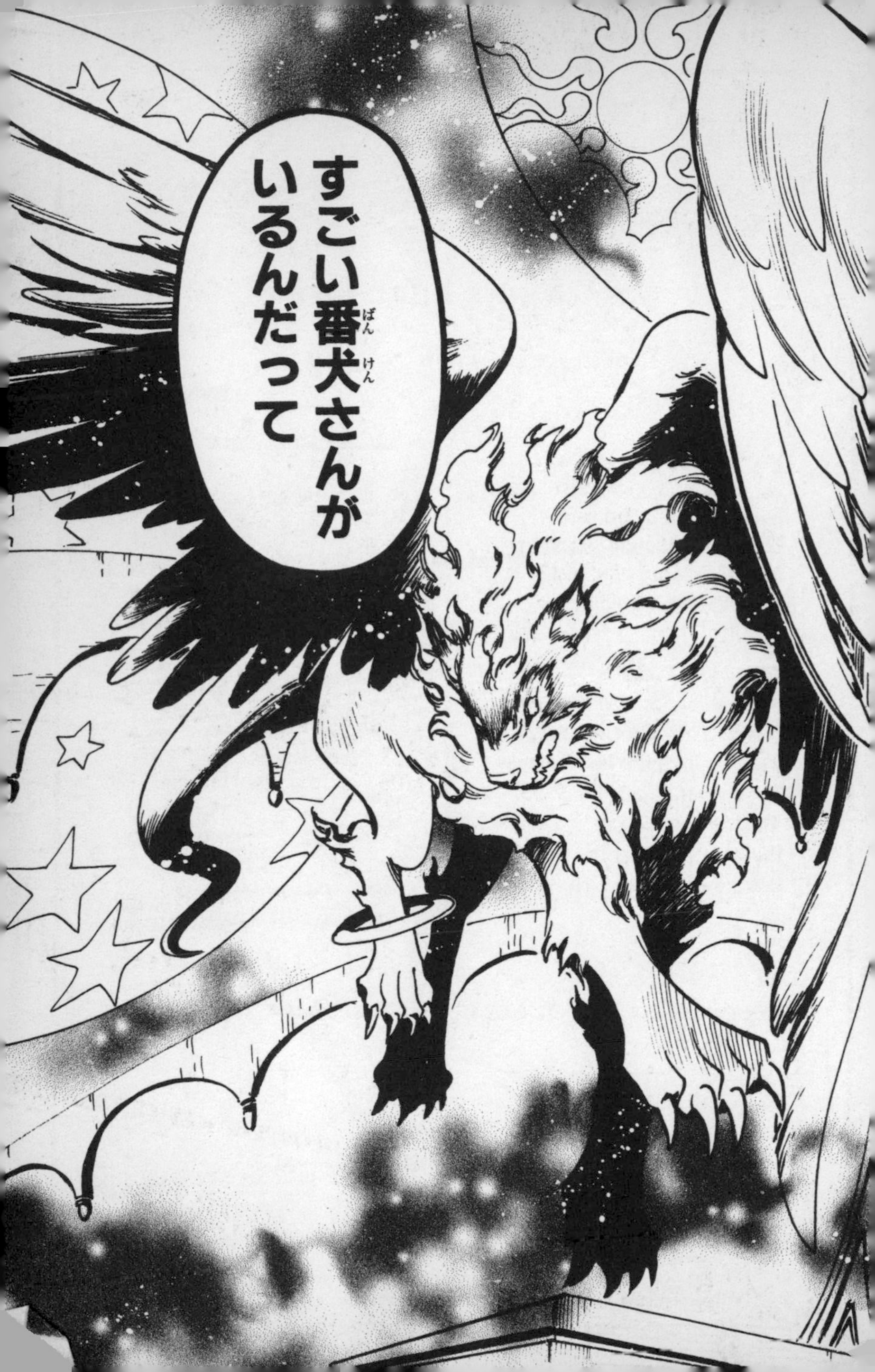
すごい番犬さんがいるんだって

DRAGON EYE

BY KAIRI FUJIYAMA

HUMANITY'S SECRET WEAPON

Dracules—bloodthirsty, infectious monsters—have hunted human beings to the brink of extinction. Only the elite warriors of the VIUS Squad stand as humanity's last best hope.

Young Leila Mikami is one of the squad's most promising recruits, but she's not only training to battle the Dracules, she's determined to find the magical Dragon Eye, a weapon that will make her the most powerful warrior in the world.

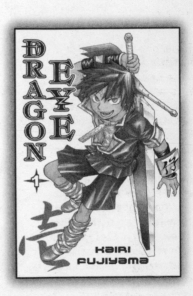

Special extras in each volume! Read them all!

VISIT WWW.DELREYMANGA.COM TO:
- Read sample pages
- View release date calendars for upcoming volumes
- Sign up for Del Rey's free manga e-newsletter
- Find out the latest about new Del Rey Manga series

RATING   T AGES 13+

 DEL REY MANGA デルレイ

The Otaku's Choice.™

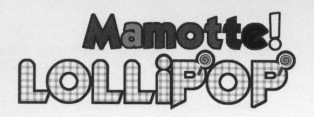

Michiyo Kikuta

BOY CRAZY

Junior high schooler Nina is ready to fall in love. She's looking for a boy who's cute and sweet—and strong enough to support her when the chips are down. But what happens when Nina's dream comes true . . . twice? One day, two cute boys literally fall from the sky. They're both wizards who've come to the Human World to take the Magic Exam. The boys' success on this test depends on protecting Nina from evil, so now Nina has a pair of cute magical boys chasing her everywhere! One of these wizards just might be the boy of her dreams . . . but which one?

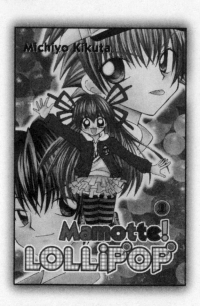

Special extras in each volume! Read them all!

VISIT WWW.DELREYMANGA.COM TO:
• Read sample pages
• View release date calendars for upcoming volumes
• Sign up for Del Rey's free manga e-newsletter
• Find out the latest about new Del Rey Manga series

RATING T AGES 13+

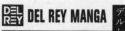

DEL REY MANGA

The Otaku's Choice

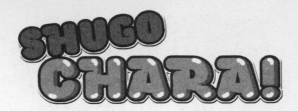

SHUGO CHARA!

PEACH-PIT

Creators of *Dears* and *Rozen Maiden*

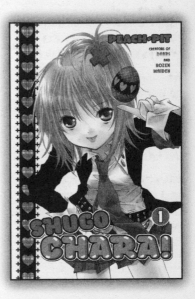

Everybody at Seiyo Elementary thinks that stylish and super-cool Amu has it all. But nobody knows the *real* Amu, a shy girl who wishes she had the courage to truly be herself. Changing Amu's life is going to take more than wishes and dreams—it's going to take a little magic! One morning, Amu finds a surprise in her bed: three strange little eggs. Each egg contains a Guardian Character, an angel-like being who can give her the power to be someone new. With the help of her Guardian Characters, Amu is about to discover that her true self is even more amazing than she ever dreamed.

PEACH-PIT
CREATORS OF DEARS AND ROZEN MAIDEN
SHUGO CHARA! 1

Special extras in each volume! Read them all!

VISIT WWW.DELREYMANGA.COM TO:

- Read sample pages
- View release date calendars for upcoming volumes
- Sign up for Del Rey's free manga e-newsletter
- Find out the latest about new Del Rey Manga series

RATING T AGES 13+

DEL REY MANGA デルレイ

The Otaku's Choice

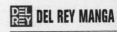

School Rumble

BY JIN KOBAYASHI

SUBTLETY IS FOR WIMPS!

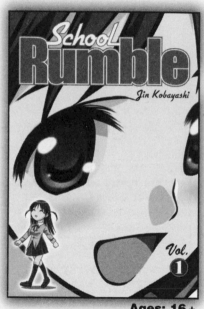

She . . . is a second-year high school student with a single all-consuming question: Will the boy she likes ever really notice her?

He . . . is the school's most notorious juvenile delinquent, and he's suddenly come to a shocking realization: He's got a huge crush, and now he must tell her how he feels.

Life-changing obsessions, colossal foul-ups, grand schemes, deep-seated anxieties, and raging hormones—School Rumble portrays high school as it really is: over-the-top comedy!

Ages: 16 +

Special extras in each volume! Read them all!

VISIT WWW.DELREYMANGA.COM TO:
- Read sample pages
- View release date calendars for upcoming volumes
- Sign up for Del Rey's free manga e-newsletter
- Find out the latest about new Del Rey Manga series

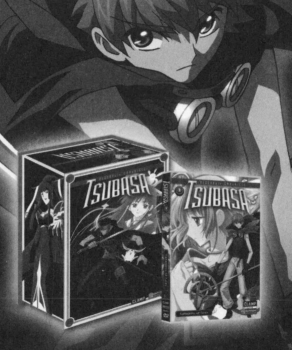

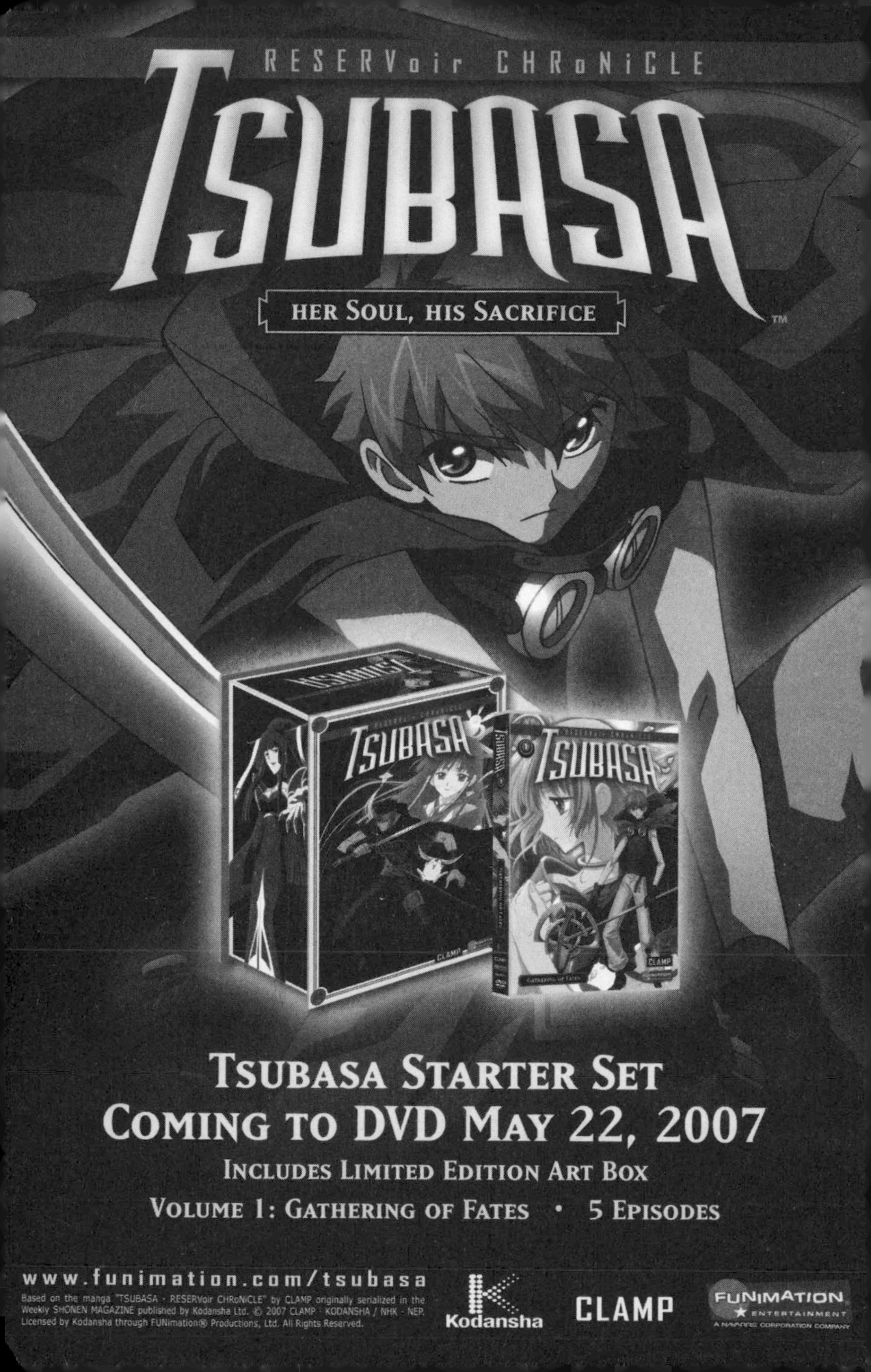

TOMARE!

[STOP!]

You're going the wrong way!

Manga is a completely different type of reading experience.

To start at the *beginning*, go to the *end*!

That's right! Authentic manga is read the traditional Japanese way—from right to left. Exactly the *opposite* of how American books are read. It's easy to follow. Just go to the other end of the book, and read each page—and each panel—from right side to left side, starting at the top right. Now you're experiencing manga as it was meant to be.